Sport in the Global

Series Editors: J. A. Mangan and Boria Majumdar

THE MAGIC OF INDIAN CRICKET

BEST OF LUCK!

KIRSTINE & CATHERINE

SPORT IN THE GLOBAL SOCIETY

Series Editors: J. A. Mangan and Boria Majumdar

The interest in sports studies around the world is growing and will continue to do so. This unique series combines aspects of the expanding study of *Sport in the Global Society*, providing comprehensiveness and comparison under one editorial umbrella. It is particularly timely, as studies in the multiple elements of sport proliferate in institutions of higher education.

Eric Hobsbawm once called sport one of the most significant practices of the late nineteenth century. Its significance was even more marked in the late twentieth century and will continue to grow in importance into the new millennium as the world develops into a 'global village' sharing the English language, technology and sport.

Other Titles in the Series

Disreputable Pleasures
Less virtuous Victorians at play
Edited by Mike Huggins and J.A. Mangan

Italian Fascism and the Female Body
Sport, submissive women and strong mothers
Gigliola Gori

Rugby's Great Split
Class, culture and the origins of rugby league football
Tony Collins

Women, Sport and Society in Modern China
Holding up more than half the sky
Dong Jinxia

Barbarians, Gentlemen and Players
A sociological study of the development of rugby football
Second edition
Eric Dunning and Kenneth Sheard

Sport in Asian Society
Past and present
Edited by Fan Hong and J.A. Mangan

Sport in South Asian Society
Past and present
Edited by Boria Majumdar and J.A. Mangan

Lost Histories of Indian Cricket
Battles off the pitch
Boria Majumdar

The Magic of Indian Cricket

In the last twenty years, Indian cricket – like India itself – has been transformed. With the arrival of global television networks, mass-media coverage and multinational sponsors, cricket has become big business and India has become the economic driving force in the world game. For the first time, a developing country has become a major player in the international sports arena.

This fully updated and revised edition of Mihir Bose's classic study of Indian cricket is a unique and involving account of the Indian cricket phenomenon. Drawing on a combination of extensive research and personal experience, Bose traces the development of the Indian game from its beginnings as a colonial pastime to its coming of age as a national passion and now a global powerhouse. This illuminating study reveals Indian cricket's central place in modern India's identity, culture and society.

Insightful, honest and challenging, Bose tackles the myths and controversies of Indian cricket. He considers the game in terms of race, caste, politics, national consciousness and ambition, money, celebrity and the media, evoking all the unpredictability, frustration and glory that is the magic of Indian cricket.

Mihir Bose is an award-winning cricket and sports news correspondent for *The Daily Telegraph*. He is also the author of a number of books, including *A History of Indian Cricket* and *Raj, Secrets, Revolution: A Life of Subhas Chandra Bose*. He lives in London.

THE MAGIC OF INDIAN CRICKET

Cricket and society in India

Revised edition

MIHIR BOSE

Routledge
Taylor & Francis Group

LONDON AND NEW YORK

To the memory of Ramesh, who knew nothing about cricket but taught me so much about life and who I miss greatly,

And to Munir, Gulu and Vidya, with whom I have shared so many wonderful cricketing moments.

First published 1986 as *A Maidan View: The Magic of Indian Cricket*
by George Allen & Unwin (Publishers) Ltd, London

This revised edition first published 2006 by Routledge
2 Park Square, Milton Park, Abingdon, Oxon OX14 4RN

Simultaneously published in the USA and Canada
by Routledge
270 Madison Ave, New York, NY 10016

*Routledge is an imprint of the Taylor & Francis Group,
an informa business*

© 1986, 2006 Mihir Bose

Typeset in Times New Roman by
Newgen Imaging Systems (P) Ltd, Chennai, India
Printed and bound in Great Britain by
Cromwell Press, Trowbridge, Wiltshire

British Library Cataloguing in Publication Data
A catalogue record for this book is available from the British Library

Library of Congress Cataloging in Publication Data
Bose, Mihir, 1947–
The magic of Indian cricket: cricket and
society in India / Mihir Bose – Rev. ed.
p. cm. – (Sport in the global society)
Includes index.
1. Cricket – Social aspects – India. 2. Nationalism and
sports – India. I. Title. II. Series.
GV927.5.S63B67 2005
796.358' 0954–dc22   2005011556

ISBN10: 0–415–35691–1 (hbk)
ISBN10: 0–415–35692–X (pbk)

ISBN13: 978–0–415–35691–6 (hbk)
ISBN13: 978–0–415–35692–3 (pbk)

Contents

Plates can be found between pages 174 and 175

Acknowledgements

Twenty years ago when I first wrote this book, books of this nature on Indian cricket were totally unknown. It resulted, like so many things in life, through a happy accident. I was originally meant to write a biography of a great Indian cricketer, but I was diverted into looking at what made cricket take root in India.

It came about this way.

Some years ago I had written a biography of Keith Miller for George Allen & Unwin. It did not, as I had fantasised, make my fortune – none of my books have – but my publishers were pleased and suggested that I write another book. We eventually settled on a biography of Ranji. I was half way through the book when we learned that Alan Ross was about to publish his biography of Ranji. The project was abandoned and it was then that an idea of a book on Indian cricket, which would look beyond the hype and the mystique, suggested itself. John Newth encouraged the idea but above all Derek Wyatt mixed the carrots and sticks in the right proportion to induce me to come up with the goods.

Much has changed in Indian cricket and society in the last twenty years and I have had to completely revise and update the book including adding new chapters to reflect the emergence of Indian as the economic power-house of world cricket.

I am grateful to Boria Majumdar for encouraging me to look again at Indian cricket and society and to produce this revised edition, more accurately reflecting both contemporary Indian cricket and its social mores.

Over the years I have, of course, incurred many other debts.

I am grateful to John Lovesey, David Robson and Chris Navarat, successive Sports Editors of the *Sunday Times*, for their help and encouragement. John, in particular, was brave enough to hire me in the first place. I also learnt much from Nick Mason and Jim Pegg, both about journalism and cricket.

I cannot adequately express my thanks to David Welch, former Sports Editor of the *Daily Telegraph* and Keith Perry, present Sports Editor, a paper for whom I now work. They have given me scope to not only write about cricket but various other sports business and political issues. This has considerably widened my range and allowed me to learn a great deal more about cricket and society. Keith, of course, is more than an editor but a friend and, like me, as a Tottenham supporter, aware of the anguish of loving a sporting team that often fails to deliver. I would also like to thank the superb backbench team of the *Daily Telegraph* Sports Desk, and the sub-editors they marshal, who have often rescued me from my own inadequacies and made me appear more knowledgeable and authoritative than I really am. If Daniel Evans, the Deputy Sports Editor, did send me into the jaws of Robert Mugabe by asking me to cover the Zimbabwe versus Sri Lanka series, it did provide me with an experience I shall always cherish.

Paul Barker, then editor of *New Society*, accepted my very first article analysing the impact on Indian society made by Tony Greig during England's 1976–7 Tour of India. That article started me on this journey and I cannot thank him enough. Since then many others have encouraged me by publishing my ideas and views on Indian cricket, which form the basis of this book. They include Jerome Burne and Don Atyeo, then Editors of *Time Out*, Gillian Greenwood, former Editor of the *Literary Review*, and the late Sharad Kotnis of *Sportsweek*. Vinod Mehta, the doyen of Indian editors, now editing *Outlook Magazine*, has always been a great supporter and friend.

Many friends in India and England have, over the years, sustained – or suffered – my constant discourses on cricket, and particularly Indian cricket. Some, like Edwin, Bala and Hubert, feature in this book; others, like Munir, remain good friends proving distance need not always sever childhood ties. English friends, even those indifferent to cricket, have indulged my favourite preoccupation. Cricket, particularly club cricket, has introduced me to a circle of friends I would never have otherwise met and I am grateful to all of them.

David Smith, Nigel Dudley, Richard Heller, Peter Oborne and Garth Hewitt have all encouraged my fantasies of being a good cricketer and even better cricket writer. Mark and Rose Streatfeild, in their very different ways, have been marvellously helpful over the years.

My parents and their friends indulged my love for the game and without the large retinue of servants and staff that my father employed, I would certainly not have been introduced to maidan cricket the way I was. I thank them and my sisters Tripti and Panna, for their patience and under-standing, and to my father's staff for their cooperation. In particular, Shankar, Arjun and Mr Kandalgoakar, who was given time off by my father to escort me to Test matches.

My wife Caroline has had to bridge a huge cultural divide in getting to know Sachin Tendulkar and reconcile herself to accommodating my yellow bound *Wisdens* in a sitting room which she feels is more suitable for the red of *Debrett's*. She has even begun to appreciate that Tendulkar is not diminished by being in *Wisden* rather in *Debrett's*.

Above all I owe the greatest debt of gratitude to Indian cricket and its cricketers. My earliest memory of Test cricket is being taken to the house of a friend of my mother's whose verandah conveniently overlooked the Brabourne Stadium. Checking through *Wisden* I can now actually place the date. It was 15 December 1951, the second day of the second Test match between India and England. As I recall, we were meant to watch Hazare grind England to dust. But in trying to hook a short pitched ball from Ridgeway he played it onto his forehead, cutting it badly. *Wisden* says that 'not only did that affect his batting in the match, but he seemed to lose all confidence and was never the same player in the three remaining Tests'. All that history has come later. I was four then, but I can still recall the surprise and anguish felt on the balcony as Hazare retired. Since then, Indian cricket has often surprised me, caused me a great deal of anguish but also provided moments of great joy. This book, although it may not read like that, is meant to repay some of the enjoyment I have had from Indian cricket.

Mihir Bose, London
Autumn 2005

Series editors' foreword

'Anatomical dissection gives the human mind an opportunity to compare the dead with the living, things severed with things intact, things destroyed with things evolving and opens up the profoundness of nature to us more than any other endeavour or consideration.'[1]

The Magic of Indian Cricket dissects India's national obsession to understand the Indian state in all its myriad contradictions and complexities.

'It was and remains self-evident that sport has been a core cultural marker, East and West, since the mid-nineteenth century, yet it has taken several academic generations for this to become widely accepted within the historical mainstream.'[2]

This truism is best exemplified in the case of the subcontinent. In that context, *The Magic of Indian Cricket* is a singular contribution; not only to an understanding of Indian cricket, but also to the wider acceptance of work on sport as mainstream historical literature.

Just as a sculptor tries to carve out each part of his statuette with scrupulous assiduousness attempting to breathe life into every minute detail and attain perfection in the process, *The Magic of Indian Cricket*, revised and updated, attempts to enable cricket devotees and intellectuals alike to relive the magic moments from India's centuries-old tryst with this once-alien game; the joy and the agony, excitement and ecstasy, ruse and intrigue, spread over a 200-year-old cricketing eon with few parallels in the history of modern global sport.

'If you ask any Dominican what he is proudest of, he will read you a list of ballplayers. This country doesn't have much, but we know we are the best in the world at one thing (baseball). That's not bragging, because it's true. And we plan to continue being the best in the world at it.'[3]

India is not yet the best in world cricket, that accolade is reserved for the Australians. Yet, if you ask an average Indian what he is most proud of, he will rattle off the names of the nation's leading cricketers. Not without reason is it said that captaining India is the second most difficult job in the country after the Prime Minister. The richness of Indian cricket is such that Ashis Nandy's aphorism, 'Cricket is an Indian game accidentally discovered by the English'[4] often rings true.

As has been suggested in *Twenty-Two Yards to Freedom: A Social History of Indian Cricket*, 'when we turn our attention to a very particular arena of Indian sport – cricket – the narrative of "backwardness," "catching up" and "gloom," commonly associated with India, ceases. Cricket is the only realm where the Indians can flex their muscles on the world stage; it is her only instrument to have a crack at world domination. It is, to put it simply, much more than a "game" for Indians.'[5]

Berry Sarbadhikary, India's greatly respected cricket writer, was correct when he argued, 'Cricket is a fascinating subject but Indian cricket is more so because of the peculiar traits of the Indians who play it . . . To point this out is not to extol the Indian at cricket as against others, just as Gandhiji's loin cloth does not necessarily constitute the ideal in the Indian national dress nor an example to the rest of the world. Yet, both are significant; they reveal the nation through the game or through the kit – for the better or for the worse.'[6]

The Magic of Indian Cricket advances this argument to the hilt.

J. A. Mangan
Boria Majumdar

Series editors
Sport in the Global Society

Notes

1 Johann Wolfgang Von Goethe (1749–1832); We were reminded of this immortal saying while visiting the exhibition 'Body Worlds', at the Museum of Science and Industry in Chicago. 'Body Worlds' was the museum's special exhibit for the summer of 2005.
2 Brian Stoddart, 'Sport, Cultural Imperialism and Colonial Response in the British Empire: A Framework for Analysis', *Comparative Studies In Society And History*, 14, 3 (1987), p. 649.
3 Manuel Mota of the Dominican Republic, playing for the Los Angeles Dodgers; quoted in Alan Klein, *Sugarball: The American Game, the Dominican Dream* (New Haven: Yale University Press, 1991), p. 1.
4 Ashis Nandy, *The Tao of Cricket* (New Delhi: Oxford University Press, 1989), p. 1.
5 Boria Majumdar, *Twenty-Two Yards to Freedom: A Social History of Indian Cricket*, (New Delhi: Penguin-Viking, 2004), p. 5.
6 Berry Sarbadhikary, *Indian Cricket Uncovered* (Calcutta: Illustrated News, 1945), p. 1.

1

India – whose India?

Sometime in the 1930s Jawaharlal Nehru, independent India's first Prime Minister was addressing a large political gathering. He was then leading the Indians in their epic fight for freedom from British colonial rule and as he spoke that day, like so often before, the crowd shouted 'Bharat Mata ki jai' (Long Live Mother India). It was the common political greeting of Indian crowds and Nehru had heard it often. But that day, as the cry was raised, he stopped speaking and, pointing to the crowd, asked 'What is Mother India? What does it mean to you?'

The crowd were mystified. They were not used to their political leaders asking them questions but Nehru insisted on a reply and, slowly, some of them pointed to the ground to indicate that was Mother India. Nehru interrupted them with that mixture of impatience and haughtiness that so characterised him and told his audience that if Mother India, to whom they were wishing a long life meant anything, it meant them, not the earth on which they stood. 'It is you, all of you together, you are India.' The crowd cheered ever more lustily and the incident was to become famous – almost every Nehru biographer has narrated it. In later years Nehru, himself, would make that impromptu question and answer session part of his unique method of arousing and educating an Indian crowd.

But if Nehru scored an important, populist point, the question: 'What is India, what does it represent?' is not easily answered. India is as confusing to Indians themselves as it is to foreigners. Even the name India is not something given by Indians. The Persians and the Greeks, trying to define the people who lived along the river Sindhu, tumbled on the words Indian and Hindu. Sindhu, a Sanskrit word, seemed too much for the ancient Persians and Greeks. They corrupted it to Indus – which is what the great river of the Punjab is called – and then in trying to define the inhabitants of the region around the river Indus the Persian and Greek tongues diverged. The Persian word was aspirated and came out as Hindu, the Greek one was softly breathed and came out as India. In this curious, convoluted, way Indian history was made, India came to stand for the subcontinent beyond the Indus bounded by the Himalayas, while Hindu became the word used to define the religion of the people who inhabited the region. Sixteenth-century European travellers arriving in India had called the Hindus by various names, the Portuguese for instance called them Gentio, meaning heathen, which was corrupted to gentoos to distinguish them from the Moors, the name these southern Europeans had long used for Muslims.

Many centuries later the Orientalists discovering India added another twist. They realised the Hindus had no name for their religion. The Hindus knew it – and still know it – as Sanatan Dharma: The Eternal Way. But Orientalists now coined the term Hinduism to describe the complex beliefs that underpinned the religion. As Nirad Chaudhuri has pointed out, on that analogy, the Greek religion might be called Hellenism or even Graecism. The Orientalists could hardly have realised the consequences of their actions. In modern India the word Indian represents all Indians of whatever religion. The country is secular, every religious group has full religious and political rights, and Indian cricketers like Irfan Pathan and Mohammed Kaif would be most upset if you called them Hindus. They are Muslims and call themselves Indians without realising that they might as well call themselves Hindus since the two words are the same.

The modern name of India could very well have been Hindusthan, land of the Hindus. In 1947 when free India emerged many of the departing British, who made no secret of their loathing for the Hindus and their preference for the Muslims, called it by that name. Indeed on 1 July 1947, six weeks before Indian independence, a meeting took place in the India Office in London when opposition leaders from both the Conservative and Liberal parties met Labour ministers to discuss the Independence Bill that Parliament was about to consider. It was this bill that led to the granting of freedom for India and the creation of the new dominion of Pakistan. The note of the meeting reads:

> Use of the title India for Hindusthan. There was a certain uneasiness about this based on a feeling that that it would antagonise the Muslims and was not justified on merits. There was moreover a feeling that the 'Union of India' should be kept for any organisation wider than either Dominion which may develop.

The documents of that period disclosed in the 12-volume British government's Transfer of Power series – indicate that had Mohammed Ali Jinnah, the creator of Pakistan, objected strongly to the term India, the British may have baulked at its use. In that case there would certainly have been problems in the independent country being called India. But Jinnah did not care. He was more concerned with the design of the flag the governors-general of the new dominions would have. And so on 15 August 1947 the new dominion got the name India without any visible fuss.

What independent India did with its foreign acquired name was not change it but have two names, one for external consumption, one for internal purposes. In Indian languages the country is called not India but Bharat and the Indian government is called the Bharat Sarkar, Bharat government. Bharatvarsha, the land of Bharat, was, after all the ancient name by which the landmass we call the Indian subcontinent was known and, as the historian D. P. Singhal has put it, 'the concept of Bharatvarsha was one of the country which lay north of the ocean and south of the snowy mountains. Kings and emperors attempted to bring all Bharatvarsha ranging from the Himalayas to Kanya Kumari (Cape Comorin) under one authority and call themselves chakravartin'. Indeed it is significant that the highest honour in independent India is called the Bharat Ratna, The Jewel of Bharat, an honour that many Indians feel should be bestowed on Sachin Tendulkar (so far he has the Khel Ratna, the Game Jewel). The modern Indian cricket fans copying English cricket's Barmy army call themselves the Bharat army. However, when it comes to singing at cricket matches they sing not Bharat but India's name. So in November 2004, as India won a thrilling victory over Australia by just 13 runs in Mumbai, in the last Test of a losing series the chant was India jitaga, India will win, not Bharat jitaga, Bharat will win, which would have been more logical. It would also been in tune with the shouts of the crowd at Nehru's meeting: Bharat Mata Ki Jai.

In this the Indians are different to the Greeks. The name Greece, too, is foreign in origin deriving from Grekos which came into use during the Turkish occupation. The original name for the country is Hellas and during the Athens Olympics in 2004. Greek fans watching the Olympics did not chant Greece, Greece, as Indians did in Mumbai but Hellas, Hellas. This chanting was particularly ferocious during the athletic events in the Olympic stadiums. Before the Olympics the Greeks had hoped to see their two stars in these events, Kostas Kenteris and Ekatherina Thanou, take the honours but a failure to provide a drug test led to their withdrawing from the Olympics amidst much controversy and the Greek crowds used the chants of Hellas to vent their feelings and reinforce their nationalist credentials. But then unlike the Greeks the Indian use of the word Bharat is somewhat selective. In Greece the Olympic Association, is called the Hellenic Olympic Association but the Board of Control for Cricket in India did not substitute Bharat for India after independence. Indeed in the Board there was no debate on this issue at all.

The problem for India is that, unlike Greece, while its history has had many glorious phases it has also been more torturous and, what is more, many aspects of its past are so controversial that even now there is no agreement about what happened. So much so that history in India can be literally lethal. This was gruesomely illustrated in December 1992 when a Hindu mob pulled down the Babri mosque in Ayodhya claiming that it was built by medieval Muslim rulers who had first destroyed a more ancient temple dedicated to the Hindu god Ram. The religious Hindus believe Ayodhya to be the birthplace of Ram. This dispute, known popularly as the politics of the Ram temple, has shaped Indian politics since the 1990s, with no agreement as to whether the Hindu claim is justified.

More recently, there was such rage generated by a scholarly biography of the sixteenth-century Maratha King Shivaji that the Bhandarkar institution in Pune, where the American scholar had done his research, was vandalised and the Oxford University Press forced to withdraw the book from India. And almost every year the Indian History Congress, composed of some of the most eminent Indian historians, meet and pass anxious resolutions deploring the tendency of politicians and pressure groups to constantly rewrite and distort history.

Indians cannot agree on their history because in Indian history there are very few straight lines. Most of them are so jagged and curved that at times it is impossible to see round the corners. What makes it worse is that through much of its long existence the history of India has largely been written not by Indians but by foreigners. India, along with China, has the oldest continuous cultural traditions in the world, much older than the Egyptians, the Greeks or the Iraqis, heirs to the Babylonian civilisation. But India has nothing like China's ancient historical records. The Indian historian R. C. Majumdar introducing *The Classical Accounts of India* – itself a collection of writings about India by foreigners such as Herodotus, Megasthenes, Arrian, Plutarch, Pliny and Ptolemy (nothing comparable from Indian sources is available) – wrote, 'there was no history of pre-Muslim India written by the ancient Indians themselves, and consequently very little was known of its political history'. Before the Muslim arrival in the twelfth century, says Majumdar, 'we possess no historical text of any kind, much less such a detailed narrative as we possess in the case of Greece, Rome or China'. Given that India can claim a history of 5,000 years this means that for 75 per cent of Indian history there are no known histories left to us by Indians. Myths and fables there are in plenty but nothing that would be considered historically authentic.

D. D. Kosambi, probably the most original, certainly the most innovative, Indian historian, responded to this lack of written knowledge by walking to Indian sites round his base of Pune to discover history, starting a new trend in Indian historical research. Since Majumdar wrote his lament in the 1950s others have followed the trail blazed by Kosambi and similar field work has been done all over India in ruins, rocks, bricks and other physical evidence left behind by the past to help reconstruct it.

Foreigners can often provide a historical view of a county that is both valid and instructive. The classic example of this is the French writer Alexis de Tocqueville's *Democracy in America*. First published in French in Paris in 1835 it remains a classic, much reprinted in America to this day. More recently, Bill Bryson, an American, has written very amusingly about Britain in *Notes From A Small Island*. Bryson would not compare himself to Tocqueville, but his book has much useful information on modern-day Britain and has been very popular with the British. However, if the only written works on America and Britain were written by a Frenchman and an American then we would get a picture of the country that is not quite complete. That is the problem we have when judging Indian history. In our times there has been no dearth of history books written by Indians but there still seems a very intriguing lack of appetite for the broad-canvas historical writing that is so common in the west. Indians are still content to let foreigners tell their story. So the one truly popular history dealing with how India got freedom, a bestseller in India, was written by two journalists: one French, the other American. And the film on Gandhi, India's greatest son, was made by an Englishman.

The Muslim period did bring great historical writers to compare with anything the rest of the world, including the Greeks or the British, have produced. The first of them shows the remarkable way Indian history has come down to us. The first truly great history book on India, and one of the classics of world history, was written by Abu Raihan, popularly known as Alberuni. His book is called simply *Alberuni's India*. A Muslim scholar, he came to India with the Mahmud of Ghazni's forces in the eleventh century and wrote this classic while the master he served was either killing the infidel Hindus or making them slaves, looting their wealth by destroying their wonderfully rich temples in places such as Mathura, Kangra, Kanauj and Somnath and taking the treasures back to Ghazni, now in modern-day Afghanistan. Every winter for 16 years Mahmud raided India gathering vast wealth and many slaves which helped him build a rich kingdom in Ghazni. Yet amidst this carnage Alberuni calmly observed the world of the Hindus, so different from his own. There is merit in the comments of the editor Edward Sachau, who in his 1888 foreword to the English edition, wrote, 'the history is like a magic island of quiet, impartial research in the midst of clashing swords, burning towns, and plundered temples'. Alberuni, in turn, profited from his work and his later status as a scientific celebrity in the Muslim world owed much to the Indian scientific and mathematical discoveries he had learnt from the Hindus and his mastery of Sanskrit.

India gives and India takes. If India took the art of writing history from Alberuni it also made him famous.

The Indians are, of course, not the only people who wrestle with their history, and make a hard work of coming to terms with their past, but they must be unique in having to wrestle with historical narratives bequeathed to them not by their ancestors but by foreigners visiting India, each of whom have had their own agendas.

No group of foreigners have had a more loaded agenda than the British and the legacy they have left behind, of which cricket is only a part, is a historical minefield as much for the British as for the Indians. Today, some sixty years after Indian freedom, there are many interpretations of British rule but very few conclusions to which both the British and the Indians can subscribe. Every now and again in the most unexpected of situations history can jar. In 2002, when the Queen Mother died, the British media made much of the fact that she was the Last Empress of India and during the mourning period her jewels, such as the Star of India, were much on display, leading to a certain amount of nostalgia about India, the Jewel in the Crown. This provoked a very pained response from Kuldip Nayar, a journalist and former Indian High Commissioner to the UK who came on BBC radio's prestigious *Today* programme to complain that such British wallowing in imperial nostalgia was meant to remind the Indians that they were once a conquered people.

Contrast this with how the British and the Americans react to their shared past.

A few months after the Queen Mother's death, Tony Blair, the British Prime Minister, addressed a joint session of the US Congress – the first British Prime Minister to do so since Winston Churchill – and a reward for having supported George Bush's policy on Iraq. During his speech he made a reference to the war of 1812 when British troops invaded the then young republic of the USA and burned down Washington. Blair apologised for that British action making a joke of it and the Americans joined in the general laughter. But that was an event in the midst of a war that the Americans had started. The British action could be said to be retaliation for the American destruction of public buildings in York (present-day Toronto).

I, personally, think such historical apologies are ridiculous and unjustified. How far back are we meant to go to apologise for what our ancestors did? But if ever an apology was needed it was for the Amritsar massacre of 1919 when the British general Reginald Dyer ordered his troops to fire at an unarmed, peaceful, Indian crowd killing or wounding more than 1,500 men, women and children. This, as opposed to killing during wars, was an unclean killing. However, when in 1997 the Queen and Prince Philip visited the site, the Queen did not apologise, merely signed the visitors book at the memorial. Philip, for good measure, questioned the figures for the dead listed on the memorial. As he passed the memorial which spoke of 2,000 being martyred he said, 'That's wrong. I was in the navy with Dyer's son.' Philip's remarks angered the Indians and coming on top of other gaffes by the British turned this royal visit, meant to mark the 50th anniversary of Indian independence, into a disaster with much bad blood between the two countries. The then Indian Prime Minister described the British as 'a third rate power' and Indians cancelled a speech the Queen was supposed to make, which angered the British. A spokesman for the Indian Foreign Ministry Talmiz Ahmed, who had been press secretary in London some years earlier, reacted strongly to the British criticism, saying:

> This is British ineptitude. I think they scheduled a speech for her in the programme assuming they would be able to bully Indians into acceptance of something completely without precedence. When they did not succeed, the thought they could find a way out by blaming bungling Indian officials.

British newspapers like the *Times* condemned the Indians saying 'the government in Delhi had let down its people'. India, said the Thunderer, had abandoned its own deeply rooted cultural and religious traditions of how to treat a guest and 'slipped back into the habits of awkwardness that Indians and the world believed that it had outgrown'.

The whole affair illustrated how very differently the British view their relationship with its two former colonies. With one it has a special, we are all one family relationship, with the other it is still, three hundred years after the initial contact, more often a case of strangers tiptoeing around each other.

One reason for this may be that the British interaction with India was unique for both the British and the Indians from the very moment it began. To say India is a land made for conquest is a truism and even the Aryans, from whom the Hindus claimed descent, invaded the country at some time in the distant past. But the British were unlike any previous foreign ruler of India. All of them, starting with Alexander, the first one for whom we have reliable historical records, came with the sword or as with the Muslims with the sword, the cannon and Koran. But in the end these foreigners stayed in India and became part of the land, even Alexander left behind Greeks who eventually became Indians. But the first British arrived with trading books, a begging letter from their Queen, and always made it clear that they were mere sojourners in India, never going to make India their home. And lest India trap the Britons, the rule in many British families in India was that every third generation should go back to

England. This rule, arguably, prevented Douglas Jardine, that most English of cricket captains, who was the third generation of his family in India to come back to England and miss out on captaining India.

Let us go back to that begging letter written in February 1583 by Elizabeth I to Jalaludin Akbar, the Mughal Emperor. The letter was given to John Newbery, one of the first Englishman to visit India, and begins thus:

> Elizabeth by the grace of God etc. To the most invincible and mighty Prince Lord Zelabdim Echebar, King of Camabaia, Invincible Emperor etc

The letter goes on to speak of Akbar's 'humanity' and says the English Queen would be 'beholden' to Akbar if he would look after her English subjects. Elizabeth misspelled Akbar's name and spoke of him being the King of Camabaia, Cambay, along whose waterfront a hundred and thirty years later British sailors first played cricket introducing the game to the Indians. But what is significant is the tone of the letter. Elizabeth comes across as the ruler of a small kingdom well aware that the greatest powers on her continent were Spain and Portugal with Spain trying to bring her kingdom back to the Catholic mainstream which Elizabeth's father had abandoned.

But then this was no more than a recognition of the reality of world politics then. As the historian Paul Kenney has written in 1500, a betting man, asked to predict which power would became the truly global power in the world, would have said that the Mughals, then at the height of their influence in India, stood a very good chance. No European country, not even Spain would have merited a bet. England were not even at the races.

This remained the position for the next century and half of British involvement with India. Britain eagerly increased its trade links with India because India was an economic superpower. It has been estimated by the economist Paul Bairoch that in 1750, seven years before Robert Clive's victory in Plassey started the British Empire in India, India had 24.5 per cent of the share of the world manufacturing output. China led the field with 32.8 per cent, whereas the United Kingdom had only 1.9 per cent. By 1860, just a century after British rule had begun, the picture had been completely transformed. Now the United Kingdom had 19.9 per cent of the world's manufacturing output and India 8.6 per cent. In 1900, at the height of the Victorian Empire, the United Kingdom had 18.5 per cent of the world's manufacturing output. India was down to 1.7 per cent, lower than the share of the UK in 1750.

It would be easy to laugh at the word manufacturing in relation to the pre-industrial age. The fact is the world did produce goods even before the machines came and that world was dominated by the luxury goods of the east such as textiles, silks, ceramics and spices. India's pre-industrial age manufacturing of handloom textiles and handicrafts was well supported by an indigenous credit and banking system. As Bairoch has said, 'More important, there was a large commercialised sector with a highly sophisticated market and credit structure manned by skilful and in many instances a very wealth commercial class.' It was their riches that lured the west to the east and the east was so superior that when the Portuguese Vasco da Gama turned up in India courts with what he thought were valuable gifts the Indians scorned at the trinkets, so inferior were they to the gold, silver and diamonds their rulers could boast.

Not that India's economic might in the pre-industrial age meant that the people of India were rich. The wealth in India was in the hands of the very few and society as a whole was very poor. As economists have pointed out, a society which has agriculture as the main component of its national product does not produce a surplus much more than what it needs for sustenance. But in the eighteenth century the disparity between the poor of what we now call the third world and the first world was not as great as in our times. India in the pre-industrial age had many traders, textile producers, and craftsmen and an Indian handloom weaver, for example, may have earned perhaps as much as half of his European equivalent. The arrival of the steam engine and the power loom that transformed the world also meant India became progressively poorer while Britain, lured to India by its wealth, grew progressively richer. It helped Britain become the world's first industrial power. In effect, Britain denuded India of its pre-industrial manufacturing dominance converting it almost wholly into a primary producing country providing raw materials for industrial Britain.

By this time the obsequious tone of Elizabeth's letter had long vanished and the British were on their way to becoming the Lords of humankind. But in another great irony, when the British were at their most rapacious in India, they had the best contacts with Indians, when they presented themselves as civilising the Indians then shunned them most. It was as the East India Company and its officials were looting India – their activities introduced the word loot, an Indian word, into the English language – that the British were most responsive and open to Indian ideas. They married Indian wives, had Indian families and took to Indian ways. The historian Percival Spear has written, 'the days of the corrupt Company officials of ill-gotten fortunes, of oppression' were also 'the days when Englishmen were interested in Indian culture, wrote Persian verses and forgathered with Pandits and Maulvis and Nawabs on terms of social equality and personal friendship'.

This was the time for William Jones and Warren Hastings, one a scholar, the other a ruler, who did much to both learn about India and indeed unearth ancient Indian learning, teaching them to an astonished generation of Indians who had forgotten what their forefathers had achieved. It was Jones, known as Oriental Jones, who set up the Asiatic Society of India and started a whole British tradition of scholarship on India which so benefited Indians. Yet even here there was a very British, we know best, attitude to India. For many years no Indian was allowed to became a member of the Asiatic Society, or attend its meetings.

This early sign of arrogance was transformed into the much more pernicious belief that the British were the master race destined to rule India after 1857 when India came under direct Crown rule. It was the high tide of the new western imperialism when everything non-western was suspect and Britons, presenting themselves as Europeans, imposed their superior civilisation. This meant, as George Orwell put it, 'You turn a Gatling gun on a mob of unarmed natives and then you establish "The law" which includes roads, railways and court-house.' It was, of course, during the period of 'a sort of forcible evangelising' that cricket took root in India.

However, despite this, the British, starting with Hastings and Oriental Jones, were the catalysts of change in India. They brought new ideas, new ways of looking and reconnected India to the world. Its effect on the Indian, particularly the Hindu mind, was immense. The most significant reforms of Hinduism, removing some of its barbaric customs, for instance, were not carried out by the British but by Indians who looked at their own society with the help of British ideas and, finding it wanting, sought to change it.

But having helped open the Indian mind the British also chained it, put a ceiling on what Indians could aspire to. The classic illustration of this is the way Everest was named. It was named after George Everest, a British colonel who, along with William Lambton, helped map India, something that had not been done before. It was an awesome achievement and it also resulted in the first accurate measurements of the Himalayas, including the world's highest peak which bears Everest's name.

But who actually calculated that the mountain we call Everest was the highest in the world? It was certainly not Everest. In the early stages of the mapping it was denoted as Peak XV as efforts were made to measure it. In Calcutta worked a Bengali called Radhanath Sikdar, a young mathematical genius whose skills had been much admired by Everest. He was the Chief Computer and he was asked by Andrew Waugh, Everest's successor as Surveyor-General of India, to provide the mathematical formula. This he did working out that Peak XV was 29,002 feet above sea level, making it the highest in the world. However, when it came to the name Waugh insisted it should be named Everest. He had already dismissed the names the Nepalis had for the mountain, saying Everest was a 'household word among civilised, nations', so for him to consider an Indian subordinate's name for the peak was impossible. This incident illustrates British rule rather well. It allowed someone like Sikdar to rise, even become the Chief Computer, but his Indian name could not possibly be given to the highest peak in the world.

The other great feature of the British connection with India was that from the very beginning the British behaved as if they always occupied the moral high ground.

You can get some idea of how deeply the British held to this notion during the Raj if you visit the third floor of the British Library in Euston. This is where the India Office Library is now located and a truly magnificent library it is, essential to anyone researching into the India of the last two hundred years. Here the British have not only carefully preserved the records of their rule but much of value relating to India. There is nothing like this available anywhere else. However, among the many wonderful things here, one set of publications is not much in demand, although in many ways it is the most revealing.

These are the annual reports presented to the British Parliament by the Secretary of State for India, summarising the activities of the government in India during the preceding year. The report underlined that the ultimate ruler of India was the British House of Commons and through this report the representatives of the British people, who owned India, could judge what had been done in their name.

Such government reports are not uncommon and the red-bound books are full of the sort of dry government facts and figures you would expect. But what is really remarkable is the title the British gave these reports. They were not called the Annual Report on British India or anything like that. Their title was: *Moral and Material Progress in India*. The message was clear. The British in India were not only improving the economic condition of the Indians – a claim some British historians still maintain is valid – but they were also improving the morals of this barbaric, decadent, people.

Such a view became the orthodoxy in the middle of the nineteenth century. But even when the British were mere traders in India, and had no expectations of ruling the country, they projected themselves as people who were always in the right and considered all those who opposed them as usurpers. In the beginning of the eighteenth century, almost half a century before Clive laid the foundations of the empire in India, the British who had trading facilities on the west coast of India had to fight a series of wars with local Indian rulers. Some of these wars involved sea battles with navies the Indian rulers had, in particular the Marathas, then a major power in India. The Maratha navy was led by the redoubtable Kanoji Angre and the British suffered many defeats at his hands. It would be entirely understandable if British histories painted him in a bad light. But the British did more than that. Although he was the Grand Admiral of what was a powerful Maratha fleet, the British refused to recognise his titles, called him a 'pirate' and the British history of that period is called the Pirates of Malabar. As John Keay puts it in *The Honourable Company* – a history of the East India Company – 'One man's pirate is another man's patriot' but the description of Angre and other Indian naval commanders as pirates was 'a peculiarly English conceit'. Angre was fighting for a legitimate sovereign seeking to police the merchant fleets along his coast-line, yet the British intruders in his native waters were not content to make money but also wanted to present themselves as the legitimate owners of the waters.

Once the British converted themselves from traders to rulers in India then this desire to portray all their actions as being on a higher moral plane to that of the Indians became an almost obsessive British concern. The British were the conquerors, yet it was British heroes who always sought to occupy the moral high ground. This started right from the moment when Clive fought Siraj-ud-daulah at Plassey in June 1757 to launch the British Empire in India.

That victory on that rainy Thursday was more like the sort of one-day cricket international that the South African Hanje Cronje might have organised with the result fixed by judicious bribing before the match (battle) begun. It rained, which affected Siraj's powder, there was some dare-devilry from Clive's cavalry but the outcome was not in doubt because Clive had bribed Mir Jaffar, Siraj's ambitious Commander-in-Chief, promising him the kingship of Bengal in exchange for remaining neutral. The result of the battle was Mir Jaffar replacing Siraj on the throne of Bengal and Clive and his men earning fortunes they could never have dreamt of. When Clive and his men entered Murshidabad, Siraj's capital, he described it as 'as extensive, populous and rich as the city of London, with the difference that there are individuals in the first possessing infinitely greater property than in the last'.

As it happens, the crucial battle of Plassey was preceded by not one deception but two, one of which involved a banker called Omichand who was the middle man between Clive and Mir Jaffar. At one stage he threat-ened to blow the whistle on the whole enterprise and tell Siraj unless he was paid very large sums of money. Clive and the English in Calcutta were convinced that Omichand was a crook. However, for their plan to work they knew they had to associate with him and, since everybody else was crooked, perhaps more so, they decided that the only way to deal with Omichand was to be as deceitful. They produced two versions of the treaty with Mir Jaffar. The true one, coloured blue, had no clause about any payment to Omichand, the false one, coloured red, with forged signatures had. Clive justified it on the grounds that Omichand was the 'greatest villain upon earth' and that it was necessary to deceive him in order to achieve the greater prize of securing these possessions for England. Many years later Clive's action was the subject of a censure motion in the British House of Commons. The proposer, Colonel Burgoyne (who was later to suffer defeat at the hands of the Americans during their war of independence), denounced Clive for his looting of Bengal and his deception of Omichand. Clive defended himself in much the same style as Napolean justifying the shooting of Duc d'Enghein. The debate showed the English at their sanctimonious worst. Part of Burgoyne's resolution was accepted, that Clive had made money, but he was also praised for 'great and meritorious service to the country'. As Nirad Chaudhuri, Clive's biographer, says, the Commons had ducked the question: how could they condemn Clive without condemning the very establishment of British power in India? 'England could not retain the stolen goods if they called Clive a thief.'

It is very interesting to see how popular British histories deal with this seminal period. Little or no mention is made of the bribery of Mir Jaffar or Clive's deception of Omichand, but much emphasis is laid on an event that preceded Plassey.

This was the notorious Black Hole of Calcutta. It came about when the wretched Siraj deciding to take on the English and teach them a lesson, captured Calcutta. In total, 146 of them were imprisoned in a dungeon in the fort which was known as the Black Hole, that being the English term for the local lock-up or a temporary jail. On a hot sultry night, one of the hottest of the year, the British prisoners suffered terribly from thirst and want of air and as the night wore on many of them just sank and died. When in the morning the door to the Black Hole was opened only 23 emerged alive. As it happens, Siraj did not know about it, was said to be affected when he heard, and it was the skill with words of J. Z. Holwell, one of the survivors, that made the story famous. Vincent Smith, author of the *Oxford History of India*, considers Holwell to be a 'plausible and none too reliable man' and while he believes the incident happened, 'the numbers involved and the details are not certain' and the whole thing, he concludes, 'should be regarded as a deplorable incident rather than as a deliberate atrocity'. For him the Black Hole is of such little historical importance that the incident is dealt with not in the main text but in a note attached to the end of the chapter describing the start of British rule in India.

Indeed for fifty years after the incident little notice was taken of it but then, as Smith observes, it 'became convenient material for the compliers of an imperialist hagiology'. Black Hole passed into the language as standing for Indian iniquity and starting in the nineteenth century it was the one thing about India every English schoolboy knew. Even today popular British writing about the start of their rule never fails to mention it. Thus Williams Pennington in *Pick Up Your Parrots and Monkeys*, a memoir of his soldiering in India during the Second World War, published in 2003, has an appendix on Clive's India. It does not mention his bribery of Mir Jaffar, let alone the deception of Omichand, but has a few paragraphs devoted to the Black Hole. As Chaudhuri puts it, 'Retrospectively, the Black Hole incident served to throw a moral halo over the British conquest of India, as it was God's punishment for iniquity.'

The fact is even if the Black Hole had not taken place Clive would have fought Siraj as vital economic interests were involved. The British attitude, as Chaudhuri notes, derives not from authentic history but is more a psychological product of history.

British rule in India was marked by such psychological moments, never more so than when the British crushed the Indian Revolt of 1857 which came within an ace of uprooting their empire. I have used the word revolt deliberately, because it was much more than a mutiny as the British termed it, and as British historians still do, but much less than a war of independence as Indian nationalists like to portray it. For a start, the rebellion was confined to a small part of India and most Indians either did not take part or wanted the British to win. But whatever term is used what cannot be denied is that it was the bloodiest revolt in the history of the British Empire and put down by the British with a severity that is quite beyond belief. There were, of course, dreadful atrocities committed by the Indian rebels, but the British responded to cruelty with redoubled cruelty, terror with even more terror, blood with even more blood. The *Times* newspaper bayed for Indian blood saying 'every tree and gable end in the place should have its burden in the shape of a mutineer's carcass'. The Baptist preacher Charles Spurgeon, addressing a congregation of 25,000 at Crystal Palace during the revolt, called for the extermination of the entire Hindu people:

> The religion of the Hindoos is no more than a mass of the rankest filth that imagination ever conceived. The Gods they worship are not entitled to the least atom of respect. Their worship necessitates everything that

is evil and morality must be put down. The sword must be taken out of its sheath, to cut off our fellow subjects by their thousands.

The historian Michael Edwards has written that even after the British retook Delhi – having stripped and then shot out of hand the sons of the Mughal Emperor, Bahadur Shah – there was no stoppage 'in the amount of innocent blood ruthlessly shed, for the city of Delhi was put to the sword, looted and sacked with the ferocity of a Nazi extermination squad in occupied Poland'.

Many of the English officers delighted in dreaming up ways they could degrade the Indian rebels before killing them. Muslims, forbidden pork by their religion, would be sewn into pork skins or smeared with pork fat before being executed, high-caste Hindus, forbidden to eat beef, had beef stuffed down their throats before they were hanged. It was common for Indians to be lashed to the mouth of a cannon and then blown apart by grapeshot. British officers encouraged rape and pillage before whole villages including old women and children were burnt and the dead were often strung up on trees, some of them resembling figures of eight. One huge banyan tree which still stands in Kanpur had no less than 150 corpses. It was in Kanpur that there had been a horrific massacre of British men, women and children, and Colonel James Neil exacted terrible revenge for this. He forced the rebels he had apprehended to lick with their tongues a square foot of the floor which contained the congealed blood, all the while being lashed by an English soldier before they were hanged.

In British eyes such things were justified because of the way the Indian rebels had behaved, but as A. N. Wilson has pointed out in *The Victorians* this is trying to establish a moral equivalence where there can be none:

The ruthlessness of British reprisals, the preparedness to punish Indians of any age, sex, regardless of whether they had any part in the rebellion is a perpetual moral stain on the Raj and it is no wonder that in most popular British histories these atrocities are suppressed altogether or glossed over with such a distasteful anodyne phrase as 'dark deeds were done on both sides'. It is not to defend the murders of European women and children that one points out such remarks suggest an equivalence where none can exist... There can be no moral equivalence between a people, by whatever means of atrocity, trying to fight for their freedom to live as they choose, without the interference of an invading power, and that power itself using the utmost brutality to enforce not merely a physical but a political dominance over the people.

Yet even now, Wilson apart, when British historians deal with this period they cannot help trying to prove the moral superiority of the British over other people. Thus Niall Ferguson in *Empire* published in 2003, which seeks to show how Britain made the modern world and was a force for good, describes a scene from the revolt just after the British had lifted the siege of Lucknow. A young boy supporting a tottering old man approaches the gate of the city. But the British officer convinced all Indians whatever their age must be rebels brushes aside his plea for mercy and shoots the boy. Three times his revolver jams, the fourth times he succeeds and then the boy falls. Ferguson writes:

> To read this story is to be reminded of the way SS officers behaved towards Jews during the Second World War. Yet there is one differ-ence. The British soldiers who witnessed this murder loudly con-demned the officer's actions, at first crying 'shame' and giving vent to 'indignation and outcries' when the gun went off. It was seldom, if ever, that German soldiers in a similar situation openly criticised a superior.

So it's all right then. Even when the British behave as badly as the SS, they are still morally superior to the Germans because there are always a few dissenting British voices.

The Indians have always found it difficult to cope with such British certainty about their moral superiority. Their answer has been to consis-tently play down their own dark side and pretend the atrocities they committed were a mistake or did not happen. Mention of incidents such as the Black Hole or the massacre of British men, women and children in the Bibighar in Kanpur is either ignored or glossed over.

When I was a child growing up in Bombay one of the things we looked forward to was the great Bengali feast of Durga Puja, a religious-cum-cultural occasion which marked the end of the rains and the start of the cold weather. At every Puja there was always a play about Clive and the emergence of British rule in India. Much was made about of the bribery of Mir Jaffar and the deception of Omichand but my fellow Bengalis never spoke about the Black Hole incident. They clearly felt that by denying the incident ever took place they could remove the moral justification for British rule.

The Indians are, of course, faced with a very awkward problem. This is, that without the active collaboration of the Indians the British could never have conquered India, let alone ruled it. At the height of the empire there was never more than 900 British civil servants and about 70,000 white troops in a country of over 250 million Indians. Even at Plassey more

Indians died fighting for Clive than British. For the record the English had 4 killed, 9 wounded, 2 missing, while 16 of the Indian sepoys fighting for Clive were killed and 36 wounded. And in 1857 the British would never have survived in India but for the help they received from the locals – in particular the Sikhs and the Gurkhas. Some of the Sikhs are still very proud of this. This was brought home to me when recently I attended a function at the Imperial War Museum in London organised by the Maharajah Duleep Singh Centenary Trust to listen to a speech about a Sikh regiment in the British Indian Army. One of the publications that was distributed was called Gurubaani (Universal Truth). It had messages from Tony Blair, Ken Livingstone, Mayor of London, Sir John Stephens, then Commissioner of the Metropolitan Police and recruitment advertisements from the British Army, Royal Air Force and Royal Navy. One chapter called 'Key Events in Sikh History' described how the Sikhs saved the Raj:

> The Sikhs helped the British to crush the Indian Mutiny uprising to prevent the return to the cruel Mughal regime aided by Hindu ministers and minor Hindu princedoms. Also, the Sikhs had not forgotten the traitorous assault on Khalsa Raj by the Indians in league with the British in 1849.

The logic here is interesting. The Sikhs were angry with their fellow Indians for attacking them but not with the foreign English for defeating their Khalsa Raj, suggesting that at that time a sense of Indian nationalism was still to be born. Perhaps, not surprisingly, what the section on key events does not mention is that the Sikhs matched and even outdid the British in the plunder, loot and killings that marked 1857. It is also worth stressing that while Dyer, the Englishman, ordered the firing into the unarmed Indian crowd in Amritsar, the troops who did the actual firing were their fellow Hindus, the Gurkhas. As he lined his troops in front of the crowd Dyer's orders on that fateful day were, 'Gurkhas right, 59th left. Fire.'

The fact that the British could recruit Indians to fight for them and even wage war against other Indians was the most remarkable achievement of the Raj. It showed the British genius at work, establishing an empire where the fighting was done by Indian soldiers guided by an Officer Corps wholly British with the money, including the money to train British officers known as 'capitation charges', coming from Indian revenues.

During the Raj the British were very proud of this achievement, and in 1911 Major G. F. MacMunn exulted in *The Armies of India* how 'the tramping disciplined legions are not the beef and porridge and potato-reared youngsters of the Isles, but of the most part men of the ancient races of Hindustan, ruled and trained and led after the manner of the English'.

In Michael Ondaatje's novel *The English Patient*, a character says of the Indian soldier Kip, 'What's he doing fighting English wars?' In all except the Boer War, which being a war between white tribes it was considered not advisable to have brown soldiers, Indians fought for the British, extending their dominions and preserving their rule. During the half century before 1914 Indian troops served in more than dozen imperial campaigns from China to Uganda, helping the spread of the pink blobs round the world. The Liberal politician W. E. Ford complained in 1878 that the government was relying 'not upon the patriotism and sprit of our own people but on getting Sikhs, Gurkhas and the Mussalman to fight for us'.

A popular music hall jingo of the time went:

> We don't want to fight
> But by Jove if we do
> We won't go to the front ourselves
> We'll send the mild Hindoo

During the First World War 1.2 million Indians were part of the war effort, 800,000 as fighters. Indian money paid for the war with £100 million given outright to Britain for the war. Between £20 million and £30 million was given annually for each of the war years. Indian troops fought on the western front, in Gallipoli – indeed they did better there than the Australians and the New Zealanders – in East Africa, Egypt and the Persian Gulf. In the Middle East, the Allenby victories owed much to Indian soldiers. If, in the taking of Jerusalem, the Indian units were not the largest part of his forces, by the time Allenby came to take Damascus they were in the majority. His third front in Mesopotamia was wholly Indian. The creation of modern-day Iraq owes much to Indian soldiers and for a time during the British occupation in the 1920s the rupee was the currency of that country. In the Second World War the Indian contribution on behalf of the British was even more extensive with a total of 2.8 million Indians fighting for the Allies in various sectors.

Both wars caused enormous collateral damage to India. Towards the end of the First World War influenza broke out in the trenches. The Indian troops fighting there caught the disease and carried it back to India. But in India the war had made the British denude India of doctors and as the returning Indian soldiers spread the disease, there was little or no medical care available. Sixteen million Indians died, almost double the numbers killed in the battlefields of the war.

The Second World War saw the dreadful Bengal famine of 1943. In a fertile land, which produced two rice crops a year, this was a man-made famine created by the wretched Bengal administration and not helped by the war cabinet in London. Recent British histories of this period accept that the anti-Indian attitude of Churchill, who believed Indians were the worst people in the world after the Germans, played a major part in the famine. The war cabinet refused to divert food to Bengal encouraged by the British government's scientific adviser Frederick Lindemann, who according to historians Christoper Bayly and Tim Harper, 'seems to have thought that the Bengalis were a weak race and that overbreeding and eugenic unfitness were the basic reasons for the scarcity'. Three million Bengalis died – the worst famine to hit south Asia in the twentieth century.

Amazingly, one group of soldiers from the subcontinent fought for the British in their wars although they were not even British subjects, or even Indians. They come from a country whose last war was actually fought against the British, nearly two hundred years ago. For the last 180 years this country has been neutral in all the wars the world has witnessed, yet its citizens under the British flag have fought all over the world including the two world wars. They are the Gorkhas from Nepal.

Nepal is the only Hindu country in the world. Between 1814 and 1816 it fought a series of wars against the British in India. In the very first conflict at the end of 1814 when 34,000 British troops, the overwhelming majority, of course, being Indian sepoys fought 12,000 Gorkhas the result was sensational. Despite being outnumbered, on three of the four fronts the Gorkhas beat the British with heavy losses. The British did recover and even marched to Khatmandu but they had seen how valiantly the Gorkhas could fight. Both sides decided it made sense to have a treaty. This saw the British making gains: Simla came to the Raj starting the whole Raj phenomenon of the hill station, but the Gorkhas preserved their freedom as a people. Under the treaty of Sargauli, Nepal was allowed to carry on as an independent state. The British promised not to interfere in its internal workings as long as Nepal allowed the British to recruit Gorkhas to fight for them.

The result was Britain got some of the most feared fighters the world has known and Nepal became a closed country, so closed that it would not even allow access to its side of Mount Everest. During the Raj every expedition to the peak of the highest mountain in the world was through the more difficult Tibet side, none of which was successful. The British had nothing to say when in 1846 a despotic Rajput Rana family seized power and made the Nepalese King their captive. Nepal was effectively put in a deep freeze for the next century with no internal development. It only came out of the deep freeze in 1949, two years after Indian independence, largely through the efforts of Nehru and despite the opposition of the British ambassador in Nepal. This also opened the southern route to Everest in good time for the first successful ascent by a British expedition coinciding with the Queen's coronation in 1953. However, the Gorkha soldiers who fought for Britain were never made British citizens and it is only now that the British are even thinking of giving their Gorkhas citizenship, finally turning the world's greatest mercenary soldiers into British subjects. (I have used the spelling Gorkha as this is the one the Gorkhas themselves use. The British trying to cope with the Gorkali language went through many variations from Goorkah, to Goorka, to Goorkha before settling on Gurkha, which is still the term used in the British army, sometimes shortened to Gurks.)

To an extent Nepal was a more extreme case of how the Raj governed India. There is no more widely held belief than that the British ruled the whole of India and when they left India they partitioned the land. Both are myths. In 1947 more than a third of the Indian landmass and two-thirds of the Indian population were not subject to British rule. They were ruled by native Indian princes who were not part of British India. They had a treaty with the Raj governing external relations. The Raj appointed a resident in each state but within his boundaries a prince could do what he liked, as long as he did not do anything to threaten overall British control. Often their most important engagement as far as the British were concerned was to make sure the Viceroy on his visit bagged a tiger. They even had their own armies, some of whom fought as part of the Allied effort in both the world wars. Neither the British courts nor the famed Indian Civil Service, which administrated India, could intervene to help any of the prince's subjects. In 1947 each of the 565 princely states on the subcontinent had the option of joining either India or Pakistan or going independent.

The integration of these states into the modern republic of India was not the work of an Englishman but of an Indian, Sardar Vallabhai Patel, the tough, no-nonsense Gujarati politician who ran Gandhi's political machine and became deputy Prime Minister in Nehru's first Indian cabinet. He bullied these princes into becoming part of India, giving up their princely states in return for a privy purse. The story goes he gathered them round him, held out the palm of his hand and said, 'You are like little insects in the middle of my palm. Anytime I want I can make a fist crushing you. Best you come in quietly.' The story may be apocryphal but whatever he said worked like a charm. Kingdoms that had existed for centuries, and even kept out of the British embrace, joined the new Indian Union in weeks. The odd ruler created problems and the new India solved the situation with the sort of show of force, as in Hyderabad, which the old Raj warriors would have approved of as it copied their methods.

The only princely state that escaped Patel was Kashmir which the British had sold to Gulab Singh for £750,000 back in 1846. A hundred and one years later the ruler, Sir Hari Singh, dithered so long he allowed

Jinnah to unleash his irregular forces of tribesmen, efficiently controlled by Pakistan. A panic-stricken Hari Singh acceded to India just in time for Indian forces to save him from defeat. But the subsequent war proved messy, the state remains divided and a flashpoint between India and Pakistan.

However, the problem in Kashmir, and the continuing insurrections in certain parts of its northwest frontier which has required the continued heavy presence of the Indian army, should not obscure the fact that in the nearly sixty years since India got freedom the country has restructured itself quite dramatically. The British had left behind provinces that were convenient administrative units for an alien, foreign, rule but made little concession to Indian realities. Even before independence the Congress had decided that India, reflecting its diversity and the fact that its people speak many languages, would be reorganised along linguistic states. It is by no means complete and new states are always being created. In 1947 India inherited six provinces from British India. This has now grown to 31 states and 4 union territories such as Delhi, the capital. Indians are constantly creating new states and since I wrote the first edition of this book, twenty years ago, four new states have been created.

This can best be judged if you pick up *Wisden* and look at the sides that now play in the Ranji trophy, the Indian national cricket championships and compare them to the ones playing in 1947. Many of the teams such as Holkar, Gwalior, Patiala, Rajputhana, Travancore-Cochin, Central Provinces and Berar, Nawanagar and Western India have disappeared. The list includes some Ranji Trophy winners like the mighty Holkar for whom Denis Compton played in an epic, losing Ranji final. They have been replaced by many new names and more can be expected as states continue to be created. The contrast with Australia is interesting. The number of states that take part in the Sheffield Shield competition have increased since Victoria first won the Shield in 1892–3 but none of the original states have disappeared. The Indian reorganisation has not been without violence. My own personal memory is of a boy, no more than 12, being killed outside our flat in the centre of Bombay during an agitation that led to the creation of the state of Maharashtra out of the old British province of Bombay Presidency. But given the wars, including a civil war, and the millions of native Americans killed during the first century of the American republic, as it went from the 13 colonies that had won freedom from Britain to a continental power, the Indians have done their internal reorganisation with much less violence and in a much more peaceful, democratic fashion. To make new countries without violence is like saying you can make omelettes without breaking eggs. Israel, created a year after India, illustrates this perfectly. But India has some distinction which is often overlooked. One of its three wars with Pakistan helped create a new state (Bangladesh) after a short, successful war when it beat Pakistan and despite opposition from the United States which, for all its commitment to freedom and democracy, did not want the people of then east Pakistan freed from the tyranny of the west Pakistani army.

There is one other feature of British India that is quite amazing. While it had the appearance of a state, it failed to meet many of the essential requirements of a state. One of these must be a commonly accepted legal system. The British India did not have such a legal system.

For the first hundred years of British rule it was the East India Company, not the Crown that ruled in India. So curious had been the nature of the British conquest that even in May 1857 – just a month before the centenary of the Battle of Plassey – a Mughal Emperor still ruled in Delhi and the British still paid homage to him. It was a piece of elaborate fiction, but instructive at that. As the British had mopped up the Indian feudal powers, banishing some, pensioning others, they did so almost as agents of the 'great Mughal' in Delhi. It was the most curious form of political leasehold tenancy. After every battle the Mughal Emperor would grant the British 'firmans' – rights – to levy taxes and control a territory and, in theory, the British still accepted the Mughal Emperor as ruler of India – and the ultimate freeholder of the country. Four times a year they presented themselves to the Emperor and offered him *nazar* – tribute.

When it came to law British India basically followed the Muslim, Mughal, law the British had inherited. In the various courts of British India a Muslim Law Officer delivered a fatwa saying whether the accused was guilty and what the crime should be. The Englishman sitting next to him then passed sentence. If they disagreed then disputes were resolved by the Sudder Court, the court of appeal. As Sir George Campbell wrote in 1852, the foundation was Mahommedan (Muslim) code, altered and added to but 'the hidden substructure on which this whole building rests is this Mahommedan law; take which away, and we should have no definition of, or authority, for punishing many of the most common crimes'.

So closely did the British follow Muslim law that in this period, long after British rule had been established, it was common for robbers in Bengal to have a foot lopped off.

Even after 1857, when India came under the Crown, the British hesitated to bring their legal system into India. There was never a complete change to the criminal, civil and domestic law the British had inherited. Indeed the Law Commission set up after the revolt of 1857 recommended that it was best to leave Hindu and Muslim law outside the legislative scope of the government of India. A common criminal law was introduced in 1860 and there were other changes including the setting up of High Courts. But throughout their rule the British never made any moves to change, let alone modernise, the personal law of the Hindus and Muslims or the other Indian communities. They remained what they had for centuries, long before the Indians had even heard about the British. Indeed the British went out of their way to reinforce such ancient customs and laws. As Michael Edwards says:

> Virtually no changes took place in Islamic personal law during the period of Crown government, because of the Muslim belief that legislation is the prerogative of God. The British interfered little in matters of Hindu personal law, partly for the usual reasons of security, and partly because of the formidable problems involved in any attempt at codification... In general the British sought to protect customary law – even, in some cases, to extend its application. In 1935, for instance an Act was passed in the North West Frontier Province which was designed to impose orthodox Muslim law on customary law, and in 1937 the Act was extended to cover the rest of British India. Various laws were also passed to give statutory definition to the customary laws of other Indian communities such as the Parsees.

Like the law, so the currency. India is the only country in the world where words like millions and billions have no meaning. Indians have their own terms. These are lakhs which stands for 100,000, and crores which stands for 100 lakhs equal to 10 million in western terms. When I was growing up in India a lakh was a lot of money and to say somebody was a lakhopati was to denote he was fabulously rich. Now it is crorepati and the Indian equivalent of *Who Wants To Be A Millionaire*, hosted by its greatest film star, Amitabh Bachchan, is called *Who Wants To Be A Crorepati*? Both lakhs and crores are ancient Indian terms and, reflecting the fact that both Hinduism and Buddhism spread out from India to south-east Asia and beyond, these terms are also used there. Just as the British anglicised the ancient Sanskrit word rupya into rupee so they just adopted the old Indian ways of denoting money. It meant that despite nearly two hundred years of British rule India has remained outside the world's commonly accepted monetary terms. Terms like millions and billions used in the rest of the world are never used in India and visitors to the country have to do quick mental calculations to work out what lakhs and crores mean.

But what about railways and the armed forces? These were two great institutions created by the British and bequeathed to a free India. Surely through these institutions the British united India? Not quite.

The railways remain a great achievement of the Raj. It opened up India in a way it had never opened up before and in 1947 the British left India a vast railway network comparable to an industrialised country, despite the fact that India had little or no industry. But as the Raj did not rule all of India railways lines did not reach all parts of India. British India was well served by railways: in princely India the reach of the railways depended on the whim of the individual ruler. In 1949, two years after Indian independence, when the railways were finally integrated into the modern Indian Railway system, the Railway Board had to combine 21 railways, some operated by the government of India, the others by the princely states. Visitors to India can quickly see what a patchwork quilt of lines this has left India. Kashmir for instance has very little by way of railways, with no train to Srinagar, the capital. Rajasthan, the modern Indian state, created by merging the many princely states that existed until 1947, has a very poorly developed railway system. Travel operators still suggest visitors take the car if they really want to see this vast and fascinating state.

The Army is even an even more revealing example of a Raj institution which, while it suited the occupying power's purpose admirably, had to be recast out of all recognition to became the army of a free country. The biggest challenge facing the new Indian nation was that the British had insulated the army from the people and the recruitment was based on a certain racial philosophy. Following the revolt of 1857 the British had completely reorganised the Indian Army developing what was called the 'martial race' theory. The western world was then in the middle of its quest to find scientific evidence that would prove that certain races were genetically superior to other races, the white races being at the top of the tree. In India this meant dividing India into races which could fight and others who could not. This was spelled out very clearly by MacMunn in *The Armies of India* – a book that had a very warm foreword by Field-Marshall Earl Roberts, the commander-in-chief of the British armies in India.

> It is one of the essential differences between the East and West that in the East, with few exceptions, only certain clan and classes can bear arms; the others have not the physical courage necessary for the warrior. In Europe, as we know, every able-bodied man, given food and arms, is a fighting man of some sort, some better, some worse but still as capable of bearing arms as any other of his nationality. In the East, or certainly in India, this is not so.

MacMunn then went on to divide Indians into martial races such as Sikhs, the Jats, the Muslims, and from outside India the Pathans and the Gorkhas. These were the only Indians recruited to the British Indian army. Other Indians like the Bengalis and the Kashmiris, being considered racially incapable of fighting, were kept out of the army.

The martial race theory remained a feature of British recruitment until it broke down during the Second World War. But even when the war forced the British to cast their net wider, Churchill was appalled the martial race theory had been abandoned. In 1943 he wrote to Field-Marshall Claude Auckinleck, commander-in-chief in India, that he should 'rely as much as possible on the martial races'. Auckinleck had to inform him that war-time 'maintenance problems' problems meant six battalions of martial regiments had already been disbanded.

But the British did not just divide the Indians into martial and non-martial races. In their army they made sure Indians did not mix and the different units were kept in watertight religious and caste units. The British did not, as the nationalists allege, create these differences amongst the Indians. They had existed long before the British arrived. But they did nothing to discourage them, made sure the divisions were maintained, indeed they nurtured them as it proved their theory that India had never been a united nation. So in the British Indian Army every platoon had a Muslim, a Hindu and Sikh section. They had separate messes, never ate together and even had their own greetings. It was only in January 1949 after General K. M. Cariappa became the first Indian commander-in-chief of the army that these divisions began to be dismantled, with Cariappa taking a decision that was both symbolic and ironic.

During the Second World War Subhas Bose, the Indian nationalist, had fled British India first to Germany and then Japan raising an army from the Indians captured by the Axis powers to fight for Indian freedom. In creating his national army Bose spent much time trying to weld the disparate Indian mercenaries who had volunteered to fight for the British into a nationalist army. He had to devise a common Indian slogan and came up with 'Jai Hind' (Hail India), replacing the many caste and communal slogans of the British Indian Army. The Raj, which did everything possible to denigrate Bose's army, banned the term in the Indian Army. But Indians outside the army began to use it and it is now the common greeting among Indians. When Cariappa, who as part of the British Indian Army, had fought against Bose's army helping defeat it, became commander-in-chief, he too started ending his speeches with Jai Hind. It was soon adopted as the greeting between the officers and men of the army.

This, along with the abandonment of the martial race theory and recruitment from all classes of Indians to the army, the establishment of the National Cadet Corps and the Territorial Army – both of which the British had discouraged – converted an army of occupation into one more in tune with the Indian people.

It is a measure of the Indian achievement in recasting its British created army that today, some sixty years after independence, the army remains out of politics. There has never been any hint that it would ever enter politics. Contrast this with most other former colonies and in particular neighbouring Pakistan. It inherited the same Raj army from the British. But the failure by the Pakistanis to change an army created for occupation into one for national needs has meant that the Pakistani armed forces soon entered politics and the history of Pakistan is a sorry story of military rule punctuated by brief periods of unsatisfactory civilian rule.

There is only one institution the British left behind that was both truly Indian in scope and which did not change after independence. That was cricket. Why and how Indians took to and have shaped it since the British left is the subject of this book. However, what is fascinating is that cricket's development in India was completely out of step with what the British were doing in other areas of Indian life.

We can best see this if we look at what was happening in the 1920s. This shaped the India that emerged in 1947.

There is much debate among British historians as to whether the British left India too quickly. The historian Lawrence James in his book *The Raj* has a chapter called 'Was It Too Quick?' This, while trying to be fair to Lord Mountbatten, the last British Viceroy, ends up blaming him, for leaving India too quickly. Andrew Roberts, the right-wing historian, goes further and alleges in *Eminent Churchillians* that Mountbatten was biased in favour of the Hindu Nehru and cheated the Muslim Jinnah. Since neither historian says when the British should have left, and Roberts's grasp of Indian history is so poor that he often comes over as a pamphleteer, these opinions sound like a long sigh disguising a certain British lament that they ever had to leave India. The fact is for all the criticisms of Mountbatten, by August 1947 the British in India were on the ropes and had little room for manoeuvre. The preceding five years had seen sustained resistance to British rule and a great deal of violence. The British could only rule India with the help of Indian collaborators and by 1947 it had run out of collaborators.

In March 1943, seven months after Gandhi had asked the British to quit India provoking a general movement against the British, General Lockhart had concluded that India would have to be regarded as 'an occupied and hostile country'. Then that year the Bengal famine killed 3 million Indians, more than three times the number that died in the killings of 1947. Following the end of the war an upsurge in both nationalist demands for freedom and violence between Indian communities had seen many killings, with the British unable to control the situation. What made it worse for the British was that they could no longer rely on their Indian soldiers as they had for centuries. The end of the war saw mutinies by Indian soldiers and sailors of the British Indian Armed Forces. At times, as in Bombay, virtually the entire Indian navy mutinied. And even the British soldiers, demob happy after such a long war, were wondering what they were doing in India when the Indians clearly did not want them. A popular song among British troops in India went as follows:

Land of shit and filth and wogs.
Gonorrhoea, syphilis, clap and pox.
Memsahib's paradise, soldiers hell.
India fare thee fucking well.

But the 1920s was different. Britain was still in control and I agree with Nirad Chaudhuri that was when Britain missed the boat in India. The decade had started with India, after its great war effort in support of Britain, expecting some reward. But instead of presents it got a kicking, and quite literally as well, in the form of the Amritsar massacre. This, aside from innocent men, women and children being gunned down, also saw Dyer forcing Indians to crawl on their hands and knees through a street where a British missionary woman had been assaulted. Gandhi launched the first of his non-violent campaigns calling for swraj, self-rule. However even at this stage Indians were not asking for independence, let alone withdrawal from the Empire. Gandhi never said swraj would mean India would have to leave the Empire. In the early 1920s that idea had not entered the heads of Indian politicians. All they wanted was to be treated like the white dominions of the Empire who had all been allowed to form their own independent governments within the Empire. It was only on the very last day of the decade, on 31 December 1929, after repeated British refusals to consider any Indian requests, that Gandhi was forced by younger radicals like Nehru and Subhas Bose to became, as he put it an 'independence wallah'. That was the day when for the first time in its history Congress called for complete independence.

While all this was going on in India there was a parallel debate in high government circles in Britain about what was called Indianisation of the British services in India such as the army and the medical services. In other words could more Indians be allowed to become officers in the Indian Army, could more Indians be allowed to become doctors in the medical service?

As far as doctors were concerned, the British accepted that more Indians had to be recruited to the Indian Medical Service, but made it clear that steps should be taken to ensure that British officers and their wives should be treated by people of their own race and not by Indian doctors.

The debate on whether to increase the number of Indian officers in the British Indian Army revealed all the old fears the British had had about granting equal status to the Indians. At this stage there were only a token number of Indian officers. The officer corps was predominantly British, commanding an army whose soldiers were all Indians. In 1921 a report prepared by Sir John Shea, then the officiating chief of general staff in India, had recommended that the British should try and aim to completely Indianise the army. Shea was no revolutionary. He suggested this should be done over the next thirty years. But even this idea was horrific to British generals and politicians. On 12 January 1922 it came up before a cabinet committee where Chief of the Imperial General Staff, Sir Henry Wilson, said that he, along with a considerable section of military opinion, would oppose the entry of Indians to the Royal College of Artillery. There were misgivings about allowing Indians into Sandhurst as well. True, in the Indian Civil Service more Indians were being allowed in, but Wilson argued the army was different. Having Indians as civil servants meant English civil servants might share an office with an Indian. Having more Indians in the army would mean English officers having to share the same mess with Indians and that was impossible. Also, equality would mean British officers serving under Indians and that was totally unacceptable. Throughout the decade this issue of having more Indian officers kept coming up and politicians feared that more Indian officers meant the British would refuse to join the Indian Army. As Indians alleged that this showed that the British were following a racial policy, public statements were made to try and counter the charge. However, in private British ministers did not disguise their intentions. In November 1927 Lord Birkenhead, then Secretary of State for India, told the cabinet subcommittee that 'the falling off in the number of British candidates of the right classes for commission in the Indian Army' was due to 'the reluctance of parents to send their sons to serve under Indians and to live with Indians as mess mates'.

That very month Birkenhead made another decision that was to have far reaching consequences for India. He chose a commission of MPs and peers headed by the Liberal politician Sir John Simon to visit India and report on whether Indians were capable of governing themselves. The Simon commission was part of the ten-year review promised in the 1919 reforms to help the British parliament decide whether Indians should be given more powers to manage their own affairs. Birkenhead had no doubts that Indians would ever be capable of managing their affairs. Towards the end of his life he wrote a book called *The World* in 2030 which predicted many things such as the automation of industry, mass air travel, synthetic food and the atom bomb, but even in 2030 he predicted Indians would be incapable of ruling themselves and the English would always remain in charge. Birkenhead, of course, also fully subscribed to the Raj's view of the master-race theory that underpinned the Raj. Essential to this was to make sure that Indians were always kept at arm's length from the white women. In 1926 there had been some reports about some of Nizam of Hyderabad's retainers at a London theatre 'leering at inadequately dressed dancing girls'. Birkenhead wrote immediately to the Viceroy 'that few things are more damaging to our prestige as a people than the exposure of the bodies of white women before Indians'.

And while Birkenhead was one of the great British politicians of the early twentieth century and considered the finest legal brain, having been Lord Chancellor, he found India and Indians boring. As part of his job he had to meet Indians, but was often rude to them. Once he introduced an Indian as a new member of his advisory council when that Indian had already been serving on the council for five years. Now in the casual style he reserved for India and Indian affairs – in his regular letters to the Viceroy he would often amuse himself by writing about cricket, in particular England–Australia Tests and events at Wimbledon tennis – he offered Sir John Simon, a Liberal politician, the chairmanship of the commission on the golf course.

The announcement of the Simon Commission provoked a furious response in India with the Indians further incensed by the arrogant way in which Birkenhead made the announcement, telling Indians that if only they could understand they would see they had been given more power. For Indians it smacked of racial despotism and a contempt for India. Indians began to realise that whatever they did they would never be considered the equal of an Englishman. The Simon Commission led to a lot of talking, two round table conferences, but the demand of nationalist India that Indians should run their own affairs was never conceded. Simon, far from taking India any nearer self-government, actually united the whole of political India, which just then had been in a slumber and, more crucially it destroyed whatever little trust the nationalists had for Britain. From now on there was little faith that Britain would ever deliver on its promises on India. Within three years Gandhi launched his great civil disobedience campaign, leading his famous march to the sea to make salt as an illustration of the iniquity of British rule.

Contrast all this with how at almost the same time the British, or rather the MCC, was behaving with Indian cricket. When it came to cricket the English authorities did much to help India became a proper cricketing nation.

The year 1927, when Birkenhead was setting out policy for India, was also a crucial one for Indian cricket. On a February evening in 1927 a meeting took place in the Roshanara Club in Delhi. Four men gathered on the well-manicured lawns of the club and as they settled in the comfortable wicker chairs, and bearers rushed round with pegs of whiskies, the international future of Indian cricket was decided. One of the men urged his companions to consider setting up a proper Board of Control for Cricket in India. If they did so, then he promised to go back to Lord's and make the case for India to be admitted as a full member of the Imperial Cricket Conference.

The man who made this case was an Englishman called Arthur Gilligan, a former captain of England. That winter he had brought the first MCC team to ever tour India, playing matches all over India.

When the idea for this tour was first mooted it had nothing to do with Indian cricket. It was meant to help English cricket or rather European cricket in India. The British in India did not call themselves British. They called themselves Europeans; in other words, they emphasised that they were a special ethnic group of white people. All their organisations had the title European and the first political organisation in Calcutta was called The European Association. In clubs and railway carriages that excluded Indians the signs read 'For Europeans only'.

In 1926 a certain A. Murray Robertson thought it would be a good idea to get an MCC team to tour India and play European sides. The Europeans occasionally played with Indians, but in Calcutta they had not done so for a long time, and this tour was meant to show the English at home how strong European cricket in India had become. In the summer of 1926 Robertson was in England where he joined up with another English businessman from Calcutta, Sir William Currie, and they approached the MCC. Lord Harris, former Governor of Bombay, was President of the MCC and therefore presided over that year's Imperial Cricket Conference. Harris was a diehard imperialist and he was no different to Birkenhead in the way he thought about Indians. Gokhale the great leader of the Indian moderates, and the mentor of Gandhi described Harris's reign as governor as an 'unsympathetic and reactionary administration' and Harris in his letters makes clear his contempt for Indians. As he put it in his letter to Lord Cross on 4 June 1891, after a year as governor, 'We can do infinitely more work in their climate than they can, and they get fat and lazy as they rise in rank, whilst our civilians are as active as young men.'

But Harris had no problems in encouraging Indians to play cricket. And now, probably because the two representatives were English, in a very Harris-like decision he on his own initiative invited Robertson and Currie to attend the ICC meetings where they were described as 'India's representatives'. There was no Indian Cricket Board and, of course, neither Robertson or Currie considered themselves Indians. They would have been horrified to be described as Indians. Their fellow delegates who were all of English stock did not ask how they could speak for India. That question would not have occurred to them.

At this stage the cricket story was in sync with the wider political one and even the wider cricketing picture round the world. The English had taken their game round the world but the people the MCC recognised as playing the game were, as the phrase went, sons of the English race. They inhabited far-flung corners of the world in Australia, New Zealand and South Africa, but they all traced their roots back to England. The West Indies did have people from other races but they were always led by people of English stock and their representatives at the ICC were always white.

But Gilligan's tour of India changed things and the result was that Indians got involved with the international game at the highest level. For various reasons the tour Murray Robertson or Currie wanted did not come about. Gilligan's tour was financed by the Maharajah of Patiala and Gilligan, himself, did not share the master race ideas of his fellow Englishmen. He not only played Indian sides but what is more did much to encourage Indians to organise their cricket.

How very different Gilligan was can be judged from the behaviour of another Englishman. This was Cecil Headlam of the Oxford University Authentics Team which had toured India some years before Gilligan's visit. Headlam then wrote a book about the tour which has a revealing description of the problems he faced trying to get a railway ticket and his encounter with an Indian booking clerk. Headlam got very upset that what would have taken a minute and a half at Euston took nearly an hour and a half. This is how Headlam reacted:

> I put the toe of my riding boot round the rear leg of this three-legged stool and gave it a sharp jerk. In a second it capsized and my Aryan brother capsized with it. Never shall I forget the look of mingled astonishment and awe upon the faces of his gaping underling, never the look of fear and injured pride upon the countenance of that sprawling and obese black gentleman. Without saying a word he got up and bowed and deferentially led the way to the ticket office. In two minutes I had got my tickets and paid for them.

Gilligan, in contrast, met Indians on terms of perfect equality and the meeting that February evening at the Roshanara club was one of many such meetings, if the most important. Sitting round Gilligan on that Delhi lawn were Patiala, Grant Govan, an English businessman in India and an Indian he employed, Anthony De Mello. It showed how Indians and the English could work together if only the English were prepared to shed their ideas of being a race meant to rule and subdue Indians. By the end of the evening the Indians were so encouraged by what Gillian was saying they decided to form an Indian Cricket Board. Gilligan's influence was immense. De Mello wrote, 'We felt if a man so cricket-wise as Gilligan considered Indian cricket had reached a state in its development where it could challenge the world then we had certainly achieved something. Gilligan promised to state our case when he returned to Lord's.'

Gilligan kept his word. Two years later India gained admittance as a full member of the ICC and in another three had made its Test debut at Lord's. In the 1920s political Britain could not imagine Indians, or any non-white people for that matter, as being capable of governing themselves. They could not even treat them as their human equals as Birkenhead's behaviour shows. But in cricketing, England, or at least some of its representatives, could see the merits in Indians and this opened the door for cricket when the political door remained shut.

The MCC's departure from the norms that governed the Raj was all the more striking because in another part of the sporting field the British were striking a very different attitude. The year 1928 was also the one when India made its mark on the international hockey scene. In many ways this was a more dramatic entrance than anything Indian cricket had achieved at that stage.

That year saw India take part in Olympic hockey for the first time at the Amsterdam Olympics. Indian hockey's rise had been dramatic. It was only two years previously that India had played its first international matches against New Zealand. In Amsterdam India won gold and after that for the next 5 Olympics it kept on winning the hockey gold. It only lost its first ever hockey match in the Olympics in 1960, 32 years after it had played its first match and 13 years after Indian independence. During this period India played 30 matches in the Olympics and won them all, scoring 197 goals while conceding only 8 – a stupendous winning run in any sport.

But there was a revealing British reaction to these Indian triumphs. The moment India emerged as a hockey nation in the 1928 Olympics Great Britain withdrew. Until India emerged Britain had been the supreme hockey nation in the world. It had won gold in 1908 and 1920 (the only two Olympics before 1928 when the competition was held). But with India rampant Great Britain did not want to take part. It only came back in 1948 a year after Indian independence when for good measure, despite playing in front of its home crowd, it was thrashed 4–0.

David Wallechinsky the historian of Olympic records writes:

> Ever since India first appeared on the international hockey field Great Britain had studiously avoided playing the Indian team, apparently afraid of the embarrassment of losing to one of its colonies.

Certainly the very nature of Olympics where national anthems are played made India v. Great Britain much more of a nationalistic contest. This was emphasised in the 1936 Berlin Olympics, popularly known as the Nazi Olympics due to the propaganda use of it made by Hitler. Although India marched out under the British flag before the match the team gathered in the dressing room and saluted the tricolour of the Indian National Congress. It was said to be the idea of Dyan Chand, the greatest player in hockey history. It inspired the Indians and they beat Hitler's Nordic supermen 8–1, with Dyan Chand, himself, scoring 6 goals playing barefoot. The manner in which he scored the goals was Indian hockey at its best, the fact that he did not wear shoes marked out his Indianess in a manner that no Indian cricketer could have emulated. Not that Indian leaders cared much for this. In 1932 with the Indians struggling to send a team to the Los Angeles Olympics Gandhi was approached for help and asked, 'What is hockey?' The British, however, understood well enough its potent nationalist power. But if the British avoided Indian hockey for twenty years, fearing that defeat might make white Englishmen look inferior to brown Indians and cast a shadow over the Raj, they clearly had no such concerns about encouraging Indian cricket.

It is worth stressing that India's admission to world cricket marked a major change in the international game. For the first time a non-white country with its own cricket structure had been admitted and India remained the exception in the cricket world until the 1950s when Pakistan joined the ICC. All the other cricketing countries were either white, or as in the case of the West Indies, led by whites. For the West Indies this only changed in 1960 after a bitter struggle when for the first time a black captain, Frank Worrell, took over. But even after that change white South Africa not only insisted on playing only against its traditional rivals Australia, England and New Zealand but also dictating who these countries could select with South Africa making it clear that if they selected a non-white person they would not play them.

However, in one respect both Birkenhead and the MCC were in agreement. This was that a second or third string team from England was always good enough for India. Birkenhead's choice of Simon and his commission members illustrated this perfectly. Simon was a senior Liberal politician but at that stage his star was in decline along with his party which was about to be marginalised. He only agreed to be chairman if the Conservatives promised not to contest his seat which Birkenhead managed to arrange with some difficulty. The members of his commission were all nonentities, except for one – Clement Attlee, then unknown but would go on to become Prime Minister and preside over India's freedom.

Birkenhead had tried to get more distinguished men but they refused. He had originally wanted Lord Hewart, the Lord Chief Justice, to head the commission but he could not spare the time. The heavyweight peers Birkenhead approached turned him down and he had to settle for nonentities with one man getting the job because he had married the sister of Lord Irwin, the Viceroy.

The MCC faced similar problems. A. W. Carr had regained the Ashes in 1926, ending a long run of Australian triumphs stretching back to before the First World War. He was reigning captain but declined. MCC had to go back to Gilligan who had led England to defeat in Australia in 1924–5, losing 4–1. Neither did the great players who had helped win back the Ashes go to India. Holmes, Sutcliffe, Woolley and Kilner all said no. Fred Root accepted but his county Worcestershire, said he must rest. Even then the Gilligan team was more representative of English cricket than Simon was of British politics. It had Tate, Andrew Sandham, Astill and Wyatt but Gilligan had to keep reassuring Indians that this was the strongest side MCC could muster. However, the tour was so curious it was not until 1937, a decade later, that it was ruled that the matches were first class; even then only 26 of the 34 matches were considered first class.

The MCC side set a pattern that was to be part of English team selection for the next half century. Whenever an Indian tour came up the leading players opted out. A whole galaxy of cricketers never toured India with England: Peter May, Denis Compton, Trevor Bailey, Godfrey Evans, Alex Bedser, F. S. Trueman, Jim Laker, Ray Illingworth, Brian Close, John Snow, Len Hutton – names that would figure in almost everybody's list of the greats of post-war English cricket. As late as 1972–3 it was the convention before an Indian tour for the leading cricketers, including the captain, to opt out. The selectors would then appoint a tyro captain such as Tony Lewis for the 1972–3 tour.

The nadir was reached in 1951–2. Nigel Howard, the Lancashire captain, who had never before played for England was chosen as the captain of the first MCC team to tour India since independence. He played four Tests, won one, then was injured for the fifth which India won, its first-ever Test victory. Howard returned to England, never played for his country again and has the most unique record in cricket: played four Tests, all as captain and all against India. On that tour he led a team of a few seasoned professionals but mostly young players coming to the top. Thus Tom Graveney and Brian Statham went when they were making their reputations but did not tour India once they were established players. It was only in 1976–7 that for the first time a reigning captain, Jardine apart, took an England cricket team to India. As it happens during that tour plans were being laid for Greig to join Kerry Packer and that was the last time series he captained England in a series.

The leading cricketers were not the only ones disinclined to visit India. The top people in all walks of British life avoided India if they could. No British Prime Minister between Wellington and Ramsay McDonald, that is between 1831 and 1924, went to India. So in this crucial period in British history nobody at the top level of government had any firsthand knowledge of India, the country that was the source of British power and which had made her the mistress of the world.

Instead, the British relied on British experts on India who themselves never visited. John Mill wrote his *History of India* – a standard history book on India for generations of British students – without ever setting foot in that country. John Maynard Keynes worked in the India Office and wrote books setting out how Indian finance should be organised. He helped create the Reserve Bank of India. But he never visited India. Indeed he said that he never needed to or wanted to visit the country. His closest contact with an Indian was a student called Bimla Sarkar. They may well have been homosexual lovers, Keynes's biographer cannot be sure. In that case Keynes, one of the greatest minds of Britain, clearly felt taking one Indian to bed was one thing, actually meeting millions of them was entirely different.

In many ways this was the most amazing dichotomy about British rule in India. The British talked about India being the Jewel in the Crown, Paul Scott's novel when transformed to television was renamed *Jewel in the Crown*, yet the jewels of Britain shunned India. India had financed Britain's rise to greatness. When Britain lost its first colony, America, it found a second, more splendid one in India, with Cornwallis having surrendered to Washington in Yorktown going on to became Governor-General in India. Yet even when Britain had a truly top-ranking man to govern India, they often failed to reach the heights back home, with Curzon the most notable example. He was probably the greatest British Viceroy in India but failed to become Prime Minister and was held in such contempt by Lloyd George who never visited India that he once said of Curzon, 'He always bears the marks of the last person who sat on him.'

This convoluted nature of British rule in the Indian subcontinent may explain why the British went in for a remarkable degree of spin-doctoring to present their rule in the best possible light. In the process words were literally turned upside down to mean the exact opposite of what they really meant. So for instance the two words much favoured by the Raj were service and loyalist. The British who worked in India and got very handsome material rewards for their work, far higher than anything being paid to Indians, never said they 'worked' in India. They always described themselves as 'serving' India, as if to denote a much higher, more selfless, calling.

The Raj used the word 'loyalist' to describe the Indians who supported the Raj. 'Collaborator' would have been the more logical word. But that was considered not to have the right moral overtones, whereas 'loyalists' promoted the idea that it was the natural order of things for India to be ruled by the British. In contrast, the Indians who demanded that they should be free were dubbed as extremists as if for India to be free was somehow unnatural. Even as late as the 1930s the British in India considered the demand for independence, as one British official wrote, 'as either visionary or dangerous' and not at all 'practical'.

The gap between what was said and what was done widened during the twentieth century. In public after 1917 the official policy of the British government was so that there was 'a progressive realisation of responsible government in India as an integral part of the British Empire'. Many assumed that this meant India would soon be put on the same footing as Australia and other white dominions of the Empire. But cabinet papers of the time which have since became public show that this was never the British intention. The 1917 policy was agreed by the then war-time British cabinet. Sitting round the cabinet table was the Prime Minister David Lloyd George, Lord Curzon and Arthur Balfour. The cabinet agreed that Indians might be ready to rule themselves in 500 years time. In 1943, after another British declaration promising Indians a post-war right to choose their own destiny, Lord Linlithgow, the Viceroy, in a private conversation said he did not think India would be ready to rule itself for another 50 years. Even then this would require much English guidance and now that air-conditioning had been invented Linlithgow felt five or six million Englishmen and women could make their homes in India and teach Indians how to govern themselves.

The British conceded the right of subject countries to nationalism but set an impossible condition: they could not organise against the British. The dichotomy was well expressed by H. R. James, Principal of Calcutta's Presidency College, during the heyday of the Raj, 'One thing that patriotism in Bengal should not do,' he warned some students once, 'is to direct the national spirit into an attitude of hostility to British rule. There would be something I should call patricidal in such an attitude.'

This attitude remains the most sophisticated and remarkable cover-up for occupation by an alien, superior, power. It allowed Linlithgow to mourn the death of a prominent Indian collaborator as the loss of a man of 'wide citizenship'. And it enabled Lord Lytton in Pundits and Elephants – a memoir of his years as Governor of Bengal – to praise S. N. Mullick for his 'sacrifice' in choosing the 'hard road' of collaboration, with its high salary and all the privileges of office.

The time is Bengal in 1923. It is two years since Gandhi has launched his first civil disobedience campaign and Gandhi and thousands of Indians are in British jails. The Raj is trying to shore up support amongst its collaborators through a reform called dyarchy where Indians are given very limited powers in provinces. The nationalists are out to prove the reforms are window dressing meant to fool the world. Lytton is, desperately, searching for collaborators who will maintain the facade of the threatened reforms. He finally gets two Muslims and a Hindu called S. N. Mullick, to work with him. Let Lytton take up the story:

> he [Mullick] was the finest type of Indian nationalist whom it was my privilege to work with. It was the object of his life to prove that Indians could be as good as any European in public life, and he always maintained himself and required from others the highest standard of honesty and efficiency... when I was looking for a Hindu minister in 1923, I sent for Mullick and asked him if he would take the post. At the same time I warned him that it was a sacrifice rather than a promotion which I was offering him.
>
> 'Are you prepared to exchange a bed of roses for a crown of thorns?' I asked.
>
> He asked for twenty four hours to think the matter over. When he returned he told me he had consulted Sir Campbell Rhodes the chairman of the British Chamber of Commerce with whom he had often sparred across the floor of the Legislative Council and asked him, 'The Governor has asked me to become a minister. Shall I accept?' Rhodes had replied, 'Well Mullick if you are thinking of yourself, don't. If you re thinking of your country do.'
>
> 'That was enough for me,' said Mullick, 'and I have come to accept your offer.'

Lytton was writing in 1942 and phrases such as Mullick's object in life was to prove that he was 'as good as any European' show the essential master race mindset prevalent at that time. But to say that Mullick, who, for his collaboration was being handsomely rewarded – a salary of Rs5,000 a month (a fortune in India in 1923) and all the perks and privileges of office – was accepting a 'crown of thorns', while the nationalist who opted for British jails was lying on a 'bed of roses' shows how far British rulers were prepared to twist facts to suit their argument. Try substituting Lytton with a Nazi ruler of occupied France saying this to a Vichy official during the Second World War, or a Japanese, at any time between 1931 and 1945, saying this to a Chinese warlord in order to make collaboration acceptable. We would rightly consider such an idea grotesque. But because the British Empire is held to be morally far superior to the German and the Japanese ones, nobody examines, let alone challenges such views. No occupying power in history has spun the story of occupation so well.

Had the British been content to say, as they had every justification, that their imperial rule was far superior to other imperial rule be it Russian, both Tsarist and communist, German, Japanese, French, let alone Belgian, there could be little argument. You only have to travel to Korea, as I did both before and during the 2002 World Cup, to realise how much the Koreans hate the Japanese for their colonial rule. So much so that despite the fact that they shared the World Cup Korea would always be upset if Japan's name was mentioned before Korea and even days before the start of the World Cup the Korean press was full of articles documenting the evils of Japanese rule. The British have never provoked such a response in India.

But the British were not content with such an honourable position. Perhaps because of what Keay has called this 'peculiar English conceit' they claimed much more. Their claim was that they were the best rulers India had ever had, better than any other ruler in India's long history. What is more that they knew India better than the Indians, particularly the educated Indians.

There were the Indians who were emerging from the English-style universities the British had set up in India. Reared on John Stuart Mill they hoped to be treated as equals but the British denounced them as dangerous radicals who did not understand their own countrymen. Lord Curzon railed against the monstrous army of infernal lawyers that the British had created in India and reserved a special scorn for the British-educated Indian. A scorn that was most vividly expressed by Sir Reginald Craddock who spoke for much of the Raj when he said:

> We British who have served India are accused of lack of sympathy. But with whom should we sympathise the most? With the millions who are poor and helpless or with the few who have always exploited them? ... The intelligentsia of a country should be the voice expressing the thoughts of the people, which they can understand even though they might not so well express themselves. This is not so in India. The language the intellectuals speak is not understood by the people.

Nothing in British history is as inexplicable as this act of intellectual infanticide, disowning not your blood children but your intellectual progeny. These were children educated in British created institutions which had held out the promise that the best Britain had to offer could be theirs. But when these Indians asked for their inheritance, they were denounced as 'denationalised' – people who were no longer Indians and could never be British. In this the British were in marked contrast to the French who not only set out to create an elite which was French in culture, taste and opinion but embraced the resulting products.

The most vivid illustration of this came in the spring of 2002 when Issa Hayatou, a Cameroonian and President of CAF, the African Soccer Federation, decided to challenge Sepp Blatter for the Presidency of FIFA, world soccer's governing body. This was the first time an African was standing for this prestigious position and just before he made the announcement CAF held an executive meeting in Cairo. It was after this meeting had ratified his candidature that Hayatou announced he would stand.

However Hayatou's formal announcement did not take place in Cameroon, or even in Africa. Instead, immediately after the Cairo meeting he flew to Paris and it was in a hotel in the French capital that he gathered the world's press to declare his challenge. His campaign was advised and financed by French businessmen, and while it was a dismal failure, the one thing that stood out was that Hayatou was both a proud Cameroonian and also a black Frenchman. It is impossible to imagine an Indian campaign for FIFA Presidency, being based in London. The Indian elite were British educated but they were never made to feel they were accepted by the British in the way the French accepted their colonial elite.

The Indian reaction to all this British spinning has been to spin its own tales about pre-British India. To answer the British claim that before the British arrived India had never been united, Indians stress the cultural unity which long predated British rule. There was certainly cultural unity in India but the fact remains that pre-British India never had political unity. Neither Ashok, nor Akbar, the two great rulers of pre-British India, ever ruled the entire landmass of the Indian subcontinent. And even when it comes to cultural unity there are limitations. Indians for instance do not have an agreed day for the New Year. In much of India it comes in the autumn at the time of the Diwali festival. Yet in the east and north it comes in the spring, around April.

The most elaborate Indian spinning relates to how India won independence. In this version Mahatma Gandhi worked the magic of non-violence, even as the British conqueror fought against it he came to admire the method, and India got freedom. Gandhi is the Father of the Nation in the same way George Washington is the father of the United States. A visit to Delhi's Rajghat where Gandhi was cremated is obligatory for all official visitors. Yet, unlike Washington's defeat of Cornwallis at Yorktown, historians cannot point to one decisive moment when Gandhi seized power from the British. He led four non-violent campaigns against the British, the last of them five years before the British left. His campaigns transformed

India and Indians. As the Indians say he made Indians walk and talk and taught them they had nothing to fear from their colonial masters. Yet on 15 August 1947 Gandhi refused to celebrate freedom, preferring to spend the day with Muslims in Calcutta trying to calm tensions between Hindus and Muslims and mourning both the division of India and the violence it had brought.

The independence of India came about through a whole host of circumstances not least Japan's initial victories in the Far East in 1941–2. As the British military historian A. J. Barker has put it, 'Indian freedom was probably assured by the events of 1942 when Japan destroyed the mystique of white supremacy in the Far East.' As we have seen there were Indians like Subhas Bose who tried to use the Japanese to secure India's freedom, while many other Indians fought the Japanese and Bose. So how does India reconcile these two? Indians simply juxtapose these two as if there is no contradiction.

On 26 January 2004 when Indians celebrated Republic Day, the day that marks the birth of the modern Indian republic, newspapers carried advertisements hailing Bose and his part in making Indians free. Papers were full of his stirring speeches saying you could only get freedom through blood. Yet at the Republic Day parade, where awards are given and India displays its military hardware much was made of the camel corps of the Indian Army which had seen action in the western desert under the British general Allenby during the First World War.

Among the participants in the parade was Subedar Umrao Singh. The next day the *Asian Age* ran an article saying how nobody had noticed his presence. Not only was he 84 but the only surviving Indian Victoria Cross holder. The paper went on to describe the action which won him the award:

> On 15 December 1944 he repeatedly beat enemy attacks in the Kaladan Valley, Arakan, Myanmar. In the final assault on the objective he struck down three of the enemies in hand-to-hand fighting and later, when found wounded beside his gun, there were 10 of the enemy lying dead around him

What the article did not go explain was that the enemy Umrao Singh was fighting was of course, Bose's INA and his Japanese allies. However the paper did remind its readers of the racial discrimination the British practised:

> Until 1912 the Victoria Cross could not be awarded to Indians in the Indian Army and only Europeans and the Anglo-Indians, could receive this honour. The Indians were given the India Order of Merit award until that time.

This curious way of presenting history can baffle visitors. In January 1985 an English visitor, the writer Mathew Engel covering David Gower's tour of India, was very puzzled when he encountered this at first hand. Walking from his hotel to the Eden Gardens he found two statues within a few metres of each other. One was of Subhas Bose, his right arm raised in a salute, and almost pointing to a column opposite him commemorating the Glorious Dead of the wars, which had the names of Indians and English who fought and died for King and Emperor during the two wars, including, of course, his own Indian National Army. To Engel's eyes the two statues juxtaposed in that fashion, made no sense. Which of them represented India? Was Bose the hero and the Indians who fought for the British traitors? Or, as the British claimed, the other way round?

If this Indian cherry picking of history seems strange to non-Indians then it comes naturally to Indians. And Bose, himself, cherry picked. Widely seen as the most radical and extreme of nationalists, who would go to any lengths to get rid of the British, while he was in India he was very eager to try and make the Calcutta Corporation, a very British created institution, work. He was its chief executive officer and then its Mayor and very proud of what he achieved there.

The novelist Amitav Ghosh, writing in *The New Yorker* India special issue, marking 50 years of Indian independence, captured this ambivalence beautifully:

> I was born several years after India's independence and the stories my parents told me about that time were so dissimilar that they could have been about different countries. My mother grew up in Calcutta and her memories were of Mahatma Gandhi, civil, non-violence, civil disobedience and the terrors that accompanied partition in 1947. My father came of age in a small provincial town in the state of Bihar. He turned twenty-one in 1942, one of the most tumultuous years in Indian history. That was the year the Indian National Congress, the country's largest political party, launched nationwide movement calling on the British to quit India; it was when Mahatma Gandhi denounced the Raj as a 'poison that corrupts all it touches'. And in that historic year of anti-imperialist discontent my father left to became an officer in the British colonial army in India. My father's stories were of war and his fellow-Indians who fought loyally beside the British. My mother's stories appealed to me more, they had a straightforward, compelling plot line and in Mahatma Gandhi an incomparably vital and endearing protagonist. Yet now fifty years after India attained its freedom stories of men like my father – soldiers in the British Indian Army – seem to me to shed a special light on Independence, for it was people like who, through their betrayals and divided loyalties, both made and unmade the British Raj.

Nations like individuals need to shut out awkward phases of their lives, reconcile conflicting elements. In some areas of Indian life this had worked very well, particularly in the army. In 1977 when for the first time the Congress lost power in the centre and a coalition let by the Janata party – meaning people's party – came to power, the defence minister wrote to the then Army chief of staff General Raina saying it was time the Army got rid of such British ideas as Beating the Retreat and European musical instruments. The dhol and shahnai, Indian musical instruments, should be used. Raina, according to army historian, Major K. C. Prawal, wrote back saying:

> There was nothing Western in the beating of the retreat, and that even at the time of Mahabharata martial music was played and fighting ceased at sunset. He emphasised that traditions built over two centuries should not be discarded lightly. After all, most armies borrowed from other countries in the matter of dress: the Russians from the French and the British from the Germans. There was nothing regressive about retaining European martial music; was not the county's administrative system what the British had left? The country's laws, the chairs, tables the minister used and the dress most educated people wore were not indigenous. Even the shahnai it was pointed out were not indigenous being of Persian origin.

The reply proved so effective that the defence minister fell silent and the subject has never again been raised.

When India got independence there was no war crimes trials of Indians who had collaborated with the British, not even a truth and reconciliation commission like the South Africans had after apartheid. On 15 August 1947 the collaborator with a shrug joined the freedom fighter.

Santimoy Ganguli a revolutionary associate of Subhas Bose who was jailed during the war by the British tells a story of that day which reflects the fundamental frustration that the events of August 1947 brought.

On 15 August 1947 Ganguli stood at the junction of Lower Circular Road and Lansdowne Road in central Calcutta. All around him crowds were shouting, 'Jai Hind!', strangers were embracing one another and young people atop lorries and buses were waving Indian flags and crying, 'Inquilab Zindabad!' (Long Live Revolution).

Suddenly he felt a hand grip his shoulder. He turned round to stare into the face of a notorious CID officer from Elysium Row. The officer was beaming and shaking Ganguli violently. He said, 'Cheer up! What's the matter? Don't you know what day it is? Today we have become brothers!'

Ganguli just managed a smile and a silent nod; but to this day he still does not know how he managed to restrain his tears. Suddenly the jailor and the man he had jailed were brothers through the simple act of the Union Jack being lowered and the Indian tricolour being hoisted in its place.

You could take the charitable view that this is a reflection of an amazing, wonderful, Indian ability to forgive and move on. James Cameron said Indians are the most forgiving people on earth. It can be beneficial and one cricketer who has benefited most from this is Geoffrey Boycott. For almost a decade Boycott was one of the most hated figures in Indian cricket and with good reason. He did not want to tour India and behaved very badly when he did. To make it worse he left the tour half way through and while he was there he was secretly plotting to tour white South Africa with a rebel group of English cricketers. Then it did not seem possible he would ever return to India.

Today he cannot keep away from the country. He is one of the most popular and highly valued cricket commentators in India. Youngsters love to mimic his Yorkshire accent, newspapers write warm articles about him and he is also very close to the Indian team. In the summer of 2002, just before India played at Headingley, he entertained the Indian team at his home, advised them on tactics and they went on to beat England by an innings in their most impressive performance in a Test in England. If this is proof of Boycott's ability to reinvent himself, becoming reincarnated into a Boycott that bears no resemblance to the old Boycott, it is also proof of how readily Indians will forgive and forget. Nobody in India ever mentions the Boycott of the 1980s and his problems with India then. It is as if it never happened.

Such an attitude can cause problems and lead to neuroses but it also means India is always full of surprises. India is too vast, too confusing for any person to present anything more than a personal view. The western method which in many ways the Indians have copied, is to try and synthesise India in a manner that makes it sound like a western country. But you cannot do that with India. There are just too many conflicts and attempts at synthesis lead to despair and resignation. For example, in England middle class means *Daily Telegraph* and Conservative; in India it very often means a lower-income urban group which reads the Indian equivalent of the *Morning Star* and votes Communist. The Indian well off definitely do not like to be called 'middle class'. In recent years the phone revolution in India has produced another very novel Indian inversion for this western invention. In the west the use of the mobile phone is a symbol of what used to be called yuppiness, in India that is not the case. It has been estimated that by mid-2006, 100 million Indians will have mobile phones, dwarfing the numbers with fixed land lines. Sunil Mittal, chief executive of Bharti Televentures one of the largest cell phone providers in India says, 'In India mobile phones are for ordinary people and fixed-line phones for the rich. We used to think it was the other way round.' India always provokes such changes to conventional thinking causing confusion not only to foreigners but also to Indians themselves.

My book is an attempt to present India and cricket's role in it in its proper historical setting. It is no more than a personal view – the view of one Indian, born in India but educated and moulded by England – a view that both the British and Indians might find unpalatable but which is more valid than the wild romanticism that India and its cricket have been subjected to in the past.

2

Khel-khood as cricket

The day before England met India in the Kolkata Test on their 1984–5 tour, a small reception was held at the Grand Hotel where the two teams were staying. Such receptions are now part of the cricket circus but this one was held to publicise a book by an Indian publisher about the Olympic Games. The irony was lost on the Indians. Cricket is such a potent force in the country that a cricket international provides an irresistible marketing occasion, particularly a Kolkata Test. The publishers accurately divined that Indian journalists covering the Test would like free booze and food. Cynical as this may seem, much of PR is based on such calculations. I was happy enough to get my copy of the Olympic book – a tribute to the increasing sophistication of Indian publishing – but what took the evening out of the PR rut was a speech of surprising insight by Ashwini Kumar.

Kumar is a hugely controversial figure in Indian sport, hated by many, loved by others. He has held high positions and for many years was India's sole representative on the International Olympic Committee where he rose to be Vice President. There he was considered something of a security expert although in India he is more famous for his long reign over Indian hockey. He has had some success with Indian hockey, even if his years of stewardship also saw the beginning of its decline, and the successful challenge by other nations to what had become an Indian monopoly. However, his focus that evening was not nostalgic, but philosophic. I had heard a great many Indian administrators talk about sport, but this was something very novel. In a few crisp sentences he demolished the whole idea of Indian sport:

India has no base for sports despite its enormous population. India does not have the wherewithals. Sport in our country is khel-khood [just a bit of fun]. It goes against the grain of our country, against our tradition to play sports the way they do in the West. If a child in our country returns from the playground he is not asked by his parents how he fared, but slapped for missing his studies and wasting his time in khel-khood. Sport is against our Indian ethos, our entire cultural tradition. In all modern countries sport is accepted as a part of life. In our country the authorities do not even know what playing facilities are available in our schools...Out of some 600,000 schools we have – and this figure is not verified – some 1.8% have playgrounds. And I am not talking of the vast playgrounds as in the West, but just a little piece of open land behind the school where the children can run, maybe. In a country of 800 million people there are only 11 gymnasiums. The sports budget of the country is 80 million rupees [£5.5 m]. We are just not organised for sports. The central government does not run it, education anyway is a state government subject so it falls between two stools. There is no dynamic relationship between player and the organisers who run the different sports in this country. Though we are producing coaches they cannot get jobs because the whole thing is not properly organised. In any case the hunger for coaches will not be satisfied till 2059. What we need to do is to encourage school sports between the ages of 8 and 11, something not very expensive to organise.

The views reflected Kumar the military man – he had been head of the prestigious Border Security Force – and probably the anguish of trying and failing to mould Indian sport, particularly the Indian Olympic movement which is a sad story of the bureaucrats trying to make capital of honest, often poor, ill-educated sportsmen. Yet they are quite astonishing. Sporting declines often produce heartrending inquests. Exaggerated pessimism is as much part of the sporting vocabulary as romanticised hyperbole. Just as supporters of winning teams easily convince themselves they are world beaters, so supporters of losing ones readily descend into the slough of utter, inconsolable despondency. But Kumar's analysis is more than that. For it raised the question: How on earth did the Indians ever take to cricket?

It is easy to understand a nation that has no sporting traditions taking to Olympic games like running, swimming, wrestling, even boxing. These have a universality that transcends culture, tradition, organisation. But cricket by its very nature is probably the most organised of games, with a chemistry that is at once subtle and, to the uninitiated, infuriatingly complex. No one who has ever organised a Sunday afternoon cricket match can have illusions about the time and effort required to get twenty-two men, plus helpers together to make it possible. Khel-khood, a bit of fun in some desolate playground, barely adequate to run on, is hardly enough.

So how is it that cricket has prospered in India? Today India's love for the game and its undoubted prowess can hardly be doubted. In a country which has, hockey apart, few sporting successes to its name – it is still to win an individual gold medal at the Olympics and in the Athens Olympics this nation of over a billion won just one silver and that in shooting – Indian cricket can claim to able to be match if not at times beat the world's best. It is yet to become the best cricket nation in the world but it has won the World Cup and has produced a host of cricketers led by Sachin Tendulkar who are the best in the world.

There is a paradox, though not quite the obvious one which appears at first glance. The paradox is that cricket, the ultimate of team games expressing a philosophy that goes beyond the game, has in India produced neither a philosophy, nor a team, but some great individuals. It is a measure of the remarkable talent of some of these individuals that India, at various times, has given the appearance of being a team. As the Nawab of Pataudi has said, 'In India cricketers are produced in spite of the system, not because of it.'

Writers on Indian cricket talk of Indians taking to this English game, as the Brazilians took to football. Nothing could be further from the truth. India, as a nation, has never taken to cricket. Certain Indians, starting with the Indian community, the Parsees, followed by the princes, for various personal reasons, took to cricket. Now more and more follow cricket in India, it is big business and in recent years it has become the sport of the urban Indian. But it remains what it was when the British first took it to India, a game played by certain Indians, often quite accidentally, wretchedly organised, shambolically run which, with the sort of magic difficult to explain, produces cricketers of quality. Pataudi has rightly pointed out that it is absurd to talk of the decline of Indian cricket for this assumes 'there had been a gradual incline'. If his phrasing is odd the meaning is clear. India has never produced a great team, strong in most departments of the game. At certain times there have been good, possibly great batsmen, at others great spinners, then for nearly two decades starting in the 1970s a fine fast-medium bowler and later still, possibly, a great leg-spinner. But the various elements have never really fused together. There is no Indian equivalent of Hutton's great sides of the 1950s, or Worrell's West Indians of the 1960s, or Ian Chappell's Australians of the 1970s, let alone the long dominance exercised by Clive Lloyd's West Indians or the current Australian team. Such teams renew themselves, as one bunch of great players depart, others take their place. Indian cricket is more like a tide, it ebbs and flows. Every now and again India seems on the verge of fashioning a team that could take on all comers. In England in 1986 India won the series 2–0, could have won it 3–0. The then chairman of the selectors hailed the team as the second best in the world, then the best was the West Indies. But the team went home and could not beat Australia and did not win a Test series away from the subcontinent for nearly two decades. In the winter of 2003 the Indians came close to winning a series in Australia, drawing 1–1 and were hailed as the only team capable of beating the Australians, who had taken over the mantle of the West Indians of the 1980s. But then back home India lost abjectly to Australia, their first home defeat to the Aussies for 35 years.

India has had its moments of glory on the cricket field but they have been isolated and more often the result of one or two towering individuals who have somehow dragged their teams to victory. That is the lesson of Indian history and the story of Indian cricket. And it is only explained by the way that the Indians learnt their cricket from the English.

The story of how Indians took to cricket has often been told. Back in the seventeenth century English sailors wishing to divert themselves played the game in the Gulf of Cambay, it was slowly taken up by the Indians, particularly the Parsees, who considered themselves somewhat separate from the Indians and rather more English than Indians. Indian princes patronised it, Ranji, a minor prince, proved so brilliant that he invented a whole new cricket stroke – the leg glance – and inspired legends about him in England. Indians flocked to imitate Ranji and soon this very English game became a national Indian one.

This summary while not inaccurate is like all summaries – a distortion. For it misses out how cricket developed in England between the time the sailors of Cambay introduced it to India and Ranji emerged; or how Indians took to English education and culture. Historians of English cricket have laboured long and hard to trace cricket's origins.

Though the recorded history of English cricket dates from the middle of the eighteenth century, there is some evidence that cricket was played in Tudor times, perhaps earlier. The Black Prince's grandfather played 'Creag' which is said to be an etymological antecedent of the game, and efforts have been made to link cricket with medieval sports such as stool-ball, cat and dog trap-ball and rounders. This cricket was largely illiterate; few records survive and the ones that do are not capable of unchallenged interpretation. While the upper classes had their blood sports – cock fighting and heraldic contests – cricket formed one of the few amusements of the rural poor, part of the amorphous village fair.

Cricket is said to have begun in the forest of the Weald with a curved piece of wood as bat and a sheep-pen hurdle as wicket. This primitive cricket first came into prominence during Queen Anne's reign (1702–14) and began to rival the more popular village football.

Its transformation into the modern, national game owes much to the public school ethos establish by Thomas Arnold and the deeds of William Gilbert Grace. Arnold's Rugby was a mixture of evangelical moralism and romantic idealism seeking to produce Christian gentlemen. Arnold could write a history of the Roman Empire in a tone of such astonishing piety it could all but obscure the violence and disorder that was part of its being – he was trying to counteract the cynicism of Gibbon – and during the opium wars with China he wrung his hands in despair about 'the dreadful guilt we are incurring'. Though sports were not properly organised during Arnold's time at Rugby, by the late nineteenth century the value of team games, particularly cricket as a means of developing character, had firmly taken root. It drew its philosophic sustenance from Arnold's desire to produce an English gentleman who was Christian, manly and enlightened, and one morally superior to any other being.

Arnold's influence was so pervasive that it was soon to be said without exaggeration that 'if a composite history of all the public schools is ever written it will be, in reality, the history of England, since the British Empire has been in the main built up by the founders of the school and the pupils who gained knowledge and had their characters moulded in those institutions'. Sentiments immortalised in Thomas Hughes's celebrated novel based on Arnold's Rugby, *Tom Brown's School Days*. In it Tom described cricket to one of the masters as 'an institution'. Arthur, whom Tom has rescued from excessive scholastic work – considered damaging in public schools – says 'it is the birthright of British boys, old and young, as *habeas corpus* and trial by jury are of British men'. The master hardly needs any prompting. 'The discipline and reliance on one another which it teaches are so valuable. It ought to be such an unselfish game. It merges the individual in the eleven; he doesn't play that he may win but that his side may.' We are entering the world of muscular Christianity, the Henry Newbolt man where physical effort and intellectual satisfaction strike a ready equation.

It is interesting to consider why cricket should have been given this honour. Cricket is a subtle game. In form and appearance it can be gentle, even idyllic, yet violence is always there. A fast bowler hurls the ball at 90 mph which could kill a man – and very nearly has – a hard-hitting batsman's use of power is all too apparent to the fielder who is in the path of the ball. Fielders have been killed when hit by a cricket ball as the tragic story of the former Indian cricketer Raman Lamba illustrates. Playing in a club match he decided to field close at silly point without a helmet – he was hit on the head and died. The argument between the bowler and the batsman can be extremely violent. A fast bowler bowls a bouncer – about the most controversial weapon in cricket – the batsman retaliates by hooking. Yet it is institutionalised anger. Firmly within certain prescribed rules.

In other respects too cricket reflected the nature of British Society. It was – is – a finely structured game. The batsmen are the natural leaders, the bowlers the toiling middle classes, the fielders very much plebeian. Each has its own appointed place, each its own specific task with the game very firmly based on the Augustan principle of order in society.

A basis which was enshrined in the distinction made between gentlemen and players – a distinction considered to be fundamental to the existence of the game. Its removal in the mid-1960s is even today resented by many in England and said to have led to a decline in quality. The professional was the man who played for money. His competence was unquestioned – he was often conceded to be more skilful than the amateur – but then skill alone has never been the supreme criterion for cricket affection. The amateur represented virtues that were said to have made Britain great. He played not for money but for the love he had for the game, the pleasures he derived, the enjoyment he gave.

But, perhaps, the most unique feature of cricket is the system of appealing. In no other game is a decision by an official only made if one of the participants in the game appeals. A footballer can appeal for all his worth for a penalty but it makes no difference to a referee's decision, indeed it could earn him a booking or, if he particularly vociferous, a sending-off. But in cricket for the fielding side to get a decision, apart from when the batsman is bowled or very clearly caught, the bowlers and the fielders have to appeal. Otherwise the umpire does not give a decision and a batsman who is out can continue batting. To me this represents the genius of this English game signifying a certain shared set of values between the batting and bowling sides, implying the fielding side will not make false claims and the batting side behave honestly and own up to its errors. In football it is common to see players try to cheat, move the ball a few yards nearer the opposing goal when they win a throw or a free kick, claim a corner when it has come off their own boot, and congratulate their team mates who has won a penalty even if he has done so by pretending to be fouled in the penalty box. But in cricket there is a premium on honesty and even now much debate as to whether batsman who know they are out should 'walk'. One of the growing areas of disagreement between English and Asian cricket is on this subject of appealing with English cricketers often feeling that Asians do not understand the delicate mechanism of this aspect of the game, appeal needlessly and bring rancour where there should be polite enquiry.

It has been suggested, by the revisionist historian Correli Barnett, in his interesting but flawed book *The Collapse of British Power*, that it was this stress on evangelical idealism and character building, divorcing education from scientific and technological goals, that eventually led to the country's decline. While Germany and Japan gave their educational systems a practical thrust the British produced generations of politicians and statesmen who believed that Britain exercised a 'moral' influence in world affairs and that 'other powers would heed the pursing of British lips and the tuttings of British disapproval'. But perhaps Barnett overstresses the revisionism. If the hard-headed empire-builders, seeking the loot of other countries, were replaced in the late nineteenth century by the high-minded empire-preservers, seeing to prove that the 'British Empire was the best thing that ever happened to mankind' it came from a shrewd realisation that a philosophy was necessary to preserve this curious entity.

Brave, hungry adventurers had secured the Empire. Trade had provided the motive and the Empire surplus fed the industrial revolution, but the process had been individual and dramatic. Suddenly, in the middle of the nineteenth century, the British people seemed to discover that they had an Empire. Yet a great many were not sure why this 'tight little, right little island', whose songs and legends celebrated its own exclusiveness, should have suddenly acquired such a huge Empire. While the upper classes were well aware of the benefits of an Empire, a philosophy needed to be evolved about why such a huge acquisition had been made and how it benefited the unfed, ill-clothed masses of the urban poor. A history which had always stressed the island's right to remain free of continental involvement now felt the need for a different philosophy, one that would serve an Empire that stretched over four continents. The philosophy that was eventually evolved was service – however spurious – and cricket was to provide a ready symbol of this service.

As with all empires, violence was part of the British Empire. But it was controlled. To control the Empire the mystique of the sahib was built up: whatever happened all dark skins paled in front of that solitary white one. In some ways an even greater mystique of the white woman was built up. In the British Raj not only was the white woman put on a pedestal but every effort was made to ensure no Indian in a public place ever saw a white woman unless she was dressed in a manner considered suitable for her status as the high priestess of the Raj. In 1922 H. L. Stephenson, the Chief Secretary to the Government of Bengal, writing about the need to tighten censorship of American films wrote about scenes in which, 'white men and women (are) shown in a state of extreme drunkenness in order to portray the degradation caused by drink. Such scenes do not convey the moral idea of Western manners and ideals'. Nirad Chaudhuri, in his autobiography *Thy Hand, Great Anarch!*, describes how when, in 1925, he went to Puri, a seaside resort on the Bay of Bengal, he was told off for walking too near a beach where some white women were swimming:

It should be kept in mind that in those days swimming costumes were not what they are today. Nonetheless a policeman was standing there to protect the modesty of these White women from our gaze. This man came up to me and said when the Memsahibs are bathing no Indian was allowed to walk on the beaches and be within observable distance. So I must go up to the roads above. Of course, I had to.

Arnold and his heirs may have overstressed the evangelical romanticism but they also realised that gut jingoism, crude nationalism and hatred of foreigners which often affected the urban masses, was not enough to sustain such an Empire. The Empire was a contradiction. The British in their songs and legends conjured up the picture of an island race bravely struggling to keep itself free of continental marauders. Rule Britannia's refrain 'Britons never, never, never shall be slaves' is evocative of his national mood. Yet the Empire enslaved millions of others and this could only be squared by creating the vision of an Empire that was supernational. As Lord Acton would put it in his 1862 *Essay on Nationality*, empires like the British or the Austro-Hungarian ones were the peaks of civilised progress, accommodating inferior races who could be 'raised by living in political union with races intellectually superior'. So the supreme nation-state of our time argued an imperial philosophy that sought to deny other peoples their nationality. It was from such a moral and philosophical contradiction that cricket provided a certain philosophy for the Empire.

The British picture of their island as a beleaguered country is, of course, an ancient one dating perhaps from Roman times, a belief strong enough to convert even foreign adventures, like Henry V's conquest of France, into ballads of national resistance. Henry rallying his troops before the Battle of Agincourt with those immortal words 'we few, we happy few' could well have been the local commander seeking to repulse a foreign horde – when the reality was quite the reverse. A global Empire, however, imposed different obligations and while the legends of Agincourt were to be recreated in various parts of the world, there was still the need for a philosophy – a philosophy that would try and elevate an Empire founded by adventurers seeking profits and preserved by a strange alliance of merchants seeking to add to those profits and administrators struggling to provide an imperial gloss of service.

It is easy enough to miss the particular agenda that Arnold and Hughes had. A century later the West Indian writer C. L. R. James in *Beyond A Boundary* used a fairly selective recreation of the myth of Greek sports to link the rise of cricket and other sports in nineteenth-century England to ancient Greece. In particular, he used his own version of ancient Greece to argue the case for his trinity of Arnold, Hughes and Grace. James cannot praise these three men more often or more wondrously and he ends his book by linking them to the West Indies tour of Australia in 1960–1, particularly Worrell. It had been a magical tour, one that is credited with recreating Test cricket which was about to die of boredom. The West Indians have been beaten but they have won the hearts of the Australians and none more so than Frank Worrell, the first black captain of the West

Indies. James is transfixed by the effect Worrell has had on the Australians. Now read the closing lines of James's book:

> He expanded my conception of West Indian personality. Nor was I alone. I caught a glimpse of what brought a quarter of a million inhabitants of Melbourne to the streets to tell the West Indian cricketers good-bye, a gesture spontaneous and in cricket without precedent, one people speaking to another. Clearing the way with bat and ball, West Indians at that moment had made a public entry into the comity of nations. Thomas Arnold, Thomas Hughes and the Old master himself would have recognised Frank Worrell as their boy.

No thought could be more absurd. The idea that either Arnold or Hughes would ever have claimed Worrell as their own is preposterous. It is extremely doubtful whether even Grace would have accepted him. As Ian Buruma has said, Arnold was more concerned with Christianity than muscles. And while Hughes, whose writing helped create the impression Arnold was the creator of games and was clearly a moralist, his values were very parochial and narrow. Early on in *Tom Brown's School Days*, Tom Brown talks about his native Berkshire village and regrets the passing of parochial loyalties.:

> We were Berkshire, or Gloucestershire or Yorkshire boys and you're young cosmopolites, belonging to all counties and no countries. No doubt it is all right, I dare say it is. This is the day of large views and glorious humanity, and all that; but I wish backsword play hadn't gone out in the Vale of White Horse; and that that confounded Great Western hadn't carried away Alfred's Hill to make an embankment.

The point cannot be overemphasised. Arnold and Hughes were working to a particular agenda – one that, unlike the picture James presents, did not include all of humanity. Here is Buruma again:

> Sport built character, specially the character of empire builders. The empire was built on the belief in racial superiority. Just as the Germans did later, British sports enthusiasts often identified themselves as the true heirs of the ancient Greeks. And just as the Greeks confined their Olympics to athletes of pure Greek blood, Englishmen in the 1890s talked of holding an 'Anglo-Saxon Olympiad'. This scheme, wrote the main promoter J Astley Cooper 'ought to act as an antidote to the debilitating effect of luxury, wealth, civilisation, for, should it be carried out in its full conception, the

honours which it affords should be those for which the flower of the
Race would chiefly strive'.

It is interesting to follow through how this nineteenth-century English
view of sports finally inspired the modern Olympic movement. Pierre de
Coubertin, not having any French sporting examples to choose from, had
to choose between the German sporting traditions, which were largely
derived from gymnastics, or turen as they were called, or Arnold's English
public school model. Courbertin could not quite take up the Germanic
sporting ideal, not after the traumatic defeat suffered by the French at the
hands of the Prussian in 1871. Instead he turned to the public school
sporting ethos which thanks to Hughes was now seen as Arnold's legacy.
Courbertin even came to Rugby and literally worshipped at the tomb of
Arnold. A sincere, if misguided idealist, Courbertin believed it was
possible to get peace and brotherhood through games and did not see the
fallacy in his own argument: that by promoting competition between
nations you got not harmony but war, not peace and amity but strife. His
French opponent Charles Maurras, who hated Dreyfus, democracy and all
foreigners, saw this well enough and supported international sports
meetings on the grounds that he felt the more the French competed against
barbarians the more the French would come to hate foreigners.
Courbertin's idealism was finally prostituted by the Nazis in the 1936
Olympics. He was too ill to go and his recorded voice spoke of, 'the most
important thing at the Olympic Games is not to win, but to take part, just
as the most important thing in life is not to conquer but to struggle well'.
Even as he spoke Hitler and his cohorts were staging a Games which were,
in effect, a celebration of Nazism with Hitler perfecting his plans for
world conquest.

Cricket's role was to not to make world conquest, the British had
already done that, but to preserve the conquests a previous generation had
made. 'Cricket's influence,' writes Barnett, 'on the upper-middle class
British kind with its sense of orthodoxy and respect for the rules and laws
and the impartial authority of umpires can hardly be exaggerated.'
Barnett's theme may be mocking but the point is well made. Yet even as
the British were fashioning a philosophy for their Empire, their
educational policy in India had already begun to produce the first of the
Indian leaders who would challenge the Empire.

The Indian educational system was the work of Macaulay. His
celebrated *Minute on Education* has been much quoted and misquoted but
what has been missed is the debate that preceded it. Macaulay was a
liberal of the free trade school with a contempt for Indian education and
literature. As he put it in his celebrated *Minute*, 'I have never found one

among them who could deny that a single shelf of a good European library was worth the whole native literature of India and Arabia.'

Macaulay arrived in India to find a furious argument raging between the Orientalists, who believed that Indians should be taught in their own language, and the Anglicisers, who believed that Indians should be taught in English. The debate was framed by the pattern of education in India that prevailed before Macaulay's intervention. It has been best described by Michael Edwardes in *British India* (London, 1967, p. 10):

> The type of education the British had found when they arrived in India was almost entirely religious, and higher education for Hindus and Muslims was purely literary. Hindu higher education was almost a Brahmin monopoly. Brahmins, the priestly caste, spent their time studying religious texts in a dead language, Sanskrit. There were a number of schools using living languages, but few Brahmins would send their children to such schools, where the main subject taught was the preparation of accounts. Muslim higher education *was* conducted in a living language – Arabic, which was not spoken in India. But there were also schools which taught Persian (the official language of government in India until 1837, when it was finally abandoned) and some secular subjects.

Hindu and Muslim education had much in common. Both used, in the main, a language unknown to ordinary people. Both systems stuck firmly to traditional knowledge.

The East India Company which had steadily, occasionally stealthily, conquered India, had little or no clue about educating Indians – or, for that matter, much desire. They had come to India to trade, had become rulers in furtherance of that trade and wanted to do nothing that would disturb their native subjects and thus harm the profits they were making. They took their cue from the ancient Indian rulers who, except in times of war, left their subjects well alone, content to make money from the land and commerce. It was only in the Charter Act of 1813 that there was a specific sum allocated to education – all of Rs100,000 (£10,000 at the then rate of exchange) but for many years after that even this piffling sum was not disbursed. As late as 30 April 1845, nearly ninety years after Clive had established the British Empire at Plassey, a total of 17,360 Indians were being taught at government expense in all parts of the British dominions.

These were the result of concessions won by evangelists keen to make Christians of the heathen Indians, and the growing British commercial community in India who saw the value of an English-educated Indian upper and middle classes that could further trade. Macaulay shrewdly combined commerce and evangelism in his celebrated *Minute*. It was best expressed in his classic speech in the House of Commons on the Charter Act of 1833:

> The mere extent of empire is not necessarily an advantage. To many governments it has been cumbersome; to some it has been fatal. It will be allowed by every statesman of our time that the prosperity of a country is made up of the prosperity of those who compose the community, and that it is the most childish ambition to covet dominion which adds to no man's comfort or security ... It would be, on the most selfish view of the case, far better for us that the people of India were well-governed and independent of us, than ill-governed and subject to us; that they were ruled by their own kins kings, but wearing our broad-cloth, and working with our cutlery, than that they were performing their salaams to English collectors and English magistrates but were too ignorant to value, or too poor to buy English manufactures.

If pure altruism was not the only motive that inspired the British in India, just as significant is the fact that the educational system that Macaulay installed was the classic liberal one. Thus at Calcutta's famous Presidency College, which in years to come was to produce free India's first President as well as Subhas Bose, the education required:

> A critical acquaintance with the works of Bacon, Johnson, Milton and Shakespeare, a knowledge of ancient and modern history, and of the higher branches of mathematical science, some insight into the elements of natural history, and the principles of moral philosophy and political economy, together with considerable facility of composition, and the power of writing in fluent and idiomatic language an impromptu essay on any given subject of history, moral or political economy.

In English public schools the playground was becoming the hothouse for the young, in India the same public school-educated administrators concentrated on the classroom. Everything outside it was a void. This has been vividly illustrated in yet another book on British India, Philip Mason's *The Men Who Ruled India*. Mason, a former Indian civil servant, in describing the British in India, asks that they should be judged not by their worst actions, or even by their best but by what they aimed at. The introduction eloquently describes how unique amongst nations the English ruling class subjected its young to the bodily rigour of 'cold baths, cricket and the history of Greece and Rome' in order to make them fit to rule India. Yet lyrical as the book can be about the British and their rule there is no description, let alone explanation, of how this bodily rigour translated onto the sporting fields of India.

The index listing for sports – and that includes hog-hunting – is marginally longer than that for servants and there are only three references to cricket. Mason is meticulous in detailing the good the British wrought in India. So why ignore cricket? The answer is that the British never actively promoted cricket in India. The English played cricket in India, and the odd administrator encouraged cricket – a Harris or Brabourne in Mumbai, Willingdon as Viceroy (though his role was more dubious and political) but there was no master plan to get Indians to play cricket, no educational policy that made cricket part of school life. It was *ad hoc*, depending on the personal taste of a particular schoolmaster or district official.

It is not that the Indians did not have a sporting tradition. The Indian princes indulged in riding and shooting and soon recognised that one way to curry favour with the English was to organise shoots. The prince who let the Viceroy bag the biggest tiger when he came to visit, found that this soon translated into useful political returns. Polo was another great favourite with the princes. But this was at an élite level. The sports the princes favoured were the historic ones chosen by ruling classes down the ages – sports as a preparation for war.

Sports as a substitute for war – as in the development of the modern Olympics – was a late nineteenth-century concept resulting from the massive changes wrought by industrialisation. England as the first country to be industrialised was to make this idea a central plank of its educational policy. Even today the sporting ethos is probably strongest in this country, and continentals often express amazement about the English obsession with sports. In India the concept never developed.

For Indians, English education was a window on the European world. But a window framed by Indian references. The British changed the language of instruction and the curriculum; instead of religion and accounts, there was a whole host of literary, political and historical subjects – but they did not alter the method of Indian learning.

The classical Indian education in the country's golden age, many centuries before the British arrived, had been wide-eyed and enquiring. By the time the British arrived this had decayed and the Indians who first took to British education – in Bengal they almost demanded it in preference to their own – hoped this would be recreated by the improving alien influence. But while the English education was comprehensive, the methods used to educate Indians destroyed much of its value. Indians may have seen the college-based Oxbridge model as ideal but what developed in India was a mockery of this. Instead of a university or a college where students went not merely to learn from books but from their tutors and peers about life and living, the Indian universities became mere examining bodies. They were like MOT centres of education, checking whether a particular person was good enough to obtain a particular degree. As Judith Walsh, observing the spread of English education in India through the middle and late nineteenth century notes:

> They had no teaching staff and offered no courses. Preparation for their examinations was given by the private schools and colleges that began springing up even in far-flung areas. There was little control over the establishment of these programmes. In fact virtually anybody with the funds to rent space and hire teachers could open a college or preparatory school. A combination of student fees and government grant-in-aid made survival likely and prosperity a distinct possibility.

The British had two methods of changing this system: to deny grant-in-aid to schools that did not pass their inspections, but more effectively to regulate the examination system so that it provided a uniform system all over the land. Course topics were announced two years in advance and the questions were stultifyingly factual: list the names of the 'twelve Caesars', describe 'some of the chief of our liberties established by the Magna Carta'. Judith Walsh concludes:

> Success demanded a ready memory uncomplicated by imagination or critical judgement. Teachers and students, if they hoped for safety, were well advised to rely on assigned texts, or if they had to choose an alternate, to select one which mirrored the first in organisation and point of view... The major, if not the only concern of the student was to pass the requisite examinations.

Their parents had realised the value of English education. They knew a pass meant financial success, failure led to ruin. So much so that students who failed even took to putting behind their names 'BA – Failed' just to indicate that they had taken part in English education. The pressure to pass examinations had the unfortunate result that, with few exceptions, the education institutions became glorified crammers where the name of the game was to learn by rote questions likely to be asked in examinations – a tradition that, distressingly, survives to this day.

This emphasis on cramming helped to create a Hindu work ethic whose tenacity matched the Protestant one. A work ethic that told its children in the words of the Bengali ditty:

Porasuno kora jey   Those who study hard
Gari gora chorey shey   Get to ride in carriages.

A work ethic based on studies and examinations that is instilled so well that even in his moment of greatest triumph (three successive Test centuries on his debut during the 1984–5 season), Mohammed Azharuddin felt obliged to refer to it. Asked what his childhood ambitions were he replied, 'Look, I was never that good in studies to become a doctor or something like that. I always saw myself playing in a Test match; that used to be my childhood fantasy...I used to play a lot; studies never really suffered if you know what I mean. I managed promotion each time though as a student I was just about average.' And then the final revealing comment that explains why he was so different from most of his fellow Indians, 'Parental interference was out of the question: I used to stay with my grandfather.' Azar, as he came to be known, has ascribed much of his success to his grandfather – a devout Muslim who encouraged him to 'pray and play side by side'. All grandparents are indulgent, Indians, perhaps more so, and Azar might have had a very different upbringing if he had lived with his parents. He might have succumbed to the 'good boy' syndrome.

A 'good boy' in India is defined as one who obeys his parents and diligently memorises his schoolbooks. Not surprisingly the unimaginative nature of Indian examinations often gives the mugger an almost natural advantage over the imaginative scholar. The knowledge it leads to can be, at times, like a laser penetrating in a single stream, but it throws no wider light outwards. Some great Indians have confessed how much they hated the Indian way of imparting education and how this turned them away from books in general. Here is Gandhi talking about his education in his autobiography:

> As a rule I had a distaste for any reading beyond my school-books. The daily lessons had to be done, because I disliked being taken to task by my teacher as much as I disliked deceiving him. Therefore I would do the lessons, but often without my mind on them. Thus even when the lessons could not be done properly, there was no question of any extra reading.

Gandhi's school actually made cricket and gymnastics compulsory, no doubt because the headmaster was a Parsee, the first amongst the Indians to take to cricket. But Gandhi 'disliked both' and never 'took part in any exercise, cricket or football, before they were made compulsory'. By the time he came to write his autobiography at the age of 56 he recanted his youthful belief that 'gymnastics had nothing to do with education'. A recantation that echoed that of other prominent Indians – Subhas Bose, for instance, who felt his youthful dislike of sports had probably made him more introverted.

But despite the middle-aged Gandhi's regret he saw no harm in neglecting cricket or gymnastics. 'That was because I had read in books about the benefits of long walks in the open air and, having liked the advice, I had formed a habit of taking walks which has still remained with me. These walks gave me a fairly hardy constitution.' Even for the middle-aged Gandhi, embroiled in a historic struggle with the British, sport was just a means to physical fitness. There was nothing wider or deeper to be gained from sporting activity.

Gandhi had ducked, or tried to duck out of gymnastics because he wanted to nurse his father. Certainly parental influence played and plays a big part in the sporting development of the child – more so in India where the family is so predominant. But one reason for the disassociation of sports and general education in India was that by the time it was acquiring its prominence in England a second generation of Indians were being brought up in the English culture who did not share their fathers' values.

Their fathers had hungered for English education, and in the words of one second-generation English-educated Indian, 'our fathers, the first fruits of English education, were very violently pro-British. They could see no flaw in the civilisation or culture of the West. They were charmed by its novelty and strangeness'. The fathers could remember the pre-British days of which their sons had no memory. While the sons and their heirs would unconsciously accept many of the criticisms levied by the English against the Indians, it was the fathers who precisely realised the logic of such English diatribes.

Lack of manliness was a constant British jibe against the Indians and many were the analyses to explain this supposedly unique Indian phenomenon: climate, lax morality, wretched diet and above all, the 'sedentary habits' of the higher classes. There was no dearth of British remedy for this. A. C. Miller in *Seven Letters to an Indian Schoolboy* had warned against excessive scholarship, 'A boy's character is far more important than cleverness at work.' In contrasting Indian and English schoolboys he noted that while not all Indian boys were bad and all English ones good, 'I do go so far to say that English boys as a whole are loyal, just, devoted sportsmen.' The Hunter Commission had felt physical exercise 'would have especially good effect upon the minds and bodies of most Indian students. We therefore recommend that physical development be promoted by the encouragement of native games, gymnastics and drill and other exercises of each class of school'.

By the time the second generation of Indians, like Gandhi, were being given an English education, they no longer saw, or at least not with that clarity, what their fathers had seen as a struggle between the ideals of the west and the demands of the old Indian ways of life. Nirad Chaudhuri – probably the greatest writer to come out of the Indo-British encounter – rejected his father's advice to use the gymnastics equipment he had bought for his sons. Regretting this youthful impulse in later life he concluded that he did not have a strong 'constitution' because 'I neglected his advice and in matters of physical culture pursued the bad old traditions.'

Also by this time in the late nineteenth century, just as sports and cricket were becoming the dominant philosophy in English public schools, the second-generation Indians were growing up in a world where western values were increasingly integrated into their lives. This, as Judith Walsh has observed, meant 'all memory of the foreign origins of these values vanished'. Or if they were remembered it was in a fashion far removed from their origins.

Thus Subhas Bose implicitly accepted the British jibe that Indians were weak and when in London, rebuked his friend for sitting cross-legged. What would the English think of this strange Indian custom? Bose, incidentally, was one of the few Indian leaders who later took an interest in sports and looked critically at the fact that British education in India shunned the need for physical activity. During the 1930s, when he was exiled by the British to Europe, he wrote a synopsis for a book on India in which he argued that British education in Indian was too literary and felt there was great 'need of sport and gymnastics and military training as part of education'.

In England, and for that matter in most of the western world, it is part of the school curriculum to teach certain basic physical skills such as swimming. My daughter born in England was taken to the swimming pool from the age of around four, once a week by her school. Yet despite the fact that Mumbai is an island no effort was made to teach us swimming. Mumbai has the sort of bay that rivals Sydney and Hong Kong but has nothing like the river transport those cities can boast. The sea around Mumbai is filthy and no well off Indian would want to dive into it. This is left to the poorer classes. In India it is a common sight to see little kids dive into rivers and water tanks but well-off urban Indians rarely know how to swim. I only learnt swimming much later in London at the ripe old age of 35, thereby never really conquering my fear of water.

And by the time my generation of Indians – the Midnight's Children of Salman Rushdie's evocative phrase – came to cricket the memories of the English introducing cricket were very dim indeed.

C. L. R. James has described how he took to cricket gulping down *Vanity Fair* with the facts about Grace and Ranji. Neville Cardus's essay on Ranji was part of our prescribed text at school but that was in the tradition of acknowledging the foreign tributes to a great Indian. In the cricket I played in my Mumbai school, any link between England and cricket was not so much denied as never alluded to. The two major schools' tournaments in Mumbai are the Harris shield for senior boys and the Giles shield for junior boys. Both are inter-school tournaments of great popularity and appeal and I, along with most of my school friends, followed both of them closely. But we had no idea, or even interest in who Harris was, and in any case never quite pronounced Giles's name correctly. We were taught to pronounce it 'Guile' with the 'G' as in Guy and probably thought it had something to do with cows, since *guy* is the Hindi word for cow.

It was many years later, in England, that I learnt about the role played by Lord Harris, Governor of Mumbai between 1890 and 1895, in promoting and establishing Indian cricket. I doubt if even a handful of Mumbai schoolboys know who the Harris of the coveted Harris shield is, despite the fact that the centre of the shield has a medallion portrait of Lord Harris, surrounded by a laurel wreath. As for Giles even less was known. He was Director of Public Instruction and helped save the Mumbai High School Athletic Association after the problems in the city following the plague of 1896.

This disassociation between the English creation and the Indian adoption of it, explains a certain Indian contradiction about cricket. The casual English visitor to India, observing the tremendous popularity of international cricket, may conclude that this means that England, too, is very popular. In fact the exact reverse is true. Those who patronise, administer and provide the money and the fervour for cricket in India today, are perhaps the most sceptical of Indians as far as the wider English connection is concerned. The popularity of cricket is not to be equated with the popularity of England or any values associated with this country. Indian attitude to England is a complex subject, to which I shall refer later, but it is necessary to understand that the Indian love for cricket does not denote a love for England.

True, in India cricketing values are accepted, indeed, as many observers have commented, as standards of English cricket have declined, the Indians appear to uphold the age-old traditions of the game. But those Indians would be very surprised to hear that the link between the two is English society.

So if cricket was not rammed down the throats of Indian schoolboys by the English – as clearly it was not – then how did it take root? One possible explanation could be nationalism. This certainly explains the rise of Australian cricket. A colony peopled by the British working class – some would say criminal class – saw in cricket a means of getting back at the upper classes of the mother country. As early as 1897 an Australian writer could detect an 'unfilial yearning on the part of young Australia to triumphantly thrash the mother country'.

C. L. R. James has told us how West Indians used cricket to shape their political nation:

> West Indians crowding into a Test bring with them the whole history and future hopes of the Island. English people have a conception of themselves wreathed from birth. Drake and mighty Nelson, Shakespeare, Waterloo, the few who did so much for so many, the success of Parliamentary democracy, those and such as does constitute a national tradition...we of the West Indies have none at all, none that we know of. To such people the three W's, Ram and Val, wrecking English batting, helped to fill the huge gap in their consciousness and their needs.

This happened as the West Indies Federation was struggling to come to political manhood with the different islands agitating for their independence. But no such links developed between cricket and nationalism in pre-British India.

If anything the pre-independence link between nationalism and sports was provided by football. In fact, just about the time that Harris, in Mumbai, was trying to promote manliness through cricket, another Indian was telling his countrymen:

> We speak of many things parrot-like, but never do them; speaking and not doing has become a habit with us. What is the cause of that? Physical weakness. The sort of weak brain that is not able to do anything: we must strengthen it. First of all, all our young men must be strong. Religion will come afterwards. Be strong, my young friends...you will be nearer to heaven through football than through the study of the Gita...you will understand the Gita better with your biceps, your muscles a little stronger. You will understand the mighty genius and the mighty strength of Krishna better with a little strong blood in you.

That Indian was Narendranath Datta who would become known to his worshipping admirers as Swami Vivekananda, the first, and probably the most prominent, of the modern Indian gurus. Vivekananda was to successfully preach a form of muscular Hinduism, almost matching the muscular Christianity preached by Charles Kingsley, and a bastard Socialism which was to inspire an entire generation of Indian nationalists and political activists. His theory that India was materially poor but spiritually rich was both an explanation for British rule in India and a balm for nationalist feelings. His belief that India could reclaim her greatness if only she acquired strength would prove so intoxicating to many that it would form the basis for Indian revolutionaries seeking to use Irish-style insurrectionary methods to overthrow the British.

Vivekananda's strength through football ideas were to be brilliantly vindicated on 29 June 1911, when an Indian football team Mohun Bagan club defeated the East Yorkshire regiment in the IFA Shield Final in Calcutta. To quote the understandably overblown rhetoric of the Mohun Bagan club that day is 'a red letter day in the history of Indian football – a day that has gone down in the history of the nation's struggle for freedom and independence'.

It is worth dwelling on the match. Like all Indian teams, its players played in bare feet. To play on Calcutta's maidan – the vast expanse of green in the centre of the city – was itself an experience. To play in the IFA Shield Final, the premier soccer tournament in India (and the second oldest in the world after the English FA Cup), against a British team kitted out in full regalia, was more than just a soccer match. Overlooking the Maidan was Fort William which, since the days of Robert Clive, had symbolised British military presence in Calcutta and over which flew the Union Jack. Only a few years had passed since Indian football teams had been allowed to play the British and poor Mohun Bagan, with their tiny delicate Indians, gingerly sidestepping the boots of the British, were given no chance against the East Yorkshire regiment. The East Yorkshires led by a goal at half-time, but in the second half, in quite extraordinary circumstances, Mohun Bagan came back to win by two goals to one.

The story goes that as the referee blew the final whistle and the crowd swarmed onto the pitch, one Indian went up to the Captain of the Mohun Bagan team and pointing in the direction of Fort William said 'Brother, you have lowered England's soccer colours. When are you going to lower those other colours?' The story may be apocryphal but some of that euphoria is reflected in the Mohun Bagan historian's view of the match that 'it gave hope and pride to all Indians and sustained and strengthened the peoples' feelings of patriotism and helped to rouse a national consciousness. In winning the match and the Shield, the Club had contributed in its own way towards the independent movement'.

The British certainly were worried about the nationalistic effects of this match and banned a short film on the match with the Censor Office of the Bengal province seeing this as a projection of the colonised overpowering the colonise.

Logically, after independence, football should have become India's number one sport. It is cheaper, certainly permeated greater layers of Indian society – even down to the semi-rural areas – than cricket and there were the obvious links between nationalism and football. It is possible that had India won its independence from Britain in different circumstances, cricket might not have occupied the position it does in India today. Had the British been thrown out of India in the violent, revolutionary way, proposed by Subhas Bose, rather than agreed to withdraw peacefully, football rather than cricket could have become the major game. Or had the Bengalis who initiated the freedom struggle, retained their control then football – which is very strong in Bengal – might have become the national game.

But by the time freedom came, the national movement was led by Gandhi and his Western Indian allies, with its headquarters in Mumbai, where cricket had a greater hold. Cricket's path was also smoothed by the fact that Gandhi's campaign was motivated by love, or at least so it appeared. He wanted Indians to hate the actions and results of British policy in India, not the British themselves. Unique amongst nationalist movements, it taught Indians to accept the good that was in the British, while rejecting the harm that they were doing to India and its people. This meant that after independence there was no contradiction in accepting cricket – it could very simply be seen as one of the British goodies which ought to be retained. It was British systems, not the British, the Indians had been fighting, and cricket could be seen as part of the British way of life which the Indians approved.

However Gandhi was murdered within six months of India becoming free and modern India and cricket owes much more to Gandhi's anointed successor Nehru. It was his decisions that shaped the India that emerged. India proclaimed Gandhi Father of the Nation, elevated him to the status of a God – he is always referred to as Gandhiji, a term of respect – but shunned his beliefs. Today lip service is paid to Gandhi's anti-modernist hymns such as discarding machines for hand-made products. In every city in India there is a Khadi Bhandar, it means a store, for Khadi and handloom products which are marketed as if they were historical relics. The stores are more often frequented by foreign visitors for whom a visit to them is akin to going to a museum. Instead, free India enthusiastically embraced the industrialisation that Nehru advocated. Nehru also took one major political decision which had a far-reaching affect on Indian cricket.

The decision which was to keep India in the British Commonwealth. When India became independent in 1947 it became what is called a self-governing dominion within the British Commonwealth. A constituent assembly met in Delhi to frame the constitution. In some ways it was similar to the founding fathers of the American constitution meeting in Philadelphia in the last years of the eighteenth century to frame the American constitution. Except by the time the Americans met they had severed all links with the British Crown. Their debate was over what kind of republican government they should have.

The situation in India in 1947 was entirely different. India had become free but it still accepted the King of the United Kingdom as the King of India. The question was what would happen to the position of the Crown when India got her own constitution?

The Congress policy on this was clear and had been so for decades. That India would become a republic and while there would be friendly ties with Britain there would be no formal ties with the British Crown. The basic nationalist position had been stated by Subhas Bose.

Independence which India aspires after today, is not 'Dominion Home Rule' as we find in Canada or Australia – but full national sovereignty as obtained in the United States of America or in France.

Bose was writing in 1933. By 1947 nationalist India was even more determined to have an India totally free of British control in any shape or form.

In 1947 the British Commonwealth was essentially the white Commonwealth. India and Pakistan were the first non-white dominions to become self-governing. The white dominions accepted the King as their head of state whose representative in their country was called the Governor-General. This is still the position in Australia, Canada and New Zealand, although over the years there has been much debate in Australia, even a referendum, about becoming a republic. It is important to note that in 1947 such self-governing white dominions included South Africa although within a year the whites would vote for the National Party which would eventually declare it a republic and take it out of the Commonwealth. There was no concept of a republic, headed by a president, remaining part of a Commonwealth whose head was still the British monarch.

The Indians saw dominion status in 1947 as a temporary measure until they finalised their constitution, declared themselves a republic and left the Commonwealth. But the British, still unwilling to lose their links with this Jewel in the Crown, began to pester the Indians to stay in the Commonwealth. Leading British politicians came up with all sorts of ideas which would keep the King at the head of the new Indian state. Churchill suggested that even if India became a republic, in the style of republics in the Roman Empire India could remain a republic within the Commonwealth and still accept the King. The King seemed to like the idea and both men thought of the King becoming the President of India. Attlee wanted India's constitution to have a specific role for the British

King, wondered if a republic was really in the traditions of India and suggested a title might be found for the King from India's heroic age. He talked about the royal family being of a universal nature transcending creeds and races.

Nehru found such ideas 'juvenile' but politically he felt there was merit in staying within the Commonwealth. The Soviet Union was very hostile to India and Pakistan was hoping India would leave the Commonwealth so it could became the Northern Ireland of the subcontinent. Although there was fierce opposition in India and from within his own Cabinet, led by Patel, Nehru agreed to keep India in the Commonwealth. The Commonwealth had to be reinvented, convert itself from its historic role as a white man's club into one where other races could all aspire to equality. The position of the King also altered. India would become a truly independent country with its own President but it would also remain part of a wider club whose permanent President was the monarch of the United Kingdom. The club as such had no power and the British monarch had no power in India. But India accepted 'the King as the symbol of free association of its independent member nations and as such the head of the Commonwealth'. The decision met with much hostility in India but such was Nehru's power that the nation accepted. It took nearly two years for all this to be sorted out and agreement was only reached at the Commonwealth Prime Ministers Conference in London in April 1949.

For Indian cricket this decision was to have far-reaching significance. On 19 July 1948 when the debate about the Commonwealth was its height with the very secret letters flying between Delhi and London, the Imperial Cricket Conference met at Lord's. At that conference, the first since India had become a self-governing dominion in 1947, the matter of India's changed status came up. It was decided that India could remain a member of the ICC but only on a provisional basis. The matter would be looked at again after two years. It is clear that the ICC, unsure whether India would remain part of the British Commonwealth, was waiting for the politicians to decide.

India's cricket status was not finalised until the ICC held a two-day meeting on June 27, 28, 1950. Six months earlier on 26 January 1950 India had finally become a republic but had also remained part of the British Commonwealth. The ICC, reassured by this, moved the new India from provisional status to full membership. In its decision the ICC stressed that it felt the separation of Pakistan had not materially affected the standard of play in India. But the crucial fact was that the cricket body had to be a member of the British Commonwealth. Rule 5 of the ICC was very specific on that point. It stated that membership of the Conference shall cease should a country concerned cease to part of the British

Commonwealth. Had Nehru not agreed to keep India in the Commonwealth then Indian cricket would have failed the basic test of ICC membership. In that case it is almost certain that at its 1950 meeting the Indian Board's provisional status would not have been made final. India would have been cast out in the cricketing cold.

It is true that eleven years later the ICC came to a very different decision when another country left the Commonwealth, but that was done in a very roundabout way and reflected the mindset of the then white rulers of international cricket. The issue at the ICC meeting on 20 July 1961 was what do with the cricket status of South Africa. White South Africa had been tolerated in the new multiracial Commonwealth for eleven years but in March 1961 Nehru made it clear that the Commonwealth must take a stand and declare it could not have such a racist regime in its club. Not only did it deny basic human rights to its non-white citizens but so wedded was it to white supremacy that it had refused to have any diplomats from the non-white Commonwealth in its country, making a mockery of the Commonwealth being a club of equals. Britain, led by Harold Macmillan, and Australia, by Robert Menzies, were reluctant to abandon their white friends. They tried hard to keep white South Africa in the club. But Nehru insisted a choice had to be made and it was white South Africa, fearing expulsion, which eventually withdrew.

That decision came too late for that year's ICC agenda to be changed. Yet this was the first time a full member of the ICC – and a founding member at that – had left the Commonwealth and there was an hour and a half's discussion of what to do with South Africa. No final conclusion was reached. The ICC thought it was best left to the next meeting in 1962 but it did decide that 'Test matches between South Africa and New Zealand in 1961–62 would be unofficial.' However, both the MCC and Australia also made it clear that whatever happened to the apartheid regime on the world stage they would continue to play cricket with their white friends. The ICC should have discussed South Africa in 1962 but did not and through a mysterious process which no cricket historian has been able to unravel the 'unofficial' Tests of 1961–2 became official. Rule 5 was forgotten. Mathew Engel, editor of the *Wisden*, believes that all cricket in South Africa after 1961 should count as unofficial, but that is a minority view.

I suspect a private, verbal, deal was done between the good white cricketing friends who ran English, Australian and New Zealand cricket. As far as they were concerned nothing had changed. Even before South Africa's departure from the Commonwealth the cricket world was split along racial lines. The MCC had always accepted the 'whites only' basis that South Africa insisted on. South Africa only played white countries but England,

Australia and New Zealand played everyone and now South Africa's departure from the Commonwealth made no difference. England and the other white countries felt the fact that they played all nations established their tolerant and generous attitude towards the non-whites. Indeed in those years the MCC used to boast of this racially divided cricket world saying how it was necessary to build bridges to the whites in South Africa. Before every South African tour English cricket officials and the captain of the day would declare how South Africans touring England would see how races lived together amicably in England, even attend cricket matches sitting next to each other (something not allowed in South Africa where non-whites were caged in separate sections – Nelson Mandela has a vivid recollection of watching a Test against Australia in this fashion) and this would make the whites in South Africa over time accept non-whites as equals.

Change was only forced on the ICC when in 1968 the South African Prime Minister John Vorster suddenly turned English cricket selector and banned Basil D'Oliveira, who unable to play for his country because of his colour, had qualified for England. But although that tour was cancelled, a year later Australia toured South Africa and in the summer of 1970 English cricket was ready and keen to welcome the white South Africans. It was only tremendous public pressure and government diktat that finally forced them to cancel the tour leading to the cricket isolation of white South Africa.

It is interesting to speculate that might have happened if in 1961 the Commonwealth had not acted against white South Africa. Nehru had told his sister that in that case he would pull India out of the Commonwealth. And what would have happened to Indian cricket then? It is extremely unlikely, given that India had none of the close personal and racial ties white South Africa had with the then white dominated cricket world, that India would have been treated with such generosity by the ICC. India then were the dull dogs of cricket, having earned that nickname when they were thrashed 5–0 in 1959 in England. So dismal was India on that tour that during one Test Colin Cowdrey, captaining England, announced in advance he would not enforce the follow-on to ensure that there was play on the Saturday. In the winter of 1961 England went on a tour of India with a B team missing several leading players. An Indian tour was a hardship tour for English cricketers. There was no money to be made, India was very far from the powerhouse it has since become, and often struggled to finance tours. India could have been easily discarded from world cricket. This would have been even easier in 1950 had India not chosen to stay in the Commonwealth.

To appreciate this let us see how the ICC saw international cricket in the immediate post-war years. At the meeting in 1948 when India had been given provisional status much of the discussion concerned a report on the future of International Tours by the MCC Selection and Planning Sub-Committee. It may seem strange that the ICC discussed an MCC document but then – and for many years afterwards – the ICC despite its fine sounding title was essentially the international division of the MCC. The MCC president presided over the ICC and the MCC secretary acted as the ICC secretary. ICC meetings were routine affairs generally after a Lord's Test.

The report drew a sombre picture of post-war English cricket. Cricket had not recovered because full employment at high wages meant many useful players did not think of cricket as a career. National Service did not help, and a post-war reaction had set in which concluded the report had caused some 'uncertainty in the players' outlook towards the game'. New players were not coming through. For the Trial Match of 1948 no player born after 1921 had been selected. This meant, said the report, that England could no longer continue to bear the burden of promoting cricket by sending teams abroad. Between 1919 and 1939 the MCC had sent 19 teams abroad including two teams on the same dates to the far ends of the world to bring Test cricket to West Indies and New Zealand. In contrast, the same period had seen six visits between the five other countries. India had toured England three times and just completed a tour of Australia. But there had been no Indian cricket contact with New Zealand or the West Indies. There was, of course, no question of contact with the South Africans. Australia was yet to tour India or the West Indies. But while the report argued that the MCC must cut back on tours, and did not want overseas tours in the year before an Australian visit, 'The MCC feel bound to give priority of consideration to their older traditional foes in the international field i.e. Australia and South Africa.'

Also interestingly, the future tour programmes of 1948, extending up to 1952, did not list any visits to or by India. Indeed, the winter of 1950–1 was left blank and it was agreed Australia would tour England in 1952, being the traditional four-year gap for Australian visits to England.

Observe the dramatic change to this tour programme when the ICC met in the wake of the Indian decision to stay in the Commonwealth. The future tours decided on at the meeting in June 1950 was for the MCC to tour India, Pakistan and Ceylon in the winter of 1951–2 and for India to visit England in 1952, back-to-back Test series. In order to do this the Australian visit was put back to 1953, making it five years – the longest gap between Australian tours to this country.

So here we have one of those great ifs of Indian sporting history. What if Indian cricket had been thrown out of the ICC but the same year Indian soccer made its debut on the world stage? In 1950 India qualified to play for the soccer World Cup, the only time it has done so. But there were many problems, including foreign exchange, transport – the tournament was held in Brazil – and also the Indian insistence that they play in bare feet. FIFA refused to sanction this and India, in a decision that was to haunt its soccer, withdrew.

Imagine that on 26 January 1950 India on becoming a republic leaves the Commonwealth. Six months later the ICC meet and downgrade India from provisional member to non-member. However, even as they come to this decision Indian footballers, playing with boots, are taking part in soccer's first World Cup since the Second World War – the ICC meeting took place in the middle of the World Cup in Brazil. And building on the impression they had created in the 1948 Olympic football tournament they make a mark on the biggest world stage for team sports. Indian cricket, on the other hand, cut off from the world withers. Ifs are fascinating because they allow speculation without being tested by reality. But we need to appreciate how fragile Indian cricket was in much of the 1950s and how much stronger Indian football was.

In 1950 Indian cricket had achieved nothing on the world stage. It had yet to win a Test – it only did so two years later. Nor through the 1950s did India do much in cricket and for much of the decade Indian cricket struggled to attract worthwhile opposition and for some seasons they had to make do with playing unofficial Tests against so-called Commonwealth sides composed of players of many lands organised by the former Lancashire wicketkeeper George Duckworth. The decade ended with a mind-numbing 3–0 defeat at home to the West Indies, when India had four captains in five Tests, and then a 5–0 drubbing in England in 1959.

In soccer, on the other hand, India won the Asian Games gold in 1951, again in 1962, and came fourth in the Melbourne Olympics in 1956. Had soccer grabbed its chance, and Nehru followed populist sentiment and left the Commonwealth, who is to say that today football, not cricket, would be the main sport of India?

But soccer did not. There were, of course, immense problems for the way soccer was played in India. Unlike cricket, the game in India did not follow the game as it was played in the rest of the world. Indians not only played in bare feet but until 1960 India did not even play the full 90 minutes in their domestic matches. Indian matches lasted only 70 minutes and this led to India, when playing abroad, often losing a match they had dominated in the last few minutes as their players ran out of puff. It was wretchedly led and, what is more, never really organised an All-Indian structure in the way cricket had. There was nothing like the princely support cricket enjoyed. The Raja of Santosh did support it and India's soccer equivalent of the Ranji trophy is called the Santosh trophy, a knock-out competition in the style of the World Cup between the various Indian states. The Ranji trophy was also donated by a prince, Patiala, but there the similarities ended. Indian cricket developed a nationwide structure, states being the equivalent of English counties, playing each other annually for a championship. After independence other tournaments were added and the Ranji trophy has been reinvented often but the basic structure has not changed.

In contrast football in India remained parochial. There was no national league until the 1996–7 season, a century after soccer had first started in the country, and fifty years after independence. Unlike the Ranji trophy the state teams mean nothing. Power rests either with club teams as in Kolkata or teams formed by corporate organisations as in Mumbai. English football had emerged from English cricket. The formation of the Football Association was heavily influenced by cricketers, the Football League took the country championship as its template and the origins of many English clubs originate with cricket, such as Tottenham. The Hotspur Cricket Club, seeking a winter game to keep its cricket season alive, formed Tottenham Hotspur. And while the days of the double international has gone from English sport, English players still have links with cricket. The Neville brothers of Manchester United were very good cricketers and could have played professional cricket had they not been lured by the greater riches of football. The Indian cricket historian Boria Majumdar has shown that the early history of Indian cricket also had clubs which played both cricket and football and I can remember a time when a double international was not impossible in India. The best example of this was Chuni Goswami, probably India's greatest footballer. He led India to Asian Gold in 1962 and while he did not play Test cricket, he came close – captaining Bengal and scoring Ranji hundreds.

But such links were soon lost. Perhaps football's greatest failing was that it was never taken up by the well-off Indians, except in Bengal. While I played both cricket and football in my Mumbai school, cricket was a game all my school mates followed. I cannot think of anybody who was not interested. But football was, to use that Mumbai phrase, a 'maca pau' game, the slang we used for Goan Catholics living in Mumbai. They formed a significant portion of our school team, and most football teams of Mumbai. A Mumbai cricket eleven always shows a great many players whose names end in kar, like Gavaskar and Tendulkar, denoting Maharashtrian Brahmins. In contrast, football teams of Mumbai have names like D'Souza, Pinto, Castro, Fernandez and D'Mello, indicating the Goan–Portuguese heritage of the players.

My own Bengali origins meant I was made aware of soccer in a way my other Mumbai schoolmates were not. Both my parents had been introduced to soccer in their youth. The two big Kolkata teams are Mohun Bagan, which represents the western part of the old united Bengal and East Bengal the eastern part. My father, an immigrant to Mumbai from the east, supported East Bengal and passed it on to me, my mother, who grew up in Calcutta, supported Mohun Bagan. These two teams would play in the Rovers Cup in Mumbai and once when the two teams met in the semi-finals on a brilliant winter Sunday afternoon our whole family went. East Bengal won through an own goal from Mohun Bagan's Indian defender Jarnail Singh, the ball deflecting into the net off the knot of hair Sikh men have on their head, I was overjoyed but my mother was mortified. This was the only time I can recall our whole family going to a sports match – I went to cricket only with my father.

It also helped that my father, a prominent businessman and a leader of the local Bengali community in Mumbai, was very friendly with Jagadish Maitra, a Bengali journalist who ran the Western India Football Association. We were given privileged status for the matches there and the WIFA also played an important part in our social life. Every Christmas it had a children's Christmas party with races and prizes which my father encouraged me to join and which I often won.

But in independent India as a whole football did not have such an upper-class social acceptance. Nehru certainly did not display the affection for football that he felt for cricket. It would be absurd to say cricket played a part in Nehru's decision to keep India in the Commonwealth, but unlike Gandhi who was indifferent to cricket (he only once commented on the game and that was to condemn matches between different religious communities in India which he thought encouraged religious sectarianism), Nehru lent the game his enormous prestige. He had played cricket at Harrow and though something of a misfit there (Nehru was at Harrow at the beginning of the twentieth century) his love for Harrow deepened as the years went by. Long after he had left Harrow, he became, says Sarvepalli Gopal his official biographer, 'very conscious of his Harrovian connections'. Imprisoned by the British for his politics 'he stuck pictures of Harrow in his prison and drew up lists of poets and politicians who had been to Harrow. He even sensed a certain affinity with Byron on the grounds that they had both been to Harrow and Trinity, and he used to sing the school songs with the younger members of the family . . . He was doubtless far happier as an old Harrovian than in his actual years at that school'.

In independent India it was common to see photographs of Nehru, in all white and padded out properly, his head now quite bald but his back fairly straight, playing in the annual Indian Parliamentarians' match. Nehru regularly attended Test Matches and other matches in Delhi, and it was his encouragement that made Delhi a Test match centre. Nehru's biographer provides no clue as to why Nehru should have taken to cricket after he became Prime Minister of independent India. But just as Nehru felt more Harrovian as he grew older, so, I think, he felt more attracted to English things as he sought to shape an English-free India. There was much talk about Nehru being the first English Prime Minister of India, and probably cricket benefited from that feeling. The departure of the British had removed the moral stumbling block about accepting cricket and this played its part with Nehru, as it did with other Indians.

It also helped that Nehru was keen that Indians should not nurse their sense of grievance as to the harm British rule had done. He worked hard not make Indian glory in victimhood. In 1955 the Lok Sabha, the Indian House of Commons, wanted to build a mural of the Jallianwala Bagh massacre, the garden in Amritsar where Dyer had shot unarmed Indians. Nehru wrote:

> I understand that the Lok Sabha Secretariat has asked the UK High Commission in Delhi for a portrait picture of General Dyer for use in connection with a mural in the Parliament building. I am rather surprised to learn this. It is obvious that such a request would embarrass the UK Government greatly ... I am entirely opposed to the idea of having any mural in Parliament building depicting the Jallianwala Bagh massacre. I think that we should not depict incidents, which, though important, excite ill will.

Nehru's generosity of spirit is remarkable. When he wrote this letter relations with Britain were bad and what is more the Jallianwala Bagh massacre was one that Nehru had himself investigated and was one of the seminal moments of his life. He had shared a railway carriage with Dyer and heard him boasting of shooting these 'niggers'. Nehru's attitude was shared by his colleagues. On 15 August 1947 Indian crowds surged to plant the Indian flag in place of the Union Jack at the Residency in Lucknow which had withstood the siege during the 1857 revolt and where the British flag was a symbol of their eternal possession of India. But the crowds were stopped by Govind Vallabh Pant, the new chief minister of Uttar Pradesh whose capital is Lucknow. He had, himself, been badly beaten by British troops when agitating for India's freedom and often been jailed. He told the crowds to go home 'and leave in peace a spot sacred to the British dead.'.

It is interesting to contrast the very different attitudes that another old Harrovian had to historical memory. Winston Churchill's hatred of Gandhi and the Indian Congress never left him. After the war while writing his

History of the Second World War he continued to vent his anti-Gandhi feelings. In a draft chapter Churchill alleged that Gandhi wanted to create a Hindu Raj, seeking to give the Japanese free passage through India to link up with the Germans so he could use Japanese military help to hold down the Muslims. These allegations were ridiculous but Churchill, like many British leaders of that period, hated Hindus, in particular Brahmins – although Gandhi was not a Brahmin – and preferred Muslims to Hindus. However, after objections from some who read the draft, Churchill omitted these passages. But his published memoirs still had one canard against Gandhi. During one of Gandhi's war-time fasts Churchill had maliciously asked the Viceroy to find out if his Hindu doctors were feeding him glucose with his water. Now he revisited that charge and wrote, Gandhi was 'being fed with glucose whenever he drank water'. The historian David Reynolds in *In Command of History*, a book which expertly analyses how Churchill both fought the war and also made sure his version of history prevailed, says this caused a furore in India. Gandhi's doctors contested the claim and it was taken out of the subsequent editions.

Leaders set the tone for their people. Churchill unable to forgive, let alone forget old quarrels has helped create a country where old battles are constantly being fought over. The British media, particularly the tabloids, can never stop reminding the Germans of what they did during the war, or even at times the Spanish of what they tried and failed with their Armada four centuries ago. In India on the whole the media took its cue from Nehru and did not go on about the awfulness of British rule.

So to my generation of Indians, the first to grow up in independent India, cricket came triply blessed. Blessed by Nehru, who was 'Chacha' Nehru, the universal uncle of all children – his birthday was celebrated as children's day – blessed by the school and blessed by the community. But it was not presented as a nationalist game, as football might have been. It was not presented as an English game, just a wonderful game which had strong English connections. Though we grew up surrounded by nationalism and with the echoes of the struggle against the British ringing round us, there was no contradiction in promoting and supporting cricket. V. S. Naipaul has suggested that Indians can reconcile historical contradictions only by ignoring historical facts. In others it may lead to neurosis, in Indians it leads to detachment and acceptance. Naipaul is being characteristically severe on Indians, who are not the only ones to ignore historical facts.

There was merit in this Indian amnesia. After all if they had really taught us about Harris they would have had to say that he held Indians, particularly educated Indians, in contempt and did not believe Indians could be ever be the equal of the English. It is unlikely that would have endeared Harris to us, let alone the game he sponsored.

They would have also had to explain how Indians took to cricket despite the apartheid the British practised in India. Nirad Chaudhuri has described how in 1928 in Kolkata, just six years before Kolkata hosted its first ever Test, he was warned off from walking on the wrong side of Eden Gardens – the side reserved for Europeans. So limited was contact between Indians and the English that in 1986 Alan Ross, one of the finest of cricket writers and editor of the *London* magazine, researching for his biography of the Indian businessman Ghanshyamdas Birla made an astonishing discovery. His father was a businessman who worked in an office within walking distance of Birla in Kolkata. Ross, himself, was born the same year, in the same Alipore district of Kolkata as Birla's youngest son. Yet while there was some official contact there was no social contact between the British and the Indians:

> As a child in India, as an adolescent with Indian connections, Indian history for me was the history of the British presence. About Indian families of the same period almost nothing has been written in English. The British in India had virtually no contact, except officially, with Indians and little curiosity.

For Ross the writing of Birla's biography was like 'a form of self-education', revisiting his Indian childhood but this time with Indian characters, missing from his original story, painted in.

This apartheid was, of course, nowhere near as total as that the whites imposed in South Africa. The very nature of British rule in India meant there had to be contact. So the first-ever Test India played in India was staged at the Bombay Gymkhana which in those days did not allow Indians as members and whose racism shocked Learie Constantine, but which for this one occasion made special arrangements. The British clubs like Bombay Gymkhana did not open its doors to Indians until well into the 1960s, fifteen years after independence. I vividly recall the commotion that was caused in Mumbai in the early 1960s when a black American diplomat, who had gone with his white colleague, was thrown out of the Beach Candy swimming pool, the club being open only to Europeans, as the British called themselves in India. The agitation to remove this colour bar was led by the English wife of an Indian.

The reaction of my father's friends reflected how the Indians saw this British colour bar. One of them, a leading Mumbai journalist said, 'If the English don't want us, why should we hanker after them.' In the end the English had to give in because otherwise it was economically impossible to maintain the clubs.

It could also be argued that the Indians did not so much forget their history but they, like others – including the English – re-interpreted it. In this version the English subjugation of India was explained in terms of a technological failure. India had nothing to learn from the west in spiritual terms, so the message went – an argument that was reinforced during the 1960s and 1970s when young westerners came to India to learn about spiritualism. What had caused the great Indian failure was its inability to keep pace with the technological change in the west. If India was to be the equal of the west, she must remedy this technological gap. Of course the theory was flawed since the technical gap had been the result of a moral and educational gap – but Indians could hardly be expected to understand that.

This desire to catch up with the west in technological terms is reflected in every aspect of Indian life. This is vividly illustrated in the reaction to Indian cricketing triumphs. In 1971, for the first time in its history, India beat England in England. In 1983, much to everybody's surprise, India won the World Cup. Both events were joyously acclaimed and the returning Indian cricketers feted like conquering heroes. The Indian mood was summed up by Mrs Gandhi's reaction to the World Cup triumph when she said, 'This shows we can do it.' It was the comment of a technologist who has finally mastered a craft he or she has been searching for. Interestingly Mrs Gandhi's comments were re-echoed some time later in an Indian magazine describing the manufacture of India's first Rover – a welcome break with the rather monotonous old Morris Oxford that used to clutter the Indian roads. But any suggestion that it marked the emergence of India as a nation would have been quite extraordinary. It would have occurred to no one.

This view of cricket explains why the roots of Indian cricket remain shallow, certainly much shallower than in England, Australia or even the West Indies. Soon after the war Neville Cardus, philosophising about cricket, wrote 'if everything else in this nation of ours was lost but cricket – her constitution and the law of England, of Lord Halsbury – it would be possible to reconstruct from the theory and the practice of cricket, all the eternal Englishness which has gone into the establishment of that Constitution and the Laws aforesaid'.

Such a statement would make no sense in India. If everything else in India but cricket were to be destroyed, we would get no sense of the country just from the practice of cricket. We would have some sense of the spectacle of Indian cricket, and some idea of cricket fever that could grip India during international matches, but nothing more. Cardus may have laid on the aesthetic cream a bit too thickly, but his broader point about the place of English cricket in English society can hardly be doubted. English cricket is woven into the fabric of English society through village, club, county and Test cricket in a very special way. English poets have written about the game, English men of letters like J. B. Priestley have chided their friends who 'have not grasped the simple fact that sport and art are similar activities'. Cricket is the subject of poems and drama and a great deal of literature, much of it contributed by Cardus. There is nothing remotely comparable in India.

No major Indian novelists, or come to that any Indian novelist, has written about the game. In the last twenty years Indian authors writing in English have created a new class of fiction winning the major literary prizes of the western world. But no Indian Nick Hornby has emerged, writing about his love for his beloved Arsenal as he did in his classic *Fever Pitch*. Writers, poets, philosophers reminiscing about cricket in England could fill many volumes. One such volume *Summer Days*, edited by Michael Meyer, had contributors ranging from Kingsley Amis and A. J. Ayer to Melvyn Bragg, Thomas Keneally and V. S. Naipaul. A comparable list in India would be absolutely impossible. The dramatist and novelist Simon Raven's *Shadows In The Grass*, is essentially a cricketing memoir, beautifully illustrating how central cricket was to his life. I cannot imagine a comparable figure in India producing such a memoir. America's leading novelists like Bernard Malamud and Philip Roth have written about baseball and there is no shame in a baseball writer becoming a major mainstream writer. Ring Lardner, one of the greatest short story writers in America, was the classic example. In America, journalists who make their mark as political writers do not feel they are debasing themselves by writing about sport. David Hallberstam, a Pulitzer prize-winning journalist, has written beautifully on baseball and basketball for that matter. This is inconceivable in India.

When I first wrote this book twenty years ago I could also confidently say Indian cricket does not feature in films except incidentally. Since then we have had the path-breaking film *Laggan* where for the first time cricket is the cinematic theme. I shall have more to say about this movie later but even then Bollywood has to go a long way before the celluloid history of Indian cricket matches that of baseball in America. Hollywood movies like *The Natural* and *Field Of Dreams* seek to recreate American dreams through baseball. In India cricket is not the subject of songs or verses, or anything remotely connected with art. Curiously, the only literary book I have seen on Indian sport was written by a Bengali author and was a short story about a football goalkeeper. Now it could be said that this merely reflects the fact that Indian culture is rather more of a verbal one. But even in the West Indian world, where again verbal culture predominates cricket is reflected through calypsos. There are odd Indians who buck this trend. Vinod Mehta, editor of *Outlook*, is the shining example. One of India's most prominent editors he is not ashamed to broadcast his love for cricket and even, at times, writes about it. But, generally, Indians tend to think that those who write about sport are in charge of the kiddies department. And it is impossible to imagine an Indian Michael Manley – this former Prime Minister of Jamaica wrote the classic *History of West Indies Cricket*.

Critics could point to the fact that there is a growing Indian literature on cricket. Since I first wrote this book twenty years ago India has produced more books on cricket, although it is still a long way behind English cricket literature. There have always been essayists like Sujit Mukerkejee and N. S. Ramswami and *The Times* of India's own K. N. Prabhu whose Cardusian flourishes shaped my early cricket understanding. A few years after the first edition of this book was published Ashish Nandy, a psychoanalyst and one of India's leading intellectuals, confessed to his love for the game in print and wrote *The Tao of Cricket*, a very engaging, provocative, book. More recently historians trained in other fields such as Ramchandra Guha and Boria Majumdar have taken to cricket writing. But even then when Guha came to edit his cricket anthology he could, apart from himself, find only four Indians worthy of inclusion in a book featuring 82 contributions. In the main, the books on Indian cricket are still written by journalists, or ghosted by them for cricketers. Indian sports magazines do very well out of cricket, and even the general magazines boost their sales during the cricket season by featuring articles on the game. But that does not constitute a literature and is rather on a par with film magazines which do very well on the popularity of the Bollywood film stars. Indian magazines and books may reflect cricket's status but they do not invalidate the argument that there exists no real cricketing literature in India. The game, as it is played now, has failed to develop real, meaningful literary roots in the way cricket has in England or baseball has in America.

The shallowness of Indian cricket can be gleaned from the analysis prepared by Dr Richard Cashman, an Australian historian writing on Indian cricket. Between June 1932, when India made her Test debut, and February 1979, 143 players represented India in 166 official Tests. Of these Cashman has been able to find the birthplace of 128. Fifty-one of them came from Maharashtra, which includes the city of Mumbai, 18 from neighbouring Gujerat and 13 from Punjab. Eighty-two out of 128 came from just 3 states.

If certain regions have been overrepresented then so have upper castes and upper classes – they do tend to be synonymous in India. Boria Majumdar's analysis of Indian cricket shows that it is only in the last few years that the upper-caste, upper-class bias of Indian cricket has been corrected:

> With a significant number of players among the current lot of cricketers playing for India at the national level coming from relatively modest backgrounds, Indian cricket is on its way to becoming a

meritocracy. Sanjay Bangar, Harbhajan Singh, Zaheer Khan, Virender Sehwag and Mohammed Kaif are men from middle class and relatively modest backgrounds, who have become national icons in the years 1998–2003. The presence of men from humble backgrounds in the team is significant, because Indian cricket, till recently, continued to be dominated by the economically privileged, affluent sections of society. In India, caste and class status has, in most cases, tended to overlap, and the economically privileged stratum has been for decades, and remains, predominantly upper caste. An analysis of the composition of India's national sides in the years since independence is indicative of this phenomenon, which has been noticeable since the inception of the game in the country from the middle of the nineteenth century. Contrary to arguments in existing literature, which make a case to the effect that cricket in post independence India has been representative of Indian society, the history of cricket in independent India demonstrates that prior to the country's triumph in the Prudential Cup of 1983, the game was dominated by an affluent, educated, upper caste elite. The victory in 1983 opened up among the middle classes and underprivileged sections of Indian society the possibility of cricket being a viable career option, allowing lower caste, economically underprivileged men to come to the fore and don the national colours.

In that sense Indian cricket developed very differently from West Indian cricket and this is well demonstrated if you compare the two great writers these two regions have produced: C. L. R. James and Nirad Chaudhuri.

They were born within years of each other, at other ends of the world, in small semi-rural areas. The only thing they had common was that they were both products of Britain's far-flung empire. Chaudhuri was born in 1897, the year Victoria celebrated her diamond jubilee, in Kishorganj, a small country town in east Bengal composed of tin and mud huts or sheds. James was born in 1901 in Tunapuna in Trinidad, a small town of 3,000 people in the sugar-growing region in Trinidad. Both men would leave their birthplaces lured by the lights of the big cities in their region, Chaudhuri for Kolkata, James for Port of Spain. Both men would travel even further. They would die within a few years of each other in England, James in a flat in Brixton in London, Chaudhuri in his house in Oxford

The conventional view of both men is well established. James was the Marxist who fought the Empire, Chaudhuri, the apologist who mourned the departure of the British from India. Yet the astonishing thing is that when you examine their writings in detail a very different picture emerges.

It is Chaudhuri who has written much the most trenchant criticisms of the British and their Empire, particularly the behaviour of the British *in* their Empire while James, for all his great Marxist analysis, has hardly had a harsh word to say about the British and in some ways has created quite a misleading image of the British and why they propagated team sports such as cricket.

James's *Beyond A Boundary* is one of the classics of our age, probably the most challenging book on sport, where James comes in various guises – novelist, critic, social historian – to argue that cricket is art. A good deal of the book is taken up by the men who made sports, and in particular cricket, so prominent in nineteenth-century England, James's holy trinity being Arnold, Hughes and Grace. At the heart of James's thesis is the link between English sport and ancient Greeks. He argues that the creators of English sport sought to propagate ideas of universal brotherhood and fellow feeling for all humankind.

James speaks of how his love for cricket and English literature was akin to that of boys in ancient Greece combing poetry and games:

> If for them games and poetry were ennobled by their roots in religion, my sense of conduct and morals came from my two, or rather my twin, preoccupations, and I suspect that it was not too different with a Greek boy. [So much so that when James left school he felt he would be more at home in ancient Greece.] If I had been French or German or African I would have thought differently. But I was British, I knew best the British way of life, not merely in historical facts but in instinctive responses. I had acquired them in childhood and, without these, facts are merely figures. In the interval of my busy days and nights I pondered and read and looked about me and pondered and read again. Sport and Politics in Ancient Greece. Sport and Politics in nineteenth century Britain... the luminous glow of the Greek city-state seems to penetrate more searchingly into every corner of our civilisation. Into the immeasurable chaos of his Guernica, lit by the electric chandelier, Picasso introduces a Greek face with an extended arm which holds a primitive oil-lamp. The Greek lamp burns today as steadily as ever. They who laid the intellectual foundations of the Western world were the most fanatical players and organisers of games the world has ever known.

James demonstrates that the ancient Greeks treated sports very seriously. While the Greek states fought each other unceasingly, every four years a truce was called to stage the Olympics. Even a philosopher like Lucian, who sneered at the games, could not but, through the mouth of Solon, speak of 'the courage of the athletes, the beauty of their bodies, their splendid poses, their extraordinary suppleness, their tireless energy, their audacity, their sense of competition, their unconquerable courage, their unceasing efforts to win a victory'. Pindar, the great lyric poet, wrote odes to the successful athletes.

James urges us to follow the ideals of the ancient Greeks, take athletic activity seriously and honour athletes. It is sheer intellectual snobbery, he says, to disregard the achievements of men such as Grace, or Headley or Bradman. Their cricketing achievements were not mere sporting matters and extended beyond the cricket field. All this may be accepted as fair, even unarguable.

However in the process James confuses many things about the Greeks, or rather does not allude to them. The effect is to create a false impression, first of the Greek invention of sports and then of the way the English took up the Greek baton. True, the Greeks did think sport was important but they would have made nothing of a team game like cricket because to them sporting glory meant individual glory. The Greek Olympics had no team games. For them glory shared was glory spoiled. The other point is that the Greek only cared about winning. Modern sport is about creating and breaking records. A game like cricket is about style, records, and many other things. We like David Gower not because he won many matches for England but for the beauty and grace of his batting. The Greeks would not have cared for him unless he won and their attitude would be like the one English selectors displayed towards Gower when they cruelly discarded him because he was not felt to be a winner.

In cricket, victory, while always welcome, can sometimes mean less than a stylish innings in a losing cause. Or, as with Michael Atherton's great innings in the Johannesburg Test of 1995–6, an effort that saves a match can mean as much as a victory. The Greeks would have been nonplussed by such a view. It is surprising that James does not appreciate this for he makes many such cricketing references particularly when he is talking of his hero, Headley. To the Greeks much of what James says of Headley would have made no sense. At their Olympic Games there was no precise time keeping. They did not care whether the victory had won by 0.03 of a second slower than the previous year. It was enough the athlete had won.

James does accept that, contrary to what Victorian headmasters liked to pretend, Greek sportsmen won more than the mere garland of wild olive. But his passage describing how the Greeks treated the winners is done in such a fashion that it obscures the fact that the Greeks were very materialistic when it came to sports. The Greek victor would get a cash award equivalent to several years' pay and free meals for life. In addition to all this there was fame and probably even a cult status after death.

James is right to stress that the ancient Greeks would have laughed at our hypocritical assertion that it is only a game. For them sport was very much a part of life, part of the whole man. Unlike modern man who divides and specialises, the Greeks saw things as an organic whole. So Solon was a political and economic writer, a man of business and a poet. H. D. F. Kitto in his book, *The Greeks*, has written:

> The Greek made physical training an important part of education, not because he said to himself, 'Look here, we mustn't forget the body', but because it could never occur to him to train anything but the whole man. It was natural for the polis to have gymnasium as to have a threatre or warships, and they were constantly used by men of all ages, not only for physical but also for mental exercise.

But if we accept this view that for Greeks sport was an integrated part of their existence, we must ask what was the ancient Greek conception of the whole man? And this is where James's thesis begins to fall apart. The Greeks were a very exclusive people. Not only did they have slaves but they treated all foreigners with great disdain. Sparta admitted foreigners but only grudgingly and from time to time expelled them. Athens was more liberal but again there was no question of naturalising foreigners. And as far as the actual Olympic games were concerned they were a men-only affair with strong homosexual overtones. All the participants had to be naked. This may explain why married women were not even allowed to watch, although virgins were.

James does not mention any of this. Instead he is so taken by the idea of being the heir to Greek civilisation that he says we will be able to answer Tolstoy's cry of what is art, 'only when we learn to integrate our vision of Walcott on the backfoot through the covers with the outstretched arm of the Olympic Apollo'. The imagery is typical James but quite absurd. The fact is had Walcott found himself in ancient Greece he would have been treated worse than a slave and certainly there would have been no question of him taking part in the ancient games, let alone playing off the backfoot. The Greeks only allowed people of pure Greek blood to take part in the Olympics.

James, the Marxist, should have been expected to see all this. Instead he burnished the myth of an English sporting Eden as one where the whole world was welcome Where did James get such a view of English sports? It is clear what his inspiration was. James refers to it again and again – it is the belief in the English public school code:

> I learnt and obeyed and taught a code, the English public-school code, Britain and her colonies and the colonial people. What do the British

people know of what they have done there? Precious little. The colonial peoples, particularly West Indians scarcely know themselves as yet.

It was not that James was unaware of the racial situation in the West Indies or what he calls the national question, the question of West Indian self-government and the formation of a federation of the islands. But in school these things did not matter and James, in any case, was much taken by individual Englishmen who may have been politically reactionary or even chauvinistic but were personally kind and tolerant. All this made James think that they were following the right policy even if they could not at times help being partial to the white boy in the class in preference to James. And just as he saw the school as a bulwark against the world where James was to receive hard knocks, he saw the English world of sports as a bulwark against the reality of life.

Interestingly, V. S. Naipaul reviewing James's *Beyond a Boundary* was one of the few to pick up James's references to the code of the English public school and commented, 'twenty years ago the colonial who wrote those words might have been judged to be angling for an O.B.E. or M.B.E'.

Now contrast James with Chaudhuri. Chaudhuri, who has written extensively about the Indo-British interaction, is generally seen in India as an apologist for the Raj and often abused quite virulently. The poet Nissim Ezekiel described one of his books, *Passage to England*, as slavish in its love for England. Chaudhuri's image as the poodle of the English stemmed from the fact that he dedicated his autobiography to the memory of the British Empire, an empire which had conferred subjecthood but withheld citizenship but 'all that was good and living within us was made shaped, and quickened by the same British rule'.

Yet now rereading James and Chaudhuri there can be no doubt as to who is both more critical and perceptive about the British impact on their colonies. It is Chaudhuri who is very severe on the British in India: at one stage he compares the British in India to Nazis whose personal behaviour towards Indians ruined the impact that British letters and British learning had made on the Indian mind. James, in contrast, has very little to say that is harsh about the English in the West Indies. In the 1950s, totally misunderstanding the situation in South Africa, he even opposed a boycott of sporting South Africa on the grounds that this would mean that for the first time a black man would captain a West Indian team, albeit it would play only a black south African team and accept the racial distinctions created by apartheid. Nevertheless, while Chaudhuri is reviled in India, in the West Indies, James, partly because of his Marxist past, partly because of *Beyond a Boundary*, is seen as the great radical historian of the West Indies.

The contrast in the treatment of the two writers tells us much about how these two societies, India and the West Indies, viewed sport. In the Caribbean cricket has enjoyed an intellectual prestige it has never done in India. In the Caribbean a man of letters could also be a lover of cricket – that was rarely the case in India. For men like Chaudhuri their imbibing of English learning was the culture of the eighteenth century long before sports entered the English cultural equation. James came to it when the nineteenth-century sporting ethos had been formed.

So unlike James, Chaudhuri has little to say about cricket, except for one brief reference in his autobiography to the discovery of a picture depicting English cricket in a school textbook. It made a profound impression, so much so that although he loved cricket and played it he could not but compare the drab efforts of his team 'by the side of the cricket world revealed in that coloured picture. The game was transformed, it was cricket suffused with the colours of the rainbow'. This, it seemed to him, was how the game was played in England. After that he could not take the Indian efforts seriously; not even Father Prior at the Oxford Mission in Calcutta could get Chaudhuri to play any sport, even badminton. The glow cast by English cricket seemed to turn Chaudhuri away from the sport in India, instead of towards it as with James.

It probably did not help that while James met Englishmen from an early age Chaudhuri did not meet an Englishman until he was 55, his exposure to England was through books and art. But this, curiously, enabled Chaudhuri to make the more insightful observations on the contradictions of the English colonial experience. So while Chaudhuri is appreciative of the British influence in India, particularly Bengal, he is, unlike James, also aware of how the British did not follow through on what they had created. James praises Greeks and debunks Rome saying the heritage of imperial Rome is 'more than ever a millstone around our necks and a ball and chain on our feet'. This is the only reference to Rome by James in 254 pages – and it is a very jarring one. Yet Chaudhuri makes the more perceptive point that the British in their civilising mission failed because they did not follow the Roman imperial logic. This was that even slaves could become Roman citizens provided they accepted Roman ways. So a Berber from North Africa could help colonise Britain because he was a Roman.

The British in India opened the door to English education but mocked Chaudhuri and his Bengali ancestors as 'babus' who would never be able to speak English properly. Chaudhuri blamed the English in India for destroying the good which British ideas and values were doing in the country, James sees no contradiction in the ideals of the British and they way the British abroad behaved. Indians in India, like Chaudhuri, were well aware of how far short of British ideas the British sojourners in India, to use Chaudhuri's phrase, fell. This shaped their appreciation of cricket.

In many ways the real, astonishing thing about Indian cricket is not its popularity but the nature of its popularity. It is not cricket so much, but international cricket that is popular. India made its Test debut even before it had a proper national cricket competition and in modern India, international cricket has become *tamasha*, a rich Indian word which means fun, excitement and glamour all rolled into one. Just as the Bollywood film stars are part of the tamasha – as occasionally are the politicians – so are cricketers. International cricket attracts vast crowds in India and visiting cricketers are mobbed like celebrities and allowed tremendous publicity, even very quickly given endorsements and used to advertise products. In the winter of 2004–5 the Australian cricketer Brett Lee who spent the entire tour carrying drinks on the field and did not play a single Test nevertheless often appeared on television advertising products. Yet the game outside Tests and one-day internationals is hardly noted.

Indian newspapers barely manage to report the scores of the Ranji Trophy matches. Apart from the finals of the Ranji Trophy and a couple of other matches, it is difficult to even get the full score card. I give an example from the winter of 1984–5 when England was touring India. Take the Mumbai *Sunday Observer*, an English-style Sunday paper, of 25 November 1984. Its lead story on the sports page is a report of a match between England and the West Zone. The story of the match is fairly comprehensive and includes the photograph of Dilip Vengsarkar, the double centurion. Tucked away next to it, with only six lines devoted to it, is a report of a Ranji trophy match between Bengal and Assam. England and West Zone's score card is printed, but there are only brief scores of the Bengal–Assam match. The space given to the Ranji trophy match pales into virtual insignificance compared to a report from Australia on the Test match between West Indies and Australia. Interestingly, the second lead on the page is of a local football match, and is quite well covered.

In India all this is accepted as very much par for the course. It is astonishing to notice the change that comes over an Indian city or town when a Test match or a one-day international is on. In the days preceding these matches, local newspapers are full of news, advertisements and build up of what they call 'Test fever'. Net practices of the Indian and visiting teams take up more space than would county cricket reports in most English newspapers. Photographers are regularly present and almost every act of the two sets of international cricketers is extensively reported. There are even snippets about the spivs trying to promote a black market in tickets. But as soon as the international finishes, the fever, like some strange Indian disease, seems to subside. The end of the international is taken as the end of cricket and it often vanishes from the newspapers. The newspapers, which brought out special editions for the match, rarely manage to report domestic cricket scores. Not that ordinary cricket is not popular. It is played by Indians every day on the maidans but in Indian cricket there is no balance between the fervour shown for international matches and the total antipathy for the domestic game. So great is this antipathy that Ranji Trophy matches hardly attract crowds unless there are special factors such as the all-too-rare presence of Sachin Tendulkar. In many cricket centres admission is free to Ranji Trophy matches.

The explanation for this international fever lies not in the deeds of Indian cricketers, but rather the nature of urban India. For Indian cricket is more than a game; it is an essential part of modern industrial India. Ruled by an élite anxious to convince the world that it heads the tenth-largest industrial power, one capable of producing atom bombs, exporting food – India is the third-largest producer of food items in the world – and machinery, and now the home of call centres, cricket is an essential status symbol.

In the social set-up of modern urban India, cricket is one sure way of obtaining acceptance. For the urban poor and lower-income groups it forms a valuable distraction from their appalling poverty and struggle to survive. It is important to stress that cricket in India is essentially an urban game, which has yet to really penetrate the rural regions which have their own games, very different from the organised family of ball games to which cricket belongs.

It is not very difficult to see why cricket occupies such a position in modern India. The sixty years or so since independence have seen great changes led by a massive, ill-directed, industrial revolution converting villagers into urban dwellers, and producing cities where Manhattan-style skyscrapers co-exist with dismal hovels. The progress is very uneven, creating several Indias. Parts of India such as Bangalore and Hyderabad in the south – where the majority of call centres are located – have progressed very rapidly. Yet there are parts of northern India, such as Bihar, which seem to have gone backwards. Boria Majumdar has called this the panoply of anomalies. Forty-four per cent of Indians spend less than a dollar a day, 70 out of 1,000 Indian children die before their first birthday, another 25 before they are 5. The relentless urge to urbanise means that every day hundreds of villagers pour into the cities looking for jobs and security and into Mumbai with its film industry come the seekers of fame and fortune. Most of these villagers end up as shoeshine boys, mournfully singing film tunes.

The urbanisation has occasionally threatened to get out of hand. During Mrs Gandhi's emergency rule in 1975–7, the local government in Mumbai thought of introducing an entry permit to regulate the flow of such El Dorado-seeking villagers. Mumbai is essentially a group of islands connected to the mainland of India and it would be rather easier to control the flow of people into Mumbai, than it would be, say, into London. But the very fact that such an idea was proposed reflected both the nature of the problem, and the mind of urban India. Not that such a movement is peculiar to Indians. Cricket became the English national game during the eighteenth century when a predominantly agricultural society transformed itself into an industrial one.

In India, for almost four decades since the 1950s, Test cricket not only brought together the otherwise strictly segregated classes of urban India, they also made up for the lack of pleasures generally. A five-day Test match with its seemingly endless variations was ideal entertainment and when the cricket got dull, the crowds devised their own situations to amuse themselves.

The location of the Test grounds in the centre of modern Indian cities emphasise the *tamasha* aspect. The cheaper stands are to one side of the ground, generally known as the East Stands. Here on hard concrete, sometimes precariously balanced on planks of wood, thousands gather for their daily excitement, equipped liberally with their own tiffin carriers and makeshift potties, the favourite being empty coconuts.

Movement during play is often impossible. A single gesture can cause whole ranks to sway, and when the play becomes boring the crowd invents its own amusements – occasionally fights. Endless chants which may not be melodious can be effective: B-O-W-L-E-D, as the fast bowlers run up to the wicket; P-L-A-Y-E-D, as a tail-ender, like Chandrasekhar, for instance, makes contact with the ball. Fences separate the popular stands from the élite who gather in the colonial-style club houses and elegant marquees. Unlike English grounds, it is almost impossible to walk round an Indian cricket stadium. In that sense Indian cricket stadiums are more like football stadiums in England closer to Manchester United's Old Trafford than Lancashire Cricket Club's Old Trafford. In any case, such is the crush during international matches that it would be hardly worth trying to go walkabout.

For those not fortunate enough to get tickets, there is television. During international match days every urban *pan* shop (the Indian equivalent of the corner shop specialising in betel nuts), replaces Hindi film music with television commentaries. Work in many offices comes to a standstill, typists, clerks, even the officers, furtively try to catch the latest score. One Indian economist has estimated that cricket internationals cause greater losses in production than absenteeism or sickness!

In the last two decades since India won the World Cup, the enthusiasm for Tests has declined. Crowds for Tests are becoming more discriminating. Not only in Mumbai, India's most sophisticated city – unless Tendulkar is playing – has Test fever been abating but now it is not unusual to see empty stands during Tests in other centres including Kolkata. But this is more than made up for the enthusiasm for one-day internationals. Then stadiums are heaving and packed to the gills as they were in Tests before India took to one-day cricket.

Since the 1990s all the major Indian grounds have been equipped with lights, a process that was helped by the huge financial success of hosting the World Cup in 1996. This has meant that day-night one-day internationals are now the staple diet of Indian cricket. India, having only started playing one-day internationals in 1981, has made this form of the game its very own. When the one-day game started in England in the 1960s it was a 60-over game. Indeed India won the 1983 World Cup batting and bowling in a 60-over match. This victory enabled India to co-host the World Cup in 1987, the first time it had gone outside England. Sixty overs in the natural light available during a subcontinental winter's day was impossible and the matches were of 50 overs. Since then this has become the norm for one-day matches around the world.

India has also reversed the position of Tests and one-day internationals. In England Test cricket is still the centrepiece of the game. While the old five-Test summer series has been replaced by the seven-Test summer and two opponents, even during an Australian summer, Tests take precedence. One-day internationals are essentially a snack, between the main meal provided by the Tests. In India it is Test cricket that is more often the snack while the one-day matches are the gourmet meal. In many seasons India plays many more one-day internationals, both in India and abroad, than Tests. In the process India has made other innovations to one-day cricket that would have been unthinkable in my childhood.

In 1997 to celebrate the 50th anniversary of Indian independence a one-day quadrangular series was organised during May. When I first heard of this plan during India's tour of England in 1996 I could not believe what I was hearing. In the India I grew up we did not, could not, play much cricket during the terrific heat of May. This was despite the fact that this was the only month when we had no school and no pressure to study from our parents. It was just too hot. We would play in the morning and then again towards evening before the natural light went. Cricket experts at Lord's scoffed at the idea saying this was just another money-making scheme of Jagmohan Dalmiya, the man who runs Indian cricket. But when I spoke to him he seemed surprised I should doubt his plan. With artificial lights matches would begin in late afternoon, when the blazing heat of the day had begun to abate, and would carry on till late into the evening. So it proved. The Independence Day Cup began on 9 May and ended in Kolkata on 27 May, quite the hottest weeks in India. If the three subcontinental teams of India, Pakistan, Sri Lanka, which won the Cup, could be said to be used to the heat, New Zealand also took part and the crowds were immense. Lights had changed Indian cricket and such tournaments are no longer unusual.

India, as it so often can, has moved quickly from a generation that expected no more than draws in five-day Tests to always looking for excitement and glory in one-day day-night matches. And as long as modern industrial India supports cricket, the game looks secure, providing perhaps the most interesting development since the British left. And it is this cricket Raj that we need to examine if we are to understand Indian cricket.

3

Middle India and the cricket Raj

On the afternoon of 1 December 1981, just after 2.30, Bob Willis, the perennial England number 11, plodded forward in his characteristic fashion to a delivery from Kapil Dev. It was the fourth afternoon of the first Test between India and England being played at the Wankhede stadium in Mumbai. England left 241 for victory, were 102 for 9. In fact, when Willis had come out to bat, England's position was much worse – 75 for 9 – and Willis and Bob Taylor were involved in a stubborn little stand. But as Willis pushed forward to the second ball of Kapil Dev's thirteenth over, the umpire upheld the Indian's appeal for a catch behind, and almost immediately the emotion and the euphoria that had been building up all day, burst.

For the English it was an unnerving, unreal moment. Keith Fletcher, the losing England cricket Captain, looked beleaguered and hunted. When I interviewed him for the post-match comment, he could barely articulate: 'I have not come here to lose. But there are only sixteen of us against...' He didn't have time to complete his sentence as another giant firecracker exploded a few feet away. I was keeping a diary of the tour and I noted some reactions as the firecrackers exploded:

> 'I know how the Christians felt', says one awed English man, though I doubt if, even at the height of Nero's rule, there were quite so many firecrackers going off, some even from the Pavilion. One disgusted Indian remarks, 'This sort of thing would never happen at the Brabourne stadium [only a mile away and a much more upper crust Indian place]. Too many nouveaux riches and smugglers have become members of the Wankhede stadium.'

At that stage, we rightly concentrated on the cricketing aspects of the defeat, which was to shape the entire series, and put paid to Fletcher's captaincy. But that little snippet about the clash between the Brabourne and the Wankhede is more illustrative of the cricket Raj which rules India. For it summarised what has been happening in India and the new power barons that control the game in India. Throughout that Test, and a couple of earlier ones I had covered at Wankhede, old Indian friends had bemoaned the loss of decorum and dignity as a result of the move from the Brabourne to the Wankhede. Clubhouse members of the Wankhede had jeered Gavaskar, the winning Indian Captain, when he was made batsman of the 1981 Test match, and even the odd orange and piece of rubbish had been thrown from the clubhouse.

It was more than a decline in manners that they were bemoaning, they were actually railing against the new Indians who had usurped the administration of the game from the old maharajas and upper-class Indians. They were the new Indians, who had benefited most from the undoubted economic progress of independent India, and who were keen to advertise this to themselves and to the world; Indians who were part of what I had called, in a *New Society* article, 'Middle India'.

> It is an India that has an embarrassingly high reserve of foreign exchange; it seriously contemplates the export of surplus grain; has discovered off-shore oil; exports machine tools to Czechoslovakia and trekkers to England. It is where Mother Theresa is somebody you read about in the newspapers. It is constantly outraged that the West always spurns its generous overtures.
>
> It would be easy to mock Middle India. It would be possible to doubt it ever exists. Unlike Middle America, it has no distinct geographical area. It is distinct from the familiar stereotypes of opulent Maharajas and diseased Oxfam kids. Basically it represents those who have reaped all the benefits from India's uneven post-independence: the ones who have never had it so good and are quite determined to enjoy it, whatever the West might say.

The term 'middle India' may suggest journalistic licence. But the article, from which I have just quoted, was published in December 1977, a few months after Mrs Gandhi had been sensationally rejected in the polls. It was meant to illustrate a certain aspect of Indian elite society neglected, even scorned, by the west. An elite that has been the engineer of the remarkable growth in interest in international cricket in recent decades in India.

I myself have been part of this middle India ever since my birth. But if hanging concentrates the mind, as Samuel Johnson said, then living abroad brings a totally different perspective on your home country. I returned to India in the mid-1970s after some years living and working in England. Though my ideas were confused, and my life far from happy, the intention was to live in India for good. It was what my parents devoutly wished, and something to which I, with a sense of inevitability and acceptance that I find astonishing now, willingly submitted; a working out of the Hindu 'karma'. As it turned out I found it impossible to live in India.

The Jesuit rationalism that Father Fritz had inculcated at St Xavier's asserted itself and I eventually returned to this England. But that is another story.

The India I returned to, for what turned out to be a brief sojourn in the mid-1970s, was at a crucial stage. Two months after I returned to the country, Mrs Gandhi's election was set aside by a high court judge in her native town of Allahabad. Indian democrats congratulated themselves on India's democracy – a touchy point in India. Mrs Gandhi, however, saw the judgment as threatening her own private democracy and immediately imposed emergency rule – arresting politicians and censoring the press. India can be a terrifyingly open country, where privacy is hard to find, and not much cared for. Though the bureaucratic maze is horrific – the Mughal bureaucracy built on by the British and run by the most pedantic Hindu civil servants – the system leaves gaps all over the place for individuals to exploit. Thus, for instance, an unlisted telephone number is unheard of in India and home telephone numbers of most politicians, and even senior civil servants, are listed in the telephone directory. Indians love politics and gossip, and freely indulge in both. Mrs Gandhi's emergency, almost overnight, completely changed that. A society which endlessly talked about politics now talked of everything else but politics.

This was brought home to me very sharply a few days after the emergency, in the library of the Calcutta club (it still carries the old British name of the city). This is one of the three great clubs of Kolkata, and it had been impressed on me that I ought to belong to one of them if I wanted to make a success of life in the city. Apart from the library, there was little in the Calcutta club that I found interesting, and it was there that I repaired as often as I could. On that particular June day it was very inviting. The front page lead story in the *Times* was about underground resistance to Mrs Gandhi's emergency rule with the promise of a main article on the subject and an editorial in the inside pages. When I turned to the centre pages, I found that somebody had removed the entire centre section of the paper. I assumed it was the work of some less than dutiful member who wanted to read it in the privacy of his own home rather than the club. As I made my way out of the library, I passed the librarian, and casually mentioned this to him. His reaction was extraordinary. His face became very dark, very heavy, and he said, almost in a whisper, 'Sir, this is a very serious matter. It will be investigated.'

I was somewhat puzzled by his reaction but thought no more of it. I was busily relearning Indian habits and treated the librarian's comments as the sort of overreaction some Indians are capable of. Soon after that I met a relation of mine, who had actually sponsored me for membership of the Calcutta club. He confirmed the librarian's words. The loss of the centre pages of the *Times* had been taken so seriously that the club committee had met. Never, in the long history of the club, had the centre pages of the *Times* gone missing. I don't know what exactly was said at the meeting but something to the effect, I suspect, of the world going to the dogs. If the *Times* was not sacrosanct in the library of the Calcutta club, then what indeed was sacred? The committee decided to seek out the member responsible for this dastardly deed and blackball him. Even then I couldn't take this story seriously and it was only the look on my relation's face that convinced me that this was no laughing matter. Eventually, the committee did find out who had committed the foul act. Alas, it turned out to be the censor at Kolkata airport and not a member of the club. Soon after that Mrs Gandhi tightened her emergency rule even further and the censor stopped the *Times* from actually entering the country.

I don't think many middle Indians felt deprived. Mrs Gandhi's emergency rule was very popular in this India. Middle India has always been convinced of its 'work ethic', almost as firmly entrenched as the Protestant kind, and confident that its endless financial calculations will not be damaged by any milk-and-water welfare socialism. Soon after Mrs Gandhi's defeat at the polls in 1977, her successor as Prime Minister, Moraji Desai, firmly rejected parliamentary demands for the dole. Apart from the horrendous financial problems (there are just no estimates of the number of unemployed but they must amount to tens of millions), Desai was convinced that the dole would encourage laziness. In fact, most middle Indians, returning from their annual visits to Britain – something they like doing – still express surprise that in Britain you can get money for not working. A not untypical comment is 'People over there are paid for not working. No wonder the country is in a mess.'

Middle India welcomed Mrs Gandhi's emergency, because law and order and firm government are favoured ideas. Mrs Gandhi's emergency rule brought together a package that these Indians had always wanted. No sudden power cuts, which can make life in many cities a living hell, no *bandhs* (strikes) that can immobilise cities for days and no rioting students or workers. Although middle Indians as a class have benefited most from Indian democracy, they are also its greatest critics. It is this paradox that explains the fact that Kemal Ataturk had long been every middle Indian's favourite 'benevolent' dictator. Soon after Mrs Gandhi's emergency arguments were quickly found to support her decrees: a poor peasantry, a huge army of illiterates, and a lack of communal sense of discipline.

What was interesting was that even the rigours of emergency did not completely erase Mrs Gandhi's reputation as a liberal compared to the rigidity of her successor Morarji Desai. This was not because of Mrs Gandhi's economic or political policies, but because she touched those aspects of life which middle Indians hold dear. She soft-pedalled prohibition and relaxed foreign travel – things that always meant more to middle India than a free press or an independent judiciary. At the height of the emergency rule I complained to one of Mrs Gandhi's admirers that she had killed free speech. He laughed, 'killed free speech? Why, I have been saying what I like. People who come here can talk freely.' As he did so he waved his arm round his well-manicured lawn, clearly showing the area of free speech that mattered to him. Democratic liberalism, it was felt, excited unbridled populism and Mrs Gandhi's warnings about 'unlicensed freedom' (a very revealing phrase) won universal middle-Indian approval. It reflected the genuine fear among many of being sucked back into the growing jungle of mass poverty from which many middle Indians have just emerged.

Not that middle India is a perfectly homogenous group. There is a distinction between those who have fully inherited the mantle of the Raj and those who would like to do so. The former are descendants of the much derided 2 per cent who were Anglicised during the Raj and are proudly colonial. Here, almost everybody of some importance knows everybody else. There is a regular flow of political and social gossip, whose intensity and variety overshadows the established media. This is a society that has taken over all the institutions of the Raj down to the last hallowed club tradition, and even the obligatory Friday buffet lunch. This tradition developed during the days of the Raj, when, having written the weekly letter home and deposited it on a 'homebound' steamer, the sahibs repaired to their clubs and had a large, carefree lunch. The weekly letter home and the homebound steamers departed long ago, but the Friday buffet lunch still continues.

It is a world where able imitators of Kipling's Mrs Hauksbee are firmly in charge – and income, status and positions are carefully monitored. Soon after I arrived in Kolkata in the mid-1970s, a Kolkata citizen distinguished the city's three major clubs – Bengal, Calcutta and Saturday – as follows: the Saturday is for young people and those earning about Rs1,500 (about £150 a month at the then rate of exchange); the Calcutta is for those earning up to Rs3,000; and the Bengal is for the real 'burra' sahibs and the top executives.

After independence you would have expected the Calcutta Club to become the top club. Indians were not allowed into the Saturday and the Bengal – except, of course, as servants. Malcolm Muggeridge, who worked in Kolkata in the 1930s, as assistant editor of the *Statesman*, has confessed in his memoirs how ashamed he felt at this colour bar but nevertheless belonged to the Bengal as membership of that club denoted one's position in the British hierarchy in India. The Bengal then was the greatest club in India, the place where the British administrators went to relax after work and there was no question of allowing an Indian as a member. On one occasion the Viceroy made a special plea. He wanted to honour Lord Sinha, the first Indian to be made a member of the House of Lord's, with a dinner at the Bengal. But the committee of the Bengal refused his request. So the Viceroy joined hands with some Indians to form the Calcutta Club where the colour of a man's skin did not decide membership. The Bengal did not remove its European-only policy until the 1960s when there were so few Britons left in the city the club was no longer viable. But the moment it did so the Indian 'burra' sahibs took over, making sure that membership was restricted to the top executives of a company. The Calcutta Club was once again relegated to becoming the second club of the city, as it had always been.

Top executive, in fact, is a favourite middle-India phrase. All the classy advertisements and the increasing range of consumer products produced by rapid industrialisation are aimed at capturing his attention. Some years ago when the domestic airlines decided to accept advertisements on products marketed during its flights, it projected itself as a 'powerful new media' to advertisers:

> Top Notch executives, successful businessmen, affluent holiday makers. These constitute a high potential market for all possible goods and services and in India over four million of them commute by air every day. Do you have something to sell them?

Despite the naked commercialism – and Indian commercialism can be very unsubtle – this has great appeal to the second, more powerful, group that makes up middle India. They are part of what is derisively called 'nouveau riche'. Unlike the old established rich, who inherited the Raj mantle, this group's Anglicisation is more recent and its grasp of what are considered essential social graces still far from perfect. They are the endless butt of jokes by their colonial elite – jokes that are envious and spiteful. The most despised are the Marwaris – India's fantastically efficient business community. Marwaris originally came from Rajasthan, an arid, poor state in northern India. In Indian legends the Marwaris are pictured as having arrived in the rich cities of Mumbai and Kolkata, with just one *lota* (pot) and one *kambal* (blanket) and being so ruthlessly successful in their business methods that while they inherited the riches of the city, the original inhabitants of the city were left with just one *lota* and one *kambal*. It is a favourite pastime in Indian elite society to picture pot-bellied Marwaris, their fingers greasy with counting money, emerging from a Mercedes and, then, immediately spitting *betel* (nut juice) on the roads. It is an image that juxtaposes their wealth and their lack of social manners. The joke goes that if on a hunting trip in the jungle you should encounter a tiger and a Marwari, make sure you kill the Marwari first!

Yet it is the money and power of this nouveau riche group that makes middle India increasingly important. 'Clubwallah', middle India, may resent this but it cannot ignore it. This was well illustrated, some time ago, when I went to interview Shoba Kilachand (she is now Shobhaa De, having remarried), then editor of *Stardust*, one of the country's leading film magazines. *Stardust* had made a reputation for itself as being full of racy, film gossip, but Kilachand herself was dismissive of the lives and loves of the Hindi film stars she chronicled. 'I hardly ever see Indian films. I don't know film people, I don't even like them.' She had a shrewd estimate of her public, 'What our readers are interested in is who goes to bed with whom. Many of them are not sophisticated enough to understand what we write. They just cut out our colour blow-ups and worship them, or worse. I don't know. I don't even care.'

Shoba has since made a great reputation for herself as a cross between Joan Collins and Julie Burchill, always ready to comment on the issues of the day and never afraid to be controversial. But her words that day to me were the authentic voice of 'clubwallah', colonial elite India, happy to make money out of the new usurpers, but distancing itself from their tastes.

Perhaps too much should not be made of the differences within middle India. Certain things are common to all middle Indian groups: food, money and power. Indeed they must be the most food conscious group since the disappearance of the Edwardian gentry. Four meals a day – breakfast, lunch, tea and dinner – are obligatory, and these are supplemented by innumerable snacks. Wedding feasts and public festivities are rated by the quantity and quality of food served. For many years there were Government Guest Control Orders limiting both the number that could be invited to weddings and other private functions and the range of food served. Despite this, conspicuous wastage of food remained a mark of social standing. Government newsreels constantly exhorted people not to over-eat or waste food. Now that India exports food, guest-control orders have long since vanished and Indian weddings are conspicuous by their lavish arrangements.

In recent years the society has become keenly aware of the need for diet control, and American-style crash diet programmes are very popular. Middle Indians may not have joined the jogging craze of the west, but they do talk about the need to eat less, and avoid the diseases that affluence and over-eating bring. In the last few years there has been lively controversy about slimming programmes and much media discussion about the best way to lose weight. Nevertheless, the success or failure of a social evening often depends on the brand of Scotch served, and an inability to distinguish between *Chivas Regal* and *Black Dog* can be almost fatal. There are bars in Kolkata where you find a greater range of Scotch whisky than in almost any pub in Britain. The casual traveller could make a small fortune from reselling a couple of bottles of *Royal Salute* – a much prized whisky in India. Indians have begun to market their own whisky, under the generic title of 'Indian made foreign liquor', but to serve it at a middle-Indian party, without adequate backing from Scotch, is to invite social disaster.

This liking for Scotch, inherited from the Raj, is one of the many English factors that bind middle India's extremely diverse communities together. (In Indian terms, English and British are synonymous.) Middle Indians call it westernisation which means grafting certain pleasurable western ideas onto a basic Indian, essentially Hindu, framework. Thus the various middle-Indian communities follow their own system of separate but equal development: they socialise, celebrate each other's social customs (particularly Christmas), they fraternise at clubs, discos and parties but they rarely inter-marry. Intermarriage, even between different Hindu communities, let alone between Hindus, Muslims and Christians is rare and something of an adventure.

The most important bond for all the communities in middle India is the need to be educated in English-speaking schools and colleges. When India struggled to attain independence from Britain, abolition of the English language was one of the main planks of the nationalist Congress Party. The Indian constitution decreed that in 1960, English would be replaced by Hindi. But, though Hindi is spoken and understood by many Indians, it remains a northern Indian language, distrusted and derided by most other parts of the country. Attempts to impose it nationwide have been a failure and some years ago, in the great Indian tradition, the constitutional requirement of replacing English with Hindi was neatly sidestepped.

Forty-five years after its supposed demise, English has never been more popular. The great English-speaking schools, where all subjects are taught in English cannot accommodate all those who want to join. Almost all of them have lengthy waiting lists, starting with nursery classes. Parents register their unborn child at both boys' and girls' schools. Many of these schools are convents or, like St Xavier's, Jesuit controlled. But whatever their structure, the essential and most attractive feature of the schools is the fact that the students there will receive what Indians call an English education. They will learn to speak English from a young age, speak it properly and have some of the celebrated English discipline and values instilled in them. Some years ago on a visit to Mumbai, I was told by an old schoolmate of mine from St Xavier's of the harrowing time he had in trying to get his daughter into one of these English schools.

The school required that his young girl, about four years of age, pass a very rudimentary test before she was admitted. It involved no more than the child showing an ability to talk in English. But unfortunately this child found this impossible in front of strangers, and school after prominent school in Mumbai was forced to reject her. Eventually with all hope gone, she suddenly opened her mouth and secured admission. Had she not done so my friend would have found it virtually impossible to find an English-speaking school for his daughter – with unimaginable consequences.

Though my friend was far too gentlemanly to actually express it that way, the recital of the story was itself a rebuke of the nouveau riche clamouring to get their children into the English-speaking schools. It is this that has created the rush and produced what is known as the 'daddyji' and 'mummyji' culture. Almost all the nouveau riche children come from a home background where little or no English is spoken. Suddenly at the age of four or five, they are taken to a school environment where everybody speaks English and where some of the education is in the hands of Anglo-Indians. The Anglo-Indians are the physical products of the curious and limited sexual contact between the Indians and the British. There was much social and sexual contact in the early years of British rule but this changed from the middle of the eighteenth century largely due to the arrival of the 'fishing fleet' from the UK – so called because they brought English women looking for English husbands. Their arrival forced English men to give up their Indian wives. The change has been brilliantly chronicled by William Dalrymple in *White Mughals*. During the Raj, the Anglo-Indians enjoyed certain limited privileges at the hands of the British, but found themselves in an awkward position. The British never accepted them as equals – and felt ashamed of these products of inter-racial sex – while the Indians saw them as half-caste interlopers who pretended to be more British than the British. The Indians, interestingly, share the British horror of miscegenation and the Anglo-Indians are still referred to slightingly as '*firinghee*'. But as one prominent Anglo-Indian ruefully confessed, this does not stop Indians taking up 'our values – talking English, drinking, dancing – these have become national values, part of the Indian elite'.

The problem for the elite has been to square such foreign, half-caste, Anglo-Indian values with the very traditional Hindu home background. The answer is through 'daddyji' and 'mummyji'. At school the children are taught to call their parents, not by the Indian words for father and mother, but by the English terms of daddy and mummy. At home, using a very traditional Indian compromise, the very Hindi word 'ji', which denotes respect, is added to the name. Thus, daddy (English) plus 'ji'

(Hindi for respect) = daddyji, a comforting word that seeks to harmonise the English world and the pure Hindu one. Similarly uncle and aunty are referred to as uncleji and auntyji.

One side effect of the 'daddyji' culture is that Indians are now encouraged to intersperse their English with Hindi words. Thus even Indians who have had a convent English education, will use some characteristic Hindi words like *yaar*, which means mate or pal, or *maha* which means great, producing a sentence like 'Are, yaar, that was a maha disco' (Well, mate, that was a great disco).

The old colonial elite suffer this corruption of the English language, something they hold dear, as patiently as they suffer the other corruptions all around them. Corruption, to an extent, has always been part of political and commercial dealings in India and sanctions for corrupt practices can even be found in the Hindu religious text. Nor is India unique in this, for corruption can be found in almost every society. But in India it seems to be omnipresent, an inescapable part of Indian life. Furthermore, while everybody in India is not corrupt, everybody is believed to be corrupt. It was this that drove Mr B. K. Nehru, a cousin of Jawaharlal, a former ambassador in Washington and High Commissioner in London, and Governor of Jammu and Kashmir, to say in a lecture in Madras at the end of 1981:

> so inured have we become to it that instead of reacting to it as destructive of all morality and decency, we accept it as a recognised way of life... Why have we degenerated in one generation from being an honest society into a dishonest one? Part of the cause is the conversion of a static into a comparatively dynamic society. The changes upset old values but our exposure to wealth is so new that no new values have taken their place.

Nehru, as befitted a man of his experience, concentrated more on the political corruption and the fact that the Westminster style of parliamentary elections in a country as large as India inevitably leads to a 'direct relationship between money contributed and favour granted'. But in many ways his observations about the change from a static into a comparatively dynamic society, and the effect this change has had on values is reflected on the cricket fields and in the cricket stadiums of India. There can be little doubt that much of the growth of Indian cricket mania, the millions of rupees that have led to the rise of new stadiums, have been fuelled by 'black money'. This is money accumulated by Indians in all walks of life at the expense of the tax payer. Money which fuels a parallel economy where every transaction has two parts: a white part and a black part. The white part is the one you declare in official contracts and reveal to the tax man. The black part is the genuine one, not written down, not accounted for but without which the transaction would not take place. Thus in Mumbai, where flat prices are higher than in London, you would have to pay 60 per cent of the price of your flat in 'black' money and only 40 per cent in 'white', tax-accounted money.

There can be little doubt that some of this black money, or 'number two account', as the Indians call it, has gone into cricket and contributed to the fever for international cricket in India. There are no statistics available, but the simultaneous growth of international Cricket fever and number two accounts seems more than mere coincidence. Almost anybody in Mumbai will tell you that a good many of the season ticket holders, whose prepayment funded the Wankhede stadium did so through their number two accounts. This may be the malicious gossip of those who lost out to the nouveau riche, but nobody who has monitored the progress of Mumbai since the 1960s can doubt the existence of black money.

The Mumbai I grew up in the 1950s and 1960s was still a very colonial town. The highest building was the Standard Vacuum Old building, a seven-floor structure which was considered such a novelty we would often gaze at it in wonder. During the 1970s Mumbai went in for building Manhattan-style high-rise buildings and new land reclamation. Perhaps a symbol of this change was the extension added to its most famous hotel, the Taj Mahal. This is probably one of the greatest hotels in the world. Nobody who has experienced its service, or its luxury, can easily forget it. The hotel itself is ideally located – it overlooks the Arabian Sea and sits right opposite the Gateway of India, the very spot where George V arrived in India in 1911 to hold his famous *durbar*. Yet the old Taj Mahal had an oddity that one could never quite explain. You would expect the front of the hotel to face the Gateway of India and the arch that commemorates George V's arrival. Yet what looked like the back of the hotel faced this while the front, with its tree-lined gravel driveway was approached through a rather dingy, mean street at the back.

There was an explanation for this, and this lay in the method used by the Taj Mahal Hotel's owners, the rich Parsee industrialists, the Tatas. Some time before the Tatas decided to build the Taj Mahal, one of them sought entry to an English club in Mumbai. As per Raj policy the club did not allow any Indians and the rich Parsee was refused. In fact he was further insulted to find that there was a sign outside the club saying 'Indians and dogs not allowed'. His response was to build a hotel, the Taj Mahal hotel, and put up a sign outside saying 'British and cats not allowed'. Of course, this is an apocryphal story and is meant to indicate the clever way in which Indians responded to British racial arrogance. But as the story was told to us it had a sad end. The rich Parsee industrialist hired a European architect to design the hotel and send the plans over to India. But when the plans were received in Mumbai, they were either received wrongly, or interpreted wrongly, and the hotel was built back to front. The architect is supposed to have committed suicide, though this could not prevent the oddity of the Taj's main entrance facing away from the sea.

The Tatas have always denied the story but almost everybody in Mumbai believes it. More significantly, and this underlines what I was saying about change in Mumbai, several years later the owners of the Taj Mahal Hotel decided to do something about their entrance. Next to it there had been a small, but rather well regarded hotel, called Greens. This was one of those classic, colonial hotels in Mumbai, very popular during Christmas and New Year's Eve and much valued for its cuisine and its Anglo-Indian and Goan dance bands. The Tatas acquired Greens, decided to expand their hotel and this time there would be no question of where the entrance was. The old entrance was demolished and converted to a swimming pool. A new entrance, complete with a modern driveway, was built, and unlike the old one, this new main entrance led straight from the Arabian Sea and the Gateway of India into the Taj. The Taj, if you like, had righted itself.

However, the rooms in the old wing are still prized and people who know the Taj still ask for them. Moreover, and just to make sure they feel nothing has changed, they come in not through the new entrance but through another, rather discreet, entrance, as used by many before the new one was built, straight into the old Taj. The feeling that is generated is that they are getting something very exclusive.

To me this change has always seemed to symbolise what has happened to Mumbai since the 1970s. If you like, it is the difference between cricket at the Brabourne stadium and cricket at the Wankhede stadium.

For almost four decades from 1937, cricket in Mumbai, and very nearly cricket in India, was represented by the Brabourne stadium. It was named after Lord Brabourne, the British Governor of Mumbai at that time, and to most people in Mumbai it was known as CCI, short for the Cricket Club of India. In Indian eyes it was the Lord's of India with CCI having status almost equal to that of the MCC in this country. To gain entrance to the pavilion of the Brabourne stadium you had to be a member of the CCI, and that was never easy. There was always a long queue and membership cost thousands of rupees. Not only was it a magnificently constructed stadium, but the pavilion-cum-clubhouse had luxurious rooms where players could stay and, if they so wished, watch play in their dressing gowns. Frank Worrell always maintained that he loved playing at the CCI because he could be in his dressing gown until he was required to bat. Apart from normal club facilities – a lounge, card and ladies' rooms and a cocktail bar – the end of the day's play would see the ground itself converted into an open-air restaurant with tables laid out for food. On some special occasions even a dance hall with a wooden floor would be erected on the outfield, near the clubhouse. The major difference from Lord's was that while the pavilion at Lord's would not admit ladies, except the Queen, the CCI quite encouraged society ladies to be guests. On important match days they could be seen seated, in their glittering saris, in the Governor's pavilion next to the clubhouse.

But if CCI was cricket to most of us, its relations with the rest of Indian cricket were never very smooth. The official cricket body in Mumbai was the Mumbai Cricket Association, which actively resented the haughty colonial style of the CCI management. The main problem was the allocation of Test match tickets. A whole block of seats, over 17,000, were given to the Mumbai Cricket Association for distribution to its various clubs, gymkhanas and associates. But the BCA never considered this adequate and every Test saw a familiar battle develop between the CCI and the BCA about the allocation of tickets. There were strong personalities involved: Vijay Merchant, on behalf of the CCI, and Mr S. K. Wankhede, on behalf of the BCA If Mr Merchant had his cricket pedigree, he had been one of the country's finest batsmen and a well-known broadcaster, Mr Wankhede was prominent in politics, including a spell as the Finance Minister of the State of Maharashtra. Perhaps the row was inevitable. Mr Wankhede and the Mumbai Cricket Association were flexing their administrative muscles in the way the Maharastrian cricketers of Shivaji Park had done almost a decade before, while Merchant was a Gujerati, from one of the old money families of Mumbai. But it would be wrong to see the fight that developed between the CCI and BCA, and which led to the development of a separate stadium, as a purely Maharastrian versus non-Maharastrian conflict.

It was more of the old money versus new money argument. Certainly nobody could doubt the existence of the new money as Mr Wankhede and the Mumbai Cricket Association made its response. Almost as soon as the last Test of the India versus England 1972–3 series was finished in Mumbai, the BCA made it known that it was to be the last Test to be ever played at the CCI. It was as if the Test and County Cricket Board had declared war on Lord's. Mumbai had heard many such arguments before, though never so emphatically, and it did not believe Test cricket would vanish from the 'dear old CCI'.

Even as the West Indies arrived in India in the autumn of 1974, it seemed most unlikely that a Test match at Mumbai could be staged anywhere but at the CCI. Mr Wankhede had promised a new stadium, even selected the place, but the stadium was far from constructed and it was difficult to see how, within a few short months, it could materialise. However, when the West Indies returned to the city in early 1975 to play the final Test of the cliff-hanging series, they found that the Wankhede stadium had, in fact, come into being, with the result that Mumbai has two first-class stadia within a mile of each other.

It was one of the swiftest constructions in Mumbai history. It seemed to demonstrate the power of money in Mumbai. As Dilip Sardesai had said, contrasting Mumbai with Madras (now known as Chennai), 'in Madras money was solid', while in Mumbai 'money flows' – in this case between businessmen who had learned to manipulate Nehru's Fabian socialism to make their own fortunes.

The clash between old and new money is not confined to India, or cricket, nor is it all that recent. My father was exposed to such arguments some fifty years ago. A business acquaintance invited him to dinner in his palatial home in Malabar Hill. The house looked rather decrepit from the outside, but was opulently furnished inside. The contrast seemed remarkable but during the dinner, the business acquaintance explained to my father 'You see Bose Sahib, we are not like these new business people who have come to Mumbai and made a lot of money. We are *baniadi* rich (the old landed rich), we don't have to display our riches like these new people.' It was this that explained the difference between the decrepitude of the exterior and the lushness of the interior. My father later learnt that actually the business acquaintance was very much part of the new rich. He had made his money recently, then bought the decrepit house but was so keen to be seen as part of the old, landed gentry rich, that he had left the outside decrepit, while furnishing the inside lavishly.

The new rich of Mumbai, or for that matter India, no longer feel it necessary to present themselves as part of the hereditary, landed rich. They may, or may not, be proud of the ways in which they have acquired their money. The Hindu system imposes few sanctions and the post-independence growth has removed the colonial-cum-ritualistic Hindu reticence which made my father's acquaintance so eager to be part of the *ancien regime*. Now they are keen to explore avenues which will display their newly acquired wealth. Even a casual visitor to the main Indian cities can see the new rich in the bars and restaurants of the mushrooming five-star hotels, swanking down mean, rutted streets in Mercedes – much prized as a status symbol in middle India – and at important social and art world functions. But it is cricket, this very English game with its very English nuances, which provides the ideal theatre. In that sense cricket could be said to have been created for middle

India. Just as Pascal felt that if there wasn't a God we would have to create one, middle Indians might well say that if there hadn't been cricket, they would have had to invent it. Some of them, sometimes, give the impression that they have indeed invented it.

It is easy to see why cricket should appeal to this group of Indians. Cricket, probably more than any other game, is, essentially, an intensely ritualistic game. The charm lies in the fact that within strictly defined parameters and rituals, it provides scope for infinite variation. Suspense builds up during the length of play, as for instance in the memorable Headingley Test of 1981 between England and Australia or in the epic Kolkata Test between India and Australia in 2001. In both Tests the team forced to follow on looked certain to lose but then suddenly ended up as victors, Australia being the victims in both cases. It is difficult to imagine such a turnaround in another game. In soccer it would be like a team losing 5–0 winning the match in the last ten minutes, in tennis a player, leading by two sets to love and 5–0 up in the third, going on to lose a match. In theory it is possible; in practice it never happens. In cricket it is rare but, as England and India have demonstrated, not impossible.

Soccer has played for 90 minutes and does not quite allow for the slow build-up of tension as does cricket. Both the Kolkata and Headingley Tests illustrated this perfectly well; until lunch on the final day most realists had to go for an Australian victory, only to find England and India dramatically turning the tables on the final afternoon of play.

Cricket and its rhythms have just the right feel for middle Indians. As one Delhi journal, observing the crowds gathering at Ferozeshah Kotla said, cricket was 'just another of the props for a successful day-long picnic'. It was during the first Test in Delhi, in the 1972–3 series between India and England that the Indian newspaper *Statesman* captured the way middle Indians could take to a Test match.

The Modis are rich industrialists based around Delhi. For the Test match they had established their own 250-square-yard barricaded enclosure right in front of the pavilion, surrounded with four fairly large signs of 'luminous green and red', that proclaimed it as the 'Modi Enclosure'. Throughout the day's play the enclosure was a hive of activity, but it was at lunch that it acquired its real significance:

> A low table approximately 4 yards × 12 yards was laden with food. Behind it stood two drumfuls of drinking water. A liveried servant, impressive in his all blue, gave the signal and the guests, including evidently the scions of the D.D.C.A. [Delhi and District Cricket Association] patron family, left their chairs nearby to be served ... A former Cabinet Secretary and a former Inspector-General of police

were among the frontliners in the enclosure. There was any number of other officials, including a former Union Deputy Minister and a Rajya Sabha [Indian House of Lords] member.

It is cricket as *tamasha*, that rich Indian word which conveys fun, excitement, glamour and suspense, all rolled into one. It was *tamasha* which made international cricketers rival film stars and Mrs Gandhi (when she was alive) in popularity. There are some good economic reasons for *tamasha*. Just as the Bollywood film industry mixes glamour with money, so does international cricket in India, particularly for the businessmen who support it so lavishly. Tests and one-day internationals bring together the rich, the not-so-rich and the aspiring rich in one convenient setting. The Indian lower-income groups tend to describe themselves as middle class, a term which does not have the same meaning in India as it has in England. In India the word middle class can be used by the low-income clerk who fervently supports the communist party to the fairly well-positioned executive, whose views are somewhere to the right of Genghis Khan and his income almost ten times that of the clerk. Both executive and clerk probably work for the industrialist who sponsors cricket. Outside the office their lives would rarely meet, except in a stadium where a Test or a one-day international match is being played. This is what makes Test and international cricket in India such a unique cultural, even political, occasion.

But this is not all. International cricket also provides a golden commercial opportunity. Gathered in one convenient place are most of the people who have purchasing power in the Indian urban economy. Sponsoring cricket means reaching this crucial public immediately. This explains the nature of commercial sponsorship in Indian cricket and the existence of a plethora of awards. So many that when Chris Tavare was made man of the match in the Third Test in Delhi during the 1981–2 series, for his century, he found himself with not a solitary award, as in England, but with nearly half a dozen: a television set, a thermos flask, an attaché case and even a scooter. Wisely, Tavare had already arranged to exchange his awards for Indian rupees, rather than lug them all back. More than twenty years later the growth of the televised same had brought even more money into Indian cricket but this penchant for showering commercial gifts on cricketers had not changed. In November 2004, as India beat South Africa in Kolkata, to win the series 1–0, both the man of the series and the man of the match, Virendra Sehwag and Harbhajan Singh, got – in addition to their cheques – a large television set. Harbhajan got a 28-in screen model, Sehwag received a plasma screen one. Both posed against the sets as if they were teenagers getting their first toys.

The commercial sponsorship of cricket and the money it has attracted from middle India has undoubtedly been good for Indian cricketers. As I arrived in Mumbai in November 1981, to report the India versus England Test series, it seemed that nearly all the English cricketers had been recruited by Indian advertising agencies to promote some or other Indian product. Boycott, amidst cover driving, was advising Indians either to drink Seven Seas cod liver oil or fly Cathay Pacific jets, the adverts taking up almost a quarter of the sports pages of most Indian papers. Botham had linked up with Gavaskar to promote tea, and nearly every Indian newspaper or magazine seemed to have the syndicated thoughts of Botham, Fletcher and many others. There was some talk in Mumbai of the English players being a bit too greedy but I could only admire their self-restraint. The game seemed to be used by almost every consumer company in town to sell its products. On the drive from the airport to the city, past some of the biggest and most wretched slums in India, there were numerous advertising awnings using cricket to sell their products. One local butter manufacturer showed its mascot struggling to tie the laces of his cricket boots underneath the slogan reading: 'If you dilly-dally, butter will melt', a reference to the boot problems that Graham Dilley had on that tour. All this made me feel that the cricketer visiting India could well take the position adopted by Clive when he was accused of making too much money in Bengal in the eighteenth century. He replied: 'given the riches that were offered to me, my Lords, I am surprised at my own modesty'.

In recent years the riches on offer to visiting cricketers have if anything increased and cricketers as diverse as Vivian Richards, Hansie Cronje, Jonty Rhodes, Steve Waugh and Brett Lee have all found how easy and profitable it is to become a great marketing symbol in India.

Some of the industrialist patrons of middle India have frankly acknowledged the reason for their cricket patronage. In the 1970s Virenchee Sagar, then managing director of the Mumbai firm Nirlon, which employed Sunil Gavaskar, made a determined attempt to establish itself as one of the leading commercial cricket teams in Mumbai. Sagar made no bones about the fact that since success in cricket brings the company free publicity and goodwill, cricket costs should be seen as a reallocation of the annual advertising budget. Promoting a product or a company may not be the only objective and many of the middle-Indian industrialists talk of using cricket to develop a more professional and businesslike approach in their own company. Discipline is something highly valued in India – but rarely found. Urban India, as Professor Galbraith, a former US ambassador to India has said, can be a functioning anarchy. It was this that made Sanjay Gandhi's talk of discipline and slogans of 'talk less, work more' quite so popular with so many middle Indians. India's besetting problem, they believe, is 'indiscipline' and the discipline and concentration required to succeed in cricket is much valued.

Promoting cricket as *tamasha* can have side affects. Just as everybody wants to see a successful show, so everybody in urban, middle India wants to go to the Test match or a one-day international. This may be changing because of the spread of television. But perhaps the most evident effect of Test cricket as tamasha is to be seen in the long hours local journalists spend just before a Test match, arranging and deciding who gets the tickets. The reason is that there are so many applicants that the cricket authorities have decided that press tickets are best handled by local journalists' associations who can detect the genuine from the less serious. Every little hick journalist, it seems, wants a ticket even if it be the annual *Tandoori Recipe Cookbook*. In Mumbai, for the first Test in the 1981–2 series, the local journalists' association had to whittle down requests for tickets from 135 journals to a more manageable 85. As one local journalist put it 'sometimes we get requests from street publications and how could we put its editor next to John Woodcock? What a shame it would be for India.' Even then, for that Test match I sat next to a press man who was in fact the marketing manager of his newspaper; he was clearly not reporting the cricket – getting a Test ticket was one of the perks of his job. It indicated social standing in the community.

Perhaps the best way to capture the flavour of cricket as *tamasha* is to visit Kolkata during a Test match. I did that for *The Sunday Times* during England's tour in the winter of 1984–5. This is how I reported the preparation for the Kolkata test:

> For the past week the Kolkata police have been guarding the home of a middle-aged Indian businessman. Though his house is only a few hundred yards away from the homes of the British diplomatic community, the police are protecting him not from possible enemies, but from 'friends' wanting tickets for the Third Test match, against England starting tomorrow. For 43-year-old Jagmohan Dalmiya, secretary of the Cricket Association of Bengal and Mr Fix-it of the match, all of this is part of the phenomenon that is a Kolkata Test. A phenomenon that produces an estimated 85,000 crowd for each of the five days of the match (Dalmiya claims a more precise 78,811) with possibly a few thousand outside clamouring to get in. Despite poor crowds so far on this tour, Dalmiya, like an impresario sure of his product, has never had doubts. 'There has been a decline even in Kolkata', he admits, 'but my requirement has always been 300% of capacity, so "house full" is no problem.' He's in a good position to

judge. Within hours of the end of the Delhi Test, his telephone had started ringing: 'Normally I don't get calls till after eight in the morning. Now it starts ringing at half-past six, and mostly from people who have just remembered that they are my friends.'

Some of the interest is due to England's surprising win at Delhi to level the series, but even before that locals were convinced that Eden Gardens would not fail to come up with that special magic of India the younger England players had been told about, but have yet to experience. Indians call it 'Test match fever' and that is perhaps not an inappropriate phrase. For very like a real fever, it has been building up, almost visibly, on the streets and round the England team's hotel.

Almost every activity of the England players, including the Christmas Day fancy-dress party, was extensively reported. As the England team left their, Kolkata hotel for last Thursday's one-day international in Cuttack, a crowd of several hundred suddenly gathered in the way they do in this city.

For many in Kolkata, that is the closest they will come to seeing the cricketers. For others with a little more money, the last two weeks have been a search for a 'ticket'. In Kolkata, you don't have to explain what the ticket is for. Businessmen have had tax inspectors drop hints that a ticket or two would help with assessments, bank managers have suggested a similar leniency towards borrowers and to accommodate the demand for press tickets Dalmiya has had to divide journalists between 'working' and 'non-working'.

Perhaps nowhere can you experience Kolkata's special Test fever better than in the tent opposite the cricket ground that is the home of the Kolkata sports journalists' club. Normally it is like any other journalists' club, perhaps a bit shabbier, with writers trading stories that are part of journalism's charm and cynicism. But in the past week it has taken on the look of an Indian railway station as leading Indian cricket journalists have queued to get their 'tickets'. In most Test centres, press tickets are distributed by the people who run the match. In Kolkata, the authorities have happily abdicated this responsibility to the journalists simply to avoid charges of favouritism.

So last week the most wanted men in Kolkata, after Dalmiya, were the executive committee members of the journalists' club, whose job it has been to whittle down the 1,000-odd applicants to 250. As Kishore Bhimani, sports editor of the local *Statesman*, puts it 'We get applications from all sorts of people. One year we even had people claiming to represent *Paris Match* and *Der Spiegel*. In the weeks immediately before a Test, we suddenly have sports magazines being published that nobody has heard of, and they disappear almost as soon as the Test is over.'

One reason for this great hassle is that in Kolkata you can't just go to a ticket counter and buy a ticket. No daily tickets are sold, or even 'season', meaning five-day tickets, as elsewhere in India. The only source open to the general public is a curious lottery where some 900,000 lottery tickets are sold, out of which emerge 8,500 lucky Test-ticket holders. Otherwise you have to 'know somebody', or belong to the right organisation.

Dalmiya argues that this very odd system evolved in order to deal with the problems created when day tickets *were* sold. In 1969 a stampede, as thousands queued for tickets, led to seven deaths. In those dark days it was common for Kolkata cricket administrators to issue more tickets than there were seats, and such characters often went 'underground' to escape the wrath of the public.

The mechanics of distribution are only part of the explanation for ticket fever. The rest lies in the curious nature of the city. It is predominantly a centre of Bengalis, but where the money is in the hands of the acquisitive and fantastically successful Marwari business community. The Bengalis despise the Marwaris as carpet-baggers, and hold them responsible for the post-independence decline which has seen Kolkata fall from being the first city of the East to one that most Indians try to avoid. Plagued by power-cuts of several hours a day and incessant political strife, Bengalis find there is little to celebrate except their very typical Bengali 'hujuks.'.

The word means roughly 'intoxicated enthusiasm' and in the past Kolkata's 'hujuks' have included riotous welcomes for such disparate characters as Khrushchev and Pele. In India Test cricket is an occasion for the various sections of urban society to come together in a fiesta. But as television eats into this audience, Kolkata retains its enthusiasm for the real thing.

Much has changed in Indian cricket in the twenty years since I wrote that. Nobody could have imagined how far Dalmiya would come and how feared he would be in international cricket. Even in Kolkata the 'hujuk' for Tests is no longer that great but it can still be ignited for some teams such as Australia, and the 'hujuk' and hunger for international one-day cricket is undiminished.

To return to the question of patronage, Dr Richard Cashman, in *Patrons, Prayers and the Crowd*, has analysed the role of contemporary patrons, highlighting their changing nature, and the impact of the *Times of India* inter-office tournament. As he says, this must be one of the most unique tournaments in the world – when he carried out his analysis nearly 300 office teams played in a tournament divided into seven divisions. What is interesting about the analysis is the light it throws on the old money versus new money development of middle India. Early winners of the *Times of India* tournament were old established organisations: utilities and government concerns, such as the Bombay Electric Supply and Tramways Company, BEST for short. In fact BEST was the most successful of the pre-independence *Times of India* teams, winning the shield six times in eight years between 1937 and 1944. It was one of the first teams to realise the need to recruit good cricketers and the need to give cricketers time off for daily net practice. Indian independence marked the heyday of the BEST cricket team – though it did win the shield again in 1952 – but as post-independence industrialisation progressed, the old utility companies, the railways and the customs teams fell away to be replaced by commercial firms.

Interestingly, the initial successes in the new phase of the *Times of India* tournaments were achieved by Tatas, very much a firm from the old money Indian tradition. The Tatas had been led by a succession of Tata family members interested in sport. They began to make their mark with the foundation of the Tatas sports club in 1937 and won the *Times of India* shield for the first time in 1941. In the days of my own boyhood maidan cricket in Mumbai of the 1950s and early 1960s, much of the cricket in the city was characterised by what we saw as the epic clashes between Tatas and another Indian company called Associated Cement Corporation, ACC for short. The Tatas–ACC matches in the *Times of India* shield used to rival Ranji trophy matches at the Brabourne stadium and at times attracted a bigger crowd.

ACC had started life as a British company though it was slowly, successfully, being Indianised. In the 1950s, with rapid industrialisation and urbanisation, making cement and cement products became all the more important ACC expanded quickly. So did its cricket team as it successfully recruited some of the top Test cricketers: Desai, Sardesai, Wadekar and Indrajitsinghji. Yet despite this talent, ACC often lost to Tatas, largely because of the performances of Bapu Nadkarni, the mean Indian left-arm spinner. In a sensational move, which was the Mumbai equivalent of the English-style soccer transfers, ACC successfully poached Nadkarni from the Tatas by offering him a better job. The poaching came just after Nadkarni's feats had led to ACC's defeat in a fascinating *Times of India* shield final. The excitement generated by this transfer was not matched until another cricketer was poached, this time from the ACC – and almost twenty years later. That cricketer was Sunil Gavaskar and the poaching was done by a very new firm, reflecting very new money, Nirlon.

Virenchee Sagar, then Nirlon's managing director, was in many ways the archetypal new middle Indian. Though not much of a cricketer, he was a keen student of the game, close to it and a contributor to many Indian cricket and sporting magazines. Sagar was dismissive of the old patrons of Indian cricket, like the princes, and his company's stated aim was to build up a good team recruiting Mumbai state players on the threshold of their careers. While Sagar generally held to that policy, in 1978 he made a significant decision in recruiting Gavaskar and this established Nirlon as the most important team in Mumbai. Led by Gavaskar, it had a near Test side which included Ravi Shastri, then widely tipped as India's future captain, Sandip Patil, the then great heart-throb of Indian cricket, and the former opening bowler Karsan Ghavri. Nirlon, specialising in synthetic textiles, was part of the new industrial scene of India and interestingly its cricketing rise challenged the dominance of Mafatlal, which in some ways represented the somewhat older industries of the cities. Mafatlal started in textiles but then diversified into chemicals, garments and even plywood. Its prominence in the *Times of India* tournament almost exactly mirrored its economic expansion. It first won the shield in 1969–70 and then established a virtual stranglehold, winning it continuously between 1971–2 and 1977–8. The company recruited shrewdly and widely, among them Nari Contractor, now the wise elder statesman of Indian cricket, Ashok Mankad, son of the great Vinoo, Eknath Solkar and rising stars from other Ranji trophy teams. By the end of the 1970s Mafatlal was the team of Mumbai, glittering with stars that very nearly made up the Test side. However, in 1984, splits within Mafatlal decimated the company and the cricket team. Mafatlal, largely a company owned by the family, split up as a result of dissension between the Mafatlal brothers. The effect on the cricket team was immediate and catastrophic, it was so badly affected that for a time Sagar's Nirlon team was left as the undisputed champion of Mumbai cricket.

For a time in the mid-1960s and 1970s it seemed as if commercial sponsorship would face a challenge from state institutions – particularly the State Bank of India. The State Bank represents neither new nor old money but the power of the bureaucracy, and provides an aspect of middle-Indian involvement in cricket which should be considered. The State Bank of India is a nationalised bank – the largest bank in the country. After Mrs Gandhi nationalised the major banks of India in 1971, the State Bank began to acquire an important role as pivotal bank in the economy. Mrs Gandhi had her own political motives for nationalising the banks but the economic argument she advanced was that nationalised banks would lend more to the impoverished rural economy and so encourage enterprise there.

The results were very different. While nationalisation led to the growth of banking in India, the growth was more in the urban and semi-urban areas rather than in the rural areas. The banks themselves, and their managers, became very powerful and connections were formed between Indian industrialists keen to secure loans and bank managers. The managers were eager to cultivate the industrialists as they knew they could provide for their retirement, perhaps by a seat on the board of their companies.

The State Bank of India's heavy promotion of cricket in the mid-1960s and early 1970s was dramatic. Not only did it win the *Times of India* shield four years running between 1966–7 and 1968–9, but at one stage the State Bank of India team could probably have fielded an eleven that could do battle with almost any Indian eleven. Players included: Bedi in Delhi, Visvanath and Kirmani in Bangalore, the elegant left-hander Ambar Roy in Kolkata and the mercurial Milkha Singh in Madras.

But between 1970 and 1976 cricket recruitment virtually ground to a halt as it was decided that sportsmen should receive no special favours in terms of recruitment and that they should enter the bank through the regular competitive channels. During the 1970–6 period the State Bank did not recruit a single player and the one first-class cricketer who entered the bank did so on his own academic merits. It was feared that Indian cricket would suffer if the State Bank did not resume its patronage. However, this has not occurred. New sponsors have come up, and keep coming up. As industrialisation progresses, and new industries emerge, they need an outlet for their products and cricket provides an ideal medium.

But there has been a change. The change has come in the nature of cricket sponsorship. For almost fifty years from the 1940s to well into the 1990s a company in India seeking to publicise itself acquired a cricket team. This was almost mandatory. The only company that did not follow this pattern was Reliance. A Mumbai firm whose founder had started as a small businessman in Mumbai, it became one of India's greatest companies. When in 1987 the World Cup came to the subcontinent for the first time, Reliance choose to sponsor the World Cup realising that this would publicise its name not only in India but throughout the cricket world.

Since the 1991 liberalisation of the Indian economy, opening it up to global competition, the new Indian companies that have emerged either see cricket sponsorship in a very different, more global, way or do not sponsor cricket at all. So companies like Wipro and Infosys, located in India's Silicon Valley in Bangalore, and global brands in their own right, see no need to sponsor cricket. Others like Sahara, a more Indian-style company, sponsors cricket not by having a cricket team of its own but by sponsoring the entire Indian cricket team. Every Indian cricketer wears a shirt bearing the logo Sahara and wherever India plays that shirt is displayed to millions of viewers round the world through the medium of television. In that sense Indian cricket sponsorship has caught up with the world. Between the 1950s and the 1990s India's cricket sponsorship had a feudal look. Sagar may have railed against the Princes but the fact that his firm had a cricket team, and the fact that he boasted about signing Gavaskar, made him not all that different from the Maharajah of Patiala who also sponsored a cricket team and employed professional cricketers.

In contrast, Sahara sponsoring Indian cricket is no different to Vodaphone sponsoring Manchester United. Both are using a well-known sports brand to reach a wider public.

The 1991 opening up of the closed economy has also had a dramatic impact on the nationalised banks and their recruitment of cricketers. The initial thought was that the government would privatise the banks. This has not happened but it has allowed private-sector banks to emerge. Such banks as Citicorp or Standard and Chartered do not have an office cricket team. They do spend money on cricket, sometimes using cricketers to promote the bank, but they do not feel the need to employ cricketers merely to play cricket. At the same time the nationalised banks, faced by competition, have stopped recruitment, dealing a dramatic blow to their once-powerful cricket teams.

The result has been that the *Times of India* Shield is no longer the tournament it was. From the 300 teams that Cashman estimated played in the tournament in the 1970s, now no more than 160 teams take part and the great names of the past have disappeared. Nirlon has gone, so has Mafatlal, although nominally it still employs Sachin Tendulkar. Tatas remain but apart from the Indian captain Saurav Ganguly who, again, is nominally a player for them, it is largely a team of Mumbai-based players. The result is a tournament that once boasted teams that showcased the nation's cricketers now struggles to display even Mumbai's best.

The changes were inevitable once India discovered television and global marketing and sponsorship. But it is worth emphasising that the link between business and cricket has not disappeared, the nature of the link has changed.

The changes in India's economic situation since 1991 have also affected what was perhaps the oddest thing about the growth of middle-Indian cricket – the civil service connection. Without the help (indeed the blessing) of the civil servants, cricket in India could never have expanded in the way it did through much of the post-independence period. In India, as elsewhere, cricket is built around tours. India entertains overseas teams and in turn, tours abroad. In India such touring arrangements require government sanctions, not for political reasons, but for purely economic ones. During the Second World War India had built up formidable sterling balances but this was dissipated in the 1950s, and by the early 1960s India suffered from a severe foreign-exchange crisis – so severe that at one time Indians traveling abroad received just £3 in foreign exchange. That was certainly the amount I was allowed to take out of the country when I left it for the first time in 1969.

Yet this was also the time when the pattern of reciprocal tours between India and the major Test-playing countries was established. In those days the weeks preceding a Test tour of India always provided a familiar scenario. The Indian Cricket Board would announce the tentative dates of the tour and then murmur, almost *sotto voce*, that it couldn't guarantee the tour because it would have to secure permission from the Indian Finance Ministry for the release of exchange. The Board officials would hurry to Delhi to hold discussions with ministry officials. There would be leaks and whispers in the newspapers, and eventually, as the public veered between despair and euphoria, the news would come that the tour had been saved and the Finance Ministry had released the exchange. Of course, this may have been the ministry officials playing their part in an enjoyable cricket drama, but it has always seemed extraordinary to me that Indian Test cricket began to blossom in the 1960s at a time when the country was cutting back on many things. The civil servants approving the tour could not have approved them on the basis of the performance of the Indian team. As we have seen, India had returned from the 1959 tour of England having lost all five Tests. Again in 1962 India returned from the West Indies having lost all five Tests. However, Finance Ministry officials, persuaded by the Indian Cricket Board, provided cogent reasons why the hard-pressed Indian Exchequer should release scarce foreign exchange to finance disastrous cricket tours.

An example of the power of the civil service was revealed when in November 1981 attempts were made to block the England tour because the English team contained Geoff Boycott and Geoff Cook who had played in South Africa. After a great deal of drama the tour was approved. When I got to Delhi I was curious to know how the controversy had started. My friends in Delhi suggested that it was all the work of certain dissatisfied senior civil servants. It seems that during the previous Delhi Test, these civil servants did not get as many tickets as they wanted. This considerably angered them and they decided to teach the Indian Cricket Board a lesson. It made some nice publicity for India in the right Afro-Asian circles and, in the end, established Mrs Gandhi, who finally allowed the tour, as a benign, considerate statesperson. All the while the Indian Cricket Board was sweating and wondering what would happen. No lesson could be more dramatic. Apocryphal the story may be, yet it is quite plausible and provides an illustration of the power of Indian bureaucracy. Without the support of this bureaucracy Indian cricket could never have prospered in the early years after independence. In many ways the bureaucrats were like the new middle Indians using cricket to advertise their power. Just as India's post-independence growth had given money to the middle Indians, so India's Soviet-style planned economy had provided the civil servants with the power to influence events. Modern Indian cricket derived its early strength from the money of the industrialist allied to the power of the civil servant. Now with Indian cricket earning vast sums of money from television the power of the civil servants to stop tours has gone, although a nominal permission is still required. If anything, it is now the turn of the bureaucrat to marvel at the money-making power of Indian cricket.

Perhaps the most emphatic illustration of the old money attitude to Indian cricket is provided by Vijay Merchant and his family firm of Thackersey of Mumbai. This is one of the old established mill-owning families of Mumbai, part of the Gujerati textile owners who shaped the city. Merchant's name is actually a misnomer, because he should be Vijay Thackersey. But when he was trying to explain his name to his English principal, he took so long and got so involved in the intricacies of the Gujerati family, that the principal decided that, since Vijay clearly belonged to the merchant class, he would have the surname Merchant. Vijay was to make his reputation as a cricketer under that name and, was later to happily confess that 'I am the only Merchant in the Thackersey family'. Merchant's contribution to Indian cricket was immense. He was, arguably, the first Indian Test cricketer to display the professionalism and dedication normally associated with English cricket. After his retirement Merchant was active as a commentator, and a fundraiser for various charities. Yet, despite the wealth his family had, and his own position in cricket, the Thackerseys have never had a prominent cricket team in Mumbai. They were far too well established, far too well known, to require cricket to achieved their name. Vijay Merchant, one suspects, must have felt an odd sense of satisfaction that he achieved his cricketing reputation not under his ancient family name, rich and secure as it is, but under a borrowed name given to him by an impatient Englishman. It is unthinkable that any middle Indian would have accepted such a situation.

4

The gully, the maidan and the mali

When I started writing this book, the kindly man who edited it suggested to me that I should explain how a seven or eight year old in India takes to cricket. We know how he does so in England but surely the Indian process is very different? Indeed it is. If English cricket is essentially rural and village cricket, in George Orwell's picturesque phrase of the light falling towards evening and a ball hit for four killing a rabbit on the boundary, Indian cricket is urban. Its roots lie in the lanes of India's teeming cities and on the broad patches of green, called the maidans, that occasionally break up the monotony of concrete. Talk to almost any Indian Test cricketer, particularly of the last fifty years or so, and he will trace his cricketing roots back to the maidan and the gully. The wonder of the maidan is well captured by Budhi Kunderan, in this recollection of how he started playing cricket as recorded by Richard Cashman in *Players, Patrons and the Crowd*:

> Since my parents moved to Mumbai, when I was eight years old, I hadn't seen cricket in my native place. None of my family members [have] ever seen or played cricket in their lives. The first time that I saw a cricket match on a maidan in Mumbai I fell in love with the game . . . this is the only game we could play on the maidan, apart from running, to play any other game in Mumbai [in] those days you had to be a member of big clubs, where you could play tennis or other indoor games. But I had no opportunity as such.

An evocative picture of Kunderan, the villager moving to the big city and being claimed by cricket, sufficiently early for India to have a remarkable wicketkeeper and batsman. Similarly, gully cricket, often with a tennis ball, was part and parcel of the make-up of almost every Indian cricketer – as much part of Visvanath's batting, as Chandrasekhar's bowling or even Azharuddin's rise to fame. It was gully cricket at the old MLA ground of Hyderabad that started Azharuddin off and he and his mates getting together and forming a gully team provided him with his first taste of cricket.

All this can be simply stated. But how does one convey gully cricket? It does not have the natural cadences or the rhapsodic melody that comes naturally to English cricket. It can be hard, brutish, often messy, though with a beauty of its own. It would be tempting to draw shrewd analogies between cricket in England and gully cricket in India, as has been attempted with beach cricket in the West Indies. But I can best convey it by reminiscing about the gully cricket that I played at Mumbai's Flora Fountain – the very heart of this great city.

The centres of the world's major cities are well etched in the mind: New York's Times Square, Paris's Champs Elysee, London's Piccadilly Circus. But even now I feel a curious magic about Mumbai's Flora Fountain. We called it the heart of the city and so it was. The Flora the fountain commemorated was lost to history, even the various ladies who made up the fountain could barely be discerned and only occasionally did their mouths and nostrils and breasts spout water. As a child I could remember Flora Fountain trams but as the city removed trams, the fountain took on its more recognisable Indian shape of a haven for urchins, layabouts and stray dogs amidst a large parking lot. Round about it swirled Mumbai's commercial traffic.

We used to say with pride, and occasionally from my mother, a little disgust, that all roads led to Flora Fountain. My mother's disgust was due to the fact that our house acted as a magnet for all sorts of visitors, most of them uninvited. To me, from my bedroom window, it seemed to provide a panoramic view on the world: here the cinema, there the bank, here the school, there the playing field, here the sea, there the restaurants. Much has changed in Mumbai in recent years as Manhattan-style tower blocks have gone up and the city has fallen prey to property developers. The rhythm of Flora Fountain hasn't changed.

Flora Fountain at seven in the morning is expectant: the sound of a passing bus distinctive. By nine it is a cacophony of noise, as cars, buses, taxis, handcarts, lorries and horse-carriages make their way towards the various business houses round the area. By twelve the hubub is pierced by the rhythmical chants of the 'box-wallahs' balancing tin boxes on their heads and carrying hot lunches for the hungry clerks. This must be the most remarkable food service in the world, with almost every individual office worker in Mumbai receiving and eating the lunch faithfully prepared by his wife at home. By three the constant afternoon noise is again pierced – this time by a different cry, that of the news vendors selling the evening papers; 'Evening, Evening, Bhumi'. By six the noise has hardly abated but now the centre is a maze of queues as commuters patiently wait for their buses. By nine the streets are virtually deserted, or as deserted as they ever get in India, and such is the contrast in noise that a fast-moving taxi braking hard can produce a jolt. It is twelve before silence really falls and then the streets surrounding Flora Fountain are a sea of human bodies: the homeless of Mumbai making their beds on the pavements. It was a rhythm I had grown up with, yet it so fascinated me that even on holidays I would often sit at one of my bedroom windows and observe the pattern, so regular and yet so capable of wonder.

Our flat was on the second floor of an office block almost exactly opposite the Flora Fountain. The block itself was one of a chain of linked houses which stretched across what the American would call a 'block', and for reasons that I never fathomed out, all the houses in the block had names associated with the sea Our house was called Sailor Building but I had never seen any sailors in it, the house next to it and linked with it was called Darya Building, which literally means 'the house of the sea'. Down below was Mumbai, with its swirl of traffic, its hawkers and its almost endlessly fascinating variety of shops. Just past the American dry food shop and the picture gallery, which appeared a bit too highbrow and snooty for us, ran a lane where my father's company had its main Godown-store room – and just to the right of this lane, past the cold drinks shop, the betel nut place and the area's most elegant tailor, was my friend Hubert's magical cricket gully. From my flat to his gully was no more than two hundred, perhaps three hundred, yards – a walk of less than a minute, yet our worlds could not have been more different. It was our amazing St Xavier's School which brought us together but it was cricket, and gully cricket, that cemented our friendship.

There was nothing sweet about Hubert's gully. The entrance to his gully was narrow, as if it were a pencilled afterthought of the architect designing the area. On one side there was a high wall that enclosed the *Parsi Agiari* – the Parsee religious place, a formidable barrier. The other wall opened with the area's sewer and ended with Hubert's house. The sewer part of it was open, while underneath Hubert's house was situated a press which reeked of gum and paste and sticky molten substances, a shop of sorts and then a gymnasium where in the evenings the local boys – poor but enterprising – could be seen developing their puny bodies.

The structure of Hubert's gully was of some importance. Its narrow entrance meant that cars – or in fact any form of transport – was never particularly welcome – the high wall of the Agiari and the definable boundary of the open sewer on the other gave the area the appearance of an enclosed space. It provided a sort of mini-cricket field all to ourselves, where Hubert and I, mimicking cricketers we had admired, could play out our fantasies. Even here our relationship was defined: I, the Bengali Hindu, assuming the names of Indian Test cricketers, while Hubert, the western Indian Catholic, invariably assuming the names of English or Australian cricketers. Years later he was to tell me that he had gone to watch his first cricket match – the 1956 Australian Test match at Mumbai – in expectation that one of the Australians would go down with stomach trouble and Hubert, from the cheap-priced East Stand, would be drafted in to fill the breach. To me the fantasy in the story was Hubert being asked to play Test cricket at all. It did not seem strange to me that Hubert, whose skin colour and appearance were not all that dissimilar to mine and millions of other Indians, should expect to play for Australia – with a name like Hubert Miranda that seemed very natural.

Neither Hubert nor I had ever been properly coached in cricket. At weekends or holidays we watched proper cricket on Mumbai's maidans; I had read a few instructional books, seen a bit of Test cricket and generally discussed the game with my friends. Now Hubert's gully fashioned all this into a very strange game. I emphasise, it appears strange now but then it seemed most natural, even the stench of the sewer which was always strong in our nostrils. Our pitch was the road – stone chips and coal tar; three lines drawn on the wall that divided the gully from the rest of the world were our wickets. The road was sufficiently long to simulate a full-length cricket pitch and, conveniently at the point where the bowler's crease would be located, there was a manhole with a cover. It seemed ideal to mark the spot of the bowler's wicket. Beyond that there were another few yards where the bowler could indulge in a run-up and, if necessary, this could be increased by running parallel to the wickets, alongside the gymnasium, a run that was not only quite long, but rather elegant since it provided a curve as you approached the wicket.

The hazards of the gully seemed to increase our appetite for play. Though we had drawn the wickets on the wall as straight as we could, the wall markings as wickets added an element of doubt. We could never be sure whether the wicket had actually been hit or not, doubts that were not always easy to resolve since the bowler's interest invariably clashed with the batsman's. To this was added the hazard of the sewer. The very nature of the gully, a wall at one end, shops at the other, meant that we could only bat at one end. This made the sewer our permanent square-leg and a firmly hit ball, or even a rustic swing, down the leg-side, often landed right in the middle of the sewer. Not that we were squeamish about going in to collect our ball. We, generally Hubert, would balance on the wall and precariously fish out our rubber ball. However, this did cramp our leg-side shots and our general tendency was to play on the off-side.

Both Hubert and I had played our early cricket with a hard ball and were petrified of being hit on the legs. So our normal tendency was to retreat from the ball down the leg-side and poke it away on the off-side. In Hubert's gully this was also a very paying stroke. A mere five yards from the wicket was the wall of the Parsee Agiari and to stab it in front of us and towards cover, our most favoured stroke, ensured it would hit the wall. The convention Hubert and I had devised meant that any hit on the wall of the Agiari was worth two runs. We occasionally managed to drive straight ahead and hit the doors of the gymnasium or the printing press. This counted as four, a mighty hit landing on the first floor verandahs outside Hubert's house counted as six. Very occasionally our swings cleared Hubert's house, which was roughly mid-on, and disappeared somewhere into south Mumbai.

Every now and again it cleared the high wall of the Agiari. The Agiari was cover, to sewer's square leg, but here the problem, if anything, was much worse. From the sewer you could retrieve the ball, the Parsee Agiari was a total loss. To approach the Agiari with its closed wall and forbidding atmosphere demanded a courage which neither Hubert nor I possessed. We had occasionally tried it and had been mortified by being confronted with Parsee gentlemen, skull cap on their heads, and wearing the all-white Parsee garb of vest and loose trousers, standing sternly at the entrance, almost defying us to try and retake our ball. In histories of Indian cricket, much is made, and rightly, about the role played by Parsees in fostering it. We knew little about this history, our knowledge of English cricket history was substantially more than that of the Indian one and for us, Parsees, at least the Parsees of the Agiari, were not initiating our cricket but destroying it.

There was one other source of interruption. I have said the seclusion of Hubert's gully made it ideal. But it could not be entirely protected from what went on in the wide streets surrounding it, and every now and again the interaction of the Mumbai police with the Mumbai hawker stopped our games. Hubert's gully, as I have said, was a mere two hundred yards from my home, and the main road through south Mumbai which ran right up to Victoria Terminus, the gothic Victorian building which was Mumbai's main railway station. All along the pavement, from our block of buildings right up to Victoria Terminus, a whole group of hawkers sold their goods to the public. Their place of business was the pavement, their method of selling highly fascinating and their whole operation quite illegal.

The problem was that the hawker was not left unmolested. He had to contend with the police, not so much the man on the beat, who probably received a regular sum of money from the hawker called *hafta* which allowed the hawker to carry on his pavement business. It was the sudden police raid, in a very black police van, which caused the hawker and our cricket, problems. Sometimes the local policemen would tip the hawkers off and they would take precautions but occasionally the raids came as a surprise. No sooner did they see the police van approach, than the hawkers quickly gathered up their things. Hubert's gully, a quick run away from the police, but secluded enough from the rest of the world, was a very convenient hiding place. Suddenly in the midst of the most tense

India–England Test match, with me as Umrigar trying to avenge myself on Hubert Trueman, we would find that we had acquired an extra wicketkeeper, or a couple of slips, or even a hawker-fielder at silly mid-on. It would become impossible to continue playing. Occasionally the panting hawkers, running for shelter into the gully, would be chased by the police fanning out from the van. Armed with *lathis*, they would rain blows on these unfortunate hawkers and frog-march them, whimpering and complaining, to the police van. I must confess that such was our dedication to Test cricket, that we shed few tears about this. We were definitely on the side of the police dealing with 'hawker nuisance', a favourite Mumbai phrase, as this meant we could carry on with our cricket.

Of course when all else failed, when it rained, or it grew dark, or Hubert's gully was somehow occupied, there was always the landing outside my flat. It was no ordinary landing, reflecting the fact that the house was never meant to be lived in but just used for offices. Our flat had really been carved out of a large office floor, the main and best part of it – facing the road – was our flat and the one at the back, my father's office and store room. The result was that when you arrived on the landing outside the flat, any number of doors faced you. The first one as you came up the flight of stairs was a door that led to a row of toilets. Next to it was a much larger door which led to my father's office and storeroom. Next to it was another door which was always shut, a third led to our kitchen and then finally there was the main door. This started off by being a rickety, rotten door, smeared with heavy chalk marks which denoted wickets. It slowly developed into a better-looking, more permanent door, against which we placed a specially constructed set of wooden stumps fixed to a base.

Its advantages were obvious. It was enclosed and gave the feel of an indoor wicket, we could easily play at night as the landing was fairly well lit. It was, however, much narrower than Hubert's gully and did not give us the same feel of a cricket pitch. The landing itself formed the wicket at the point where the staircase from the floor below curved on to our floor, marking an imaginary bowler's wicket. But this severely restricted our run-up which had to be of a curving, slanting type to have any meaning whatsoever. The only way we could increase our run-up was to open the door that led to the row of 'loos', immediately behind the bowler's wicket. Running along the length of this, and emerging from the darkness, one could gather some speed and simulate the feel of what we imagined was a quick bowler.

As in Hubert's gully, cover was again a problem. In Hubert's gully it was the forbidding wall of the Agiari. Here, cover point was a window. At some stage early in our India–England–Australia Test matches, a window had been broken and never replaced and a sizzling cover drive, or what passed for it, meant the rubber ball whizzing through the open window and dropping two floors below right down the common sewer of the three buildings. To collect this ball was an extremely difficult feat and invariably I had to seek the assistance of some of my father's servants, or, more usually, have it replaced.

But perhaps the gravest problem with my landing was that it was, after all, a landing of a flat and, therefore narrow. A leg-side stroke was almost impossible since the wall on the leg-side was a few inches away from where we took guard at the wicket. And then there were the problems of the two staircases – the one that came up from the floor below and the one that went to the floor above. Very often a straight drive that beat the bowler would ricochet off the wall and go bouncing down the wooden stairs – right down to the flat of an old lady, who would complain piteously.

It is possible Hubert and I fashioned a unique form of cricket but I doubt if our experiences were all that different from many of the midnight children growing up in India in the 1950s and 1960s. If anything, our experiences of cricket were typical of India then, and now.

From gully to maidan was a natural transition. In fact we journeyed back and forwards between the two forms of cricket very often, as do almost all those who play cricket in India. The maidan is, probably, the most evocative place in Indian urban life. It has been called the equivalent of an English park but this is grossly misleading. The only similarity it has with a park is that it is a vast, open area, very often at the centre of cities. But beyond that there are no similarities. It is not merely that the grass in an English park is much greener and finer than that of the maidan, but that whereas an English park is an oasis of calm, a shelter from the hustle and bustle of city life, the maidan reproduces Indian city life with all its noise and clamour. The grass is matted, raggy, struggling to stay alive amidst the dirt and rubble. Flowing through the maidan are little canals, the surface is pock-marked with ditches, even what looks like small ravines and the whole area is filled with people from every walk of life. It is amidst such confusion and noise that Indians learn to play their cricket.

The photographs in this chapter, taken at the Fort William maidan in Kolkatta, on the rest day of a Kolkatta Test, illustrate what maidans and maidan cricket are like. There is the maidan cricketer who fancies himself as Dr W. G. Grace, a pavilion under the tree, tea with cakes from a tin box, the bewildering variety of cricketing styles and dress and above all the sheer wonder of playing cricket on a ground so inhospitable you might think it would deter walking, let alone the pursuit of such a delicate game.

But just as the lotus, that great Hindu flower, springs from the dirtiest and most inhospitable of surroundings, so does Indian cricket arise, grow and blossom on these maidans dotted all over the urban landscape.

Nowhere can maidan cricket be better appreciated than Mumbai, particularly south Mumbai, where I grew up. That area is dominated by three great maidans: Azad, Cross and the Oval. Azad, meaning free, had the distinction of being the home of the club to which Vijay Merchant, one of India's great batsmen, belonged. Opposite is the Cross, so called because at one end of it there is a huge cross bearing the inscribed legend INRI. Azad is a regular venue for many of the matches played in the inter-schools tournaments of the city. Cross often attracts large crowds to watch famous Tests, or ex-Test players playing in the inter-office *Times* shield tournament. When I was growing up the competition, organised by the leading local daily, the *Times of India*, was very well reported and, at times, an even better draw than the Ranji trophy. It cost nothing to watch and it was not unusual for a few thousand people to gather along the boundary edges, sometimes spilling over onto the adjoining roads, to watch the stars of today and yesteryear do fierce competitive battle. This is what may be called *mali*-dominated cricket.

Malis generally live in the shacks that dot the edge of a maidan and efficiently police the pitches on the maidans. These pitches are distinguished from the rest of the field not merely in the normal cricket sense, but by special arrangements. No sooner is a cricket match over than the mali comes trundling in with wooden staves and ropes and encloses the whole area of the pitch. It would not take much to remove the wooden staves and dismantle the ropes but such is the aura possessed by these illiterate, but shrewd guardians of the pitches of the maidan, that nobody dares. Also playing on these pitches is part of a package that you have to earn. Along with pitch comes a tent, specially erected for the match and acting as a pavilion, changing rooms with a little cubicle attached to it serving as a lavatory. It is when the malis start erecting the tents that the people on the maidan know that a proper cricket match, on a proper pitch, is about to be played.

The maidan pitches are also used for net practice – mostly on weekday afternoons. The Azad maidan lay between school and home, and on my way back from school I would occasionally pause to watch these cricket nets and find nothing surprising in the fact that the batsmen, with their boxes happily attached outside their trousers, practiced at the nets. Today when I revisit Mumbai, and occasionally visit Azad maidan, the sight of hundreds of batsmen in full cricket regalia proudly displaying their boxes as they practice the forward defensive stroke seems odd, even faintly obscene. Then it was part of normal mali-maidan-cricket.

Most of my maidan cricket and, for that matter, most people's, was played on dirt tracks with some grass on it which formed the space between the pitches. This wasn't the only impromptu part of our cricket. There was the problem of equipment. I had been generously provided with full cricket gear, some of it from my father, and some of it gifts from friends and relations. But most of the members of my team were not quite so happily placed, and in most of our matches we had at best two pairs of pads, and very often just three pads. I mean not three *pairs* of pads, but one pair of pads and another solitary pad! So for much of the time, since most of us were right handed, we wore a pad on the left leg, leaving the right unprotected. Gloves were a scarcity and, though I had a set of stumps, only very rarely did we play in matches where we had two sets of stumps. Generally we had four stumps which imposed its own constraint. Three stumps would constitute the wicket at one end, the solitary stump the bowler's wicket at the other end. This meant that at the end of overs the batsman would cross over, not the wicketkeeper or the fielders. Again the bat which had been a gift of a friend of my father was our prize bat, and very often the non-striker would have to do with a broken bat, or a wooden plank. At the end of an over, or when it was his turn to bat, he would exchange his bat, or plank, for a proper one. These are, of course, personal recollections but they mirror cricket as it was played then and now.

Not surprisingly maidan cricket gave rise to a new vocabulary. Thus maidan cricket uses the expression 'runner' in a totally different way from the common cricketing meaning of the term. In cricket a runner is one who runs for a batsman who has been injured during the game and cannot run for himself. In maidan cricket the number one batsman is called the 'opener', his partner is called the 'runner'. Very often in this class of cricket there are only three stumps and the stumps at the bowler's end are indicated by a pile of *chappals* – Indian slippers – heaped at the spot where the proper stumps would be. The 'runner' is the one who immediately takes up his position at the chappal end.

There is also 'twoodie'. In maidan cricket boundaries have to be laboriously fixed. There are often very serious arguments about where the boundaries are. This is not surprising since the ground is not marked out, there are very many matches taking place all at the same time and the square-leg of one match is the cover point of another match. Often there are objects on a maidan which conveniently indicate a boundary: a roller, a tree, perhaps the spot where a pitch has been protected by the mali's wooden staves and ropes. But very often there are insurmountable objects on the ground. They are too near the wicket for the hit to be classified as a four should the ball hit the object. So in maidan cricket it counts as two runs and in order to given it a name the hit is signalled as twoodie, meaning two runs.

But perhaps the most important innovation of maidan cricket is the reinterpretation of the two fingered salute. Now, normally in cricket the index finger of the right hand raised upward into the heavens is seen as the traditional mark of the umpire's decision in favour of the fielding side. This is all very well when the umpire is giving a decision in favour of the fielding side. But what if he is signifying not out? How does he do it? He could say 'Not out', but in maidan cricket this is considered not enough. So an innovation has been introduced whereby one finger raised to the heavens is out and two fingers raised to the heavens are not out. In maidan cricket, the umpire wishing to turn down an appeal doesn't say 'not out' or shake his head – a gesture which in India has a very different meaning – but raises two fingers of his right hand.

But what sort of cricket is this maidan game? Let me reminisce again and talk of the maidan cricket I played as I grew up in the 1950s. For some reason, and maybe because I provided much of the essential gear – stumps, bat, gloves, pad – I was the Captain of my maidan team. In the early years I also provided two very important players: Shankar and Arjun. Shankar was my father's driver and Arjun one of the many servants which my father employed. Both of them were young men in their prime and though they hadn't really played cricket properly, their ability to clout the ball hard and bowl it faster than we could added considerably to the strength of our team. This enabled us to boldly challenge older boys and hold quite an advantage over most teams. Later, as work commitments made Shankar and Arjun unavailable, I formed a team that perhaps reflected that area of Mumbai rather well.

Apart from Hubert, whose cricket skill was perhaps slightly inferior to mine, there was Bala. He was some years senior to us and of his origins, we knew nothing. One day while we were practising at the Oval he had turned up and become part of our team. He would often come in bare feet, or at best wearing thin, fragile chappals. I think his father was some sort of labourer and his family lived in a *chawl*, a tenement not far from Flora Fountain though, prudently, we made no enquiries.

Then there was Eddy. He was the same age as Bala but came from the same Catholic mileu as Hubert, though from Goa and, of course, was much more sophisticated and cleverer than Bala. Both Eddy and Bala, I believe, appeared for the matriculation at the same time, with Eddy doing somewhat better than Bala. This gave Eddy and Bala a certain awe in our eyes. In school, matriculation was always being held up as the great exam that would crown our school career: passing it was considered essential if our lives were to have any meaning, and we hoped to follow the example set by Eddy and Bala.

I was personally intrigued and enchanted by Eddy's infatuation with *The Guns of Navarone*. This was around 1962 and *The Guns of Navarone* had just been released in Mumbai. It was proving immensely popular and easily notched up a silver jubilee, twenty-five weeks of continuous showing. Eddy, if I remember rightly, saw it half a dozen times and appeared to have memorised every scene. His particular favourite was the moment when David Niven and Gregory Peck discover that Peck's girl friend is really a German spy. Eddy, in a typical Goan accent, that would now be described as a take-off of Peter Sellers's Indian one, would love declaiming David Niven's speech to Gregory Peck urging him to kill his girl friend. 'Do it for England', Niven urged Peck in the movie and this became Eddy's war cry during our matches. Eddy, who was quite a decent bat, would often share stands with me and in the middle of a stand, as we crossed over, or consulted in the middle of the pitch, Eddy would seek to encourage me by quoting Niven's speech and saying, 'Do it for England'. I don't know how often we 'did it for England' in those matches but we found nothing incongruous in Eddy's exhortation.

But perhaps our most colourful cricketer was Ching, the Chinaman. It was an indication of our cricket, or at least of my team, that we never really discovered his proper name, nor even made any effort to do so. He lived not far from the dock areas of Mumbai and had been introduced to the team by Bala. The most distinctive thing about him was not his origin, which we accepted without question, but his style of play. His most effective, in fact his only, stroke would be to cross his legs in front of the wicket and then hold his bat in the gap formed by the crossing of the legs. If he kept the bat straight then he would drop the ball dead centre. Occasionally he would twist the bat either on the leg-side, squirting the ball through fine leg, or on the off-side, sending it through slips. I think the shock of the style proved so great for most bowlers that they often found no way of dislodging Ching.

Bala, Hubert, Eddy, Ching and I would form the hard core of the team. We would be supplemented by other players, cousins of Eddy's or friends of Bala's but at times we struggled to complete the team. Then total strangers would be incorporated into the side. Some of them just people lounging at the Oval while we were about to start the match. This gave our already exotic team an even more exotic flavour and probably accounted for our success.

Some of our most colourful matches were played against a team made up from the residents of Rehmat Manzil, a large block of flats on Veer Nariman Road, the road which ran past the Oval and houses some of Mumbai's restaurants. Many of the boys in the team were from my own school, some of them from my own class, and they were the archetypal 'building' team (all being from one building). There was Gupta, who happily allowed everybody to mispronounce him as 'Gupte', thus appropriating some of the glory that was attached to the name of Subhas Gupte, India's legendary leg-spinner and a hero of our youth. The cricketing similarity between Gupta and Gupte was remote, since Gupta's leg-breaks very often turned out to be gentle up and down stuff. Worse still, not all members of Gupta's team accepted his captaincy, though the gravest problems for him were caused not by his middle-class school contemporaries, but by Sammath, the son of the 'building' durwan, an Indian-style porter. Durwans in India generally hail from Afghanistan or the north-west frontier provinces and are called Pathans. Most of them are called not by their names but by a general term, Lala, and this Lala was a tall, fierce man who fitted every Indian stereotype of the Pathan and looked capable of fulfilling his job of protecting the building. Sammath, his son, in our cricket terms was just as fierce – a tearaway fast bowler who took a long run-up and appeared to deliver the ball with exceptional speed. Unfortunately for Gupta's team, Sammath also had the fast bowler's temperament and did not like being taken off at any time. This caused some merry rows between Sammath and his Captain Gupta, much to our joy.

No doubt individual memories of maidan cricket will differ. But in essence I doubt if it has changed all that much. It is still the world of twoodies, runner, the V-sign signifying not out, the mali as a shambolic man but with real power protecting his pitch from the assaults of the multitudes and the maidan team made up of many elements reflecting the fantastic mix that is urban Indian life.

5

An English sporting Eden in India

So we know how an Indian takes to cricket. But what about the sporting world he inhabits? What shapes it? India is changing all the time but the sporting world that existed in the 1950s and 1960s when I grew up in India has rarely been examined and in many ways its influences still weigh heavily on contemporary India.

My generation was brought up to believe that England was the ultimate sporting heaven: a unique, wondrous world where skill reigned supreme and sportsmanship was never in doubt. I had first glimpsed this world as a nine-year old when I saw Tom Graveney score a hundred in each innings of the match played at the Brabourne Stadium to celebrate the silver jubilee of the Indian Board. To mark the occasion an England A team toured India.

The beauty Graveney produced was so great that not even Fred Trueman, who broke the fingers of Vijay Hazare – my favourite Indian batsman – could dim it. Trueman, who was playing in India for the first and only time, may have been the great English saitan, devil, who ate Indian batsmen for breakfast but my mind was filled with Graveney, the English enchanter. I can still see him elegantly stretch his left leg and stroke the ball through the covers, so sweetly that he had hardly finished the stroke before it was hitting the concrete just in front of the East Stand where I sat. Elegant, said the retainer my father had assigned to escort me to the match, and elegant repeated I, not quite sure what the world meant but certain it was a term of approval.

Not long after this my cousin had presented me on my birthday with Graveney's *Cricket Through the Covers* which I read and reread many times not least for his praise of my hero Subhas Gupte. I particularly savoured his prediction that in 1959 Gupte's leg spin would devastate England. It did not come true and was angry but this was nothing like the anger I felt when someone, I believe the servant who every morning dusted the furniture with a piece of felt cloth, tipped a pot of ink on the book. It stained it a hideous dark blue, including the picture of W. G. Grace, but I insisted on keeping the book and refused to let my mother throw it away. At around that time I had also became a Surrey supporter – they were in the middle of their seven champions in a row sequence – and eagerly lapped up Jim Laker's *Over To Me*, although I wasn't sure how to take his criticisms of Peter May. However, when Surrey banned Laker from the Oval I felt personally slighted. I was even more devastated when I read in the *Evening News* how Yorkshire had ended Surrey's run in 1959.

And besides that of course, at school and at home I had received a whole host of signs which made England seem all the time like the land of super sportsmen, the veritable factory of sporting dreams. After the first football match I had played in at my Jesuit school, Father Fritz, who took us for sports and English, fixed a photograph on the school notice board purporting to be from the match.

It turned out to be a photograph of an English first division game which had been reproduced in an Indian sports magazine and, if every memory serves me right, it showed Dave Mackay of the Tottenham Hotspur Double Winning Team of 1960–1 – the first English team to do the domestic double in the twentieth century – tackling some other burly player. Fritz had just scratched out their names and put the names of two of my school team mates. He explained it was a not a deception. He wanted to show us the standards we should aim for when playing football.

Even without Fritz's bizarre way of providing an English role model, reports and descriptions of England at play were all about us. Every week there was the *Sport and Pastime*, the awkward-looking A5-sized magazine which you could neither fold when trying to read under the bed clothes or bend but which was full of articles and action photographs from English sport. In winter it was mostly football, in summer mostly cricket, but all year long there were reprints of articles from the English press describing the goings on in English sport. Since these articles were often from the newspapers like the *Daily Express* and the *Daily Mail* they were an early introduction to the popular style of reporting, so different to the almost Victorian prose used in the *Times of India*. So, far away in India, I and many other Indians, read the same sports articles that people in England were reading, albeit a few days, or at times a few weeks, later.

As for the Tottenham Double Winning Team the doors to that sporting Camelot had been opened for me on 8 May 1961. It was a Monday and the *Times of India* led its entire sports page – it only devoted a page to sports then – with a photograph showing the Spurs Double Team parading the Cup and League trophy through the streets of north London. The trophies were being carried on an open top double decker bus that looked very like the BEST, Bombay Electric Supply & Transport buses which were a familiar sight in Mumbai, hardly surprising given that Mumbai had bought the old buses that London Transport did not need.

Recently I looked up the photograph and it was a grainy black and white print, the bus looks startlingly white with two signs reading Private, Private. As it makes it way up the Tottenham High Road between

Edmonton and Tottenham town halls it seems to be escorted by a line of policemen shepherding a large, happy, crowd who look more curious than boisterous. Behind them are visible council flats packed with people and overhead the tram cables. The photograph also reminded me that Ron Henry held the championship trophy and Peter Baker the FA Cup. I cannot in all honesty claim I remembered all those details and my devotion to Tottenham never reached that of Irving Scholar, the former chairman, whose test for every aspiring girl friend was: Can you name the double team. And if they couldn't instantly recite: Brown, Baker, Henry, Blanchflower, Norman, MacKay, Jones, White, Smith, Allen and Dyson the relationship did not progress much further.

But my love for Tottenham was sufficiently strong so that the following season the first thing I turned to on Monday mornings were the results of the previous Saturday's English league matches (they came too late for inclusion on a Sunday) only to find a club called Ipswich, which I had never heard of, pip Tottenham and rob them of a second successive double. It saddened me but also, in a curious way, confirmed my judgement. I was used to my favourite sporting teams flattering to deceive, a phrase I had often seen in the *Times of India*. Having fallen in love with Tottenham I was determined not to abandon the club, even when my friend Umesh introduced me to his adoration of Manchester United. We argued long and hard about the respective merits of Dennis Law and Jimmy Greaves and I followed Greaves's unhappy move to Milan and return to Tottenham. How I raged when Ramsey dropped Greaves in the final stages of the 1966 World Cup. The only truce I had with Umesh was when the name of Bobby Charlton came up. Much as I loved Tottenham, Charlton was like a god who occupied a special plane, epitomising the promise which the English sporting world held out to me.

The *Times of India's* decision to lead its sports page with a story of English domestic football was not unusual. In the summer the *Times of India* easily, effortlessly, allowed English sports like cricket and tennis to take over its sports pages. It fitted in neatly with the rhythms of the sporting season in India which are mainly in the cooler winter months. That is when Tests and domestic cricket, and also the major hockey, football and other tournaments are played. Come May, and with it the unbearable heat, organised domestic sport, takes a back seat. The heat and the rains do not put a complete stop to sport in India – Mumbai in the midst of rains has the amazing Kanga League – but the sports editor of the *Times of India* seems to recognise that Bombay's Harewood League, the city's soccer competition, cannot match the lure of a Lord's Test or Wimbledon tennis.

So from about early May, through to the end of August, the *Times of India*, while reporting local sports, often led its sports page with English sporting stories. At that time in the early 1960s there was always the Indian hope that Ramanathan Krishnan, who had twice got to the Wimbledon semi-finals in 1961 and 1962, both times losing to the eventual winner, would actually win the tournament. But even in the years when he failed, Wimbledon made the headlines. And English Test cricket, whoever England were playing, always led the sports pages, even in 1960 when South Africa were the visitors to England.

Nothing could have illustrated England's sporting hold on us more emphatically. On the editorial pages the *Times of India* hardly had a kind word to say about South Africa. This was hardly surprising given that South Africa was in the middle of bolstering its hated apartheid policy. We were all aware that white South Africa did not want to have anything to do with us Indians and treated people of our colour abominably. But as far as the sports editor of the *Times of India* was concerned when South Africa played England at cricket, apartheid was not the issue. This was Test cricket from England and deserving not just a mention but often the top billing. So through that 1960 series I followed South Africa's progress, including the amazing throwing controversy of Griffin, who finally ended up being no-balled during the Lord's by the umpire Syd Buller.

And even when we read about Indians', progress in sports like cricket it was often refracted through English eyes. Vizzy, the Indian prince who looked like an owlish Indian Billy Bunter and despite being no more than a club cricketer had intrigued his way into the captaincy for the 1936 Indian tour of England, about whom I shall have more to say later, had now became a commentator. To every Test one of his assistants carried a thick book which was full of cuttings from Cardus. Every time Vizzy wanted to describe a stroke his assistant would open the book, Vizzy would select the appropriate Cardus phrase and reproduce it. Many years later I was to learn that this produced a quite extraordinary incident during an England tour of India.

Vizzy had donated the pavilion at Delhi's Kotla ground where Test cricket was played. This entitled him to two seats at the press box. However on the day before the Test against England, E. M. Wellings, the correspondent of the *London Evening News*, arrived and decided that he and a colleague would book those seats for themselves.

On the day of the Test Vizzy's assistant, carrying the book of Cardus cuttings, arrived to find Wellings and his friend occupying Vizzy's traditional seats. He suggested to the Englishmen to move . . . This was met by a very short, sharp reply from Wellings: 'Fuck Off'. After that a few more words were spoken and a sort of Mexican stand-off ensued. Wellings wouldn't move and Vizzy did not have a seat. However, as was his custom, Vizzy had put up a marquee during the Test where the English cricket journalists were invited for lunch and tea. Wellings could hardly go there so he got Ian Todd, a young reporter for the *Daily Mirror*, to bring back some bananas for him. Eventually the matter could only be resolved by the intervention of Paul Gore-Booth, then Britain's man in Delhi, and Wellings was persuaded to move.

I heard this story many years later from Ian Todd but had I known it then it would have confirmed my opinion of Vizzy. Despite quoting Cardus, his unfortunate speaking voice, not remotely suited to radio, it being somewhere between a hoarse whisper and a strangulated cry meant he more often than not sounded quite comical. Vizzy could be so eccentric that once during a Kolkata Test against Pakistan in the 1960–1 season his reactions to the fall of a wicket made All Indian Radio end the transmission. During that Test Chandu Borde was bowled by the last ball of a day's play. Vizzy, overcome with emotion let out a cry, which went on for minutes. All India Radio, aware that the day's play was done, and assuming the noise coming from the stadium was the sound of static, decided the commentators had nothing more to say and went back to the studios. The result was that the listeners did not know India had lost a wicket and only learnt about it from the next day's papers.

We preferred our Cardus straight – as for instance his essay on Ranji which was part of our prescribed reading – or as it came to us through K. N. Prabhu, the *Times of India's* cricket correspondent. Not only did Prabhu often quote Cardus but his attempts to explain India, even our own Mumbai, to us, meant borrowing English imagery. So Shivaji Park, the vast, teeming ground in congested central Mumbai which has produced a whole galaxy of cricketers who have played for India through to the present-day Sachin Tendulkar was described by Prabhu as the Pudsey of Indian cricket. It did not seem at all incongruous to us that we could appreciate Shivaji Park, which we passed on the way to the airport and where my father often took me because it housed his favourite Bengal Club, only by comparing it to the cradle of Yorkshire cricket which we had never seen. As far as Prabhu was concerned by calling Shivaji Park the Pudsey of Bombay, Shivaji Park had been properly categorised, even redeemed. After all had not Pudsey produced Len Hutton? In batsmanship there could be no higher standard. Not having images and metaphors of our own we borrowed shamelessly from England and in time began to feel that they were part of our traditions.

Even when India played in England – all too rarely and all too disastrously – we heard about the Tests through English voices. We listened to the World Service's ball-by-ball commentary and read match reports written by Englishmen. So while Prabhu often covered tours abroad, when India went to England as in 1967 he stayed at home. Ian Wooldridge wrote about it for the *Times of India*. In the traditional opening match between the Indians against Indian Gymkhana he wrote rather tenderly of a corpulent Indian Gymkhana leg-spinner, clearly an expatriate Indian, who had troubled the Indian team. I read and reread that passage many times thinking how sweet it was of Wooldridge to take the trouble to produce that extra touch which he knew would appeal to his Indian readers. Many years later when I finally arrived in Fleet Street I learnt that Wooldridge was still waiting to be paid for his dispatches but by then I had realised that was a common fate for those who wrote for Indian papers. Indian editors then felt the glory of writing for them was payment in itself.

This in turn fitted in neatly with the other pictures of England that were constantly crowding in. I had been introduced to the World Service and all its wonders. The World Service news which was followed alternatively by commentary about the day's event or *News about Britain* was a must for me. In those days the ten-minute news featured only one newsreader, there were no other voices during the bulletin with the newsreader at most saying, 'a correspondent in a dispatch to the BBC says...etc.'. *All India Radio* news was so boring and so predictable, being full of government statistics and handouts, that the joke was that if the Third World War broke out it might just make the closing headlines after the latest production figures for rice and wheat. To listen to BBC news was like being transported to another world. It was on the BBC World Service news that I heard that the Russians had erected a wall in Berlin. I rushed in to tell my father. I was more than a little disappointed to find that he did not seem to take that much interest.

The shining jewel of this was the *Saturday Special*, the sports programme that would start at round 4.30 in the afternoon and end at 11.15 p.m. with *Sports Round-up* when a man in a stentorian voice read out the English football results. Before that every Saturday I listened to a second half football commentary during the winter and as often as not it turned out to be a Scottish game. So not long after falling in love with Tottenham I also fell in love with Celtic and their European Cup victory in 1967 brought great joy.

Soon after I had fallen in love with Tottenham the man I knew as my grandfather – although in reality he was my father's uncle – came through on one of his periodical visits from Pune. He was on his way to a Rotary election – and he presented me with two *William Brown* books. If I remember right they were *Just William* and *William in Trouble*. Soon I was progressing through my own English world of letters: *Biggles*, followed by *Sherlock Holmes*, Agatha Christie and finally the grandest of them all, P. G. Wodehouse.

My father often used to tell me that it was good to eat fish. Once I had read the first Jeeves story I needed no further inducement. After all was that not why Jeeves was so bright? Needless to say I did not see myself as Jeeves. When I got to London I imagined I would be like Bertie Wooster, belong to a club like Drones and get a man servant like Jeeves who I would feed the Bengali delicacy of *Hilsa*, specially flown in from India.

If following Tottenham and Surrey made me feel I knew how my two favourite games were meant to be played, then the *William* books seemed to suggest that life in England was not all that different from India. After all did not William have a cook and servants at home, and did he not tussle with his parents about school much as I did? I recently recounted my love for William books to an Australian friend and how I imagined all of England lived like that. But what about William's dropped aitches said the friend, did that not strike you as odd, he asked. I had never noticed it as odd. I was amused by it but it did nothing shake my conviction that everyone in England spoke like Alvar Liddell. The one exception was John Arlott and his cricket commentaries but then Arlott was God and like any true God allowed to be idiosyncratic.

The more we read and heard about England the more easily we imagined ourselves to be part of England. This was particularly so when the *Sport & Pastime* serialised extracts from the memoirs of cricketers, footballers and even English jockeys. It was here that I learnt from Scobie Breasley that the Derby came too early in the English season. In the late 1940s he had just failed to win the Derby with a much fancied horse owned by the Maharaja of Baroda. Not long afterwards when a friend of my father came to our house and discussed horseracing I stunned him by repeating it. When he asked, 'Have you been in England in early June' I had to shamefacedly accept I had not. When my father's friend went on to say Breasley was Australian and did not know much about England it was my turn to be stunned.

But that did not stop me from claiming a superior intelligence based on knowledge of English sports. And when a friend of mine discussed the deeds of the then leading Indian jockey Pandhu Khade I said with some authority, having read it in *Sport & Pastime*, that Khade could not possibly match Breasley, who was a fine judge of speed and the best jockey to engineer a win by a short head. Unlike my father's friend, my friend did not ask, 'Have you seen Breasley ride?' probably because he too passed on opinions of English sport he had garnered from the *Sport & Pastime* as his own. Both of us knew that in the eyes of our contemporary it made us important, marked us out as men of the world.

This knowledge, however incomplete, made us feel we knew as much about English sport as we did about Indian sport, at times even more. This was all the more important, because although we would never have put it quite like that, we felt Indian sport like Indian life was deficient, not quite complete. It could only be completed by a knowledge of English sport and the more we knew about it the more superior we felt, a superiority already guaranteed to us by the fact that we went to a what was called an English-speaking school, where the language of instruction was English, as opposed to many other schools where students were taught in Hindi, Marathi or other Indian languages. It was much later that I realised it was a typical colonial reaction, a way of looking at England as the mother country, the source of goodness, the provider of knowledge to validate our experience. Sport added a further dimension to this.

About this time my uncle, who had become a prominent Congress politician, came from Calcutta to attend the annual session in Bombay. There had been atrocities against Hindus in the then Eastern Pakistan. My uncle was unhappy about it and more so about the Indian government's rather weak response. He wanted to make a tough speech. I eagerly volunteered to be his speech writer. Summoning all the words I had recently learned, and fortified by Fritz's praise of my command of the English language, I poured them into the speech, talking of the genocide of the Hindus and appeasement of Pakistan with suitable references to Chamberlain, Munich and Hitler. With Nehru (who was to die a few weeks later) watching, my uncle delivered the speech in his best oratorical style and it quite electrified that staid Congress session. Afterwards Congressmen gathered round complimenting him. He generously pointed out that I had drafted it and that I was only 16. One of his Congress colleagues, an old man, patted me on the back and said, 'Genocide, appeasement, very appropriate words. You write like an Englishman.' It may have been a perfect illustration of Naipaul's mocking description of our mimic societies but at that moment I felt so proud.

This was India of the early 1960s, almost fifteen years after its much cherished independence from England. The Indian constitution had laid down that in 1960 Hindi would replace English as the national language but this raised such a protest that the constitution was amended to allow English to co-exist with Hindi. We would hear of Indian politicians, who had themselves been educated at Hindi-speaking schools, sending their children to convents. Our contempt for those who could not speak English fluently was cruel and shameful. Much later I realised it was a typical colonial reaction, a way of looking at England as the mother country, the source of goodness, the provider of knowledge to validate our experience.

'I am craze for foreign, just craze for foreign,' Mrs Mahindra told V. S. Naipaul when renting out a room to him in Delhi. Interestingly, Naipaul was visiting India in the very season I was puzzling over the achievements of Ipswich and mourning Tottenham's surrender of its crown, and like so much in his *Area of Darkness* he had caught the mood just right. We were all 'craze for foreign' – foreign degrees, foreign foods, above all, approval of foreign opinion. And England stood at the very apex of our foreign craze.

The evidence was all round us. Our flat was in the most famous street of Bombay, Hornby Road, renamed Dr Dadabhai Naoroji Road after one of the founders of the Indian National Congress and a man who was also the first Indian elected to the House of Commons. But if we felt ourselves to be at the centre of Bombay the streets below and around echoed to cries that made us aware we were very peripheral figures on a world stage. The cries were, 'Foreign, imported novelty', as the street vendors enticed us with items, imported and smuggled, from England and other parts of the world. The vendors did not need much to persuade us that if an item was made in England then it must by definition be better than anything India had to offer.

Strange as it may seem in now, in our eyes it was Japan that was suspect and England beyond reproach. My father's most telling example of the shoddiness of Japanese goods was derived from his own experience from the 1930s when the streets of Bombay had been flooded with cheap Japanese imitations of western goods. This memory of Japan as the home of badly made goods never left him. If you wanted quality, said my father, you bought English. Japanese may be cheap but it was rubbish.

In his business – the company made raincoats – there could be no higher quality than Gabardine and Burberry. And for him the only car worth possessing was an English car. He had great faith in Fords; Ford Anglia, Ford Popular – although Ford was an American company, the cars we had were made in Dagenham in east London. 'Whatever happens,' he would say, 'an English car will always start first thing in the morning.' His best friend had a Sunbeam sports car and while my father did not approve of the flashiness he was reassured that it was English. To even write this now is to invite mockery, given there is no English car industry left, but in India of the late 1950s and early 1960s such sentiments were commonplace and evoked no comment, let alone derision.

It was not merely that British goods were more reliable, but also that England had a superior moral system. My father's favourite example of this was the way Edward VIII had not been allowed to ascend the throne because he wanted to marry a divorced American woman. For my father it showed how family life was valued by the royal family. Had he been alive today the events with Diana would have left him bemused.

In cricket this craze for foreign meant Indians could get very upset when every spring *Wisden* announced its cricketers of the year – it was prominently featured in the *Evening News* – and there was no Indian name. In those days *Wisden* only considered cricketers who had played in the previous English season – they have a less parochial outlook now – but we in India did not understand that distinction. As far as we were concerned we took *Wisden* cricketers of the year in the literal sense – meaning all cricketers – and raged that no Indian was considered worthy. I can see this attitude now as an Indian sporting schizophrenia but then I shared it.

Much has changed in India since my childhood but this craze for foreign, particularly English, recognition, has not disappeared. In May 2002 the Indian cricket writer Suresh Menon listed his favourite all-time cricket books in *Wisden Asia*. In it he praised the award that Ramchandra Guha had won for *A Corner of a Foreign Field*. This was the Literary Award given by the English Cricket Society. I was rather taken aback by Menon's use of the word 'path breaker' to describe Guha's achievement. My *History of Indian Cricket* had won the same award twelve years earlier, being the first Indian cricket book to do so. What was more intriguing was that Menon completely excluded me from his list because he said I lived and worked in London and therefore did not count. This seemed to be a curious way for evaluating Indian cricket books. An Indian who lives in India but writes a book on Indian cricket in English and has it published by a British firm in London, entering it for an English prize, qualifies. But an Indian who lives in England and does the same does not. Also it illustrated that Indians had still not developed their own awards which could rank alongside the English ones. I was sufficiently worked up to write to the magazine:

> Why are Indians still seeking English approval, 56 years after throwing the British out of India? If Indian cricket is to come of age, it needs Indian awards, not salivating at the prospect of getting more colonial gold.

My love affair with Tottenham had begun at a crucial time for me. I had just turned 14 and felt I was an aware teenager who could hold his own in any argument. The previous winter we had an unseasonable holiday in Calcutta to see my grandmother – we usually went in the summer – and on the long 36-hour train journey, just days before the 1960 American presidential election, I poured over papers debating the fortunes of

Kennedy and Nixon and argued with my father that Kennedy would be better for India. We were aware of its great power and influence and America fascinated us. Many of my school friends were planning to go there to study. I myself sat the SSAT exams for American universities and in time MIT and Harvard were talked about as much as Oxford or Cambridge, though they could never equal Oxbridge in prestige. In the early 1960s the Indian balance of payments made foreign travel very difficult – any venture outside India required Form P for travel, a Kafkaesque bureaucratic nightmare, and anyone leaving India received just £3. But for those who got admission to Oxford or Cambridge there was never any problem for the Reserve Bank of India giving foreign exchange. The civil servants who decided such things were themselves from Oxbridge: the two universities set a standard which Yale or Harvard could not match – as did almost everything in England.

The Madras Brahmin who, on reading O'Hara's *From the Terraces*, had told Naipaul, 'You couldn't get a well-bred Englishman writing this sort of tosh', echoed many of our feelings about the powerful but crude Americans. At school the poetry and almost all the prose we read derived from English writers – Shakespeare, of course, but also Shelley, Wordsworth, Walter de la Mare, Chesterton, Robert Lynd. The only American we ever read in our school was Mark Twain. That was his essay on Bombay and then largely to point out how dreadfully certain foreigners can get things wrong about India. Fritz used to almost foam at the mouth when he referred to Twain's passage describing the Indian crow.

My father admired American marketing skills. Alfred Tack's book on selling was one of the few he had read diligently. And I was much impressed when a friend at school suddenly turned out to be a salesman for *Time* magazine and even got my father to subscribe to it. But while *Time* was useful – I noted down the difficult words I read there in a notebook – for real writing we all preferred the English. I felt I had stolen a march there for about this time I discovered a very special British library which none of my friends even suspected existed. I was still chaperoned wherever I went. If for some reason my father's chauffeur could not take me to school then he would detail one of his many company peons. To take me to Tests at the Brabourne Stadium there was always one of his clerks, Mr Kandalgoakar, who had played some cricket at Shivaji Park and considered himself an expert on the game. But on Thursdays, when our school had a midweek holiday, after lunch I was allowed to wander out into Hornby Road on my own. There I stumbled across the offices of the British Deputy High Commissioner, just opposite our flat and the other side of Flora's fountain, located on the second floor of a marvellous white stone building – the rest of it was occupied by the Hong Kong and

Shanghai Bank. I found that it had a small library which housed all the English papers, printed on paper so thin I felt I could eat them, let alone read them.

My reading was voracious and undiscriminating and the high point was the *New Statesman* and the political commentaries of Anthony Howard. Harold Macmillan was then immersed in political problems – soon the Profumo scandal would break – and Howard wrote in a style that was at once so intelligible and accessible. Political commentaries were not unknown to me. The *Times of India* carried one almost every day and once a week the editor wrote his long piece that took up almost the entire leader page, setting right the nation and the world. But they were written in a heavy neo-Victorian style that was quite difficult to fathom. Howard was like a ray of sunshine cutting through a dense fog. As I read I imagined him to look like David Niven, our idea of the typical Englishman.

The journey to the library was like going to the source of the river. The *Times of India* had a weekly 'Letter from London' from its correspondent on the goings-on in Whitehall and Downing Street. But far from carrying any of the verisimilitude that Alastair Cooke's 'Letters from America' have always had, they read poorly, sounded contrived and, as I soon realised, were no more than a summary of the British press. This feeling strengthened when I read the originals and began to detect a phrase or two the *Times of India* man had lifted, without attribution, from the *London Times* or the *Guardian*.

Perhaps what gave me the most pleasure about visits to the library of the British Deputy High Commissioner was that I knew it was like a secret treasure trove to which I alone had the key. Of course there were many in Bombay who knew about it but they were grown men and women. I alone of my contemporaries and school friends knew of this library and its treasures. We all knew of the much more famous and bigger library run by the British Council. The idea of free public libraries is taken for granted in Britain but it is unknown in India and membership of the British Council library, which was the nearest equivalent, was the great prize of our youth. But such was the demand that the British Council had rationed membership and we had to wait until we were 16 before we could become members. Of course we could become members of the United States Information Service, but it had boring books on the threat of Soviet Communism, or why collective farming was not working in Poland, by writers we had never heard about. The British Council library offered us access to the writers who were part of our school syllabus but in a more abundant and complete form.

My discovery of the Deputy High Commissioner's little library meant that while my friends waited to be 16, 1 felt I had already got access to part of the kingdom. The Deputy High Commissioner's library had no Wodehouse or Shaw that I could take home to read but the compensation was that I could always read book reviews discussing Wodehouse and Shaw.

My interest in that library was not merely intellectual; the sensual side was also catered for. The 1960s were upon us and the English girls of the High Commission had taken to wearing short skirts – if not quite mini, certainly much shorter than anything to be seen in Bombay. Lunchtime was a good time to go because just after two they all returned in one group. I only had to look up from that week's Anthony Howard political commentary to see a generous flash of thigh as they paraded past. The combination of Howard's astringent prose and the promise of those thighs made me long for Thursdays to come around.

But just as the promise of the thighs never turned into reality, and I never imagined they would, so for very different reasons I was shocked when years later I got to London and made my pilgrimage to the *New Statesman* offices then at Great Turnstile. I was ushered into Howard's office. He received me with great kindness but I could hardly take in anything he said. Far from looking like Niven he looked like one of our Nepali servant boys and to my utter shame – although I did not say this to him – as I left his office I told myself, 'How can a man who looks like Ramu write so well?'

Yet all this did not mean a wholesale acceptance of anything and everything English, indeed, our love for English sport was also a contradiction, except that at that age we saw no contradictions. It was only much later, after I had read C. L. R. James and then returned to Nirad Chaudhuri and his autobiography – the two representing, as Naipaul put it, the delayed and imperfectly understood cultural boomerang from the colonies – that I began to appreciate the moral and political confusion from which our love of English sport had sprung.

It is worth emphasising that our longing for the English sporting world was mixed with our loathing for what we saw as the iniquitous way, for instance, the English cricket world treated Indian cricket. Indeed, when it came to international sporting contests it was Australia rather than England that claimed us. England playing Australia would have us all rooting for Australia and Australia got our support even when they played the West Indians. The only time we wanted Australia to lose was when they played India.

Our fanatical support for Australia was nourished by Test cricket commentaries from that country. After BBC cricket commentaries our great joy was to tune in to these cricket broadcasts from Australia by Alan McGilray and Lindsay Hassett. They were carried on Radio Ceylon, a sort of Indian sub-continental Radio Caroline. It combined advertisements, profiting from the fact that in those days All India Radio refused to carry any, with Hindi film songs and BBC World Service news. When Australia played a Test series at home, Radio Ceylon relayed cricket commentaries from the Australian Broadcasting Commission. The time difference was perfect. Whereas listening to BBC cricket commentaries meant sitting up late, often as late as 11.30 p.m. – difficult on schooldays – the Australian Test would start at six in the morning Indian time and finish by lunchtime.

I first began to appreciate this during the West Indian tour of Australia in 1960–1, the one that produced the first-ever tied Test. The last Test saw a narrow Australia win by two wickets and they took the series 2–1. The reaction of the Australians was unprecedented. As the West Indians left Melbourne, a quarter of a million inhabitants of the city crowded the streets to bid them goodbye. It was the first series where the West Indians had been captained by a black man, Worrell, and it was the most memorable series of all. Jack Fingleton would declare that it saved Test cricket and his book, *The Greatest Test of All*, soon became a favourite, almost displacing Graveney's *Cricket Through The Covers*.

By the time I read the book I had followed almost every ball of that series on the radio. Just before the series began I had finally persuaded my father to get me a proper radio that could receive shortwave broadcasts. My father had resisted this in the past because he felt it would distract me from my studies. So, during the series I would wake early and before going to school listen to all the pre-lunch session of play. So did most of my school friends and during that series much of our discussion would centre around events in Sydney, Melbourne, Brisbane and Adelaide. However, I had an advantage over them. Whereas they had to have their lunch at school, my fathers chauffeur would drive me home for lunch. Before that series began it was a routine event. During the series it acquired tremendous significance. It meant that while my schoolmates speculated on the score I could catch the last few overs before the close of play.

I would return after lunch full of myself, aware that I was the only one in school who knew what the close of play score in Australia was. Just before the master arrived I would stride up to the podium on which the master's desk perched. Behind the desk, and just underneath a large cross, hung the class blackboard. I would take the chalk from the monitor and write the score in large capital letters. This often produced comical moments. The monitor usually had the names of boys who had misbehaved and should be caned by the master. Now next to their names would be 230 for two or some such score. In the fourth Test, when the last-wicket pair of Mackay and Kline batted for over an hour to deny the West Indians victory, I, to the bemusement of the cook, missed lunch and sat glued to the radio as Hassett and his fellow commentators described quite the most absorbing closing overs of a match I have ever known. Then I rushed back to give the news to the class. The Australian victory in the final Test in Melbourne, which led to the ticker-tape parade, saw me proclaim Australia's triumph from the blackboard in class VIII to the cheers of my classmates.

We saw no contradiction in our love for Australian cricket and our vision of England as a sporting paradise. We knew nothing about Australia and were completely ignorant of its treatment of the aborigines, or even its white Australia policy which meant most Indians could not migrate to that country. Even had we known it would have made no difference. I think the only piece of non-cricketing news about Australia I ever heard at school was that very few Australians went to university. Australia meant great cricketers and, what is more, unlike top English cricketers, they were willing to tour India.

In general, Australia would get its cricket teams to stop off in India on the way back from an England tour. They often beat the Indians but this policy meant we did see all the great post-war Australian cricketers and we respected them for treating us as equals. In contrast, through the 1950s and 1960s England sent what were very nearly 'B' teams to India. It meant that India often defeated England in India, but we felt the victory was hollow as it was clearly not against the best English side. In contrast, with Australia we saw Benaud, Miller, Lindwall, Harvey, O'Neill, Simpson, Lawry and Burge. They may have had as many tummy problems as the Englishmen but they came and, often, conquered both on the field and off.

Jawaharlal Nehru had long ago explained why the Indians preferred Australians to Englishmen. In *The Discovery of India*, written while he was imprisoned by the British in Ahmadnagar Fort Prison Camp during the Second World War, he said:

> The racial discrimination and treatment of Indians in some of the British dominions and colonies were powerful factors in our determination to break from that group. In particular, South Africa was a constant irritant, and East Africa and Kenya, directly under the British colonial policy. Curiously enough we got on well as individuals with Canadians, Australians, and New Zealanders for they represent new traditions and were free from many of the prejudices and social conservatism of the British.

As in politics so in sports. The Indian sporting love affair with Australia, which started in the 1950s with those radio commentaries I heard in the early morning, continues to this day. Modern-day Indian cricketers love touring Australia and nothing gives them greater satisfaction than in beating Australia. None of them have the same feeling for England. In Australia, even when they are getting beaten, they experience a sporting fellowship and respect they never seem to enjoy in England.

6

Ranji's burden

So far we have discussed the puzzle of Indian cricket. A country that is cricket mad turns out to be not so much mad about the game as mad about the spectacle that is associated – or it has created – around the game. A game that is played in the country not in the structured, organised fashion of village to club, club to county or state and then to national team as in England or Australia but in a more ad hoc, hit-and-miss fashion. But despite the considerable number of individually talented cricketers it has produced, rarely, as one of its best-loved captains the Nawab of Pataudi confesses, have 'they combined to make a composite team which could produce consistent performances over a period of years...When Vijay Merchant or Gavaskar was flourishing, the middle order was brittle: when India had world class spinners there were no opening bowlers. And when Kapil Dev eventually turned up, the spinners had gone'.

It is just as well that an Indian prince should have made the point: cricket, a team game that allows the individual unbridled opportunities for glory should become in India a game where glorious individuals occasionally drag their team to odd moments of triumph. A prince needed to make that point for, in many ways, it is the legacy of the Indian princes' involvement with Indian cricket. The English had promoted the game in an ad hoc fashion: here a governor, there a viceroy, here a district official who particularly liked the game and wanted to see his Indian subjects take to it. The Indian response had come, initially, from the Parsees who, despite having lived in India for almost 1,300 years before the English arrived, understood, or thought they understood, the English sense of alienation in India and saw cricket as forging a bond between the Parsees, the old interlopers in India, and the English, the new interlopers. But what of the Indian princes? What of Ranji – surely here we have examples of a particular group of Indians who had royal blood, promoting and organising cricket in India?

No writer of Indian cricket can ignore the princes, yet few, it seems, have bothered to study their effect on Indian cricket. Virenchee Sagar, the modern business patron, previously mentioned, who employed Gavaskar and a number of other Indian cricketers may be overstating the case when he accused the Indian princes of retarding rather than promoting Indian cricket. But he has a point. Certainly for them, cricket and its promotion was more an outlet for intrigue, pomp and ambition in a troubled age, than a pleasure in promoting cricket for its own sake. Indian Princes had a role to play in cricket. They did shape Indian cricket. It was not quite as beneficent and benevolent a role as it has been made out to be. Princely patronage, down the ages, has always had a touch of capriciousness that is almost a princely prerogative. But if the princely patronage of Indian cricket came late, spasmodically and was motivated by political and social ambitions, it reflected individual princely fears and hopes about the future of Princely India.

Princely India was unique. In 1929 a British committee reporting on Princely India, the Report of the Indian States, 1928–9 (Cmd. 3302), said: 'It is generally agreed that the States are *sui generis*, that there is no parallel to their position in history, that they are governed by a body of convention and usage not quite like anything in the world.' So unique were they that British officials thought that the only historical parallel was provided by the position of the princes of the Holy Roman Empire at the beginning of the nineteenth century. And at one stage during the Raj, the Indian Political Department prepared a memorandum on the unification of the German states which they hoped would provide some clues as to what would be the final position of princely India, once Britain withdrew from India. It has even been suggested that Mountbatten used this memorandum to convince the Indian princes to become part of India once the British had gone, but this seems somewhat unlikely.

Princely India was the most vivid illustration of the unique, one is inclined to say curious, nature of British rule in India. The British were supreme in India, but, as we have seen, they did not rule all of India. A third of the country was ruled by native Indian princes. Their relationship with the British government was defined by treaties of the eighteenth and early nineteenth centuries and fashioned by the slow, inexorable spread of British rule in India. Princely intrigue and endless machinations had opened the way for the British conquest of India. Treaties defined the relationship between the British Raj and those Indian princes, who, shrewdly realising the new power in India, came to terms with it. This was the doctrine of paramountcy. It was a British version of a fairly ancient Indian practice where Indian princes conceded certain powers to the dominant central ruler in return for rights and privileges. The princes recognised that the British were the paramount power in India with the princes enjoying – or claiming – sovereign status in the internal affairs of their own states.

This was the broad picture but there were many variations. Only about 40 of the 562 princes who made up princely India had treaties with the crown and saw themselves as allies of the crown, but resisted British

interference in their internal affairs. Many of the princes were so small
that they were no more than county squires and, in time, the British
developed a theory of unlimited paramountcy of the crown. Their
supremacy, they argued, arose from their conquest of the country, not from
any treaties they had signed with the princes, and it was this that was the
source from which the princes derived their own internal sovereignty.
Paramountcy was the subject of endless debate and discussion between
the princes and the Raj. The British did intervene in the internal affairs of
princes, and occasionally ousted a bad ruler. But generally they allowed
the princes to get on with their own internal affairs as long as they were
loyal to the crown. The British, buffeted by the growing tide of
nationalism in India, found the princes an important bulwark against the
democracy and change demanded by other Indians. Indeed, viceroys
aware of the need to use the princes to thwart the Indian nationalists often
drew back from pressing for internal reforms when faced with princely
opposition.

The Raj in India was a mosaic of many interests. The British strategy
was to ensure that enough of the interested groups supported them and
helped neutralise the growing power of the nationalists. It was British
attempts to appease the nationalists after the First World War that altered
the princely perception of their place in the Raj and led to some of them
patronising cricket. The first and most astounding thing about the Indian
princes' involvement with cricket was that it came so late in the history of
the Raj – and it prospered for no more than two decades. As Dr Richard
Cashman has pointed out, it was not until the 1920s that Indian princes
really took to cricket, and by the late 1940s the princely patrons had been
replaced by businessmen and bankers. Those two decades were years of
princely political debate in India – they also saw the flourishing of
princely money and the patronage of cricket. Political intrigue in the
Chamber of Princes went hand in hand with patronage and intrigue on
the cricketing field. The Raj's love for cricket was used as a lever to secure
a better Princely political position.

The statement by the Secretary of State for India in 1917 that India
should work towards 'self-governing institutions' was a threat to the
princes' power. The Chamber of Princes was a sop to soothe their fears. Its
very structure was meant for what may be called the 'middle-class' prince –
not small enough to be totally disregarded, but not really big enough to
parlez directly with the British government. Thus of the chamber's 120
members, not a single one represented the 327 rulers of tiny states
who together ruled a population of just under one million. A further 127
states, which ruled eight million, had just 12 members. Only 108 princes
enjoyed individual representation. Here again, and this point is crucial, it

was the middling prince who really dominated the chamber and the standing committee of 7 princes which acted as the chamber's executive. The middling princes were as shown in Table 6.1.

These middling states had only 4.8 million of the 70 million people who were ruled by the Indian princes. The really great states of princely India – Hyderabad in the south with a population of 12.5 million and as big as France, Mysore with a population of 6 million, Cochin with a population of 1 million, Travancore with a population of 4 million, Baroda with a population of 2 million, Kolhapur with a population of 0.8 million, Jaipur with a population of 2.3 million, Jodhpur with a population of 1.8 million and Udaipur with a population of 1.4 million played no part in the chamber's affairs. They were represented, but that was nominal, they were big enough to argue their own case with the British and they resented any suggestion of parity with the lesser princes who dominated the chamber.

Just as the bigger princes had no need for the chamber, so they had no need for cricket. It was the middle-class princes calling the tune in the Chamber of Princes who also lavished their love and money on cricket.

Some of the larger states did promote cricket but, as in Hyderabad, this was the work of *jagirdars* – country squires – rather than of the ruler. The ruler of Hyderabad, the Nizam, said to be one of the richest, was also one of the meanest men in the world and his personal habits were so frugal that his parsimony became a legend. But he overcame this to become a great patron of arts and a keen scholar of languages such as Arabic, Persian, Hindi and Urdu. The game in Hyderabad developed because of Nawab Moin-Ud-Doula and Nawab Behram-Ud-Doula. Moin-Ud-Doula donated a gold cup named after him for an annual tournament which brought together the best players in the country as did his colleague, Nawab Behram-Ud-Doula. The Nizam cared little for cricket but it was these country squires, who owed their position to the Nizam, whose patronage encouraged the game in that state. Similar stories of minor aristocrats encouraging the game, either because they loved it, or because they saw it

Table 6.1 Princely states and population

Princely state	Population (million)
Patiala	1.5
Bikaner	0.6
Alwar	0.7
Dholpur	0.23
Bhopal	0.7
Kutch	0.48
Nawanagar	0.34

as a way of increasing their influence, formed part of the princely involvement with cricket in India. Thus Raja Dhanarajgiriji, another wealthy country squire, encouraged one of India's most colourful batsman, Mushtaq Ali; and Raja of Jath, who ruled a very small state of less than 100,000 people, imported Clarrie Grimmett to coach Vijay Hazare – one of India's great cricketers. Baroda, one of the heavyweight states, did come to cricket but not until the 1940s when the equation: *cricket patronage = political power* was no longer valid.

Statistics in cricket can mean a lot or nothing but Table 6.2 which shows the princely states, their size and their influence in Indian cricket, is strikingly illustrative.

One prince who became a 'name' in cricket was the Maharaj Kumar of Vizianagram. Although he was classified as a prince and passed himself off as one, he was not really a prince. And though he played Test cricket for India, captained India in three Tests in England, he was no Test cricketer, or even a first-class cricketer. The title Maharaj Kumar, in a very subtle Indian princely way, suggested this. The normal title for a Hindu prince in India is Maharaja, if he is a major prince, or Raja if he is a minor one. Muslim princes tend to have the title Nawab. Maharaj Kumar, literally, meant son of a prince – Kumar means young man – and the English equivalent would be the title of 'the honourable' for sons of peers who do not ascend to the title.

Vizianagram is a very small princely area in the southern state of Andhra Pradesh. Vizzy, as he was popularly known, did not succeed to the title, and had so much trouble with his nephew – who eventually did succeed – that he left his homeland to migrate to Benares in Uttar Pradesh, nearly a thousand miles away, to live on the Zamindara (landed estate) owned by the Vizianagram house. He was the classic case, as Indians put it, of the Maharaja of *Kuch bhi nahi* – meaning the Maharaja of nothing – and who did not do very much either! But he had a palace in Benares, which counted as a great status symbol, and a means to promote cricket. His private pitch on the palace grounds had E. H. Sewell, covering the MCC tour of India of 1933–4, in raptures – 'the appointments of the ground are well nigh perfect . . . the light is splendid. The white building of the palace, which is parallel to the pitch, and the sea green of the screen, both assisting to that end'.

It was on this pitch that Douglas Jardine's team suffered their first and only defeat of the tour. Vizzy often recruited some of the leading players of the day for his team for a match, a season or even a tour. During the 1930–1 season he organised a tour of India and Ceylon to compensate for the cancellation of the MCC tour and persuaded Jack Hobbs and Herbert Sutcliffe – neither being readily open to persuasion – to join his team.

In 1934 Constantine was brought to India. Vizzy never persuaded Donald Bradman to join his team but made a film of Bradman giving Vizzy batting lessons after the Oval Test of 1930, and proudly told Indians that 'films of these lessons have been taken and these will be shown whenever necessary and any little batting fault is corrected'. Cynical Indians couldn't help thinking that Vizzy's own batting had so many faults that not even the great Bradman could have corrected them. Players who went on Vizzy's tours did not receive money to protect their amateur status, but many gifts including clothes replete with gold buttons and the Vizianagaram crest, a silver statuette of a batsman, trophies and, often, cash purses at the end of the tour.

Had Vizzy been content with that he would have had a position in Indian cricket similar to the one occupied, and at about the same time, by Sir Julian Cahn in England – a man in love with the game using his money and influence to promote and encourage it. But for Vizzy the other side of patronage was personal ambition – a common failing it would be said with most princes. Patrons need not be altruistic but when their munificence is laced with such deadly ambition, the results can be very damaging. So it was with Vizzy. Vizzy, with a donation of Rs50,000, had helped underwrite the 1932 tour which included India's first ever Test at Lord's. Four years later India returned to England hoping to build on that first experience. Despite losing the 1932 Lord's Test, India's performance had been creditable and left the impression of much hope for the future. But the 1936 tour had barely got under way before such hopes were cruelly dashed, and by the end of it Indian cricket was in a turmoil – the international consequences of which continued to taint it for many a decade. Vizzy was at the very centre of the turmoil.

The 1932 Indian team had been led by the Maharaja of Porbandar. This was Indians mimicking the British cricket division between amateurs and professionals. In English cricket an amateur, whatever his playing merits, was always Captain. In India it was felt that the Captain of the cricket team ought to be a prince. But Porbandar was sensible enough to realise that while socially he made a very acceptable Captain, as a cricketer he was not up to much. He played in the first four matches making 0, 2, 0, 2, 2, averaging 0.66 and it was said of him that he was the only first-class cricketer in England who had more Rolls-Royces than runs. So for the Test match C. K. Nayudu, India's greatest cricketer of that era, captained the side. Keeping up with the Joneses also tends to be a princely habit – at least in India – and long before the 1936 tour Vizzy had set out his stall to acquire the captaincy. In fact he had been appointed as Deputy Vice-Captain – a post that almost defies description – on the 1932 tour but had withdrawn with the rather mysterious claim that he was 'making this

Table 6.2 Princely states: patronage and effect

Name of princely state	Size in square miles	Population (1931)	Test player	Cricket specialisation	Captaincy
Northern India					
Patiala	5,932	1,625,520	Yuvraj of Patiala	Batsman	Captain (unofficial test)
Jammu and Kashmir	85,884	3,646,243	—	—	—
Pataudi	53	18,873	Iftikhar Ali Pataudi	Batsman	Captain
			Mansur Ali Khan Pataudi	Batsman	Captain
Rajastan					
Udaipur (Mewar)	12,915	1,566,910	—	—	—
Banswara	1,606	225,106	Hanumant Singh	Batsman	—
Dungarpur	1,447	227,544	—	—	—
Western India					
Baroda	8,135	2,443,007	D. K. Gaekwad	Batsman	Captain
			A. D. Gaekwad	Batsman	—
Kolhapur	3,217	957,137	J. M. Ghorparde	Batsman	—
Junagadh	3,337	545,152	—	—	—
Nawanagar	3,791	409,192	K. S. Ranjitsinhji	Batsman	—
			K. S. Duleepsinhji	Batsman	—
			K. S. Indrajitsinh	Wicketkeeper	—

Jath	909	90,102	—
Porbandar	642	115,673	—
Limbdi	344	40,080	—
Bilka	167	45,000	Yajurvindra Singh	Batsman
Wadhawan	243	42,602	—
Central India			
Gwalior	26,383	3,523,070	—
Indore	9,570	1,318,217	—
Bhopal	6,902	729,555	—
Dewas Senior	449	83,321	—
Alirajpur	836	101,963	—
Bengal			
Cooch Behar	1,318	590,886	—
Southern India			
Hyderabad (Nawab Moin-Ul-Doula)	82,698	14,436,148	—
	—	276,533	—
Vizianagram (Zamindari Lands, UP)	21	—	Maharaj Kumar of Vizianagram	Batsman	Captain

Source: Richard Cashman, *Players, Patrons and Crowds*, New Delhi, 1980, p. 123.

immense sacrifice for the sake of the future of cricket in India'. To cynics this had sounded like Vizzy doubletalk to cover up his disappointment that he was only number three in the side, next to two other Princes, a position that hurt his ego. So, in 1936 he wished to take no chances.

The full story of how Vizzy became Captain of the 1936 tour may never be told, so enmeshed is it in princely politics of the time. But an outline is possible, and instructive. It began, amazingly, two years before the tour when the Nawab of Pataudi Senior returned to India. The son-in-law of the Nawab of Bhopal, whose influence on the Indian Board matched that in the Chamber of Princes, Pataudi was a clear frontrunner to lead India. He had made his debut for England against Australia on Jardine's Bodyline tour of 1932–3, scoring a century in his first Test. He had then been dropped (he did not get on with Jardine) and now back in India he declared himself ready to play for India. Indian cricket seemed to have found its saviour. Ranji couldn't play for India, as in his time India didn't have a Test team. He had also dissuaded his nephew Duleep from paying for India and many Indians had commented caustically on Duleep's preference for England over India. Pataudi's belated acceptance of India overjoyed them. On 29 October 1934 Pataudi was voted Captain of the Indian team to tour England in 1936, beating his opponent C. K. Nayudu by a handsome margin – Nayudu getting only four votes.

Long term is a good thing but this was still an amazing decision. The tour was eighteen months away. Pataudi was known to be in indifferent health, it had broken down during both the 1933 and the 1934 English seasons. Why then was he appointed Captain 18 months in advance? Perhaps euphoria had gotten the better of the Indians, though the cynical explanation that emerged later was that it was meant to pave the way for Vizzy to become Captain.

It is hard to deny this cynicism. As the months went on Pataudi's health did not improve and, some months before the tour, he withdrew, citing his ill health as the reason. Many doubted this and some of his friends later told an Indian cricket writer that he had withdrawn 'for reasons of state'. For reasons of Vizzy is more like it; Pataudi had served his purpose as a stalking horse for Vizzy. In 1934 had Vizzy been proposed as Captain, in place of Nayudu, he would have stood little or no earthly chance. Pataudi with the glamour of his having played for England could easily beat Nayudu. And with Nayudu defeated, Vizzy could now spin his web of captaincy intrigue.

Vizzy may have been a poor cricketer but off the field he was a shrewd politician. The federal structure of the country meant regional imbalance and Vizzy astutely promised disaffected state associations better representation in the Indian team. A selector and respected former cricketer Dr Kanga had already resigned on grounds of 'Princely interference', and there was the intriguing presence of Major Brittain Jones, who, for some bizarre reason, was representing Rajputana on the Indian Board. Behind these men was Lord Willingdon, the Viceroy of India, who was a friend of Vizzy and like all British administrators saw the Princes as a bulwark against the rising tide of nationalism. He was keen to have his man as Captain in England. The result was one of the strangest teams ever to leave on a cricket tour. Vizzy was appointed Captain and there was no Vice-Captain and no Tour Selection Committee. All the decisions rested with Vizzy, assisted by Major Brittain Jones, who became the Manager. The price of political lobbying is bloated cricket teams and the Indians finally comprised 21 players. It was not so much a team as a prince's retinue; Vizzy, travelling with 'thirty six items of personal luggage and two servants'.

Picture the scene. Vizzy, a plumpish, rather hunched figure, perpetually standing in the slips and peering through spectacles at a game he did not seem to understand. With reason one is inclined to add. England not only marked his debut as a Captain of India, but also his debut in first-class cricket. The matches in India he had taken part in were not by English standards first class, and he was yet to play in the Ranji Trophy. In the past, when he had captained his own team in matches in India, he had used the experience of players like Nayudu to help set the field, or change the bowling. In England helpful suggestions of that nature from Vizzy's team mates, and even in the English press, seemed to incense him. Vizzy's reaction was to be even more capricious and this was to lead to the tour's great explosion. Lala Amarnath who had made a spectacular century on his debut against Jardine's England team two years previously in India, had shown much promise on the tour. He had scored over 600 runs and taken 32 wickets. But in a match against the Minor Counties, Amarnath, padded up and ready to bat, found himself waiting while others lower down the batting order were promoted. His reaction was strong, characteristically Punjabi and, no doubt, he was rather rude about Vizzy and his captaincy. All this was faithfully reported back to the prince who, egged on by Major Brittain Jones, and perhaps, Lord Willingdon, decided that Amarnath had to be sent home.

During his lifetime Amarnath never gave his side of the story. When I approached him during research for my book *The History of Indian Cricket*, he said he was about to reveal everything in his book. That never emerged, but in 2004, four years after his death, his son Rajender published a biography of his father *The Making of a Legend: Lala Amarnath, Life & Times* which for the first time contained some details of Amarnath's side of the story. This is what Rajender says:

> The match against Minor Counties was especially important as he had struggled with form due to injuries. With the weather playing

spoilsport and performance not up to expectation, Amarnath wanted desperately to score runs to boost his confidence. The Indians won the toss and batted first. The captain asked him to be ready as he was to bat at number four or five. At the same time, Mushtaq Ali was asked to pad up as well. When Hindlekar got out, Mushtaq went in and played out the day to remain not out along with Merchant. The following day, when Mushtaq got out after a fruitful partnership, Vizzy sent in Amar Singh to bat with Amaranth waiting padded up. He waited patiently till another wicket fell. He got up to pick his bat when he saw C. S. Nayudu marching towards the ground. Unable to control himself, he went up to the captain and asked if he still wanted him to keep his pads on 'Yes, keep them on, you'll be sent in,' Vizzy replied curtly. Confused at this treatment, he kept quiet but was beginning to rage with anger.

Amarnath had his pads on all afternoon as well and, yet at the fall of the fourth wicket, Wazir Ali was ordered to go ahead of him, frustrating him further. Such moves clearly demonstrated that the captain was playing everything but cricket. By now, Amarnath's sore back had become stiff and painful from sitting and waiting for his turn to bat. The shadows had lengthened and Amarnath presumed there would be a night-watchman padded. It was at such a moment that Wazir Ali got out. Vizzy looked at Amarnath and said 'Your turn.' Reluctantly, Amarnath went in and played out time, remaining one not out. Furious at the treatment by the captain, he returned to the dressing room an annoyed man. Removing his gloves and then pads, he threw them one another into his kit bag in one corner of the room. In typical Lahori Punjabi, he then mumbled aloud 'xxx xxx aasi vi bari cricket khel li hai char saal tonh, asi koi bevkoof nahi haan saano sab pata hai! (I have played enough cricket in the last four years and I'm no fool, I know what is transpiring!)' The treasurer, Hadi, then walked up to an unhappy Amarnath and asked him if his sore back need a massage. 'I don't need any bloody massage,' Amarnath shot back. Vizzy was sitting and watching everything but, like his colleagues from the southern or western parts of India, could not understand any Punjabi. Yet, he asked Amaranth if he was talking to him. 'I am not talking to anybody, in particular, nor do I wish to speak to anyone,' he replied. Many years later, Amarnath told me in private 'That is all that transpired in the dressing room before the players dispersed to the hotel.'

That evening, there was a conference attended by the supporters of Vizzy in his room, since the majority of the players did not understand Punjabi, a distorted version of the incident reached the manager who had not been present in the dressing room. After the day's play, Major

Jones asked Amarnath to meet him in his room. Changing into fresh clothes, he reached the manager's room. Without wasting any time, Jones produced a letter signed by several players, prominent being those from Vizzy's camp and a couple of others. They had demanded strict action again Amarnath for his behaviour in the dressing room. This came a shock to him and he tried to reason with the Englishman. He was ready to apologise if he had hurt someone's feeling. He also promised to control his emotions and behaviour. No amount of persuasion had any effect on the fastidious manager, who it seemed had already made up his mind. Amarnath was to be sent back home on disciplinary grounds!

Amarnath never explained the slang words he used, just saying they were common slang terms, and it is interesting to observe that even in the twenty-first century Rajender cannot bring himself to tell everything that Lala said that day marking some words with 'x,x,x', suggesting they were swear words. Whatever they were they had their effect.

India's cricket historians are still divided about who really showed Amarnath the red card. Was it Vizzy? Or was it Major Brittain Jones? One theory, perhaps suffering a bit from latter-day nationalist revisionism, states that it was Major Brittain Jones who really wanted Amarnath sent home. As a member of Lord Willingdon's staff, he treated the Indians as people belonging to a subject country. He, so the theory goes, had every reason 'to magnify the Amarnath episode for political gains in order to prove to the world that even a few Indian cricketers couldn't live as a team, let alone a whole nation'. The Government of India Act, 1935, had just been enacted and Indians were being given greater powers, but such public displays of disunity in an Indian cricket team playing in England could be a handy weapon to use to answer Indian nationalists' cry for more freedom. If Indians couldn't manage a cricket team, how could they manage a whole country? Perhaps the nationalist cricket historians are right, though one suspects that if Major Brittain Jones did the stirring, Vizzy and some of his cohorts were willing to be easily stirred.

Willingdon of course, saw himself as the kindly paternal father, bringing up his Indian wards. This was demonstrated very vividly when his wife, Lady Willingdon, decided to hold a lunch at the Ritz hotel in order to cheer up the Indian cricket team. Apart from the team the lunch saw the great and good of the British establishment in attendance including the former governors of Bombay, Brabourne and Lloyd, Lord Hardinge, a former Viceroy of India, and Sir John Simon who, as we have seen, had led the all-white Simon Commission to India in 1928 to decide whether Indians could rule themselves. In retrospect the most interesting

British guest at the lunch was Colonel Pugh Ismay and his wife. Ismay was then the military secretary to the Viceroy – later he would be chief of staff to Winston Churchill and later still, in 1947, chief of staff to Mountbatten presiding over Britain's withdrawal from India. That prospect would have been unthinkable to Willingdon and his wife, as it would have been to the entire British establishment in 1936.

The India Office was very keen to publicise this lunch and wrote to the editors of various newspapers and agencies in England enclosing the guest list along with a short note urging them to give as much publicity as possible. These letters were written by H. MacGregor. The one to the editor of the *Morning Post* said, 'If you can find room for the enclosed you will be doing a real service to our Indian cricketers. It is characteristic of Lady W. to take them in hand when they are down on their luck.' The one to the *East India Association* said 'This is Lady W's method of pouring oil into troubled water and putting new heart into the team. She proposes to send them onto Wimbledon after the lunch.' The one to A. E. Watson, the then editor of the *Daily Telegraph*, said 'Public notice of this little party would mean a great deal to the all Indian team in circumstances, of which you know, are not as happy as they might be.' Earlier MacGregor, in a letter to E. T. Campbell MP, had said about the Indian cricketers, 'They like Indians are the foster children of the Indian office.' And he had tried to generate publicity when the Indian cricketers had visited Parliament early on in the tour. However, while the British provincial newspapers had given it much publicity the London papers had ignored it. Macgregor wanted to avoid the same fate for the Ritz lunch and was keen that the London papers should also mention how concerned the Viceroy and his Vicerene were for these cricketing children who had come from India.

The scenes that followed Amarnath's return to India have a fictional touch about them. According to Anthony de Mello, the secretary of the Indian Board, demonstrations were planned in Mumbai to greet Amarnath as his ship docked and de Mello had to 'kidnap' Amarnath, by smuggling him aboard the pilot launch before the ship docked. He then hid him for a while at the Taj Mahal hotel and when asked where he was gave misleading answers suggesting he might have left Mumbai. This was meant to disperse the crowds that had gathered to see Amarnath and were getting agitated at not being able to greet their hero. De Mello's tactics worked. The crowds spent some hours that day vainly trying to locate him, visiting both railways stations and hotels. That night De Mello was seen dining at a restaurant by some journalists and he agreed to take them to Amarnath whereupon Amarnath sounded conciliatory and was prepared to leave everything to the Board. Led by the Nawab of Bhopal efforts were made to fly Amarnath back to England but Vizzy could not back down and the tour limped on without Amarnath.

Inevitably the dramatic sending off led to a committee of inquiry headed by the then Chief Justice of the Mumbai High Court, Sir John Beaumont. The Beaumont inquiry felt that the action against Amarnath was too severe and stern. As for Vizzy, his performance at social functions where he was 'brilliantly successful' was noted, but the committee found that his batting was below Test standard and that 'he did not understand the placing of the team or the changing of the bowling, and never maintained any regular order in batting'.

The committee had got it just about right. Vizzy was knighted during the tour but the tour was a disaster. But if the Beaumont enquiry meant the end of Vizzy's playing career, the cricket politician in him never gave up and for the next three decades, until his death, his hand and his purse pursued many a scheme, doing some good but wrecking many plans.

In the process he sustained a princely legacy that has continued to haunt Indian cricket. A legacy of unbridled individualism, which could often be destructive, of sudden caprice followed by sudden munificence, of charming generosity destroyed by wilful malice, and of a game which was meant to combine the highest of individual talents and the noblest of team spirits, converted into an exotic display of individual arrogance. Some flavour of this can be found in this description by H. G. Wickham, a member of the northern Indian police service between 1904–22, of the Maharaja of Kashmir at play:

> At 3 o'clock in the afternoon the Maharaja himself would come down to the Ground, the band would play the Kashmir anthem, salaams were made and he then went off to a special tent where he sat for a time, smoking his long water-pipe. At 4.30 or thereabouts he decided he would bat. It didn't matter which side was batting, his own team or ours. He was padded by two attendants and gloved by two more. Somebody carried his bat and he walked to the wicket looking very dignified but very small and with an enormous turban upon his head. In one of the matches I happened to be bowling and my first ball hit his stumps, but the wicketkeeper quick as lightning called 'No Ball' and the match went on. The only way that the Maharaja could get out was by lbw. And after fifteen or twenty minutes batting he said he felt tired and he was duly given out lbw. What the scorer did about his innings, which was never less than half a century, goodness only knows.

The eccentric Maharaja is not always destructive. The house of Patiala was India's most beneficent princely patron. Yet Rajendra Singh, who started the cricket tradition at Patiala, took to the game because he was bored. In the nineteenth century, like all Indian princes, Rajendra Singh had taken a keen interest in polo and pig-sticking. The early 1890s had seen Rajendra Singh's polo team win the Punjab Polo cup four times, the Simla-based Beresford Cup three times, with his horses also winning two Viceroy's cups, and four civil service cups. The year 1895 saw a marvellous victory over the rival royal house of Jodhpur in the Punjab tournament and this seems to have satiated Rajendra Singh's appetite. He required a new challenge and took to cricket. Within three years the Patiala Eleven was one of the best in the country, consisting of Ranji, English professionals like Jack Herd, the Middlesex bowler, W. Brockwell, the Surrey batsman and Arthur Priestly, MP for Grantham, friend of Ranji and a decent enough amateur cricketer. In addition to these, the Patiala team had several very good Indian players including the leading player K. M. Mistri.

Rajendra Singh's impact on cricket was great. The Patiala team set a standard that others followed. Rajendra Singh's son, Bhupinder Singh, successfully combined cricketing pleasures with other pleasures. He surrounded himself with several hundred wives and concubines and his palace included a scented swimming pool. He often went to bat in bright pink and blue turbans adorned with expensive pearl earrings. Once when he was playing for the MCC one of the earrings was lost and play was held up for several minutes. Bhupinder, like most cricketing princes, used cricket to promote his politics and vice versa. Like his father he too brought out leading English professionals to India; George Hurst, Wilfred Rhodes, Maurice Leyland, Harold Larwood and the Australian-born Frank Tarrant. In many ways Bhupinder Singh went further than his father. Whereas Rajendra Singh had concentrated mostly on cricket in Patiala, Bhupinder organised, financed and captained the 1911 tour of an Indian team to England, helped establish the Indian Board of Control, donated money for pavilions and trophies, including the Ranji trophy, and did much to encourage the game. His son, the Yuvraj of Patiala was probably one of the finest cricketers to play for India – albeit in unofficial Tests – and had he had some relish for the cricketing intrigues so intrinsically part of Indian cricket he might well have been the Captain of the ill-fated 1936 tour. A tall, hard-hitting batsman, the Yuvraj seemed to combine both the batting dash associated with cricketing princes – his grandfather once scored 21 runs in just eight and a half minutes – and the chivalry which is the hallmark of any prince. In one of the unofficial Tests that he played in, the Yuvraj, coming in with the score at 66 for 4, hit five 6s and one 4 in just 30 minutes. It could not prevent the Indians from being soundly beaten but it embellished the princely legend of batting.

Although Bhupinder, like his father, did a great deal for Indian cricket, inevitably his cricketing and political interests clashed. Often while he was immersed in politics, coaches would find they had nothing to do but kill time. They would lose interest in cricket coaching and drift away in disgust. Perhaps the whole nature of princely patronage of Indian cricket and its consequences would have been different had Ranji played a part in it. But he didn't and it is his legacy that is the most difficult for Indian cricket.

Of Ranji's place in cricket there can be no conceivable doubt. In *The Complete Who's Who of Test Cricketers*, Ranji is the legendary prince who 'brought Eastern magic to the cricket fields of England, America and Australia'. One of his biographers, Alan Ross, was convinced that Ranji was one of only half a dozen in the history of the game who have added something new to it. 'His true memorial is in the memory of those who saw him, transmitted down the generations: a shiver of the spine at Hove or Lord's, the air fined with that latest of late cuts, that silkiest of glances. The Indian prince, in all his finery, abroad in an English summer.' Ranji was a giant in the golden age of cricket – indeed his deeds, and his cricketing style and genius, made the golden age. But that was an English golden age of cricket. How much of an Indian prince was he? What could he do for Indian cricket?

Alan Ross accepts that Ranji was alienated from Indian cricket. His biography ends with two postscripts. The first of these assesses Ranji's contribution to the game, the second presents what is called 'An Indian View'. The Indian view is that of Anthony de Mello, one of India's great cricket administrators and a founder of the Indian Board of Control. Writing in *A Portrait of Indian Sport* in 1959 de Mello bluntly states:

> Ranji did absolutely nothing for Indian sport and sportsmen. To all our requests for aid, encouragement and advice, Ranji gave but one answer: Duleep and I are English cricketers. He could not have been more blunt. In short, Ranji was a different man in England than in India ... In most other walks of life he was a model Indian Prince. But the Ranji who settled in Jamnagar after the First World War was an all together different man from the great cricketer who delighted English crowds in earlier years ... it is understandable that when he finally left England to live in India he should leave something behind him. There was talk too of an unhappy love affair; and certainly as an Indian Prince Ranji could not have married an English girl, if true, it would take us a step nearer to the explanation why Ranji left his heart somewhere among the green fields of England.

De Mello, while acknowledging Ranji's work in Nawanagar, is scathing about Popsey the 'ironic, bitter parrot, who seemed closer to him than any man'. De Mello concluded that 'towards the end of his life, he gave the impression that he was disillusioned', waiting for something he knew he would never have. Ross suggests extenuating circumstances. Ranji came into cricketing prominence when there was no Indian cricket at Test level, or for that matter, at national level. All of his serious cricket was played in England and, inevitably, he was happiest with the friends he had made in the formative period of his cricketing life. But something more than this mere recital of historical facts is necessary to understand de Mello's expression of Ranji's alienation.

For a start he was not only alienated from Indian cricket he was also, in many ways, alienated from Indian life. Ranji's official biographers accepted that he felt more at home in England than in India. Roland Wild, in his official biography published in 1934, a year after Ranji's death, wrote. 'More than once it is remarked that the Jam Saheb seemed to attain the peak of his enjoyment only when in the company of his English guests.' Wild did not appreciate how ironic this was. Some years after Ranji left Rajkumar College for Cambridge, Lord Curzon, then Viceroy of India, came to the college to make a speech-day address and reiterated the philosophy that guided the institution. The aim he said was not like Macaulay's, to turn Indians into Englishmen. 'The Anglicised Indian is not a more attractive spectacle in my eyes than the Indianised Englishman. Both are hybrids of an unnatural type. No ... After all, those Kumars who became Chiefs are called upon to rule, not an English but an Indian people; and as a Prince who is to have any influence and to justify his own existence, must be one with his subjects, it is clear that it is not by English models alone, but by an adoption of Eastern prescriptions to the Western standard that he can hope to succeed.' Ranji, educated to be an Indian who could use English methods to improve his rule turned out to be the exact opposite: an Indian who could teach the English something about their own national game. What is more, he left his heart in England when he finally returned to India.

Until recently Ranji's biographers have said little about his love life. Indian Princes, as de Mello said, were indeed discouraged from marrying English girls. Wild, writing when the Raj did not believe its rule in India would end, said nothing. Alan Ross, writing long after the Raj was history, is eloquent about Ranji's cricket and his role as a prince, but is mysteriously silent about his private life. We are not told why Ranji never married or, if, indeed, there was an English love in his life. De Mello's insinuation there may have been an English girl involved is quoted, but not explained.

Since the 1990s biographers have become less reticent and there has been more research done on Ranji's private life. From all this it is clear that Ranji's love for England was deepened by his love for an English woman. But there still remains a mystery as to whether there was more than one Englishwoman involved.

The first peek at Ranji's private life came in Simon Wilde's biography of Ranji in 1990. Wilde said the love of his life was Edith, the daughter of Louis Borissow, the chaplain of Trinity College, Cambridge. For obvious reasons this was a love he could not declare when he was alive. The love had to be so clandestine that, says Wilde, he had a secret passage built in his palace connecting their two rooms. The idea of intermarriage scandalised both the English and the Indians, and the idea of an Indian ruler marrying a European seriously alarmed the India Office. It raised all sorts of diplomatic and social problems for the Raj, built as it was on the idea that the white woman was sacrosanct and any Indian going to bed with her would defile the whole idea of the Raj.

But Wilde, while the first Ranji biographer to talk about his private life, uncovered no firsthand details of this love affair. More recently the historian Boria Majumdar has broken fresh ground by discovering real evidence of a love affair complete with letters from Ranji that indicate beyond doubt that there was one, possibly two women Ranji was in love with while in England. Neither of them was Edith.

The beginnings could not have been more romantic. It is 1890. Ranji, then a student in Cambridge, is cycling past a huge grocery store called Bond and Holmes located at Sidney Street. The owner of the store has two daughters, Mary and Minnie, who are immediately captivated by this Indian prince; there could not have been many Indians in Cambridge then, let alone Indian princes. They immediately signal to him in the style of the time: one of them drops her handkerchief, Ranji picks it up and the romance begins.

Ranji visits them, slowly discovers the girls names, gets to know their parents who he calls father and mother, and writes letters. In the first letter to Mary he addresses her as 'M.H', by the time of the third letter she has become 'dear Madge'. Some of the letters are in verse. Ranji claims they are either verses he has himself written or that he has translated from the vernacular Indian languages. In fact he had copied them from Shelley's *Lines to an Indian Air*. Some of the verses to Mary leave little doubt Ranji was in love:

I loved thee once, I love thee still

And fell this world asunder
My loves eternal flame would rise
Midst chaos crash and thunder.
Two rubies on those lips of thine
Unrivalled in fresh glory
Happy is the man to whom
They whisper their love story.

Ranji in his letters comes over as any other love-torn youngster. Once, on the advice of a friend called Hussain he tried to make Madge jealous by saying there was another girl in London he was friendly with and when that failed apologised abjectly. 'I shall never forgive him for the trick. I am so awfully ashamed of acting accordingly but you must forgive me for doing so unless you wish to make me unhappy and sad. I love you only and I did not think I could be fond of anyone as I am of you and of Minnie. I hope you will forgive me.'

Ranji also gave the girls many presents, including bicycles and jewellery and took them on picnics and expeditions. Ranji's extravagance often landed him in debt but there was no marriage. Majumdar, concludes:

> While Mary had married in 1898 seeing that her affair with Ranji was going nowhere because of their colour difference, Minnie was deeply attached to him and preferred to stay unmarried all her life. This seems possible, for Ranji was in constant touch with Minnie even when he had not written to Madge from India. However, Mary had never forgotten her first love and had a large photo portrait of Ranji with his bat with her in her old age. What we don't know is whether Mary, whose husband had abandoned her and six surviving children, and who was on the verge of destitution, received any support from Ranji after he became the Jam Sahib of Nawanagar in 1907. We will also not know whether Ranji would have preferred to stay unmarried to honour his relationships with Mary or Minnie Holmes. This suspicion is strengthened when we hear about the statue of a British woman Ranji had erected in his native state in the 1920s. His biographers have wondered whether it was of Edith Borissow, daughter of the Chaplain of Trinity, the Rev Louis Borissow, who had looked after Ranji when he arrived in Cambridge. The discovery of his letters to Mary suggests otherwise.

These discoveries also suggest that Ranji's cricketing story is more than just a case, as Sir Edwin Arnold said, indulging in the height of Victorian sentimentality, of a 'star from the east' bursting upon the cricketing world. If such a star did burst it was a cool, calculating star which knew exactly where it was going to land and how. Ranji had wonderful natural gifts, perhaps no other cricketer before or since has had such gifts. His dedication and his discipline were exemplary, enabling him to harness those talents and create a batting revolution. But at the same time he saw cricket as a weapon – a weapon for his own personal advancement. There need be no dishonour in that. For in a sense, Ranji's is a very modern story of an immigrant who seeks fame, glory and money in a foreign land, and then returns to his own land to use his foreign money and prestige to establish himself. Ranji did not earn money in England, but the prestige he earned from cricket was invaluable.

The modern immigrant does it by setting up a business or occasionally winning success in the field of sciences or medicine. Ranji was the first to do it on a cricket field. Like many an immigrant Ranji did perhaps create an impression of wealth and standing back home that may not have passed critical, modern scrutiny. Strictly speaking, Ranji was not a prince, nor a direct descendant of the rulers, but the grandson of an officer who had served the state and hailed from a village that in comparison makes Bradman's Bowral look rich. He was initially adopted by the ruler as his successor but was then ignored. When he came to England he had no official status. Nawanagar was an insignificant kingdom where plague alternated with famine – in the ten years after Ranji became ruler in 1907 there were four famines – nature had given it little, nor had its rulers done much better. But in England all this was obscured by a lifestyle that lived up to every occidental's idea of Indian princely behaviour. While this meant that Ranji was often in debt, that was a small price to pay to establish the princely cricketer. Cricket, Ranji quickly sensed, was the key that could unlock the door to social acceptability in the highest class in England.

The making of Ranji as the prince among cricketers also helped with establishing Ranji the ruler. When he returned to India in November 1904, his fame as one of the great cricketers of the world established, there seemed no chance that he would become the ruler. But Ranji kept up his socialising both of fellow princes and, more particularly, of British officials who would have to decide should a successor become necessary. This seemed unlikely as the then ruler was younger than Ranji, but suddenly he died of typhoid and British officials ruled in Ranji' s favour as the natural choice. On 10 March 1907 Ranji became the ruler of Nawanagar.

After that he discouraged all talk of cricket, but whenever the need arose he used cricket to further his plans. Thus, just after the First World War, he returned to England to play cricket. He was 48, had lost an eye in a shooting accident, and had no other cricket fields left to conquer. But he played thrice for Sussex – scoring 16, 9 and 13 – a pale, rotund shadow of the pre-war Ranji. He explained that he wanted to write a book on the art of batting with one eye, also that the king wished him to play.

To keep the king sweet, was, perhaps, the real reason. For years Ranji had harboured the ambition of making his state a major princely power. Before Ranji, it was too small to merit more than passing reference.

Nawanagar came at the bottom of the middle table of princely states and was not big enough to enjoy the status that a princely state like Baroda or Hyderabad enjoyed. It was only in the summer of 1920 that Ranji finally persuaded Edwin Montagu, Secretary of State for India, to grant Nawanagar such a status. A statue of Montagu was erected in Jamnagar, the capital, and King George V was humoured by Ranji coming out of retirement to play cricket. Ranji knew how well cricket and diplomacy could be made to work.

It was Ranji's example of combining cricket and politics that had the biggest influence on India and its cricket. His fellow princes had eagerly followed his career and noted how cricket had carved Ranji a position he would otherwise not have gained. The Ranji story suggested that they could use Indian cricket to further their own political ambitions. It marked the next stage in the development of the game in India.

This point is important with respect to Ranji because of the way de Mello and other Indians argue that Ranji did nothing for Indian cricket.

'Nothing' is perhaps rather a strong word. De Mello is not a disinterested witness and Ranji did play cricket very regularly in India until 1915 when his duties as ruler of Nawanagar took precedence. He shared cricket coaches with other states and in unobtrusive ways encouraged youngsters to play. He was the first to observe the potential of one of India's finest fast bowlers: Amar Singh. Perhaps Ranji felt it was enough to set a wonderful example by his personal deeds – propagating, as Alan Ross puts it, 'the idea of Ranji, the awareness that it was an Indian who had become the greatest batsman in the world', Certainly this idea of Ranji exercised a powerful influence on Indian minds. Even today school children in India read with delight and wonder Neville Cardus's marvellous essay on Ranji as told in a probably apocryphal story of the Yorkshire bowler Ted Wainwright. Every year Yorkshire would come down to Hove, the moist air would be heavy, Wainwright would grab a couple of early wickets and then Ranji and Fry would get together and by the end of the day the score would be 300 for 2. This essay was part of our school syllabus and certainly the idea of Ranji, the Indian, dominating Yorkshire, the might of England, had a great effect on us. Cardus tells the story through Ted Wainwright, the Yorkshire bowler, and while Indian schoolchildren struggle with Wainwright's Yorkshire dialect, there can be no mistaking the strong romantic image he conjures up of an Indian conquering the English cricket field. With India a colony of the British, and Indians made to feel that the British were their superiors in all things, this image of Ranji played an important part in fostering Indian pride and self-respect. However, Ross may be exaggerating slightly when he said that this 'contributed more than anything else to the Indian cricketer's realisation of his own possibilities'.

The more relevant question is, 'Did Ranji ever consider himself an Indian?' I do not mean it in the sense that de Mello and Ross do, of Ranji considering himself an English cricketer as opposed to an Indian one. I mean did he consider himself an Indian as I consider myself an Indian, or the editor of this book Derek Wyatt considers himself English? This is not as arcane as it may sound. It goes to the very heart of Ranji's legacy. Ranji, said John Lord in *The Maharajas*, was 'the first Indian of any kind to become universally known and popular'. Although this is rather an English-centred view, reflecting the idea that only an Indian who had made a reputation in England was truly world famous, it nevertheless emphasises the position Ranji had attained. But if Ranji did not consider himself to be an Indian, the sentence has no meaning, or a very different one from what the writer intends. In fact Ranji's alleged 'Indianness' has suffered such a curious metamorphosis that in Scyld Berry's *Cricketwallah* Ranji, amazingly, appears as an Indian nationalist fighting the British for Indian independence. According to Berry, Ranji, while Chancellor in the Chamber of Princes, had a serious disagreement with the Viceroy over India's future. 'Although English in many ways and loyal to the Crown, Ranji wanted independence for India far sooner than the British planned. A few days after this disagreement in New Delhi, he returned to Jamnagar, and died in his bedroom of heart failure.' There was indeed a disagreement, and Ranji did die a few days later, but to read into this Ranji the nationalist opposing the bureaucratic Raj is certainly overdoing things.

Ranji, though born in India, didn't consider himself an Indian, but a Rajput. Roland Wild, who Ranji chose to be his biographer, is eloquent about Ranji's ancestry. The eloquence concentrates on the Rajput race, their ability to trace the clan back through centuries, their ancient pedigree. Throughout Wild's biography, published in 1934, a year after Ranji's death, there is much about Ranji the Rajput but nothing about Ranji the Indian. Ranji's loyalties were to his state, Nawanagar, to his people in Nawanagar and to the King Emperor. Though Nawanagar was too small to have a Treaty of Accession to the Crown, Ranji, like all princes in India, saw a personal link between rule in Nawanagar and the King Emperor's rule over the British Empire. The idea of an Indian nation, let alone one free of British rule, must have struck Ranji as quite absurd.

The background to the dispute between Ranji and the Viceroy centred around the British government's plans to introduce a new method of ruling India. Although the new proposals offered only the slightest concession to Indian nationalism, the Princes refused to accept the new scheme and it was never implemented. Ranji, as Chancellor of the Chamber of Princes, was actively involved in formulating princely opinion. In July 1931, addressing an all party meeting of MPs in the House of Commons, Ranji

made it abundantly clear that he was 'absolutely opposed . . . to all this talk
of independence'. He and the princes would favour federation provided
there were safeguards for the way the princes ran their own states. Later,
when the meeting of the Chambers of Princes took place in New Delhi on
Monday 20 March 1933, Ranji made it clear that he did not support the
British scheme for a federation of states. 'I have nothing but the friendliest
and the most brotherly of sentiments for British India and I wish her
leaders well. I hope that she will attain her aspirations, but I hope she will
do this without involving the States.'

This is not the voice of an Indian nationalist urging independence
from Britain. It is the voice of a prince who keenly felt his Rajput,
Hindu, origins and who was desperately worried that even the limited
reforms the British were introducing in India would damage the ancient
rights of kings. Ranji was no democrat. He was an autocrat and his
autocracy derived its power and authority from what he believed to be
his Rajput inheritance. It was 1933, Hitler was coming to power in
Germany, fascism was on the march and democracy seemed a poor bet.
Ranji, a rather proud Rajput, would no more have advocated independence for India than he would have renounced his Rajput inheritance.
This is not to make a charge against Ranji. He was merely reflecting the
princely ideas and attitudes of the time. So if Ranji did not do much for
Indian cricket it is because he did not think of India as a cricketing
nation. He did not think of India as a cricketing nation because he could
not conceive of India as a political nation. India as a political nation was
born 14 years after Ranji died and, had he lived, as his successors'
actions show, he would have undoubtedly opposed it. He advised Duleep
to play for England rather than India and he did so because to him an
Indian team meant nothing. Had Nawanagar managed to get together a
Test team then, I am sure, Ranji would have advised Duleep to play for
Nawanagar. For, in as much as a king is ever a nationalist, Ranji was a
Nawanagar nationalist. He was, perhaps, a Rajput nationalist, if that
term can have any meaning. He was not an Indian nationalist and to
accuse him, as de Mello does, and other Indians do, of not doing much
for Indian cricket is to miss the point.

This is of particular importance because in recent years Indian writers
have begun to look at Ranji more critically. Mario Rodrigues's *Batting for
the Empire, A Political Biography of Ranjitsinhji* is certainly the most
noteworthy and quite the most controversial of these new works. Based on
extensive research, particularly contemporary newspapers, it demonstrates
how great a supporter of the British Raj he was and also that, contrary to
the image fostered by his hagiographers, he was not a farsighted ruler but

one who was an absentee landlord and much given to squeezing money out of his subjects for his spendthrift ways.

I could not agree more with Ramchandra Guha who in his foreword to the book says that given the tendency of Indian biographers to be deferential, this book represents 'a refreshing departure'. This may explain why it has raised such a storm in India.

But is it fair to present Ranji as some sort of unique villain as this book seeks to do? Guha lays much stress on how 'fanatical' Ranji was in supporting the Raj, contrasting him unfavourably with two of his contemporaries Mahatma Gandhi and Palwankar Baloo. Guha argues that Baloo – from the so-called untouchable Hindu caste, now known as Dalits – could challenge Ranji as India's first great cricketer. Baloo, says Guha, had to overcome such hardships and did it so splendidly that he was even a hero to 'the greatest of all Dalit leaders Dr B. R. Ambedkar'.

But if Ranji is a villain because he collaborated with the Raj than what did Ambedkar do? The moment you raise the question you are suddenly confronted with the horrendously complex reaction British rule produced amongst Indians, and not merely Ranji. The man who Guha hails as the 'greatest of all Dalit leaders' was, if you look back at what he did and said during the Raj, an even greater collaborator than Ranji. The Dalits have been the victims of some of the most evil practices any group of humans have ever perpetrated on others. For centuries the Hindu higher castes considered that not only was the touch of these Hindus a defilement, but in some parts of India, even their shadow could pollute a higher born Hindu. Dr Babasaheb Ambedkar, to give his full name, was a lawyer who did much to uplift his community. In modern India he has almost a god-like status amongst the Dalits, his birthday is a public holiday and Indian school children are taught he drafted the Indian constitution. Yet for all his political life he was also a very vociferous collaborator with the Raj and boasted how untouchables had helped the British conquer India. In 1942, when Gandhi called on the British to quit India, he joined the Viceroy's Executive Council and denounced Gandhi (in terms very like the ones the Raj used) as a: 'humbug and hypocrite'. But because this whole portrayal of Ambedkar would raise too many questions, mainstream Indian historians, like Guha, leave the inconvenient bits out with the result that revisionist historians like Arun Shourie, (who was a minister in the BJP government and has his own Hindutva agenda), are left with an open goal to aim at, something he does with great skill in his book *Worshipping False Gods*.

The fact is it would have been a miracle if Ranji, given his background, his upbringing and the people in England he mixed with, turned out any differently. As Subhas Bose had very perceptively written back in 1933 there was never any chance that the Indian princes would prove to be the leaders of the Indian freedom movement:

> The Princes will go as soon as English rule ends – no possibility that any Prince will have a role emancipating India as the House of Savoy did in Italy. There is the bare possibility that some Princes may remain if they democratise their administration and sympathise with the Nationalist Movement – but signs of this possibility are very few – with the disappearance of Princes the provinces will have to be reorganised on a linguistic basis.

Interestingly, Bose was then exiled by the British to Europe and wrestling with a political legacy which Ranji had helped create. This was the League of Nations. Created after the First World War, India was one of its founding members and Indian revenues financed the organisation. The League was meant to make the world safe from war and project the doctrine of American President Woodrow Wilson that the First World War had been fought to bring freedom to nations. Of course this was, as George Orwell later called it, a 'not counting niggers' thesis. The freedom these leaders were talking about was freedom for white people. Back home, Wilson was so opposed to improving the lots of his own blacks that he did not support legislation outlawing lynching and the freedom the League spoke of was freedom for the various European nations that had been part of empires such as the Russian, Austro-Hungarian and Turkish. The British had no desire to give India freedom but as part of their elaborate spin-doctoring it suited them to give India a seat at the League to convince the world that Indians were slowly being taught how to rule themselves. This meant all sorts of contradictions: India sat as part of the overall British Empire delegation which contained genuinely free nations such as the self-governing white nations of Australia, Canada, New Zealand and South Africa. But as the decade wore on the British sought to cover this up by allowing India to acquire certain trappings that free countries have. Today these may seem ridiculous and spurious but through the 1920s and 1930s they helped the Raj spin the story their way – in 1930, for instance, India House was established in London with an Indian High Commissioner – the very building that free India acquired as its first genuinely free mission abroad. And at international gatherings there was often an Indian delegation stuffed with Raj collaborators.

Ranji was the most flamboyant of them in Geneva. Curiously, Ranji's biographers including the recent by Rodrigues, have not devoted much space to this part of Ranji's life and we have to go to Ian Wilton's biography of Fry, *C.B. Fry, King of Sport*, to find out how Ranji fared. It is a fascinating story.

As Wilton notes neither Fry nor Ranji did much in the First World War. Ranji had been given some largely honorary positions which kept him well away from the fighting and his war-time injury – the loss of his right eye – occurred whilst shooting grouse in Yorkshire, not Germans in Belgium or France.

But then in 1920 as a late replacement he was asked to become one of India's three representatives at the League of Nations and took with him two Englishmen: Colonel Berthon, who helped him run Nawanagar; and Fry.

Wilton describes how the political partnership between these two batting stars of Sussex and England fared:

> Arriving at the Hotel de la Paix, Fry and Ranji found that all its sitting rooms, and most of the bedrooms, had already been snaffled by the massive Japanese delegation, which had also ensured that the building – and the whole city – was festooned with Rising Sun flags. With a pronounced sense of his own importance, Ranji objected to seeing so many Japanese emblems and even telegraphed the Secretary of State for India to insist that the Indian flag should be displayed as prominently as that of any other state. Within days of this incident, Ranjitsinhji's sensibilities – and his growing self-importance – were demonstrated on two further occasions. First, at a dinner hosted by the British Minister, Theo Russell, he was annoyed that he was not given precedence over other Dominion representatives (presumably on the basis that, despite Nawanagar's small size, he was the only sovereign ruler present). Once more, he refused to let the matter rest and, in a letter of complaint, insisted that an important principle was at stake. Although Ranji signed the letter, it was widely believed that the decision to complain had emanated from Fry. Such suggestions were compounded when Ranji took offence, yet again, at his treatment during a banquet given by Sir Eric Drummond, the General-Secretary of the League. In an attempt to avoid a repetition of the scenes experienced by Russell, the organizers had decided to seat the guests in alphabetical order but a clerical mistake meant the same seat was allocated to both Ranji and a delegate from Central America. Predictably, Fry's employer took the error to heart – threatening to walk out and testing Sir Eric's powers of diplomacy to the full. 'Although we are experimenting with dyarchy in India at present,' Drummond commented, 'the time has not yet arrived when an Indian Prince can share a seat at table with someone else.' It appears that Ranji was eventually placated – but his initial reaction to the incident was believed, by British diplomats, to show how he was being influenced by the status-conscious Fry.

As Wilton tells the story there was a fair element of farce in this Ranji and Fry political partnership. India's chief delegate was an Englishman – Sir William Meyer – like all such Raj institutions Englishmen were real centres of power. Fry, who was no good at mathematics, thought Meyer's decision to appoint Ranji on the finance committee showed a sly sense of humour. Ranji after a few meetings stopped attending and deputed Fry to attend and as Wilton observes. 'Indeed, it was odd that the Indian Princes' official delegate on the Finance Committee was someone who was quite unable to control his own spending, while their Substitute Delegate had been unable to join the I.C.S. because of his poor grasp of maths.'

By this time Ranji's spending in Geneva was already legendary. Here is Wilton again:

> Ranji had arrived in Switzerland after a massive spending spree in Britain. In the summer of 1920, for example, he had bought paintings from the Royal Academy, large quantities of diamond-encrusted jewellery from Cartier and a number of expensive race horses, including one (the Goodwood Cup-winner, *Western Wave)* which had cost him 9,000 guineas. In Geneva, he continued spending at an alarming rate, and even his hagiographer, Roland Wild, conceded that he 'brought a new technique of buying into Switzerland'. He would sit in an antique shop for several hours, drink coffee, admire the *objets d'art*, and then 'suddenly stand up, finish the interview, and remark as he left: 'I want that and that, and that and that...' The remark sometimes cost him £2,000. In addition to such purchases (many of which were soon given away as gifts), Ranji started to provide perhaps the most lavish hospitality in Geneva, believing that his lunches and dinners could bring people together and show the Indian Princes in a good light. As he later remarked, 'The keynote of this place is rubbing together with strangers over the port. You may think at first that some of the others are savages, and then you find out they are gentlemen.' Several of these events were designed for the benefit of the Press and were supposed to be organized by Fry – but he usually delegated the task to the Yuvraf of Limbdi. Others brought together some of the most important members of the League itself, such as Sir George Foster (from Canada), Sir James Alien (New Zealand), Sir Reginald Blankenberg (South Africa) and leading British representatives, including Lord Balfour and Viscount Cecil. The dinners were certainly lavish affairs: the food was excellent, the table would be decorated with small silk flags and Ranji tended to wear elaborate waistcoats with eight buttons that were, in fact, black pearls, each worth £300. The extravagance of these events is shown by the fact that, in 1920, they were costing

Nawanagar over £250 a week... C.B. was also present at a special luncheon that Ranji hosted for some of the most important – and best-looking – women in Geneva. It was a typically luxuriant affair, with special menu cards being printed, a present of a watercolour lying on each plate and every lady being presented with roses (in November) that were tied up with ribbons which matched Ranji's racing colours. The guests, like the gifts, seem to have been carefully chosen. They included: Dame Rachel Crowdy, a member of the League Secretariat, the former head of the wartime V.A.D. (Voluntary Aid Detachment) and a slim, elegant and fashionable woman with whom Fry loved to dance; the strangely named Mrs Wellington Koo, the daughter of the Siamese Ambassador to Rome, the wife of the Chinese Foreign Secretary and, in C.B.'s view, 'the best-dressed woman in Geneva'; and a secretary, called Stephanie, in Siam's delegation, who 'was about the size of a large doll, spoke goodness knows how many languages, more or less ran the Secretariat of Siam, wore the neatest black silk stockings imaginable on the neatest of legs, drove an enormous racing car, and used to tango with an A.D.C. on the staff of an Italian Military Adviser... to unstinted applause'.

Ranji was much taken by a good-looking Rumanian delegate, Helene Vacaresco, a poetess, who Ranji thought was the most interesting woman in Geneva. His other great friend was Ignacy Paderewski, the Polish pianist-turned-politician. Ranji had three spells in Geneva in 1920, 1922 and 1923 and amidst the pleasure there was some work. During this third spell he called for the tight restrictions on Indian emigration to South Africa to be relaxed and a change in the racist attitude of the government there. But although his requests were very diplomatically and moderately worded it is a reflection of the times that Sir Joseph Cook, a former Australian Prime Minister and senior delegate dismissed them as 'cheap claptrap'. But then, the League as a whole had refused to take any steps against racial discrimination.

Ranji's speech was written for him by Fry, as were all his speeches and Wilton has a hilarious account of how one speech came about. This one Fry would later claim helped reverse Mussolini's invasion of Corfu. Mussolini had occupied the Greek island of Corfu, Greece turned to the League and Ranji turned to Fry. Fry told the story in *Life Worth Living*:

One afternoon, I was in the lobby of the Salle de la Reformation... when a messenger came to tell me that His Highness wanted me.

His Highness said briefly, 'Charlo, we have got to make a speech.'

'What about?'

'Lord Balfour wants me to make a declaration on behalf of the British Empire that, in the opinion of all its Delegations, the Corfu question is within the competence of the League.' [Mussolini had argued that the League could not discuss the issue.]

I said, 'When?'

He said, 'Now.'

'But we can't get it typed.'

'Never mind. Write it out large and legible.'

Fry, says Wilton, 'went straight to work with "a green pencil, as thick as a walking-stick", and, within half an hour, the speech requested by Balfour had been hastily – but skilfully – written by Fry and was being read out by Ranjitsinhji.' Fry, who thought the speech sounded good in English but superb in French, would later claim this speech made Mussolini vacate Corfu but the decision, as Wilton points out, was taken elsewhere. The one definite effect of the speech was the three Italian delegates who were due to have lunch with Ranji cancelled saying they had headaches.

There is one other episode from Geneva worth considering. This is an apparent offer to Fry to become King of Albania. Fry in his own autobiography, *Life Worth Living*, would describe this at some length. The offer came through Ranji and, an Albanian Bishop, who looked like W. G. Grace, came to see Fry. Fry writes:

My preparations consisted in obtaining the use of the largest salon in the Hotel de la Paix, persuading the proprietor, M. Albert, to adorn it with the best furniture selectable from other salons, and I told Ranji's four personal servants to be ready, in full Nawanagar State livery, with a good supply of every kind of refreshment in the background... Ranji instructed me to get ready my very best behaviour... He impressed upon me the necessity of trying to look English and, if possible, a country gentleman, and further, if I could manage it, one likely to possess £10,000 a year... I received him with my best bow, quick down and slow up, with a resounding click of the heels, and conducted him to a circle of stately chairs. After compliments and general conversation, I invited the Bishop as to whether he would take some refreshment... Bhimji, the Rajput servant... who at the moment looked enough of a prince himself, advanced carrying an enormous silver tray on which there was a powerful battery of decanters. Another servant, Mohan, followed with another silver tray, charged with about two dozen wine-glasses and tumblers. The Bishop did not hestitate. He would have Irish whiskey. I selected a decanter on faith, hoping it was not sherry, and began pouring the liquid into a tumbler. It was whisky all right. I suggested to the Bishop to say when. The Bishop did not say when until I had half filled a tumbler. Would he have soda-water or plain water? 'No,' said the Bishop. So Bhimji handed him the whisky on a silver platter. The Bishop with his left hand pushed his great black moustache conveniently upwards and tossed off the liquor in two gulps... Then Ranji appeared in a leisurely hurry of courteous excuses, and, much delighted to have had the honour of meeting His Lordship, I bowed myself out backwards... Beyond telling me that the Bishop was quite favourably impressed with me, and that the matter was now under full consideration, Ranji never revealed to me what had occurred – except that the Bishop had enjoyed another half-tumbler... After about a fortnight I could see that the prospect of either losing my services or of having to find the £10,000 a year was beginning to weigh down the balance in Ranji's mind against my elevation. When he casually laid stress on the inconvenience of having to live in a lonely castle on an island, and perhaps of a bullet in the ribs, I could see at once that his lively affection for me had decided him against the adventure. At any rate, for some reason or other, the proposal gradually faded out.

Wilton says it would have made little sense for Ranji to finance Fry becoming king of Albania and declined to supply the money. But whether this whole thing was a joke by Ranji on Fry we do not know. Jack Fingleton claimed that Ranji had played an elaborate hoax on his friend and his authority for this was Duleep who had told him the story when he was Indian High Commissioner in Australia. Others claim that Fry knew it was a joke but went along with it.

Fry in *Life Worth Living* concluded: 'I do not say that I received a specific and definite invitation to become King of Albania, but in the indirect manner which so often characterises any affair in which an Indian is concerned it amounts to this – that I was well in the running for the billet.'

This reaction of Fry's is very interesting, particularly in the way he describes how Indians behave. Today we would construe this as a stereotypical way of looking at people and while that may not be fair on Fry the fact is that he, was very much part, an English generation which had every reason to feel that the Empire they had created was the best thing mankind had ever seen and people like the Indians who had been brought into the Empire should feel grateful for being British subjects. Fry's contemporaries were, Lord Birkenhead and John Simon. We have already seen the essentially racist mindset of these individuals and Fry to a great extent shared that.

Fry believed for instance that Indians would never have started asking even for home rule, which is what Indians were then demanding, if the

British had not said they were preparing the country for self-rule, exactly the sentiments of Birkenhead. As Wilton says, 'Indeed, C.B. believed that only three groups of people were keen on *swaraj* (home rule): the intelligentsia in the towns, "a quantity of Westernised applicants for careers which did not exist" and some merchants, financiers and industrialists who believed that, without independence, they would be unable to compete with their British counterparts on level terms.' The idea that Indians might like to rule themselves as the British did and gloried in never, never, being slaves would have struck Fry as preposterous – as it did to his contemporaries Birkenhead and Simon.

Not that Fry shared Birkenhead's almost physical distaste of Indians. Wilton tells us he treated,

> Indians with more respect than most other Britons, believing, as he later explained, that 'the only way of being pro-British then was to be pro-Indian in the right way'. It was, he added, an approach which should have been supported by 'anyone with the brains of a louse' – a group which, in his view, excluded members of the Royal Bombay Yacht Club. However, Fry's respect for Indians (and India) was not merely cosmetic: he was intrigued by many Indian traditions and tried to understand some of the beliefs which baffled other visitors. For example, he was fascinated by the caste system and attached some credence to the suggestion that someone's behaviour in one life could affect their status in a future existence.

Fry in his travels in India working for Ranji came across Gandhi and, writing in 1940, analysed him more perceptively than did some of the other, more important political supporters of the Raj, although being Fry there was a quixotic touch. This is what he wrote:

> This little man is a brilliant talker and a paramount politician ... to see him sitting cross-legged on the ground at Ahmadabad in apparent poverty and with few clothes on, with his protruding ears and steel spectacles, and to be suddenly involved in a stream of rather highbrow English, worthy of an English professor, is startling. ... (Gandhi) deals with an awkward argument just as Ranji used to deal with a fast bowler – he glances it to leg.

This was the complex world that shaped Ranji and to dismiss him as a 'fanatical' collaborator without assessing the backdrop of British rule in India is neither fair on Ranji nor a true portrayal of India at that time.

Ranji is the English face of Indian cricket; Nayadu the Indian one. Though Ranji's English deeds are carefully re-told – mainly through Cardus – and the national championship named after him, Nayadu with his mixture of pride, stubbornness and a certain Indian arrogance allied to his undoubted achievements, is seen as the true father of Indian cricket. The memorial and its setting exemplifies a certain Indian obsession with ritualised honour: casting heroes in concrete at the first opportunity. Observe the surrounding park is unkempt, and the statue having been erected amidst ceremony, will languish there. What matters to Indians is the gesture of erecting the statue, not its upkeep.

As India defeated England in Bombay in December 1984 after 31 barren Tests, crowds exulted with anticipatory cries of 'Brownwash', hoping to repeat the West Indian 5–0 triumph over England earlier that summer. A few days later, and less than 200 miles away in the hills, crowds in Pune were throwing bottles as India lost a one-day international. By the end of England's tour, much of India was thoroughly disenchanted with its cricket only to be revived by unexpected one-day successes in Australia. Indian crowds have always been fickle, but since the World Cup triumph of 1983 crowds used to draws now expect victory at every turn and take defeats very bitterly. There have been several instances of crowd misbehaviour, particularly in the semi-final between India and Sri Lanka at Kolkatta during the 1996 World Cup and then again during the Test with Pakistan in 1999. On both occasions India was on the point of defeat and the crowd took it badly.

Maidan cricket is the basis of the Indian game as these photographs taken during the rest day of the Calcutta Test between India and England in January 1985 illustrate. Calcutta's maidan is a vast central area of what passes for greenery in India: unkempt, chaotic but gratefully seized on by the city's Club cricketers. Almost every piece of the maidan is used, even if square-leg is divided from mid-wicket by a filthy canal, or tea consists of dubious cakes from a tin box. The condition of the ground may not produce a Jonty Rhodes – would you dive across a canal? – but shades of David Gower and W. G. Grace can be seen.

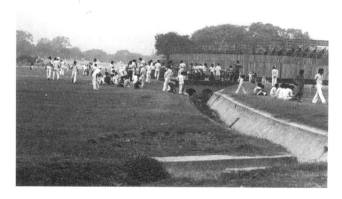

Observe how pockmarked and rugged this ground is. No pitch is discernible, as there is none; indeed there is no square in the traditional sense of the word, and no way to differentiate between the batting surface and the rest of the ground. Wickets are pitched on that part of the ground where the surface is least uneven, and clearly there would have to be a special rule for what happens to the ball should it fall into the little canal on the right of the picture. The stand on the far side belongs to one of the many established clubs of the maidan. Few of those in the picture would ever graduate to play there, if they did they would know they have arrived. That is mali-dominated cricket where there are proper pitches and all the attention to detail you expect in a proper cricket match.

Maidan cricket in all its elemental rawness also has a certain beauty and certainly an awesome compelling power. The little boys trailing their bats behind them have in all probability cobbled their equipment together. They probably have one pad between them, so if they are right-handers the two batsmen at the crease will only put a pad each, on their left legs, and might just about manage a pair of gloves between them. It is unlikely they have more than one set of stumps, the stumps at the bowling end would be a pile of *chappalls* (slippers), and in this cricket it is batsmen who change ends at the finish of the over, not the wicketkeeper as, unlike proper cricket, wickets are pitched only at one end.

The Indian W. G. Grace? Not quite but a serious maidan cricketer who has all the gear and is clearly intent on his business. When this picture was taken helmets had not yet come into use; now he would be wearing a helmet.

Two of the most remarkable batsmen India has produced and a very good wicketkeeper batsman. In the foreground is Syed Kirmani, the wicketkeeper batsman who was a regular member of Indian teams for much of the 1970s and 1980s. Sitting to his left, Gundappa Visvanath, and facing the pair, Sunil Gavaskar. Visvanath and Gavaskar were the two great batting stars of India in the 1970s and 1980s. Visvanath was the first to emerge scoring a century in his first Test but within two years Gavaskar announced himself to the world with a Bradman-like average in his first series against the West Indies. For the decade that followed the two held Indian batting together, reminding cricket lovers of another era of a great Indian batting pair, that of Vijay Merchant and Vijay Hazare. Except unlike Merchant and Hazare there was no rivalry for the captaincy and Visvanath got married to Gavaskar's sister making it something of a family affair. But while Indians admired Gavaskar there was something in him that stopped him from being loved in the way Visvanath was. A Visvanath innings could often be a thing of beauty but rather fragile, Gavaskar always seemed to know what he wanted and often got it by a determination that unnerved Indians who were more used to their sporting heroes just failing rather than succeeding.

Kapil Dev's rise marked the re-emergence of the north as a major force in Indian cricket. Before Indian independence the north had produced some of the best Indian cricketers, including the fast bowler Mohammed Nissar and the all-rounder Lala Amarnath. But then through much of 1950s, 1960s and 1970s Indian cricket was dominated by the west, in particular the city of Bombay and the south. Then Kapil emerged in answer to many Indian cricketing prayers for an Indian fast bowler who could at last answer the ordeal through pace from which Indian batsmen had so long suffered. Kapil did more than that. He quite unexpectedly led India to victory in the World Cup in England in 1983. At that stage the West Indies were the greatest one-day team. The Indian victory led to such a decline of the West Indies that they had to wait more than twenty years before winning another major one-day trophy. Kapil's victory revolutionised Indian cricket as Indians took to the one-day game, deserting Tests, and it also had a major impact on world cricket. But as in all Indian stories there is always a tale of the serpent in the apple and although Gavaskar was a very established player by the time Kapil came, and captain of India, as Kapil rose he was seen as a rival to Gavaskar and through the 1980s the captaincy often changed hands. Differences between the two men led to defeats and many problems but when the two players, expertly managed by Raj Singh, put their differences aside in England in the summer of 1986 they produced the best Indian performances outside of India.

This advertisement during the 1996 World Cup marked a seminal moment in Indian cricket. Note the slogan at the bottom of the Sachin Tendulkar picture saying, 'Nothing official about it'. It is Pepsi getting back at its great rival Coke. Coke was one of the official sponsors of the World Cup and the only product available inside the grounds. Pepsi, beaten to the rights, decided to have its revenge by gathering together some of the then greats of cricket. They include besides Tendulkar, Dickie Bird, the English umpire at the height of his powers. They were all filmed with a bottle of Pepsi and these adverts were displayed outside cricket grounds and on television. The slogan, 'nothing official about it', amused Indians greatly, and Pepsi scored a great success against its rival Coke. Coke fumed but could do nothing. Pepsi has since become one of the official sponsors of Indian cricket. Tendulkar has become the greatest sporting icon Indian cricket has produced and his image can sell everything.

7

The besieged hero

Every country gets the hero it deserves. It is difficult to imagine John McEnroe as anything other than an American hero. According to Professor Jack Higgs, while he is not yet a national hero, he is as thoroughly American as the New York Yankees. In India there are heroes and there are Gods. In the west the two terms, at least in popular usage, may be interchangeable but in India they have rather distinct meanings.

The ideal Hindu God is Rama, that wonderfully self-effacing person who, in order to keep his father's word, was ready to sacrifice his kingdom, and in order to please his subjects, was ready to sacrifice his ideal wife. Ramayana is one of the great classics of our times, though I don't suppose any western child knows the story, but that is a reflection of the effects of colonialism and the fact that we live in a world made by Europeans, where most things non-European are 'the other'. In India and South East Asia its status is far higher than that enjoyed by Homer's *Iliad* in the west.

In this great Hindu myth Rama is God incarnated as man – the eldest son of a king who reigns at Ayodhya. He is about to succeed his father when the distressed king summons Rama. Some years ago, cherished back to health and life by his second wife after a war wound, he had made extravagant promises to her. She was now cashing in her chips. The second wife wanted her son, Rama's stepbrother, to become king. Rama the perfect man immediately understands and, with his wife and another brother, he vanishes into the forest to start 14 years of exile. The story of Ramayana is actually the years of exile; the tribulations of Sita, Rama's wife, who is kidnapped, then rescued and the eventual, joyous return of Rama to Ayodhya.

Ramayana does tend to come overloaded with self-effacing heroes. The stepbrother for whom Rama vacated the throne refused to actually sit on it. Through those 14 years he sat in front of the throne that Rama was supposed to have occupied, using a pair of Rama's shoes as a symbol of the lost king.

Ramayana is a story of good triumphing over evil – and there are some marvellously evil characters in it – and its moral is not lost in contemporary Indian life. Rama's portrait stares down from a million Indian *pan* shops, he is the ideal Hindu and when he reigned there was perfection on earth. It was Mahatma Gandhi's political aim to recreate Ramrajya (rule of Rama) in India.

But Indians distinguish between Rama, as the great political God-hero and the more modern heroes. Indians, even if they cannot speak a word of English, actually use the English word 'hero' and when they do so they are thinking of the hero in Bollywood films. While occasionally Bollywood films do have heroes full of excessive goodness, such as Rama, a hero in the Indian film world, and as understood by most Indians in contemporary India, is a somewhat rakish individual. He probably has a lock of hair perpetually falling across his eyes, which he constantly brushes back, either with his fingers or with a dainty comb he keeps in his hip pocket. His clothes are just that bit too fashionable, his manner just that bit too out-landish, he is both a bit of a voyeur and a bit of a poser. The Bollywood film world hero can, sometimes, be something of a character. In fact Indians can hurl the word hero as an abuse, or at least a reproach. If somebody fails whilst trying something outlandish, or ends up looking stupid, it is not unusual for his friend or colleague to say 'What do you think you are doing? Trying to be a hero?' Heroes are difficult to live with. In India there is a problem in that while it would prefer all its heroes to be like Rama, it often finds that they are more often a caricature of the Bollywood film hero – slightly more lewd, slightly fatter, slightly more absurd and a lot less lovable. The contradiction between the ideal and reality is always going to cause problems. Problems clearly illustrated in the way Indians react to Sunil Gavaskar, one of India's greatest batsman and one of the finest in the world.

Gavaskar's place in cricket can hardly be in doubt. By the time he retired in 1987 he had scored more centuries than Donald Bradman. He did so opening the innings for a country whose batting has often been very brittle; he went out to bat knowing he could echo Louis XIV and say, 'After me, the deluge of wickets.' He burst onto the Test scene in 1971, aged just 21 and with a handful of first-class matches behind him, scoring 774 runs in his first Test series – against Gary Sobers's West Indians. It was a Bradman-like opening and if his subsequent series didn't quite match the first, he was remarkably consistent producing runs in the sort of profusion that has not been seen before in Indian cricket, and rarely else-where. Gavaskar returned from that West Indies trip as a celebrity, or as Indians like to put it a VIP, a Very Important Person. The extent of Indian adulation for a VIP produces wondrous gasps in England, and Gavaskar has been subjected to hero worship almost from the beginning.

At the height of his career he received some eighty letters a day, even his then teenage son Rohan received letters, and Sunil's *darshan* was eagerly sought. Literally the word darshan means 'sight' or 'introduction', but in India it has a quasi-mystical association with crowds gathering to be near a great man or woman. Thus Mrs Gandhi regularly had crowds gathering in front of her house every morning hoping to catch her darshan.

If Gavaskar, say, went shopping in a Mumbai street, soon after he entered a shop, word passed through the street, that the great man was around. Crowds, in that characteristic Indian fashion, gathered outside the shop as if from nowhere. They wanted nothing from him, not even his autograph; all they wanted was to be near him, and, perhaps, be touched by his magic. Film stars and politicians have always enjoyed such darshan, but Gavaskar was one of the first modern Indian cricketers to do so. At times the swarm of crowds, say at railway stations, used to be such that his son and wife had to get off on the wrong side of the carriage and escape across the tracks.

But this adulation came mixed with unease, disquiet and downright hostility. English writers, like Dudley Doust, have misinterpreted the adulation as uncritical hero worship. Gavaskar was never seen as a Rama, the epitome of good, much more like a Bollywood film hero. The Indian response to him was complex, reflecting both pride and unease: wonder about his achievements but doubt about the means he used to attain his ends. Here is how Mansur Ali Khan Pataudi in an article entitled *The Decline of Indian Cricket*, put the case against Gavaskar:

> Gavaskar was the greatest, and while no one doubted this, it is plain that only some Mumbai players paid him sycophantic homage. Perhaps the others were jealous but no matter how hard he tried, many cricketers from elsewhere were unable to give him their full trust [Dilip Doshi is an example]. They felt that Gavaskar stood for Gavaskar though he had often clashed with the authorities for the benefit of his team.

Pataudi's explanation for the unease Indians feel about Gavaskar was money. Prize money came into India in 1969. Pataudi was Captain. At a team meeting Wadekar, who was to replace him later, suggested that it be shared. Pataudi spent two years in legal fees to convince the income tax department that the money ought not to be taxed and the Indian off-spinner Venkataraghavan was given the task of ensuring that the prize money was properly split between the various players. Pataudi said that was not only because he was honest 'but he had the knack of dividing thousands by any number and arriving at an even figure'. Later Venkataraghavan's position as team accountant was to be taken up by Chetan Chauhan, and it was partly his departure from the team that contributed to the hassles about sharing prize money in later years. According to Pataudi:

> Gavaskar opened up entire new vistas of making money. He had noticed how quickly cricketers once out of limelight were actually shunned by the same people who had fussed over them, fought for the pleasure of inviting them home and queued to have photographs taken

with them. In Mumbai only money seemed to matter, and there was more than one way to make it. Gavaskar found them all. Advertising, film producing (this may have been for a lark), writing articles (on the same match but for different publications), taking a fee for organising matches, writing instant books, which were spiced to sell better, appearance money (one paid for the pleasure of entertaining the team) and signing contracts with the manufacturers of sports equipment. He became the first Indian millionaire through cricket, rich enough to buy a flat in the centre of Mumbai. In a capitalist cricketing country he would have been considered a financial genius. In India they began to call him a mercenary, and within the team he became the envy of some who felt that their contribution to Indian cricket was not being fully appreciated. Why should Gavaskar hog all the publicity as well as the money? The answer was simple: he had reached those dizzy heights to which no Indian cricketer in his right mind would even dream of aspiring. As importantly, he was articulate where others were dumb, he was controversial where others dared not to be, he could even be witty and this made him ideal material for the media and the advertiser.

Pataudi, as ever, has got to the nub of the problem. For many Indians Sunil Gavaskar is 'money-mad'. Almost everyone describes his actions, from his flirtation with Kerry Packer's World Series cricket, his appearance at some social function or the other, to his supposed lust for money. By any international cricket standards, let alone the standards of tennis or golf, Gavaskar was extremely poorly paid. At the height of his career he only earned something like £35,000 a year, some £5,000 less than what Ian Botham earned from his bat contract alone. But £35,000 is a lot of money in India – and much more than that earned by cricketers in the pre-Gavaskar era. (The sums have vastly increased in the Sachin Tendulkar era, as we shall see.) Gavaskar's supposed crime was that he did not accept the Indian dichotomy about money.

It has always surprised me to find certain westerners depicting the Indians as a uniquely non-materialistic people, not interested in this world, or its worldly goods, but only in a sort of mystical after-life. *Maya*, illusion, the west believes, is a central Indian plank. It may be a central Indian, or rather Hindu, philosophical belief but the idea that Indians are not materialistic is absurd. India is probably the most materialistic place on earth. The Hindu belief in a pantheon of Gods enables them to worship many Gods. One of the most popular, and worshipped with great fervour, is Lakshmi, the Goddess of Wealth. Perhaps the most celebrated temple in Mumbai, certainly the most popular is Mahalakshmi, where a wondrous statue of

Lakshmi is worshipped every day with milk, ghee, money, and various other offerings. The different Hindu communities have their different Gods, but almost all of them have an annual Lakshmi Puja which is marked with great devotion and enthusiasm. And in most Hindu homes the goddess Lakshmi is worshipped every Thursday. In other religions the prayer is for salvation in the after-life, Hindus ask for material rewards in this life.

The confusion in the west arises from the fact that while Indians are terribly materialistic, they do not flaunt their materialism. They do not like bragging about how much money they have, or how many cars they possess, or about their lifestyle. Indians hunger for money, perhaps more than most, but they do not like their heroes to openly proclaim this.

Gavaskar has always been honest, meticulous, about money. In 1990 when he wrote the foreword to my *History of Indian Cricket* he negotiated a fee, as he was perfectly entitled to, and not only wrote a beautiful foreword but agreed to come to signing ceremonies with me. It was all done in a highly professional manner. I can imagine other Indian cricketers who would have said they would write the foreword for free but then either not delivered it or made me feel they were doing me a great favour. Gavaskar treated it as a very a straightforward business transaction. Indeed, not long after that, another Indian cricketer who, as it happens, did not get on with Gavaskar, messed me about with a book he wanted to write. I put in a lot of work but he was never clear about his intentions, I learnt quite by accident that he had decided to publish with someone else and the whole episode made me appreciate how much more straightforward Gavaskar is.

Gavaskar possesses another un-Indian characteristic – in cricket he was very consistent. The same could not be said for the true Rama-like figure in Indian cricket -a definite contrast to Gavaskar. While it was hard to see Gavaskar vacating the crease at any time – let alone in order to redeem someone else's promise – one could imagine Visvanath doing so. He was the Rama of Indian cricket. Physically both Gavaskar and Visvanath looked similar – both small men – and they made their impact at roughly the same time. Visvanath, in fact, made his debut in 1969 scoring a century in his first Test. Before the West Indies tour of 1971, it was Visvanath who was considered the main batsman. But on the tour he suffered an injury; Gavaskar made his debut and while Visvanath came back he never quite recaptured the spotlight. Indians have always debated the merits of these two batsmen. Gavaskar, himself, generously admits that Visvanath is the greater batsman. 'I have just one stroke to every ball, he seems to have four or five.' It makes Visvanath so cherishable, so lovable, but like all the great Indian heroes, he is fallible. A Visvanath innings could be an innings of great joy, but it could also amount to nothing. It allowed Indians much speculation on their favourite subject of 'what if...' Visvanath accepted whatever was given to him modestly and with the sort of self-effacing air that the Indians find so charming.

But despite Visvanath's charm, and the evident understanding between the two men, the Gavaskar and Visvanath argument can generate extreme passion amongst their supporters. I witnessed one such scene as Sunil was making his memorable 221 against England at the Oval in 1979.

The Oval then had its cramped, almost subterranean, press box. I sat next to an Indian journalist. As Sunil slowly built the Indian innings, and turned what looked like a hopeless defeat into the most glorious victory, my Indian colleague was dismissive of his efforts. Sunil, he declared, had never really faced proper bowling. He had made his runs when the top bowler of the opposing side had been absent. Sometime earlier on that last day Hendrick, England's most difficult bowler, had limped away. My friend pointed to this as confirmation of his thesis. Even Sunil reaching his century, then his double century, then placing India on what looked like the high road to victory, did not dampen his anti-Sunil tirade. Set 438, India now needed just a few runs for victory and, with a few overs left, a remarkable five-day Test had turned into a limited-overs run chase. Kapil Dev, promoted in the order, got out and Visvanath strode to the wicket. My friend nudged me and said 'What you have seen so far is nothing, here comes God. He will take us to victory.'

As it happened Sunil was out soon afterwards, Visvanath got a rather dodgy decision and with a couple of other umpiring decisions going against them, India just failed to win the match that had looked theirs for the taking, by nine runs. I was sorely tempted to mock my Indian colleague about his God, but I resisted that. But such are the passions that Sunil arouses that even after that great innings, there were whispers in some Indian quarters that he had got out because he didn't want India to win. On that tour India was being captained by Venkat, who had supplanted Sunil, Captain for the previous home series, because of Sunil's flirtation with Kerry Packer's World Cricket series. Immediately after the Oval Test, the Indians flew home to face the Australians and on the plane, with the sort of subtlety that has made the Indian selectors famous, it was announced by the pilot that Venkat had been replaced as Captain by Sunil. Immediately the rumours began to circulate. Yes, of course, Sunil played a great innings, but why didn't he carry it to completion? Why didn't he ensure that India had won? Well, said the anti-Sunil brigade, the reason is that his 221 was a personal effort. It impressed his unique mark on English cricket where he hadn't scored as heavily as elsewhere, but it was just short of clinching victory for India. A victory for India would have meant a victory for Venkat, and the Indian selectors could hardly have dropped Venkat after that.

This is, of course, an absolutely disgraceful suggestion which has no basis in fact. Sunil played the innings with a throbbing toothache, although physical pain of that type always seems to spur him on. When, after eight hours and nine minutes he finally got out, he was a very tired man. It would have been fantastic if he had actually made the winning hit against England, but to blame a man after such a stupendous achievement seems extraordinary. It is also characteristic of certain Indian attitudes, certainly an anti-Sunil Gavaskar attitude, that out of such personal success they could construct a conspiracy. It explains the passion Sunil Gavaskar aroused during his playing career, passions that Fritzy would have understood, though not necessarily condoned.

We must, indeed, look to Fritzy and St Xavier's High School, Shivaji Park and Dadar Union to understand the remarkable phenomenon of Sunil Gavaskar.

In Sunil Gavaskar's autobiography *Sunny Days* there is a paragraph devoted to St Xavier's High School. It reads:

> I joined St Xavier's High School which had a fairly good cricket team at that time. While we were just juniors we would run during the lunch recess to watch the senior boys play. Feroz Patka was then the ideal of almost ever Xavierite and Vinay Chaudhari, the skipper, was equally popular. When St Xavier's won the Harris Shield during the Chaudhari's captaincy, every Xavierite went delirious with joy. We had inter-class matches which were very important, because the School's Junior Team was selected on the basis of performances in these encounters. Even on holidays we went to play the school matches, very often with just one leg-guard and no batting gloves. I used to bowl, also, at that time and managed to bag quite a few wickets.

In an autobiography of 264 pages, this is about the only reference, or at least significant reference, that Sunil makes to our school. When it was first published I was disappointed to find that Sunil had not dwelt a bit more on our school, and surprised that he hadn't mentioned Father Fritz, St Xavier's sports master. But then Sunil had confessed in his preface that the autobiography was 'an attempt to put down my stray and random thoughts in some order' and it followed the autobiographical style established by other famous cricketers. Later I learnt that Sunil invited Father Fritz to watch his first Test in Mumbai against England in 1973 and later still he was to speak of the influence of Father Fritz and his cricket dictum – 'A good-length ball you block and anything else, bang.'

But what is misleading is to suggest, as Sunil does, that it was natural that he should have gone to St Xavier's and not some other school in

Mumbai, natural that Xavier's should have produced the man who beat Bradman's record of 29 Test centuries and whose name has become synonymous with breaking Test cricket records all round the world. Such an impression would be totally wrong. St Xavier's had never been the great cricketing school of Mumbai. During my ten years at the school, we won the Harris shield only once, the victory to which Sunil refers.

St Xavier's, as its name suggests, was a Catholic school, a Jesuit school, administered by white-robed priests, whom we called Fathers assisted by the odd 'brother', a priest who had yet to make the grade. Not all our teachers were Jesuits, or even Catholics. For some remarkable reason a good many of our teachers were females, and a good many of them were non-Catholics. We did not encounter male teachers apart from the odd priest, until we reached the age of 14. This in an all-boys school either reflected remarkable faith or remarkable obtuseness.

Our school did have Catholic students but they were, like my friend Hubert, poor Catholics whose education the school subsidised. I vividly recalled how the presence of some of these poor Catholics in my class used to goad a Parsee female teacher, a rather stern type – attractive in a curious sort of way – into demented fury. It may have been born out of sexual frustration, but her contempt for the poor Catholics she had in her class was total. She would make their rather ill-kept clothes, their total lack of scholastic ability, their lackadaisical general demeanour a target of direct assault. She would pick on them individually asking questions which she knew they could not answer. Then she would berate them, 'You are privileged. You get free tuition here. Yet, look at the way you dress. You may be poor but can't you even spare some soap? Poor does not mean you should wear dirty clothes. You don't even make an attempt to study.'

This female teacher's views probably reflected the views of a good many of the non-Catholic teachers in our school, and many of the non-Catholic students. That she could express it so openly in a Catholic school, where her paymasters were Jesuit priests, gives some idea of the school, and the curious nature of co-existence of different communities that prevails in India. Whenever I have mentioned to my English friends that I was educated at a Jesuit school in Mumbai, their reaction has been an interesting mixture of horror and bewilderment. The horror arises from the English distrust of Catholicism which still exists, the bewilderment from the realisation that in India there are Catholics. My English friends are even more surprised when I tell them that my Jesuit school made no attempt to convert me, or at least not directly. In that sense the Jesuit Fathers of St Xavier's matched the British Raj who frowned on conversion and let the Hindus and Muslims get on with their particular beliefs.

Most of the students at St Xavier's were non-Catholics – Hindus, Muslims, Parsees from the middle- and upper-middle-class families of Mumbai. They had been attracted to the school because while the fees were relatively low, the standard of education was supposed to be excellent. We were, of course, open to Catholic influences. In all our class-rooms, just above the blackboard, there was the figure of Christ on the cross. Four times a day, we bowed our heads before this figure, crossed ourselves and said the prayers of the Lord. Twice a day we sought bless-ing before class and again after lunch; twice we sought forgiveness for our sins, just before the lunch break and finally, before going home at 4.30 p.m. In unison we all learned to mumble our prayers in low monotones, quickly cross ourselves and get on with more desirable pursuits. There was never any danger that this would convert us. The school did not expect it or want it, and our parents did not fear it.

What the school did was to promote a rational outlook which, in subtle ways, was subversive of traditional Indian beliefs. Thus Father Fritz would often try to convince us that it was natural that a man should choose his own wife. 'Your parents may tell you that the female is a cow and for years you will believe it, but the day will come when you will tell your parents that even if all females are cows, I would like to have a cow.' It was in such ways, and through moral science, that the school tried to influence us. Catholic boys went for catechism classes, we non-Catholics had moral science which was generalised, albeit Catholic-influenced propaganda in favour of God's existence.

Sunil has never spoken about the effect all this had on him and his cricket. But he cannot but have been marked by that special stamp that St Xavier's put on all of us. This stamp of exclusiveness set us apart from the rest of the community we lived in. It inculcated a superiority based on our supposed mastery of the English language, our sophistication and our worldly wisdom compared to our contemporaries. The very physical loca-tion of our school seemed to emphasise our superiority. It was right next door to a municipal school. Schooling is neither compulsory nor universal in India, and millions just cannot afford to go to school. Municipal schools are run in the major cities by the local municipality, the Indian equivalent of councils, and are meant for the slightly better-off among the urban poor who have a bit of money to spare after meeting their daily necessities. They send their children to these schools in the almost forlorn hope that this will improve their job prospects. The schools generally teach them various sub-jects in the language of the state in which they are situated, provide a few years of unsatisfactory education and release them into the urban jungle.

The municipal school was just beyond our playground, and ran along one side of it. During our lunch and other recesses, it was part of our

pastime to watch the students of this school. We were told they were poor
and they looked poor. We were told they were hungry and they looked
hungry, we were told they were ill-educated and ill-mannered, and they
looked it. I cannot speak of their feelings, but from our side of the fence
there was some pity and mostly relief that we were not part of that jungle.
They were part of the unnamed, never mentioned enemy, those who did
not speak English and were incapable of simulating our westernised
thoughts.

It was not merely the municipal school poor we despised. We also
despised those who were evidently richer than us, and for much the same
reasons: that they could not speak English. And in despising them we were
expressing certain views of society. We had a term for these people: *Guju
Bhais* and *Mani Bhen*, meaning Gujerati brothers and sisters. They were
not all Gujeratis, the very successful business community from which
Mahatma Gandhi sprang, but in our imagination any well-off person who
couldn't speak English well, was quickly dubbed an undesirable Guju. We
were aware of their riches, but we consoled ourselves with the fact that
they had no learning. They could be seen on a Sunday evening prome-
nading along the sea front at Marine Drive, their radios blaring forth loud
music, their dress and manner struggling to be modern but failing awk-
wardly and their behaviour generally clownish and unsuitable. Their riches
did not bother us because we believed, with some justification, that they
had made their money by defrauding taxes. Perhaps there was envy here
because they had clearly done well out of the free, independent India
which Nehru was constantly telling us was ours to inherit. The more they
flaunted their money, the more we despised them. They may have the
money, we said, but they do not know how to use it. We of the middle
classes may be limited in our riches, but we have the sophistication and
the wit to enjoy what we have.

This, then, was Sunil Gavaskar's school inheritance. What was there
that helped him to achieve his greatness? The school gave him, as it gave
all of us, poise, confidence, belief in oneself and command over the
English language. This last quality is not quite as trivial as it may appear.
We, Sunil and I, grew up in India in the immediate post-independence
years. All around us Nehru, through eloquence and personal magnetism,
tried to create a new, independent India, an India which was nominally
trying to move away from its English heritage and where the English language should have been shunned. Its constitution provided for English to
be replaced by Hindi as a national language by 1960. But as the English
departed from India's shores, Indians seemed to be free from the invisible
yoke that had prevented them from taking to the English language. Our
politicians declaimed the need to speak Hindi but sent their sons to

English-speaking schools, and many found that a command of the English language was very useful in opening doors.

What else did Sunil receive from school? I think he found the belief in his cricket from Father Fritz. I have said that St Xavier's was not a great cricket school and it was not. But cricket was played, incessantly, during the short mid-morning break, during the lunch recess, after school, on Thursdays, on Sundays, (the two days that we did not have classes) and at every available opportunity, apart from the four months between June and September when torrential rain swept Mumbai.

Father Fritz was tall, rather angular and, again by Indian standards, very fair of skin. The most significant thing about him, and one that never ceased to amaze us, was his accent. This was very clipped, and it seemed to us to be dreadfully English, peppered with phrases like 'You two-pice chaps', or 'You load of wash-outs'. This heightened the exotic air which made him such a novelty. We were never sure of his origins. He looked Indian, but seemed so English in his manner that we considered him a foreigner – despite his almost touching display of Indian patriotism. In fact the greater his patriotic fervour and emphasis on being Indian, the more it seemed as if he were a foreigner who had decided to be more Indian than the Indians.

All this far from diminishing Fritz in our eyes increased his status. If anything, it put him on a completely different plane from the other Jesuit padres, as we called the Fathers – though, never to their face. We liked very little about those padres, and, in fact, told mocking and even scurrilous tales about most of them. Never more so than when we saw one of our padres with a nun from a neighbouring convent. We derived much malicious delight when one of our padres, an American who looked like a film star and was supposed to have the reputation of a rake, disappeared from our school in somewhat dubious circumstances.

Our principal was a thin, frail, sour-looking man called Father Miranda. We were convinced that he had only one lung, (largely I think due to his frailness), and instantly dubbed him 'one lung kid'. There was nothing kiddish about him, if anything he was always very severe, hardly ever smiled and was not particularly approachable. He seemed to radiate a certain evil. Not all our padres were as daunting as Miranda, but they were a very mixed bunch, many of them Spanish who spoke little English and a few of them, the ones from Ireland, providing us a rich feast for our scurrilously imaginative tales.

Fritz was different. Patrician, aloof, moving in his own world he was far removed from what we saw as the machinations of Miranda and the curious goings on of lesser padres. Quite early in our school career, Fritz had been dubbed Fritzy, and this abbreviation denoted both affection and warmth. Fritzy, we came to believe, was capable of anything. I well remember the morning after I played in my first inter-class football match. Matches within the school, whether cricket or football, or any other sport, were very important and formed the backbone of the sporting system at St Xavier's. I cannot remember what happened in the match except that I played as a burly left-back who, failing to get the ball, often got the man. There were two other defenders in the game even burlier than me and, the next day, on the school notice board, Fritz pinned a report of the match. The report was fair enough though what was astonishing, and very Fritzy, was a photograph. This purported to be a photograph of the match, show-ing two very large players tackling each other. The caption identified two players as Chandra of our team and Devdas of the opposing team. In fact the photograph was not of our inter-class match at all. Nobody took pho-tographs of such matches. What Fritz had done was to clip a photograph of a match from the English First Division which had been printed in *Sport and Pastime*, then India's leading sports magazine and pretend it represented our puny football match. The idea that Chandra and Devdas, then two Indian 12-year olds, could match up to two burly English first division players was comical. But we admired Fritzy's cheek in suggesting such comparisons. Later, when we quizzed him about it, he explained that his intention was to demonstrate what a real game was like and set us a standard.

For Fritzy was a great man for enunciating the broad principle. If he liked something, or somebody, he made it very clear quickly. Mostly he disliked a great many things, and a great many people, and we were always on our guard against falling foul of Fritzy. But what Fritzy brought to our lives were his convictions and his ability to motivate others. It was this that first brought Sunil Gavaskar to my notice.

I must have been 14, Sunil was probably 12. Fourteen meant we were two, three years away from the coveted matriculation or SSC (Secondary School Certificate) as it was called in Mumbai. We had got to the age when we were just about beginning to enjoy being a senior boy at school. One evening a group of us senior boys were talking to Father Fritz. As I recall we were standing on one of the balconies that overlooked the school ground. One end of the school playground housed garages for the school buses which ferried students to and from the school. For some reason the garage doors were invariably painted red, and when shut provided a most convenient, impromptu, wicket. Suddenly, as we leaned over the balcony, we saw a solitary little fellow in front of the red garage doors. Senior boys at school tend to be dismissive of their juniors, but even without this prej-udice, Sunil looked comical. He was still wearing his school uniform of dirty beige shirt and pants, except being a junior he hadn't graduated to long trousers as we had. He even wore the recently introduced school tie. All this was supplemented by the full cricket gear. Pads, gloves, even a cap. The pads seemed to come to his chin, as he repeatedly and religiously played forward; every now and again we would catch a glimpse of the back of his shorts and his bare legs. It was too much of a temptation and we mocked and laughed with great pleasure.

I do not know whether Sunil heard Fritzy's roar of disapproval, it was certainly loud and very severe. Turning on us he said in his most clipped English accent 'You load of wash-outs. You think you can play cricket. You are just two-pice chaps. You'll never be cricketers. That boy will be a great cricketer. He will play for India.'

We were used to Fritzy's verbal broadsides, but this one was very odd. It ran counter to everything Xavier's was meant to stand for. St Xavier's was an all-round school, which gave its pupils a good general education but did not seek to make them excellent in any one thing. Though nobody would have admitted it then, or even now, St Xavier's had a slightly dilettantish air. Its good scholastic students were good at their studies but they did not match up to the best in Mumbai. In sport they put up a good fight, very rarely won and certainly did not believe in sacrificing everything for victory. In fact, dedication in pursuit of any one thing was somehow an un-Xavierite trait.

However, Sunil avoided dilettantism because his dedication was real, and because Fritzy was committed to him. Fritzy had a way of conveying his commitment which was so passionate and touching that it remained with you for many years. I experienced it myself, a couple of years after the Sunil episode, when Fritzy took us for English, and with one throw-away sentence made me believe I could aspire to be a writer. It was years before I realised how much those words were to mean to me and how much they were to sustain me when writing seemed so very far away. Something of the same Fritzy commitment must have been conveyed to Sunil.

But did St Xavier's do anything else for Sunil Gavaskar and his cricket? Here I am inclined to agree with Milind Rege, Sunil's contemporary, and the one under whose captaincy Sunil played for the school. Rege has written, 'At St Xavier's High School where Sunil studied, he was like every other cricketer. In fact there was little or no encouragement for us at Xavier's. We played cricket on a mat which was half the length of a cricket pitch. Later, we graduated to turf wickets – the turf being in the form of red mud spread evenly on a hard bumpy outfield.'

So between the half-matting and the not-quite-proper turf, we played a lot of our school cricket. Its heart and soul were inter-class matches where a good performance brought the player to the notice of Father Fritz and the school selectors. I think one year an attempt at school trials to alert good cricketers was made. But there was never any attempt at coaching cricketers or bringing them up. We played a lot of cricket, but little of it was good cricket. We played for fun and those of us who had some ability went on to play for the school. Xavier's cricket had a brittle charm which can pass for substance at that age, and that seemed to be personified by Feroz Patka.

Sunil at school never had the sort of aura that came naturally to Patka, and if the truth be told it was Milind Rege who was considered the really gifted cricketer at school. For various reasons, largely connected with his health, Rege, though he played for Mumbai, never made it in international cricket. At school the cricket pundits were convinced that he would make his name as a cricketer and display to a wider world the leadership qualities that Xavier's sought to inculcate.

At school Sunil appeared to be good but he was not particularly exceptional. The first time he had played for the school he had batted number ten, scored thirty not out and found himself in the next day's *Times of India* as 'G. Sunil 30 not out'. It was when he moved to a higher grade of cricket, the inter-schools Gooch–Behar, then the inter-collegiate Rohinton Baria competitions that Sunil revealed what an unusually perceptive cricket journalist, Sharad Kotnis, described as a 'Bradmanesque streak'.

However, it was not only Jesuit discipline that helped to shape Sunil as a cricketer, but also his own Hindu Maharashtrian work ethic. Although nobody who grew up in Mumbai, and knew of Shivaji Park or Dadar Union, or experienced the peculiar Maharashtrian *angst*, could be unaware of it, in the millions of words that have been written on Sunil, nobody has referred to it. What is this Maharashtrian angst? This Shivaji Park ingredient so crucial to the making of Sunil Gavaskar? Very simply it is wronged nationalism. Somewhat similar to the one felt in Yorkshire but infinitely more powerful. One that sees enemies everywhere and believes that the true merits and genius of Maharashtrians – as the descendants of the Marhattas were called – have not been acknowledged. Shivaji Park is a symbol of that feeling. Physically, Mumbai is an island, or a group of seven islands joined together, representing a long, thin sausage surrounded by sea on either side. Just three main arterial roads link the commercial centre of Mumbai in the south with the industrial suburban north. Shivaji Park stands in the centre of this link, and is that area's cricketing maidan: equivalent to south Mumbai's Oval, Cross and Azad.

Shivaji Park is named after Shivaji the great hero of Marhatta nationalism. In the early years of the seventeenth century he raised the standard of revolt against Aurangzeb, the last great Mughal Emperor of Delhi, and so successful was he that he not only established a kingdom, but sowed the seeds of the eventual destruction of the Mughal Empire. In the struggle against the British the Maharashtrians were in the forefront along with the Bengalis. When Gandhi's methods won the day the Maharashtrians found they had gained little or nothing.

Mumbai, the commercial capital of India, and arguably the principal city of the country, always symbolised to Maharashtrians their double loss. The loss of Shivaji's Marhatta Empire that had challenged the Moghuls and resisted the British, and the loss of the pre-Gandhian political leadership. Though Shivaji, and his descendants, had never controlled Mumbai – it had been a Portuguese and then a British enclave – in the Mumbai of my youth the Maharashtrian desire to control Mumbai was evident. Try as they might, they could not achieve this. They formed the most significant proportion of the population – 42 per cent – but not the majority. They were the drawers of water and the hewers of wood. The real power in Mumbai lay with the others: Parsees, efficient middlemen, who had helped create commercial Mumbai and, as Gandhi swept the Indian political board, his community, the Gujeratis. By the mid-1950s Gujeratis were being challenged by the Sindhis. The Mumbai legend was that Sindhis, refugees from Sind which had gone to Pakistan at the time of the Indian partition, had arrived in Mumbai wearing just one shirt and ended up selling shirts to everybody in the city.

What galled the Maharashtrians was the fact that they were lumped together with their hateful enemies, the Gujeratis, in one composite state of Mumbai, whose capital was the city of Mumbai. While the rest of India was divided up into linguistic states the central government in Delhi argued that Maharashtrians and Gujeratis must live together and Mumbai was too important, too 'cosmopolitan' to belong only to Maharashtrians. Eventually, through Gandhian-style mass action, and a certain amount of violence, the Maharashtrians won their argument. A separate Maharashtrian state was created with Mumbai as its capital. This did nothing to change the commercial power in the city, and even today Mumbai, remains a city where the capital is in Gujerati and Sindhi hands – the bosses for whom the Maharashtrians work.

Nowhere is the sense of injustice stronger than in the congested Maharashtrian middle class of Shivaji Park. Perhaps in time some researcher will tell us about the mainspring which motivates the Maharashtrian middle classes of Shivaji Park. It is already easy to discern the broad outline. The intense desire to succeed, the need to prove to the rest of cosmopolitan Mumbai and India that they are a force and a certain feeling, which they share with the Bengalis, that they have been wronged by the rest of India, ruled – or ruined – by Gujeratis and upstart Sindhis and Marwaris. The Maharashtrian middle class nurses a deep sense of wronged justice and that can always be a very powerful force, be it in politics or sport.

How much or little Sunil actually shares these Maharashtrian Shivaji Park middle-class ambitions is not known, but he was fully aware of them and must have been influenced by them. Like any good Maharashtrian, Sunil learnt the Marhatta history early, from his mother and father – and at the age of ten there was Vasu Paranjape and Dadar Union, which plays its cricket on a maidan about a mile or so from Shivaji Park. It was Vasu who gave Sunil his nickname Sunny, a name whose endless permutations along the lines of Sunny Days, Sunny Plays, Sunny Records – and even more ridiculous ones – are a delight to Indian sub-editors. If Sunil had a mentor in cricket then it was undoubtedly Paranjape. For many years he worked in the same Mumbai firm as Sunil and continued to act as a sort of father-confessor.

In December 1983 Sunil returned to Mumbai after a quite traumatic Test match against the West Indians in Kolkata. Sunil had equalled Bradman's record of 29 Test centuries in the Delhi Test a few weeks previous to this and an expectant, characteristically tumultuous Bengali crowd were waiting in feverish expectation to see Sunil actually break the record. But he was out to the first ball of the match, to Marshall. He lasted a little longer in the second innings, but he got out with a reckless, very un-Sunil-like stroke. The Indians, who at one stage had looked like winning the match, collapsed ignominiously and almost everybody in India seemed to hold Gavaskar personally responsible for the Indian defeat. Forgotten was his Delhi performance, and Indians, who can veer alarmingly from praise to abuse, showered choice epithets on him. One cricket supporter sent him a photograph of a chappal (slipper) with an arrow pointing to the picture and the inscription, 'I present this with due apologies for your performance against the West Indies.' In the Indian tradition the Order of the Chappal is damning. It is quite common for political demonstrators to indicate their disgust by hurling chappals at their political enemies. How rattled Sunil was by all this, I do not know, but he promised Paranjape that he would make amends. The result was his scoring his thirtieth century at the Madras Test and breaking Bradman's record.

Paranjape tells the story with no great dramatic flourish, almost as if it was inevitable. But then to Paranjape it undoubtedly was. He had done much to instil this Marhatta determination in Sunil. This is how Paranjape would later recall Sunil's introduction to Mumbai club cricket:

> I remember Sunny as a youngster of ten plus, coming along with his
> father to watch Dadar Union play on Sundays. Eagerly pressing for a
> knock before the start of the matches, I distinctly recall the obvious
> and conspicuous straightness of his bat. Even the seriousness during
> those knocks used to be beyond his years.

We can picture the Dadar Union scene. The tin, asbestos shed, that has
clearly seen better days – next to it, a few shacks for the malis and their
children, who can just be glimpsed playing in the mud in front of the shed.
Behind the shed, half obscured, a block of flats with its mixture of grime
and dust and Indian domesticity. And just in front of the shed, instead of a
pitch fit for a conquering hero, there is a mound of weeds that would
shame any weekend gardener.

Yet in Gavaskar's recall of his crucial Dadar Union days, there is no
mention of such disabilities. Partly this is the Indian ability, necessary for
survival, to ignore the squalor and poverty that surrounds almost every
public place. It is this that enables rich Indians to ignore the beggars outside the restaurants and walk blithely in and enjoy a sumptuous meal. For
Sunil, the Dadar Union's sumptuousness was provided by Vasu Paranjape,
the Captain of the team, and Vithal 'Marshall' Patil, good Maharashtrians
and forceful personalities. Paranjape impressed on Sunil his outlook on the
game, which was 'a blend of the carefree approach of the West Indians and
the bulldog tenacity of the Australians...as a fielder he was magnificent
and his aggressive batting won many a hopeless match for Dadar Union.
His captaincy was as dynamic as his batting, and he loved a challenge.'

Patil, or Marshall as he was called in the Indian tradition of giving
English nicknames to their compatriots, was the Dadar Union coach. He
lived and breathed cricket and encouraged Sunil by not only bowling to
him at every possible opportunity – a distinct advantage as he could swing
the ball – but also by providing him with a mental stimulus. 'Often,' Sunil
would later recall, 'he would drop in at our house later after dinner and
say "Sunny, a century tomorrow". I think he had more confidence in my
cricketing ability than I had myself.'

Paranjape's influence was so pervasive that most Shivaji Park
Maharashtrians, interested in cricket, seem to have fallen under his spell.
I remember talking about Paranjape with a staunch Maharashtrian nation-
alist, who worked in my father's firm, and was struck by the emotion that
Paranjape generated even in such a grown man. In those years, Paranjape's
Dadar Union and Shivaji Park as such had a cricketing mission similar to

the one that inspired Maharashtrian politicians. Right from the inception of the Ranji trophy in 1934, the state of Mumbai had been represented by a cricket team. However, during the days of the Raj, the state of Mumbai was huge and in addition to the Mumbai team, parts of the state were also allowed to enter the Ranji trophy. So Gujerat had a team as did Maharastra. The Gujerat team was centred around Ahmedabad, the Maharastra team around Poona, now called Pune and the actual Mumbai state team around the capital city of Mumbai. It was as if Yorkshire had been allowed to enter three teams, one centred around Leeds, another around Bradford and a third, possibly around Harrogate or Scarborough.

When the Maharashtrian politicians won their argument, the old Mumbai state was divided between Gujerat, with its capital at Ahmedabad, and Maharastra with its capital at Mumbai. The Ranji trophy continued to have three teams: Mumbai, Maharastra and Gujerat. But for the Maharashtrians living and playing their cricket in Mumbai, this produced a curious situation. There were now two Maharashtrian teams, the original Maharashtrian side centred around Poona, and the old Mumbai state side, now exclusively devoted to Mumbai city. Mumbai's cricket team reflected the cosmopolitan nature of Mumbai society. The great Mumbai cricketer and captain was Polly Umrigar. Faroukh Engineer, another Parsee, kept wicket and one of Mumbai's leading players was Gulbhai Ramchand, a Sindhi. Maharashtrians formed part of the team, but did not run it or control it.

The tension between Maharashtrians and non-Maharashtrians was reflected in the struggle between the Mumbai cricket association, which was Maharashtrian dominated, and which resented the pre-eminence of the Cricket Club of India, at that time India's MCC. The CCI was more cosmopolitan; it owned Brabourne stadium, Mumbai's Test centre, and every Test match saw a running battle between the Mumbai Cricket Association and the CCI about the allocation of Test match tickets. Eventually so bitter was the struggle that Mumbai Cricket Association decided to take cricket away from the CCI and Wankhede stadium was built a mere quarter of a mile away. By the time the first Test was played there in 1975 the Maharashtrians had asserted their control over the Mumbai cricket team. But in the decade preceding that, as Sunil grew into cricketing maturity, the battle for the control of Mumbai cricket was yet to be decided.

Sunil has never spoken or written about this. Possibly he would profess total indifference to all this Maharashtrian feeling. In the mid-1980s, a *Sunday Times* writer, Dudley Doust, went to India to write a profile on Sunil Gavaskar and I suggested to him that he might look into Sunil's Maharashtrian, Shivaji Park, background. But when Dudley asked Sunil about this he dismissed it. No, he didn't feel particularly Maharashtrian, he was an Indian. Why, his wife Marshniel was not a Maharashtrian but a girl from UP, a province in northern India, and he frankly did not bother much about her origins. To Dudley this answer seemed conclusive enough. In fact though, it is very much the answer I would have expected a good Xavierite to give. After all we were taught at school. 'You are Indian first, then anything else. When they ask you who you are, do not say you are a Bengali, or a Maharashtrian, or any other regional variation. Say you are Indian.'

Perhaps some clue to Sunil's real feelings on the subject can be found in *Idols*, which was published in 1984 and contains Sunil's reflections on 31 cricketers. Nearly all the well-known cricketers of the last two decades are there and most of the names would be easily recognised by any cricket follower. However, the style of the essays is that of fulsome praise rather than appraisal. Only one cricketing essay stands out – the one on Padmakar Shivalkar. He is also only one of two in this list who never played Test cricket or even came near to it. He is hardly known outside his native Mumbai. It is precisely because of Gavaskar's ability to portray Shivalkar's predicaments and problems, a left-arm spinner hoping to play for India at a time when Bishen Singh Bedi was at his height, which makes the essay stand out from the rest. Gavaskar neatly highlights Shivalkar's Shivaji Park background, the character and humour that gave rise to his nickname Paddy, and the cheerfulness and determination with which he nurtured his skill as a left-arm spinner, knowing full well that he would never play for his country.

Gavaskar is able to do it because he has known Shivalkar since his teens, and clearly shares the widespread Mumbai feeling of the late 1960s and early 1970s that Shivalkar was unlucky. Shivalkar's story seemed to symbolise the Maharashtrian angst. In this essay Gavaskar seems to be paying homage to the cricketing memory of a man, lost to possible international greatness because of rotten luck, and perhaps, prejudiced authorities.

There are some in India who would see Sunil's Maharashtrian background as a clue to his curious love–hate relationship with the Indian public. Indians respect Sunil but they also fear him. He is not, for instance, able to invoke the sort of warmth that was awarded to Kapil Dev, or to his own brother-in-law, Visvanath, probably the most loved of all Indian cricketers, let alone Sachin Tendulkar.

Part of the Indian diffidence may be that for all his records and his achievements, Gavaskar's domestic record has always lagged behind his Test record. By the time his career ended he had scored more runs at Test than in domestic cricket (see Tables 7.1, 7.2 and 7.3).

Table 7.1 S. M. Gavaskar: Test match career

v	Season	T	I	NO	HS	Runs	Ave	100	50	Ct
WI	1970–1	4	8	3	220	774	154.80	4	3	1
Eng	1971	3	6	0	57	144	24.00	—	2	5
Eng (Ind)	1972–3	5	10	1	69	224	24.88	—	2	2
Eng	1974	3	6	0	101	217	36.16	1	1	1
WI (Ind)	1974–5	2	4	0	86	108	27.00	—	1	1
NZ	1975–6	3	5	1	116	266	66.50	1	1	5
WI	1975–6	4	7	0	156	390	55.71	2	1	2
NZ (Ind)	1976–7	3	6	0	119	259	43.16	1	1	3
Eng (Ind)	1976–7	5	10	0	108	394	39.40	1	2	7
Aus	1977–8	5	9	0	127	450	50.00	3	—	8
Pak	1978–9	3	6	1	137	447	89.40	2	2	3
WI (Ind)	1978–9	6	9	1	205	732	91.50	4	1	4
Eng	1979	4	7	0	221	542	77.42	1	4	3
Aus (Ind)	1979–80	6	8	0	123	425	53.12	2	2	3
Pak (Ind)	1979–80	6	11	1	166	529	52.90	1	2	4
Eng (Ind)	1979–80	1	2	0	49	73	36.50	—	—	—
Aus	1980–1	3	6	0	70	118	19.66	—	1	3

NZ	1980–1	3	5	0	53	126	25.20	—	1	3
Eng (Ind)	1981–2	6	9	1	172	500	62.50	1	3	9
Eng	1982	3	3	0	48	74	24.66	—	—	2
SL (Ind)	1982–3	1	2	1	155	159	159.00	1	—	2
Pak	1982–3	6	10	1	127*	434	48.22	1	3	5
WI	1982–3	5	9	1	147*	240	30.00	1	—	4
Pak (Ind)	1983–4	3	5	1	103*	264	66.00	1	2	—
WI (Ind)	1983–4	6	11	1	236*	505	50.50	2	1	5
Pak	1984–5	2	3	0	48	120	40.00	—	—	4
Eng (Ind)	1984–5	5	8	0	65	140	17.50	—	1	3
SL	1985	3	6	1	52	186	37.20	2	2	3
Aus	1985–6	3	4	1	172	352	117.33	—	—	2
Eng	1986	3	6	0	54	175	29.16	1	1	3
Aus (Ind)	1986–7	3	4	0	103	205	51.25	1	1	3
SL (Ind)	1986–7	3	3	0	176	255	85.00	1	1	2
Pak (Ind)	1986–7	4	6	0	96	295	49.16	3	3	3
In India		65	108	7	236*	5,067	50.16	16	23	51
Overseas		60	106	9	221	5,055	52.11	18	22	57
		125	214	16	236*	10,122	51.12	34	45	108

Note
Ind = played in India
* = Not out

Table 7.2 Domestic competitions: 1966–7 to 1986–7

		Matches	I	NO	HS	Runs	Ave	100	50	Ct
M	1966–7	1	2	0	9	15	7.50	—	—	1
M	1968–9	2	3	0	54	112	37.33	—	1	2
R	1969–70	2	3	1	114	141	70.50	1	—	6
I & R	1970–1	3	5	1	176	365	91.25	2	—	2
M/I/R/D	1971–2	8	12	0	101	828	69.00	3	1	10
M/I/R/D	1972–3	12	20	3	160	757	44.52	3	2	23
M/I/R/D	1973–4	10	16	2	108	563	40.21	1	3	13
I/R/D	1974–5	8	11	3	156*	435	54.37	1	1	7
I/R/D	1975–6	6	8	1	190	681	97.28	3	1	5
I/R/D	1976–7	11	17	4	228	807	62.07	2	4	13
D	1977–8	2	3	0	169	276	92.00	1	1	3
R/D	1978–9	7	8	1	204	509	72.71	3	1	6
R	1979–80	7	11	1	153	491	49.10	1	3	2
I	1980–1	1	2	0	27	28	14.00	—	—	—
I/R/D	1981–2	9	12	3	340	971	107.88	4	1	—
I/D	1982–3	3	6	0	67	136	22.66	—	1	3
R	1983–4	6	8	3	206*	541	108.20	2	2	1
I/R	1984–5	5	9	3	106	426	71.00	1	3	1
D	1985–6	2	3	0	119	235	78.33	1	1	2
R/D	1986–7	3	3	0	92	114	38.00	—	1	6
M	Moin-ud-Dowlah	9	13	0	94	476	36.61	—	4	7
I	Irani Trophy	12	22	4	156*	733	40.72	3	1	9
R	Ranji Trophy	66	93	17	340	5,335	70.19	20	14	74
D	Duleep Trophy	22	36	5	228	1,891	61.00	6	8	16
		109	164	26	340	8,435	61.12	29	27	106

Bowling	Balls	Runs	W	Av	BB
Tests	380	206	1	206.00	1–34
M	108	98	2	49.00	2–33
I	72	61	0	—	—
R	320	148	6	24.66	1–0 (twice)
D	120	104	0	—	—
	1,000	617	9	68.55	2–33

Note
* = Not out

This is quite extraordinary. Comparable figures for Boycott and Bradman would show phenomenal run-scoring in domestic cricket far outstripping that of international cricket. Partly this may be due to the growth of international cricket, but more perhaps because Sunil is not an accumulator. Only twice in domestic cricket has he accumulated more than 500 runs a season – a benchmark in Indian domestic cricket.

But even that can hardly explain the anti-Gavaskar venom that is spewed out by the Indian press. At the end of the 1984–5 season against England, a dismal one for India, there was much press coverage on India's

Table 7.3 S. M. Gavaskar: First-class hundreds

	Season	Score	Side	Opponent	Venue
1.	1969–70	114	Bombay	Rajasthan	Bombay
2.	1970–1	104	Bombay	Gujerat	Bombay
3.	1970–1	176	Bombay	Maharashtra	Pune
4.	1970–1	125	Indian XI	Trinidad & Tobago	Pointe-a-Pierre
5.	1970–1	116	India	West Indies	Georgetown
6.	1970–1	+117*	India	West Indies	Bridgetown
7.	1970–1	124	India	West Indies	Port-of-Spain
8.	1970–1	+220	India	West Indies	Port-of-Spain
9.	1971	165	Indians	Leicestershire	Leicester
10.	1971	194	Indians	Worcestershire	Worcester
11.	1971	+128	Indians	TN Pearce's XI	Scarborough
12.	1971–2	101	West Zone	East Jone	Jamshedpur
13.	1971–2	282	Bombay	Bihar	Bombay
14.	1971–2	157	Bombay	Bengal	Bombay
15.	1972–3	160	Bombay	Gujerat	Bombay
16.	1972–3	135	Bombay	Maharashtra	Indore
17.	1972–3	134	Bombay	Hyderabad	Bombay
18.	1973–4	+108	Bombay	Rest of India XI	Bangalore
19.	1973–4	104	Indian XI	SL Board Pres XI	Colombo, PSS
20.	1974	+104*	Indians	Lancashire	Old Trafford
21.	1974	136	Indians	Surrey	The Oval
22.	1974	101	India	England	Old Trafford
23.	1974–5	156*	Rest of India	Karnataka	Pune
24.	1975–6	112	Bombay	Gujerat	Butsar
25.	1975–6	203	Indian XI	Sri Lankan XI	Hyderabad
26.	1975–6	190	Bombay	Maharashtra	Bombay
27.	1975–6	171	Bombay	Saurashtra	Bombay
28.	1975–6	116	India	New Zealand	Auckland
29.	1975–6	156	India	West Indies	Port-of-Spain
30.	1975–6	+102	India	West Indies	Port-of-Spain (2)
31.	1976–7	228	West Zone	South Zone	Baroda
32.	1976–7	119	India	New Zealand	Bombay
33.	1976–7	108	India	England	Bombay
34.	1976–7	120	Bombay	Tamil Nadu	Bombay
35.	1977–8	169	West Zone	Central Zone	Ahmedabad
36.	1977–8	+113	India	Australia	Brisbane
37.	1977–8	+127	India	Australia	Perth
38.	1977–8	+118	India	Australia	MCG
39.	1978–9	165*	Indian XI	Pakistan Banks	Karachi
40.	1978–9	111	India	Pakistan	Karachi
41.	1978–9	+137	India	Pakistan	Karachi
42.	1978–9	205	India	West Indies	Bombay
43.	1978–9	107	India	West Indies	Calcutta
44.	1978–9	+182*	India	West Indies	Calcutta
45.	1978–9	105	Bombay	Maharashtra	Ahmednagar
46.	1978–9	120	India	West Indies	Delhi
47.	1978–9	204	Bombay	Bihar	Bombay
48.	1978–9	130*	West Zone	North Zone	Delhi
49.	1979	166	Indians	Hampshire	Southampton

(continued)

Table 7.3 Continued

	Season	Score	Side	Opponent	Venue
50.	1979	116	Indians	Gloucestershire	Bristol
51.	1979	+221	India	England	The Oval
52.	1979–80	115	India	Australia	Kanpur
53.	1979–80	123	India	Australia	Bombay
54.	1979–80	166	India	Pakistan	Madras
55.	1979–80	153	Bombay	Maharashtra	Bombay
56.	1980	+138	Somerset	Surrey	The Oval
57.	1980	155*	Somerset	Yorkshire	Weston-super-Mare
58.	1980–1	157	Indians	Western Australia	Perth
59.	1980–1	108	Indians	Queensland	Brisbane
60.	1981–2	102*	Bombay	Rest of India	Indore
61.	1981–2	164*	West Zone	Central Zone	Nagpur
62.	1981–2	172	India	England	Bangalore
63.	1981–2	127	Bombay	Baroda	Bombay
64.	1981–2	340	Bombay	Bengal	Bombay
65.	1982	+172	Indians	Warwickshire	Edgbaston
66.	1982–3	155	India	Sri Lanka	Madras
67.	1982–3	+127*	India	Pakistan	Faisalabad
68.	1982–3	147*	India	West Indies	Georgetown
69.	1983–4	+103*	India	Pakistan	Bangalore
70.	1983–4	121	India	West Indies	Delhi
71.	1983–4	236*	India	West Indies	Madras
72.	1983–4	110	Bombay	Maharashtra	Bombay
73.	1983–4	206*	Bombay	Delhi	Bombay
74.	1984–5	106	Bombay	Delhi	Bombay
75.	1985–6	119	West Zone	South Zone	Bangalore
76.	1985–6	166*	India	Australia	Adelaide
77.	1985–6	172	India	Australia	SCG
78.	1986	136*	Indians	Somerset	Taunton
79.	1986–7	103	India	Australia	Bombay
80.	1986–7	176	India	Sri Lanka	Kanpur
81.	1987	188	Rest of the world	MCC	Lord's

Note
* = Not out

one great hero of the series: Mohammed Azharuddin. India's then leading weekly Sunday published a cover story about him. Within that cover story was this article about Sunil Gavaskar. An article that deserves to be quoted in full, just to indicate the emotions that Sunil can arouse.

Is Gavaskar jealous of Azharuddin?

For over a decade Sunil Gavaskar was Indian cricket. He was the best opening batsman in the world, one of the greatest Indian batsmen ever, an astute and successful captain, and the holder of just about every batting record in test cricket. In the hit-and-miss world of Indian cricket, he was a phenomenon. With success came fame, fat paychecks and the adulation and affection of millions, something which Gavaskar may well have taken for granted.

More recently, however, there have been more ruins than runs for Gavaskar, a phase which has coincided with the rise of Mohammed Azharuddin. His first series has been as magnificent as Gavaskar's 1971 tour of the West Indies and he has quickly replaced his captain as the cult figure of the game. Cricket-lovers all over the country are already lining up behind Azhar. Is Gavaskar missing his status as a Messiah? And more importantly, has he deliberately tried to place obstacles in the young super-star's way?

With Sandip Patil dropped after his suicidal dismissal in the lost Delhi test, one place in the middle order was vacant. It was Gavaskar's plan to drop down the order, not to give it a semblance of stability as was the original excuse, but to find his touch – his failures with the bat were continuing. But the selectors, the men Gavaskar had once called jokers, strongly, and this time rightly opposed his plan. This was the right time, they decided, to blood a promising young cricketer and Gavaskar would have to open the innings. And in what was one of the dreariest test matches in recent history, only Azharuddin sparkled.

Again, after Gavaskar's by-now-all-too-familiar early dismissal in the Indian first innings at Kanpur, it was surprisingly Azharuddin who replaced his skipper at the batting crease. Admittedly, Azhar was the man in form and Gavaskar's Mumbai colleague Dilip Vengsarkar the regular one-drop batsman in the side was not, but it was only Azhar's fourth Test innings and there was another far more experienced batsman. Mohinder Amarnath who has regularly batted in this pivotal number three position. And why was a young batsman pushed up the batting order just to protect an out-of-form senior batsman?

When Azharuddin did get his third and by far his best century on the second morning, his team mates applauded from the players' enclosure as the crowds rose to a man to greet their new hero. Only the man who ought to have led the applause was very conspicuously absent. Since Sivaramakrishnan had sent the English side spinning to their doom during those brief moments of euphoria at Mumbai few things had gone right for India, and this was one of the few. The Gavaskar of old, more a leader of a combative, fighting-fit team, than of a surly bunch of highly-talented individuals would have been the first on the balcony. This time he refused to make an appearance. What kept Gavaskar away during Azhar's and India's moment of glory may never be revealed. Was it pique that a man far younger and far more inexperienced had stolen his thunder? Or was he simply scared of showing his face in the enclosure and facing a crowd which has adopted Gavaskar-baiting as a bloodsport?

Then, with the wicket proving to be a traditional Kanpur sleeping beauty which even Sivaramakrishnan, the prince charming of Indian spinners could not awaken, did Gavaskar honestly expect to dismiss a side which had batted for over two days and scored over 400 runs in just over two hours? Or was it just another gesture of empty defiance, crafty enough to prevent Azhar, batting on a brilliantly improvised 54 from getting another hundred and re-writing the cricket books all over again? Gavaskar himself had admitted that God was an Englishman and so, could not have hoped for divine assistance. In any case, getting a Test team out in 80 minutes and 20 mandatory overs on a batsman's paradise would have required not only extraordinary slices of luck, but a course in black magic as well.

Is Gavaskar envious of Azharuddin? Is he trying to prevent Azhar from reaching the pinnacle of glory he himself had reached? Perhaps, the limited overs matches in Australia next month will provide the answer.

It is difficult to imagine a similar article appearing in the English press. But while this Indian writer reflected the bitterness that Gavaskar arouses, did Sunil, perhaps, contribute to it? There was the celebrated feud with Kapil Dev, the fact that he had not been able to project an all-India image and his quest for money. I am inclined to agree with Pataudi that there is a perverse streak in Gavaskar that may have been worsened by the pressure-cooker atmosphere that Indians inflict on their celebrities. While the charity and obvious generosity of Indians can be quite marvellous, it can also be overwhelming and the family focus of Indian life make – at least in the urban sphere – cool-headed contemplation difficult. But perhaps Gavaskar's career and his relationship with the Indian public prove that single-minded dedication has its pitfalls. He was certainly a hero and a great cricketer but one the public found difficult to live with.

Since his retirement Gavaskar has continued to stamp his very unique, and singular, personality on the cricketing world and the wider world. He has shown personal courage too – during the horrific riots in Mumbai in 1993 when Hindu mobs targeted Muslims he helped to rescue them. More importantly, he has kept his distance from Bal Thackeray, the former cartoonist turned politician and a very divisive, controversial, figure in modern Mumbai. The Shiv Shena leader, who started his political life on the sectarian slogan of fighting for his fellow Maharashtrians, targeting the Udipi restaurants run by people from the south of India, has now made himself the leader of a fascist Hindu party targeting all Muslims, asking them to prove their loyalty when India play Pakistan and even agitating to stop Pakistan playing cricket in Mumbai. His followers even dug up the wicket at

Wankhede. In such a situation lesser men, let alone sportsmen, would have taken the easy way and said nothing. But not Gavaskar. In 1992 Gavaskar boldly forecast that Pakistan would win the World Cup, at a time when not many in the Pakistani team were that confident. When Pakistan duly won he became a hero in Pakistan and was asked to join in the celebrations. There were those in Mumbai who felt he should keep his head down but Gavaskar, who had made his judgement on cricketing grounds, ignored such cowardly advice and went to Pakistan to be feted in royal manner.

His individual style was, probably, most evident to people in England in the summer of 1990. The Indians were touring England and during the Lord's Test it emerged that Gavaskar had turned down an invitation to became a honorary member of the MCC. This is an honour extended to famous cricketers and coveted by them. Lord's, for nearly everyone in cricket has a special magic, the headquarters of the game where cricketers want to succeed. But Gavaskar has never fallen under the spell of Lord's. He never scored a century in a Lord's Test and never seemed to regret it. But for him to turn down an invitation to be a member was sensational. It soon became clear that he was less than impressed with the offhand, even rude manner, in which he had been treated by the Lord's staff, particularly the officious gatemen. Gavaskar's decision caused such a shock that Bishen Bedi, the manager of the India touring team, came into the Lord's press box during the Test and distributed a statement saying how shocked he was. He spoke of his own delight at being made a MCC member and condemned Gavaskar for dishonouring Indians living in England. How Bedi, a visitor to England, could present himself as a spokesman for Indians in this country was a mystery. Gavaskar let the controversy swirl round him paying little or no attention.

A few years later, when the MCC renewed their invitation, Gavaskar obviously, feeling he had made his point, accepted and became a member. And later still he delivered the prestigious Cowdrey lecture using the speech to criticise Australians for their on-field sledging. At the lecture he made a point of wearing the Indian national dress, as he did when in the spring of 2004 he acted as studio-based commentator in London for Sky during the Pakistan–India series. He was making the point that he was an Indian, a proud Indian, but not one who either accepted shabby compromise or tolerated evil.

It summed up the complex man. Always willing to speak his mind. Not afraid to take up controversial positions. The first modern Indian cricketer to truly impress himself on the world stage, a man seen abroad as the representative of Indian cricket but a man who provokes more complex emotions amongst Indians themselves.

8

The Nawabi legend

In December 1980, just after India had beaten Pakistan in the third Test match in Mumbai, the following graffiti appeared on the walls of certain parts of the city. It read:

INDIA PLAYS WITH THIRTEEN PEOPLE – ELEVEN PLAYERS AND TWO UMPIRES.

Indians have a much more relaxed attitude towards their own umpires than most non-Indians give them credit for. That graffiti was still on the walls of Mumbai when I visited India almost a year later. Then, too, umpiring decisions were threatening to bedevil a Test series. The first Test between India and England was being played in Mumbai, and Keith Fletcher and his men were convinced it had already been lost because of Indian umpiring decisions. I remember talking to a few of my Indian friends the day before England lost the match and one of them was supremely confident that India would win. 'You just watch; there will be three lbw decisions – Boycott, Fletcher and Botham.' Fletcher and Boycott were indeed given out lbw, but to play back on a crumbling fourth day wicket suggested an optimism that would have been misplaced even in front of English umpires. Botham, more characteristically, was out trying to hit the ball into the Arabian Sea.

But the graffiti that had appeared on the Mumbai streets was no self-deprecatory Indian joke. It appeared mostly in the Muslim areas of Mumbai – clearly the work of Indian Muslims expressing an unequivocal opinion on that controversial Test. The whiff of controversy is evident even from the scrupulously objective reports in *Wisden*. The pitch, it said, presented problems from the first day, so much so that Gavaskar, the Indian Captain, who had decided to bat on winning the toss, was out for four by a ball that stopped. The Indians secured their initial advantage because they won the toss but the anger that prompted the graffiti was caused by the number of lbw decisions given by the umpires against the visiting Pakistanis. Four of them were out lbw in the second innings, as against only Visvanath in the Indian second innings. *Wisden*, describing Miandad's lbw said 'considering that the ball was turning so readily, he might have been unfortunate to be given out'.

To the Indian Muslims Miandad's dismissal was not chance but part of a conspiracy. They reflected the charges made by the Pakistani cricketers who not only alleged bias on the part of the umpires, but also claimed that the ground authorities in Mumbai had doctored the pitch after the match had started. For Indians, naturally suspicious of Pakistan and her actions, the fact that Indian Muslims' views agreed with those of the Pakistani cricket team raised all the old doubts. By the time I visited Mumbai the Test, indeed the entire series (which the Indians won 2–0) had reopened many of the arguments I had personally experienced some forty years ago. Then the debate had taken place behind closed doors. Now it was the subject of cover stories. Very simply it was: when India played Pakistan, what was the position of the large minority Indian Muslims? Did they support India, Pakistan or remain neutral?

We are dealing with what one of India's greatest writers, Nirad C. Chaudhuri calls 'the least of the minorities' in India. I am inclined to say we are dealing with the Indian nigger. I shall explain both terms in greater detail but first an account of the historical background is necessary.

Of India's population of over one billion, some 120 million are Muslims. The great majority of these are descendants of converts to Islam from lower-caste Hindu society. A small minority among them could, possibly, claim descent from the Muslim conquerors that arrived in India in a wave of invasions that started in the eleventh century. The Muslim conquest of India was a gradual, long, drawn out process which started in Sind in the eighth century, and ended with the Mughal rule in Delhi between the fifteenth and the eighteenth centuries. The Muslims never conquered the whole of India, or even ruled over all of it, not even at the height of the Mughal Empire. As D. P. Singhal, says in *A History of the Indian People*, while the Turki Afghan invaders were mainly interested in loot and plunder – destroying innumerable Hindu temples and icons, carrying off immense wealth and appropriating businesses – the later Muslim rulers were woven into the India pattern 'drawn by the tolerance and responsiveness of the Indian mind and their own capacity for absorption and imitation. Throughout India, an initial clash was followed by fusion and synthesis'.

The popular conception however was different. The Hindu recollection of the Muslim invasion of India was that of the classical conqueror and plunderer. The Muslim Muhammed of Ghazni is seen swooping down from the lush inviting mountains of the Hindu Kush to repeatedly invade India, destroy the wonderfully rich temple of Somnath and the perfection and beauty of the pre-Islamic Hindu Raj. In this Hindu version, which is highly selective and somewhat biased, the Hindu fall dates from Muhammed of Ghazni's repeated invasions of India. It symbolises the archetypal Muslim interloper, the man who covets Hindu wealth and rapes Hindu women. To many Hindus the Muslim is ignorant, uncouth, dirty, often has a short, funny beard and a very peculiar un-Indian (read un-Hindu) cap. What is more he does not wear the *dhoti* as most Hindus do, but a *lungi*. To most westerners the difference between a *dhoti* and a *lungi* may seem academic. Both are long pieces of cloth, worn by men, and wrapped round the body from the waist downwards. But in Hindu eyes the *dhoti* is elegant, invariably white, and draped round the body with a certain delicacy. The *lungi* is generally of bizarre, multi-colour material and wrapped round the body, rather more casually, like a towel.

The Muslim preference for the *lungi* could be explained in terms of economics, the *lungi* being cheaper, but uncharitable bigoted Hindus give a different explanation. This is that the Muslim, or at least the ghetto Muslims, preferred the *lungi* because they can discard it easily to indulge in their favourite activity: sex. Muslims, like Jews, are circumcised. And in India they are referred to, rather crudely, as *katela*, meaning the cut one. Sexual potency may or may not be increased by circumcision, but it is widely believed in India that this is one of the forces that drive the ghetto Muslim and his sexual potency is only equalled by his lust for Hindu women.

It was our driver, Shankar, who first told me about *katelas*. One evening in 1946 when the Hindu–Muslim riots had gripped Mumbai, Shankar, minding his own business, was travelling home. But his home was in Mazgoan, and he had to pass through certain Muslim ghettos to get there. He was stopped by a Muslim mob and asked 'Who are you? What is your name?' He was petrified. To have given his real name would have been to commit suicide. As he stood undecided, the mob edged closer, threatening to take off his trousers and reveal his true identity. Suddenly Shankar realised that in his pocket he had the means of possible salvation: a cross. He took it out, and pretended to be a Christian. He claimed his name was Stanley. The Muslims were convinced and he escaped.

However, alongside this general fear and suspicion, in personal situations Hindus and Muslims would often get on very well. My father employed Muslim workers, traded with Muslims and, indeed, his favourite business contact was a Muslim who became a good family friend.

Of course not all Muslims lived in ghettos. There were educated, cultured Muslims too and, as India is a secular state, there were Muslims occupying high political positions. In the years since Indian independence, India has had three Muslim presidents, a Muslim chief of defence staff, several Muslim judges, a couple of chief justices of the Indian Supreme Court, a great number of Muslim politicians and ministers in central and state politics and several senior Muslim civil servants. Also for ten years, a Muslim was India's cricket Captain. The Nawab of Pataudi, popularly known as Tiger.

Nirad Chaudhuri has suggested that this was the result of the Hindu–Muslim political collaboration between 1917 and 1922 when the two communities successfully came together to fight the British, and the personality of Nehru, who was 'by social and cultural affiliations' more of a Muslim then a Hindu, in so far as he was 'anything Indian at all'. Nehru, according to Chaudhuri, came from a family which was open to Islamic influences and found Muslims more sophisticated than Hindus. Nehru's personality may well have provided Muslims with a certain position in India after independence, but the case of the Nawab of Pataudi and the role he played in cricket suggests that the broader topic of Muslim participation in Indian cricket is somewhat more complicated than that.

This extract from a double-page spread in the magazine *Sports World*, entitled 'Face to Face with a Tiger' gives one a feeling of the position Pataudi occupies in modern Indian cricket.

> If you've got a minute, try this experiment. Take a ball, close one eye, toss it up and try catching it. The chances are you will miss. Because with one eye, you will have what is known as a 'parallax' problem. Now imagine facing Jeff Thomson, John Snow, Fred Trueman, or even Lance Gibbs with one eye. Or imagine taking a hot, low catch. And imagine doing all that with style, power, and international class. Hard to imagine an ordinary human being doing that. But what about a Tiger? Or Mansur Ali Khan-the Nawab of Pataudi? Ah! Now that's possible isn't it!
>
> Within the first two minutes of meeting him, you'll know tiger's no pussy cat. He stalks into his lair, a brown, dark den loaded with books and a few photographs and fixes you with a steady, unblinking gaze. His agile mind ripples with tough opinions and he expresses them with the tigerish conviction. Mansur Ali Khan is every inch his epithet – Tiger.

As it happens Tiger was then the editor of *Sports World* and you may think this was just a personal plug. In fact it is an advertisement feature by Air India, using Tiger to promote the airline. What is so astonishing is not so much the overblown rhetoric which is fairly common in India, but the fact that Tiger last played cricket for India in 1974 – ten years before Air India decided to use him as their advertising symbol. Few ex-cricketers, Indian or foreign, have lasted so well. Everybody in Indian cricket knows him as Tiger, he requires no other name. When interviewed, his expert, often pithy, comments are eagerly awaited; stories of his eccentric behaviour are endlessly retold and his very presence on the cricket ground, albeit in the commentary box, is still guaranteed to create a stir.

When Tiger arrived on the scene Indian cricket desperately needed a hero. In 1955–9 the West Indies, building the first of their awesome pace attacks, had come to India and won 3–0. In 1959 India went to England and lost 5–0. In 1960–1 Pakistan came to India and all five Tests were drawn. Apart from lowly New Zealand, India, it seemed, could beat nobody. Against such a background Tiger's exploits at Winchester, Oxford and Sussex seemed like manna from heaven – another Ranji and what is more one who would play for India.

Then came the tragic accident. When everybody was predicting the greatest of futures for Pataudi – as a batsman who might rival the other great Indians who had played in England, Ranji, Duleep and his own father, the Nawab of Pataudi Senior – he was involved in a car crash and lost an eye. Sudden tragedy is by no means an Indian phenomenon, but in Indian life it seems to play a big part. Almost every family tale has some tragic loss to relate. In Pataudi's case the loss was ameliorated by his ability to quickly resume cricket. Within six months of the car crash, he was making his Test debut for India, playing a swashbuckling innings, including a century in his second Test. His very first Test, the fourth in the series against Ted Dexter's England team, produced an Indian victory. Pataudi himself scored a century in the last Test and India confirmed her superiority by completing a 2–0 series victory. This is one part of the Pataudi legend. Despite his appalling handicap, he was a fine player and while Indians continuously sigh about what might have been had the car crash not taken place, they applaud the courage and skill of a player who overcame such a handicap.

Interestingly, Pataudi's great international innings always seemed to be played amidst tragedy. His memorable 148 at Leeds was played while two of his colleagues Surti and Bedi nursed injuries and could take little or no part in the match. His 86 at Melbourne, a year later, was played on one leg – he had a torn thigh muscle – while the rest of the Indian batsmen collapsed all around him. In both cases India lost fairly comprehensively and there were question marks about Pataudi's captaincy. The Indian batting collapse at Melbourne was due partly to Pataudi's decision to bat first on a lively, greenish wicket. But such criticisms were muted because of Tiger's batting exploits. Indian cricketing history is full of stories of the lone batsman, battling against the enemy while all his colleagues collapse round him in a heap. For example when India was defeated 4–0 at the hands of Bradman's Australians in 1947–8, Indian cricket drew some comfort from Vijay Hazare scoring a century in each innings of the Adelaide Test. On the equally disastrous 1952 tour of England, Vinoo Mankad's exploits at Lord's: 68 and 184 and 5 wickets led one London paper to describe the match as 'Mankad versus England'. This headline and Mankad's feats have been endlessly retold in India as if by doing so Indians could forget the damage the Australians and English had inflicted on their cricket team.

But Tiger brought to this familiar 'boy on the burning bridge' syndrome a dash, charm and style all of his own. Even his debut as India's Captain had this same feel about it. He became Captain in only his fifth Test match, at the age of 21, the youngest man to captain his country. Soon after India's 2–0 victory over England, in the spring of 1962, the Indians flew to the West Indies for a five-Test series. The Indian Captain was the left-handed opening batsman Nari Contractor. Though a dour bat, he had led India to her first serious victory over England and seemed destined to captain India for a very long time. Pataudi was appointed Vice-Captain, a decision much applauded in the country where it was seen as providing useful experience for the youngster. Nobody expected Pataudi to become Captain – at least not for some time.

India lost the first two Tests to Frank Worrell's immensely strong West Indian side, and then moved to Barbados to play the island side which, in those days, was almost as strong as a Test team. Here the second tragedy, which was to shape Pataudi's cricketing life, struck. Contractor, opening the innings as usual, ducked into a ball from Griffiths, which did not rise as expected and was led away from the field bleeding, and India was left without a Captain. Pataudi as Vice-Captain took over in the third Test but could do little to prevent the Indians being thrashed 5–0.

It was another eighteen months before India played a Test series again, in 1963–4 against Mike Smith's England team. Pataudi was appointed Captain and remained so until the spring of 1971 when, in a sensational coup, he was replaced on the Chairman of the Selectors' casting vote in favour of Ajit Wadekar. Three years later, Wadekar returned from England his team beaten 3–0 and Wadekar himself personally disgraced. Pataudi was recalled to the captaincy against Clive Lloyd's West Indians. If the first phase of his cricket captaincy was marked by defiant batting exploits, this, his last series as Captain and player was marked by undistinguished batting performances but redeemed by his skills as a Captain. India lost the first two Tests and then won the next two producing a cliffhanging final which the West Indians eventually won.

As far as the Pataudi legend is concerned it would have been totally out of character if India had actually won that final Test. The Pataudi legend was founded on dramatic losses and might-have-beens. Yet Pataudi is still considered, as the Air India advertisement put it 'one of the finest Captains India has ever had'. Pataudi himself has never had any illusions about his captaincy saying 'India has never had a good captain. In the land of the blind, a man with one eye is King!' Certainly by any international standards, Pataudi's record as Captain can hardly be described as glorious. His captaincy record is shown in Table 8.1.

Pataudi's numerous supporters say that Tiger was unlucky. By rights he should have reaped the glory that went to Ajit Wadekar when, between 1971 and 1973, India beat West Indies in the West Indies and beat England in England. These victories when the spin quartet of Bedi, Prasanna, Chandrasekhar and Venkat was at its height, provide the most glorious Test period in Indian cricket history. Tiger, so the argument goes, had prepared the team that Wadekar took to glory. With better catching, India might have won the series against Australia 3–1 at home in 1969–70 instead of losing it by that margin, and Wadekar was, undoubtedly, lucky to be the right man at the right place.

Perhaps so, might-have-beens are always fascinating in India, and something Indians love to indulge in. Yet contrast Wadekar's record (Table 8.2) with Pataudi's:

Table 8.1 Career record: Pataudi

Season	Venue	Opponent	Result
1962	West Indies	West Indies	India lost 5–0, Pataudi Captain for the last three Tests
1963–4	India	England	All five Tests drawn, 1964–5, India Australia 1–1
1964–5	India	New Zealand	India won 1–0
1966–7	India	West Indies	India lost 2–0
1967	England	England	England 3–0 (series consisted of three Tests)
1967–8	Australia	Australia	India lost 4–0 (series consisted of four Tests)
1967–8	New Zealand	New Zealand	India won 3–1 (series consisted of four Tests)
1969–70	India	New Zealand	India draw 1–1 (series consisted of four Tests)
1969–70	India	Australia	India lost 3–1 (series consisted of five Tests)
1974–5	India	West Indies	India lost 3–2

Table 8.2 Career record: Wadekar

Season	Venue	Opponent	Result
1971	West Indies	West Indies	India won: 1–0
1971	England	England	India won: 1–0 (series consisted of three Tests)
1972–3	India	England	India won: 2–1
1974	England	England	India lost: 3–0 (series consisted of three Tests)

This, in overall series terms, is by far, the best Test record of any Indian cricket captain. The 3–0 defeat in England was a bad one, involving a most humiliating 42 all out by India in the second innings of the Lord's Test, but even so it seems that the punishment Wadekar received was excessive. He lost the captaincy and was virtually made to retire from Test cricket. Pataudi was recalled as Captain and was welcomed back by the Indian cricketing public as a prodigal son. At least one cricket writer felt that it was generous of Tiger to forgive the Indian Cricket Board for sacking him in such a dastardly fashion in 1971. Few recall Wadekar's captaincy with any warmth and he certainly does not have the status that Tiger enjoys. Despite Pataudi's record, almost because of it, his captaincy reign is seen as a long, lost golden age.

I well recall a conversation I had with an Indian journalist during the 1974 tour. The journalist made no bones about his anti-Wadekar views, and, confidently predicted that the Indians would have a terrible summer. When I demurred and pointed to Wadekar's record, he said that India's victory over England in 1972–3 owed much to Tiger's recall as a batsman. (Pataudi had missed the 1971 tours of West Indies and England by trying and failing to become a politician. In the low-scoring 1972–3 series, his batting had been quite crucial.) My journalist friend then told me, with malicious delight, how the Indian Board had tried hard to persuade Tiger to come to England in 1974. But, according to this journalist the 'wise Tiger' had sensed that the tour would be disastrous and declined.

Now this may be apocryphal and is not dissimilar to stories seeking to explain Boycott's absence from Tests in the mid-1970s. What is revealing is that while Boycott's absence from Tests reinforced the image of the lonely recluse only willing to play on his own terms, Pataudi's absence from Tests only served to heighten the impression of a man of destiny wrongly cheated of his inheritance.

It is this that made Pataudi's captaincy seem so magical in India. During the 1963–4 series against England, his first as a proper Captain of India, the first four Tests ended in a fairly pedestrian draw. At the fifth Test, played on a perfect batting wicket in Kanpur, Pataudi won the toss. To the amazement of everybody he decided to put England in. There was nothing, conceivably, in the wicket or the atmosphere to justify his decision. England made a big score, well over 500, and the Indians, who went in to bat after two days in the field, promptly collapsed. Defeat seemed near but thanks to a century by Nadkarni, India saved the Test. When asked for an explanation for his extraordinary decision, Pataudi remarked that since the first four Tests had ended in draws, he thought it was time to do something to provide the long-suffering crowd with some thrills. Although the only thrill in that Test was that of India escaping from defeat, such was Tiger's aura, that there were few recriminations about a decision which had opened up the possibility of defeat in the first place. Indeed he won applause for his marvellously eccentric thinking.

It was, perhaps, this unpredictability in Pataudi, something totally foreign to most Indians, which made him so charming and exciting. As I have said Pataudi came to the helm of affairs after two decades of captaincy that had produced draws at home and ignominious defeats abroad. Any challenge was preferable and Pataudi's captaincy walked a tantalising tightrope. He always seemed to be at the point of resigning the captaincy and, always being persuaded by the Indian cricket authorities to stay on. Just before the Indian team left for Australia on their 1967–8 tour, Pataudi actually resigned from the captaincy. The Indians had returned from England the previous summer having been beaten 3–0 in the Tests and the manager had made critical references to Pataudi's captaincy. But this was not well known and the resignation, on the eve that a crucial Duleep trophy final between the West Zone and the South Zone was to start at the Brabourne stadium, came as a shock. It overshadowed all news and I and my friends, watching the match felt a deep sense of sadness that he was going. Even Indian journalists who had been critical of his captaincy wondered who could replace him and hoped that he would think again. Throughout the match a remarkable pro-Pataudi sentiment built up and this was crowned by Pataudi himself, scoring a double century for South Zone which enabled them to take the first innings lead against West Zone and win the Duleep trophy. By the end of the match there was no doubt that Pataudi would remain India's Captain.

Probably Pataudi's resignation stunt was meant to bring the normally faction-ridden Indian Cricket Board into line. Indian cricket, as Pataudi says, produces cricketers 'in spite of the system – not because of it'. The Indian Cricket Board is perpetually divided into factions: East versus West, North versus South, South combining with the West to down North, and throughout Pataudi's captaincy there was the chance of Chandu Borde becoming Captain. Had the Contractor accident not taken place in the West Indies in 1962, and catapulted Pataudi to the captaincy, Borde might well have been the Captain. He was already well established in the Indian team when Pataudi made his debut and was a reasonable Captain of Maharashtra. But Borde was condemned to be Pataudi's Vice-Captain. Preliminaries to every cricket season saw familiar speculation about Pataudi being replaced by Borde only for Pataudi to be eventually reconfirmed as Captain.

Raju Bharatan in *Indian Cricket: The Vital Phase* has provided a certain gloss on the Pataudi resignation stunt. The selection committee, says Bharatan, were due to discuss the manager's report before deciding the

Captain for the Australia tour and Tiger wanted to pre-empt them. Bharatan writes:

> On the day he dropped that brick, Chandu Borde was in Mumbai leading Maharashtra in the Ranji trophy. I rushed to his sea front hotel room at 7.00 in the morning to get his 'spot' reaction to the Pat bombshell. 'You look at last like getting the honour that was always rightfully yours,' I said. 'Don't you believe it,' said Borde, 'What's the bet he'll be back on the scene at the "psychological moment"? Don't get me wrong, this kind of thing's happened to me before. I was then promised everything and got nothing, I now just don't hope for anything. Don't believe all that you read. It's ultimately going to be Pat, and Pat alone, as Captain of India to Australia.'

Of course, in supposedly egalitarian, socialist India, Borde should have been the natural choice'. He was one of ten children born into a family not very well off and a 'non-matriculate'. In the west the term may mean nothing, but in class and caste conscious India it immediately reveals a person's economic background. Matriculation is almost the minimum qualification most educated Indians aspire to and among middle Indians it is not uncommon to hear jokes that even their *peons* – office boys – are matriculate these days. Borde made it in cricket because of assistance from the Maharaja of Baroda, and later from the veteran Indian cricketer, Professor Deodhar. But in many ways, it was Borde's origins that told against him. A very popular story during Pataudi's reign was of the occasion when during a Test match, Chandu Borde decided to wear his Maharashtra cap and go out to field. Normally all Indian cricketers were required to wear their India cap during Tests. As Borde left the dressing room Pataudi told Borde that he was playing for India, not Maharashtra and should wear his India cap. Borde is supposed to have replied, 'But Tiger, you often wear your Sussex cap.' Tiger, looking down his long impressive nose, allegedly replied, 'Yes, Chandu, but Sussex is not Maharashtra.' There were different versions of this story with Tiger being credited with wearing the Winchester cap, or the Oxford cap, both of whom he captained. Again this may be an apocryphal tale, but one endlessly retold and with every retelling, Tiger acquired a new aura. The story, however unlikely, seems to combine all the Tiger qualities.

Tiger, himself, disarmingly acknowledges that he was made Captain because he was different. 'In fact I was selected because culturally and regionally I was from nowhere in particular. I was the simplest way out for our faction ridden Board. The Indian team is probably the hardest to captain anyway. First of all you are invariably the weakest side and then you could have the problem of dealing with twelve culturally, ethnically and linguistically different people.' Or to put it plainly, Tiger was India's 'great Captain' because he was a prince, a Nawab. We have discussed the role of princes in Indian cricket but Tiger was the last of the princely cricketers to play a part in Indian cricket. Some Indian sceptics would joke that Tiger was the 'Nawab of Kuch-be-Nahi', meaning the Nawab of nothing. This was a reference to the fact that Pataudi, which gave Tiger the title of Nawab, is a very small place just outside Delhi. As Indian princely stages go it is nothing more than a pimple. But that did not matter for what Tiger carried was the 'Nawabsahib'.

There are two words to denote princes in India. If the prince is a Hindu then he is generally called a Raja or a Maharaja, the second word meaning a greater Raja. If the prince is a Muslim then he is called a Nawab. In Tiger's case there was the aura of his father's Nawabsahib. The Nawab of Pataudi Senior had played for England, scoring a century in the 1932–3 Bodyline tour, and then captaining India on the 1946 tour of England. But even without such antecedents the very word Nawab would have created the right association for Tiger. We have spoken of the poor Muslims being the Indian 'niggers'. But however much the Hindus may resent, fear and mistrust the ghetto Muslims, they also carry with them the image of the other Muslims, the Muslims who ruled them and left behind the monuments of northern India, especially the Taj Mahal that is so eagerly exhibited to foreigners. Hindu historians may endlessly debate the legacy of these Muslim rulers, but in the popular mind there is still respect and longing for the wonder of this Muslim rule.

This is the Nawabsahib. Nawbs were unpredictable but glorious, handsome but also cruel, capable of great generosity and of great wickedness. Their whimsy was part of their charm and everybody enquired what the Nawab's *mezaz* (mood) was like. The right mood could grant a thousand favours, the wrong could mean the end. The Nawab of Pataudi inherited much of this, other, Hindu feeling towards Muslims and very often when he took one of his more eccentric decisions it would be explained as 'Nawabsahib's *mezaz*'. This Indians, and Hindus in particular, knew from their own history was not something to be trifled with. In a sense by clinging to the concept of the Nawabsahib, alternatively capricious and glorious, Indians were trying to unite their very muddled history.

Apart from Pataudi no other Muslim cricketer has evoked this special feeling. This is hardly surprising since Pataudi and his father were the only two Muslim princes to play Test cricket for India, or for that matter Pakistan. Before Indian independence, and the partition which came in its wake, Muslims formed a sizeable proportion of the Indian Test team. Nearly all of them were from Punjab, a northern Indian state, and generally from the Indian lower middle classes. India's partition meant the division of Punjab, and the loss of a great many Muslim cricketers. Since then India has always had Muslim cricketers, and most Indian Test teams have fielded one, possibly two. But they have all come from the general Indian middle classes with the possible exception of the Indian Wicketkeeper Syed Kirmani, who describes his background as working class. In fact the only cricketer to remotely threaten Tiger as a romantic hero, a personage off as well as on the field, was another Muslim, Salim Durrani.

Here again there was something of the other Nawabi Muslim aura about Durrani. Salim is a magical name in India. It is the name that the Mughal Emperor Akbar gave to his son from his Hindu wife. Though Salim took the name Jahangir when he became Emperor, it was as Prince Salim that he created some of the most enduring Mughal legends. Legends strong enough to become translated into films like *Anarkali* and the epic *Mughal-E-Azam*. The name Salim evoked romance, valour and recklessness and Durrani's cricket symbolised all that. As N. S. Ramswami was to write in an appreciation in *Indian Cricket*, Durrani broke hearts not records. Handsome enough to be lured by films, though not very successfully, there was always something very challenging about his cricket.

As an orthodox left-arm spinner he was not in the class of Bedi – more in the meaner tradition of Nadkarni – but it was his approach to the game, particularly batting, that made Durrani special. 'We want six, we want six, Salim' the Indian crowd would shout and sure enough Salim Durrani, whatever the state of the game, would launch into one of his lovely, flowing drives and hoist the ball high over the bowler's head for a straight six. If India were struggling to save a Test, or win a tight game, commentators would often plead 'If only Salim gets his head down and plays responsibly, India could easily win this match.' Sometimes Salim did, many an occasion he did not. It all added to the great might-have-beens of Indian cricket. If only Salim would...

The Salim–Pataudi relationship was complex and interesting. Durrani was already established as a Test cricketer when Tiger made his debut. In the early years of Tiger's captaincy, Durrani's left-arm spin (Sobers found this particularly difficult) and middle order batting were quite crucial. By the mid-phases of Pataudi's captaincy it was clear that things were not working out well between them. I doubt if the fact that both of them were Muslims played any part in this. Tiger's hold on the Indian public was derived from the Nawabship, the ancestral royal blood that demanded loyalty from its subjects. Durrani's was the Mumbai *filmi* charm: his slightly unkempt look – the long hair falling over the eyebrows and perpetually being brushed back – combined with his ability to convert lounging laziness into electric athleticism. I well remember the last occasion

Salim Durrani played under Tiger's captaincy. It was the first Test of the 1966–7 series against the West Indies at Mumbai. India, after a bad beginning, had struggled to make a decent score, with Durrani helping Borde in the rescue act. Durrani made a lovely 55, including one huge straight 6 over Charlie Griffith's head into the CCI pavilion. If this was classic Salim, so was his dismissal, head in the air, bat askew and bowled by Sobers all over the shop. For much of the match he fielded at third man, just in front of the north stand, and throughout the innings I seem to recall him combing his hair, wearing a rather detached, vacant look. Once or twice his preoccupation with his hair led him to misfield and one could almost feel the electricity passing between the Nawab of Pataudi and Salim Durrani.

India, through some bad catching and a dreadful batting collapse in the second innings, lost the Test. Durrani was one of the casualties. He was replaced by Bishan Singh Bedi. To most Indian cricket followers Bedi was unknown and to some his inclusion was seen as yet another example of the daftness of Indian cricket selection. Little did we know the magic in Bedi's left arm. But even after we appreciated it we continued to mourn Salim, though he did not make a comeback for almost five years. By then Pataudi had been replaced by Wadekar and nothing could comfort Indian cricket for the lost years of Salim Durrani.

There could be no such feeling about Abbas Ali Baig. In cricketing terms Baig came into prominence at about the same time as Pataudi and, in some ways, made even more of an impact. Baig played so well for Oxford in the 1959 season, that, when the main Indian batsman Vijay Manjrekar, had to withdraw because of a knee injury, the young Muslim cricketer was drafted in. He proved a splendid choice and was one of the few successes for the Indians on that dismal tour. Baig played in the fourth Test, after the Indians had lost the first three, and repeatedly hooked Trueman's bouncers. Though he was hit on the head by one bouncer, and had to retire hurt, he came back to complete a fighting century – joining a select band of Indians who had scored a century in their first Test.

Baig became an instant Indian hero. Here was a cricketer who could answer fire with fire, bouncers with hooks. His status as India's up-and-coming batsman was further reinforced the following winter when the Australians under Richie Benaud toured India. Though India lost the series, they won a Test match (their first victory against Australia) and Baig was a central figure in the Indian batting revival. In the third Test at Mumbai, with India always struggling to stay in the match, Baig scored a fifty in each innings. Yet within a year Baig's cricketing world had been reduced to dust. After the 1959–60 Australian tour, he was to play just five more Tests for India in the next fifteen or so years. His nemesis came after his failure in the first three Tests of the 1960–1 series against Pakistan. His scores were: 1, 13, 19 and 1. Baig was dropped and did not play again for India until the 1966–7 tour of the West Indies when he played two Tests and was dropped. Though he toured England with the 1971 team, he did not play another Test. Baig's low scores in 1960 and 1961 are difficult to explain, though not unusual. Other batsmen, even very great ones, have had seasons and series like that. What undid Baig was very simply that he was a Muslim playing for India against Pakistan.

The years 1960 and 1961 marked a watershed in India–Pakistan Test cricket. Test series between the two countries had started in the 1952–3 season, when India had won 2–1 at home. India had visited Pakistan in 1954–5 with all the matches ending in dreadfully dull, boring draws. The dull cricket did not make either country keen to have another visit and in any case after 1954 political relations between the two countries progressively deteriorated. Pakistan became more closely involved with American-sponsored alliances, while India became a champion of the non-aligned world.

Pakistan finally revisited India in the winter of 1960. The first Test was played in Mumbai and was a sell-out long before it started. I persuaded my parents to let me visit the flat of one of their friends, which happened to overlook the Brabourne stadium. The route to the friend's flat passed Churchgate railway station and the entrance to the east stand of the Brabourne stadium. On the first day of the Test I walked towards the flat and saw a whole crowd of very Muslim-looking people entering the stands. One passerby observed the rush of the Muslims and commented 'No wonder these *Meibhais* (as some Muslims are called) come crawling out now. It is their team that is playing. No prizes for guessing who they are supporting.'

This bitter remark reflected the feeling of many Hindu Indians during the series – that Muslims in India were all supporting Pakistan. It was this feeling that was to prove the undoing of Abbas Ali Baig. A failure in non-Pakistan series, or by a Hindu in that series, might have been overlooked. But against Pakistan the natural, albeit libellous conclusion was that Baig had sabotaged his own chances so that the good of Islam, in the form of the Pakistan cricket team, could triumph. Poor Baig heard so many whispers about his 'treacherous' behaviour and received so many poison pen letters that by the time he was bowled by Haseen for one in the second innings of the third Test in Kolkatta, he was ready to throw in the towel. As *Current*, a review of India and Pakistan Test cricket between 1952 and 1984, puts it, 'Confidence was further shaken by a torrent of poison pen letters, telephone calls and telegrams. He opted out of the Indian team after the Kolkatta Test.'

Baig never recovered from the libellous accusations made against him during that series. A one-down batsman who looked like becoming one of the Indian greats merely proved the Indian adage that batsmen who score a century in their first Test for India rarely score many more runs for India. It was a hoodoo that was to afflict Indian cricket until Visvanath broke the spell by scoring a century in his first Test and then going on to score a few thousand more runs.

As it was, the end of the 1960–1 Test series with Pakistan marked the beginning of an 18-year period when neither country played each other. Interestingly this was also the period when the two great Muslim cricketers that India has produced in the modern era, Pataudi and Durrani played for India. Neither Pataudi nor Durrani played for India against Pakistan. Had they done so we might have seen how their popularity and evident appeal would have stood the test of any possible failure. By the time India resumed cricket with Pakistan by touring the country in the winters of 1978–9, the only Muslim in the side was Syed Kirmani, and he was so established as a wicketkeeper that few would dare to ascribe his failures to religious feelings. Even then, during the controversial Mumbai Test of 1980–1, there were some mischievous whispers about Kirmani's loyalty. This, despite the fact that it was his stand of 95 for the seventh wicket with Kapil Dev, with Kirmani making a 'cheeky' 41, which helped India reach 334 in the first innings and played a crucial part in its victory.

But then it is hardly surprising. For Indian Muslims' relations with Pakistan complete the three-sided way in which Hindus view the Indian Muslim. There is the view of the katela, there is the Nawabsahib and then there is Pakistan. It is the interaction of the katela and the Nawabsahib with Pakistan that brings out all the old paranoia and distrust of Muslims. Physically India and Pakistan may be very close, but intellectually and emotionally, they are far apart.

In 1977 Pakistan had a traumatic election leading to the overthrow of Bhutto and the installation of General Zia al Haq. Yet the best reporting on Pakistan in the Indian papers was filed by Indian correspondents in London scavenging reports filed by British correspondents in Pakistan. News coming straight out of Pakistan into India was almost invariably laconic agency dispatches that said very little. Some sixty years after the sub-continent was split, Pakistan for most Indians is still not a living country. It is an ogre, a devil waiting to devour India, a fantastic mistake – but not a country of a hundred million human beings. I can remember very few articles which have talked of the people of Pakistan. Apart from the Indian news agencies there are hardly any Indian journalists based in Pakistan. Few visit the country. It is as if with the traumatic partition of the sub-continent something had snapped in the Indian mind. A limb of the body had been dismembered, it was said, and the body had forgotten that it had ever had this limb. Perhaps this was the only way in which the trauma of those days could be faced.

The long cricket break between India and Pakistan intensified this feeling. In the late 1970s and early 1980s cricketing contacts resumed, but it was almost impossible to go from India to Pakistan. Those wishing to visit Pakistan invariably require a visa and the visas have to be issued in Delhi. In the early part of 1984 England visited Pakistan. I happened to be in India then and the Sports Editor of the *Sunday Times* thought it might be simpler for me to travel from Mumbai to Karachi to cover the first Test. I soon realised the difficulties. I would have to go to Delhi to make a visa application, the Pakistani Embassy in Delhi would have to refer this to Islamabad and by the time the whole thing was settled, the first Test would be over. When I mentioned all this to my Sports Editor he was, understandably, bemused.

It was only when I began to live in England in the late 1960s that I overcame my ignorance and hostility towards Pakistan. This was largely through meeting Javed, who worked with me in a small, dingy, accountants' office just off Fleet Street, where we were both training to be chartered accountants. To Javed all Indians were Hindus and therefore despicable – which revolted my secular conscience about India being a nation for all religions. Javed would call me 'Indiana'. One of his minor hobbies was to pass himself off as a Mexican with his own version of an American accent. This mixture of Lahore English with a contrived New York accent produced some quite remarkable consequences.

When we first met we circled around one another warily, like two fighters in a ring waiting to land the first decisive punch. But all around us was this alien, white, English world – a world which could scarcely distinguish between Indian and West Indian, let alone between Javed and me. Slowly we stopped circling and came to trust one another. Our friendship grew and seemed to be prospering when, suddenly, Pakistan unleashed its terrible repression of Bangladesh in the spring of 1971.

I was appalled to find Javed not only siding with Tikka and Yayaha Khans but despising the Bengalis in the sort of fascist rhetoric, which, if applied by a white to a black would have incurred all the wrath of the Race Relations Act. In my fading Bengali memory where ideas of a *sonar* (golden) Bengal still resonated, the Pakistani action was a heinous crime. The fragility of our friendship became even more evident as the repression continued through the summer of 1971. It was not helped by the fact that the Pakistani team just failed to beat England at cricket, while the Indians miraculously won a series against England in England for the first time in its history. Javed felt that events were conspiring in my favour.

He was convinced of this when in December 1971 India and Pakistan went to war. While his Embassy told him, almost every day, how they had shot down hundreds of Indian planes with all Pakistani planes returning safely, British news media told a very different story. He was no longer the cool Mexican with his supposedly neat American accent. He began to look and sound like a very angry Pakistani Peter Sellers. The Indians had cleverly allowed western correspondents to report the war, and as their dispatches filled the media Javed, desperately needing to marry this with Pakistan's dispatches, began to believe in a great conspiracy embracing the BBC, all of Fleet Street and me. When the BBC showed the fall of the Bangladeshi town of Jessore, he dismissed the pictures as belonging to a carefully camouflaged suburb of Kolkatta. At the end of the war our relationship was in tatters.

It only recovered through the intervention of an external force: an Iranian who worked with us. He was junior to both Javed and me and would often try to butter up Javed by referring to him as 'my Muslim brother'. While the Bangladesh war raged Javed inclined to his Muslim brother. But after the war and the liberation of Bangladesh the Muslim angle began to wear thin.

The Iranian's English was rather poor and he often misunderstood things. He failed his very first accountancy exams because in the general paper asked to write about the ways in which the English waterways system helped the transportation of goods, he had written about the Stock Exchange. It transpired that he had mugged up a certain number of questions and, not quite understanding what the word waterways meant, had taken it to refer to the Stock Exchange. Javed, on hearing his explanation, made malicious fun of his lack of English.

The breaking point came when one day Javed asked him to get the evening paper. Both Javed and I were very keen on cricket scores and in those days the *Standard* published a special late edition, available in Fleet Street some time after five, which contained the latest cricket scores. It had, I believe, the code number 7RR and Javed asked the Iranian to look for the number and make sure it had the latest cricket scores. But like the confusion between the English waterways and the Stock Exchange, this proved rather too much for him. He brought an edition which contained the lunchtime scores, which we already knew. Javed, furious, turned on him and said 'You are useless. You don't know the difference between the English waterways and the Stock Exchange or the difference between lunch and close-of-play scores.' The poor Iranian who knew nothing about cricket, did not know what to say and soon found that even liberal applications of 'my Muslim brother' did not mollify Javed. After that I was once again 'Indiana'.

Perhaps this anecdote proves that cricket can override religious differences, bringing together people of very different backgrounds. Yet the history of India–Pakistan cricket, and the wider role of Indian Muslims in Indian cricket, suggests that even if it does, it does so in a somewhat unexpected way.

Nothing, of course, could have been more unexpected than the relationship that was formed between Raj Singh Dungarpur and Mohammed Azharuddin although it neatly complements the long affair between Pataudi and the Indian cricket public. Whereas in the case of Pataudi it has been a story of the love of millions of Indians, many of them Hindus, for a Muslim Prince, whose wonderful cricketing gifts were blighted by a terrible tragedy, in the case of Raj Singh and Azharuddin it is the love of a Hindu prince for a working-class Muslim cricketer of exceptional ability whose career was ruined by the worst corruption crisis in the history of the game. What makes this story even more interesting is that Raj has always been close to Pataudi, indeed he hero-worships him, and one of his favourite photographs is one of Raj's father with Pataudi's father, not long before Pataudi senior died. The picture captures the pair in a jocular mood symbolising the close ties between these two princely cricketing families.

Raj Singh is probably, the last great prince left in Indian cricket, the Dungarpur in his name being the ancient Rajput kingdom from where he hails. A medium pace bowler who played for Rajasthan, but did not make the Test team, Raj, as he is popularly known, has been the leading cricket administrator since the 1980s. He has been the manager for several tours, chairman of the selectors and president of the board.

He comes from proud Rajput stock and will happily tell anyone who cares to listen that his clan of the Rajputs never gave their daughters in marriage to the Muslims as the Rajputs of Jaipurs did. This meant they missed out on the economic prosperity that alliance with the Mughals brought the Jaipurs and other Rajput rulers willing to compromise on what the Dungapurs felt was a matter of honour.

His pride in his Rajput ancestry was vividly brought out in June 2000 when he came to Lord's for a meeting of the ICC. Held in the wake of the Hansie Cronje cricket corruption expose the meeting started in dramatic fashion. Just as the then ICC President Jagmohan Dalmiya opened the meeting, Lord Ian MacLaurin, then chairman of the England and Wales Cricket Board, circulated a document which he asked all present to sign. This declared that the administrators were personally honest and untainted by the corruption crisis. This was clearly directed at Dalmiya who was facing allegations in India over television deals which was later the subject of an investigation by the Indian Central Bureau of Investigations. Everyone duly signed up. It was rather odd that the rulers of the game, meeting to convince the world the game was clean, had first to declare that they, themselves, were clean.

Raj, who had just flown in to represent India, in the absence of the then Board President, was a little too jet lagged at the meeting to raise any meaningful questions but later queried a peculiarity about the document. It was on ECB headed notepaper when, for it to be a valid ICC document, it should have been on ICC headed notepaper. He was told it had been produced by MacLaurin and as a lord he was entitled to get his own way. Raj responded, 'If you are going to brandish titles, then I can produce a royal family tree that goes back 900 years, not a Lord who got his title through his business activities giving money to a political party.'

Raj's views on corruption in cricket have been equally forthright and singular. He does not believe that it is possible for any cricketer to fix a match. With cricket being a team game, he argues, no cricketer, is good enough to influence a match on his own. The only one he thinks could do it is Sachin Tendulkar, not that he would ever dream of it.

This belief made him always reject the match fixing charges against Mohammed Azharuddin and ever since the crisis broke Raj has not only championed Azharuddin's cause but reassured him that one day he will return and play in his 100th Test – Azhar had played 99 Tests when he was banned as a result of a CBI inquiry into match fixing.

Raj, like everyone else in India, had been fascinated by Azharuddin ever since he made his sensational debut in the 1984–5 season, scoring three successive Test centuries. Raj recalls Azhar's wonder as he was catapulted into the sort of fame success in Indian cricket can bring, staring wide-eyed as he moved almost instantly from a downtrodden Muslim mohalla-ghetto of Hyderabad into a world of celebrities and Bollywood film stars.

I was first aware of the special bond between Raj and Azharuddin during the Headingley Test between India and England in June 1986. The soccer World Cup was on in Mexico and had introduced us to the Mexican wave where sections of the crowd get up and then sit down, and as this rolls round the stadium it creates the impression of a wave. During the Saturday of the Test as India, having secured a substantial first innings lead, tried to build on that platform, the Leeds crowd, frustrated by England's lack of success, started doing the Mexican wave. This was probably the first time the wave had been seen on an English sporting field. Azharuddin was batting with Dilip Vengsarkar and, as another wave was launched, Azharuddin got out. Raj, the manager of the Indian team, was convinced Azharuddin's concentration had been disturbed by the wave and he stormed into the press box at Headingley to denounce the crowd for their behaviour. When an English journalist remonstrated that crowds in India could be far noisier and boisterous Raj retorted yes they could, but they would never stand up as the ball was being bowled.

Three years later Raj demonstrated his faith in Azharuddin in even more dramatic fashion. First as chairman of selectors he picked him to tour Pakistan when his form was poor. He played in the first Test of the series only because at the last minute Raman Lamba, who was to later die tragically, pulled out. Azhar made runs and secured his place. Then when the Indians returned home Raj Singh made Azharuddin captain. The story has now became legendary in Indian cricket. Azharuddin was leading south zone in a Duleep Trophy match. Even this captaincy was unexpected as it had come because Srikkanth who had captained India in Pakistan withdrew making Azhar Captain.

Raj then went up to him and said, 'Meia [general name for a Muslim], Captain bonagay [Will you be captain]?'

Azhar, thinking he was referring to the captaincy of the south zone team, a position he just acquired said, 'Mai to captain hoon' [I am already captain].

Raj explained that he was offering him the Indian captaincy but it took sometime for a bemused Azhar to understand the prize he was being offered.

Ever since then Raj has always supported Azhar right through the corruption crisis, and despite the fact that the charges laid against him saw him banned by the Board from all cricket. Raj was the sole voice on the board which opposed the move. Raj has made it clear he should never have been banned and the charges are not well founded. In the summer of 2002 as India toured England Raj speaking at the launch of my *History of Indian Cricket* used the occasion to embark on a spirited defence of Azhar. This was the first time Azhar had appeared on a public platform since his banning and I could see how moved he was and the close bond between these two very dissimilar men brought together by cricket. Azhar remains the one cricketer to start and end his Test careers with centuries, his last Test innings being against his friend Hansie Cronje's visiting South Africa in 2000. A few weeks later the investigations of the Delhi police revealed cricket's corruption.

In many ways the stories of both Pataudi and Raj and Azhar could well be made for Bollywood movies, with the participants all having Bollywood connections. Pataudi is married to Sharmila Tagore one of the great actresses of India, and one of his sons is a well known actor. Raj knows a great deal about Bollywood as he is a close companion of Lata Mangeskar, the most famous singing star of Bollywood, and Azhar's second marriage is to a Bollywood actress. But, perhaps, because real life is so much stranger than fiction no one in Bollywood has thought of turning it into a movie.

9

Vegetarians, fast bowlers and violence

If myth is the father of belief, then no belief is more mythical than the one about Indians being mild, meek and gentle. It is difficult to be precise as to when the west began to accept this myth but it probably dates from Victorian times, strengthened by the unique, non-violent approach used by Gandhi to fight the British. Indian conversations, discussions and even arguments have a certain elliptical, very decorous, manner. While Indians can be highly inquisitive and very open about the most intimate matters, they often find it very difficult – or are reluctant – to say 'no' to situations which demand such an answer. They are more likely to say 'yes', or 'maybe' out of a quite unaccountable sense of inadequacy and, perhaps, in the hope that the problem will go away. This is allied to a severe dislike of what Victorians would have called 'robust language'.

In Great Britain, for instance, discussions or arguments between friends – of a fairly standard nature – may feature phrases like 'What nonsense', or 'That's rubbish'. It does not mean the two friends are having a violent quarrel but merely a strong disagreement about certain things. But in India, even between intimate friends, the use of such language would very nearly threaten the friendship. I was reminded of this very sharply some years ago when my nephew and niece, who then lived in India, visited me in England. During a discussion and disagreement, at one stage, irritated by what I thought was my niece's feeble arguments, I said 'Oh, what nonsense, come off it.' In a similar conversation with an English friend the remarks would have meant nothing. My niece was very upset and I had to spend much time and effort to mollify her and make her see that I did not mean it as a deep, wounding, personal insult.

In India there is still a sharp distinction between language that is spoken privately and what is considered acceptable in print. This was a distinction that existed in Britain, too, but over the years this has eroded. I can still recall the shock I, and most of the Indian cricket team, felt when in August 1979 the *Sun* led its front page with a one word headline: 'BASTARDS'. The headline referred to the IRA which had just murdered Lord Louis Mountbatten by blowing up his boat while he was holidaying off the coast of Ireland. The murder came just days before the start of that summer's last Test at the Oval and, at the pre-match reception given to the Indian team, a minute's silence was observed, indicating the special feeling Indians felt for the man who, as the last British Viceroy, presided over India's arrival as a free nation. In private, bastard was quite a polite description of what the IRA had done, but to see it in print, in 60-point bold headline right across a newspaper, was a shock to the system.

Twenty years later when I ventured in print to speak of the sort of language that Indians and Pakistani cricketers use in private, I upset a great many people from the subcontinent.

On the eve of the World Cup match between India and Pakistan at Old Trafford I wrote a piece for the *Daily Telegraph* analysing the clash between these two rivals. In the piece I wrote:

> Privately, Pakistani cricketers believe that when it comes to pressure they are better able to cope with it than the Indians and they use an expression 'Uski ghand pfut gayi hai.' Literally it means 'his arse has cracked' and is the subcontinent's equivalent of 'he has lost his bottle'. Today's match will show whose ghand does not have the bottle as it recreates the sort of communal games that was the bedrock of Indian cricket before independence.

That day when I got to the Old Trafford press box I found it in uproar. The journalists from the subcontinent were shocked that I had managed to use the word *ghand* in print (and that too in the *Daily Telegraph*). Their shock might have been less had it been the *Sun* or some other red-top tabloid. Some of the Indians did not seem to mind, but one or two Pakistanis felt I had defiled the paper. Curiously, the cricketers on either side found it very funny and much enjoyed what they knew to be the truth. It is, of course, ironic that when the Victorians arrived in India they often found the Hindu sculptures, paintings, statues and forms of gods and goddess too explicit for their liking and sometimes covered them up. The modern Indians are now borrowing from these Victorians and seeking to cover up the language which some of them use in private.

It is this open and very robust use of language by the west, and particularly by the English, that perhaps explains why in India the English have a reputation for being men, and women, of violent tempers. In contrast to the English, Indians seem meek and mild. However, the reality is very different. As Nirad Chaudhuri has explained in *The Continent of Circe*: 'Few human communities have been more warlike and fond of bloodshed... Their political history is made up of blood-stained pages.' The Janus problem has arisen because of the oldest form of historical confusion: two disparate events have combined to produce a wholly misleading theory. The first, in the third century BC, concerned the conversion of a king. The second, in the twentieth century AD, concerned the politics of a Middle Temple lawyer. The King was Asoka, one of India's greatest kings and the shining jewel of the Maurya Empire of 300 BC. Asoka conquered a state called Kalinga, modern-day Orissa, in the course of which 50,000 people were deported, 100,000 were killed and many more died in other ways. It was as Nirad Chaudhuri says, an Assyrian method of warfare – total destruction. At the end of it, Asoka, seemingly overcome by remorse, proclaimed *ahimsa*, non-violence, as state policy. About twenty-five words, explaining the creed, were inscribed on massive iron pillars which were erected all over the country. Their existence along the length and breath of Ancient India shows a certain unity of subcontinent, thousands of years before the British arrival. Twenty-three centuries later the message re-emerged by means of a Middle Temple lawyer. Gandhi decided that *ahimsa* was the only way to fight the British. Asoka's declaration was good propaganda based on shrewd statecraft. He had conquered nearly all of India and there was no practical need for violence. Gandhi's decree was also good propaganda based on the shrewd realisation that an armed challenge to the British would be futile. But between these two events, as Chaudhuri says:

> There is not one word of non-violence in the theory and practice of state drafted by the Hindus. Read all the inscriptions, and you will find that when they are not bare records of gifts or genealogy, they are proclamations of the victories and the conquests of the kings concerned. The martial boasting is found not only among the Hindu Kings, but equally among the Buddhists...the whole of Sanskrit literature, from the epics down to the latest long poems, is full of accounts of battle and exultation of war and conquest. These were the business of Hindu Kings.

The Hindus developed the concept of the just war, *Dharma Yuddha*. The righteous war, and the events leading up to it, is the story of *Mahabharata*, which along with Ramayana, forms one of the two great epics of Hinduism. The story of Mahabharata is a family row. The King dies, and the right of his sons to inherit his throne is challenged by his brother and his family. The brother's family, through evil means, occupies the throne and the rightful heirs seek justice. Finally, the two warring cousins meet in battle. But on the morning of the battle one of the dispossessed heirs expresses grave disquiet about the impending clash of arms. He cannot, he says, kill his own flesh and blood, the sons and nephews of his own uncle.

But the God Krishna, charioteer to the reluctant warrior, launches into a unique exhortation to battle. The warrior is convinced and, eventually, after an epic struggle, righteousness prevails. Krishna's arguments constitute the *Bhagavat Gita*, Hinduism's holiest book. Unique, not only because of its philosophical arguments, but because it provides the only known case of war producing a religion's 'bible'.

The *Bhagavat Gita* has been interpreted as the great classic on the Hindu theory of acceptance and denial of free will. The violence that surrounded its birth provides the real clue as to how Indians see force, both in everyday life and on the cricket field. Ever since India made its entry on to the international cricket scene, it has been obsessed by the need for fast bowlers. Opponents repeatedly humbled India through pace, particularly Hall, Gilchrist and Trueman. Every defeat increased the Indian obsession for an avenging fire. The great Hindu Goddess of strength is Kali and, for almost fifty years, Indians sought a Kali on the cricket field.

The post-1946 period has seen India produce some great spinners: Vinoo Mankad, Gulham Ahmad, Subhash Gupte, Bishen Bedi, Erapalli Prasanna, Venkatraghavan, Chandrasekhar and more recently Anil Kumble. But though they are honoured and respected none of them evoked that special adulation that Kapil Dev conjured up. He personifies the long-cherished Indian dream of answering fire with fire, pace with pace, force with force. There is nothing meek or non-violent about him.

What aroused India was not only Kapil's good looks, or the sort of cavalier approach to batting that had been Salim Durrani's hallmark, but his bowling. For Indians it brings back hallowed memories of Nissar and Amar Singh, the two fast bowlers who opened India's attack in the country's first-ever Test at Lord's in 1932. Though they opened the bowling in only six Tests, in Indian cricketing memory their names resonate in a manner similar to that of Hornby and Barlow in Lancashire, or Holmes and Sutcliffe in Yorkshire.

Both were very similar in looks – tall, strapping men, six feet two inches – though Mahomed Nissar was a Punjabi Muslim and Amar Singh was a Gujarati Hindu from Ranji's Nawanagar. Indeed, it was Ranji who spotted his potential rather early on. Kapil Dev is probably closer to Amar Singh in his cricketing outlook than Nissar. Amar Singh was not only a fine opening bowler, he was also a marvellous right-hand hitter whose clean stroke play could demoralise many an attack and quickly change the course of a match. Nissar and Amar Singh first came into prominence, or at least English notice, during India's inaugural Test at Lord's in 1932. England won the toss, Holmes and Sutcliffe who, a few days previously, had put on 555 runs for the first wicket, opened the batting. Within fifteen minutes of play both had fallen to Nissar and with Woolley run out,

England were 19 for 3. Jardine had to play a major innings for England to reach 259, but Nissar ended the innings with 5 for 93. Amar Singh came into the picture in the second innings when his figures of 2 for 84 did not quite reveal the effect he had on the batsmen. While Nissar was a classical looking fast bowler both in action and style, he could swing the ball and break back viciously, Amar Singh, who had a rather shambolic run-up approach to the wicket, relied on swing and cut. In the heavier atmosphere of England it was his pace on the wicket which disconcerted batsmen and caused Wally Hammond to say that 'he came off the pitch like the crack of doom'.

According to one Indian cricket writer they 'formed one of the greatest double-edged opening attacks any country has turned on their opponents', ranking alongside such dread modern pairings as Lindwall and Miller, Trueman and Statham, Hall and Griffith. The statistics hardly bear out such a contention. They did well enough in the thirteen Test innings in which they opened the bowling, all against England, taking 53 of the 86 wickets that fell. The Indian hyperbole reflects the despair and the near 40-year fast bowling famine that resulted after their departure. Both men were 22 when India made her Test debut at Lord's in 1932. They would have been in their prime at the time of the Indian tour of England in 1940. But that tour never took place and as Hitler's *Blitzkreig* laid waste to Europe, Amar Singh, suffering from an attack of pneumonia, died in Jamnagar. Though Nissar lived on for another 23 years, India had lost its first, and only genuine, opening pair after a mere seven Tests.

The anguish, and hence the adulation for Nissar and Amar Singh, was all the greater because they had been preceded by other fast bowlers. According to one Indian writer 'it is a matter of eternal regret that India did not enter Test cricket in the early 1920s'. The regret may have come with hindsight but that era did seem to produce a great many fast bowlers. It is difficult to gauge their international position, but certainly the idea of club, college or national cricket teams, having opening bowlers with genuine pace was not quite so foreign to the contemporaries of Nissar and Amar Singh as they were to those of Mankad and Bedi in the 1950s and the 1960s.

This era marked the rise of the great Indian spinners and their prominence on the international stage. Inevitably in an attack dominated by spinners, to such an extent that even non-bowlers like Wadekar, Pataudi and Kunderan (who was actually a wicketkeeper) opened the bowling, suggested certain arguable conclusions. India, so the belief went, was the land of spinners. The great Indian bowling gift was to produce small, gentle men who with guile, cunning and the intricacies of flight and spin deceived the batsmen. The hot climate, the slow pace of life, the contemplative nature of its people, all seemed to make this the land of mystery and spin a very natural one. Wickets were slow, the cricket was slow and in the boiling heat what could be more obvious than hour upon hour of spin patiently wearing down the batsmen.

That indeed was the picture in India through the 1950s, 1960s and for much of the 1970s. It is a picture that the Indians detested. Throughout this period the Indians mourned the loss of Nissar and Amar Singh and elusively searched for replacements. Indians hired overseas fast bowlers to try and unearth local talent. Alan Moss of Middlesex, Gilchrist, Stayers, King and Watson of the West Indies, all went out to India, all put young Indians through their paces, and all produced nothing.

As the years passed and the Indians were increasingly humiliated by pace – both at home and overseas – the memories of Nissar and Amar Singh glowed ever more brightly and the search for their replacement became ever more desperate. The Indian press regularly carried stories of 'lost' fast bowlers. Harrowing tales were told of how a promising fast bowler had been ruined by the misdeeds of the Indian Board. Even in the heyday of the great spinners the Indian Board was criticised for not including a token bowler who aspired to be quick. One critic wrote 'not even the encouragement of rubbing shoulders with the playing 11 at net practice on such occasions is available to youngsters aspiring to bowl fast'. Difficult though it was to see how a fast bowler could improve by rubbing shoulders with Bedi or Prasanna, the argument revealed the depth of feeling in Indian cricketing circles about the lack of fast bowling.

Such desperation could cloud the judgement even of sensible critics and make them doubt a spinner's worth even in the great victories against the West Indies and England in 1971. Perhaps this was because whilst India occasionally won through spin, it was pace, the pace of Trueman and Statham, of Lillee and Imran, of Hall and Gilchrist, Roberts, Holding, Marshall and Garner and almost any fast bowler that undid them. The images they had to live with were of their batsmen failing so dismally to cope with pace that their struggles became a joke. As for instance during the Trueman blitz of 1952 when an umpire is supposed to have said that what worried him during the series was not Trueman's bowling, but being trampled to death at square-leg by the retreating Indian batsmen. Sporting displays of fear are never pleasant and for Indians all the victories won by their spinners did not compensate for the terrible shame and humiliation inflicted on their batsmen by opposing fast bowlers. Some of the critics pointed to India's slow pitches. But, neighbouring Pakistan, where the wickets were just as slow, if not slower, seemed to have an abundance of fast bowlers, or at least bowlers who could adequately open the innings. Some argued for a crash programme along military lines. The Indian

military is held in high, if aloof, regard and there was at least one suggestion that Project Fast Bowler should be handed over to the army. As the
most efficient thing in India, it would produce a workable solution. Others
were more pessimistic and doubted whether it was in the Indian nature to
produce fast bowlers. When one seemed to emerge, Indian cricket writers
went into raptures. The winter of 1967 saw one, Kulkarni, unexpectedly
selected to tour Australia on the strength of one good spell of left-arm
medium pace bowling on a sunny afternoon in Mumbai. One cricket
writer, overcome by this, immediately drew analogies between Kulkarni's
selection and the West Indian selection of Ramadhin and Valentine for the
1950 tour of England. But while the West Indian hunch had proved
marvellously right, Kulkarni, like so many other bowlers before him,
proved a flop.

   In the 1950s as the search for fast bowlers led to ever more bizarre
ideas, Vizzy suggested that the Punjab, where the men were supposed to
be tall and brawny, might be able to supply the goods. It was the granary
of the country, it could become the workshop of the Indian fast bowlers.
'Give me ten Punjabis and I shall give you fast bowlers', Vizzy was
supposed to have bragged.

   The fact that Indians could readily believe that ten tall Punjabis could
be taught to become fast bowlers, merely because they were tall, strapping
lads, demonstrates the hunger of the cricketing public for a fast bowler. A
desperation that made my school friends try and bowl like Lindwall
and Bedser, and many Indians question the country's mental aptitude
for cricket, and even the diet. Could a country that lived on rice and
vegetables really produce fast bowlers to match those from countries that
ate beef and pork? It was and is one of the most fascinating arguments
in sports. Is vegetarianism an enemy of fast bowling? Fast bowlers need
to be tall and strong, so ran the argument, then how could vegetarians
with their supposedly puny bodies ever match up to the demands of fast
bowling?

   Not all Indians are vegetarians. The Bengalis, living along the great
rivers Ganges and Brahmaputra, and not far from the sea are voracious
fish eaters. In fact, the Bengalis differentiate between sweet-water, river
fishes, which are a delicacy, and shun the salt-water sea fishes. Chicken
and mutton are plentiful, even if mutton is somewhat misleading since
what is consumed in India is goat meat, rather than lamb. But Hindus as
a general rule do not eat pork and shun beef. The cow is worshipped as
Gomata, mother cow, even if historians and philosophers debate whether
this worship is actually part of Hindu religion or something that developed
out of economic necessity. The view that beef-eaters are stronger than
vegetarians is, I suspect, the legacy of Muslim and British rule. Beef, it

began to be believed, gave them the strength to overawe and conquer the vegetarian Hindus.

I had illustration of this attitude some years ago when I visited India with a friend, Jim Pegg, then Assistant Sports Editor of the *Sunday Times*. My father was already in poor health, unhappy with my decision to live away from home and discard the security and the riches of accountancy – for which I trained – for the risks of journalism. Always somewhat sickly, he was now given to saying that he didn't have long to live and I should really give some thought to settling down – meaning marriage to a good Indian wife and life in a secure job in India. One day in order to reassure him I said, 'Baba, I am sure you will live for a very long time. Look at Jim's mother. She is 93, twenty years older than you.' My father looked at me with a sadness that is still vivid in my memory and said, 'These people are different. They eat pork and beef. You cannot compare us Indians with them.'

It was an astonishing statement. A successful, well-travelled businessman, his life had far from been a struggle and while he may not have eaten pork or beef his diet had hardly been wanting in any of the required vitamins. Yet even to him the mere tradition of eating pork or beef gave people strength and longevity. He looked so sad and forlorn that I did not have the courage to tell him that the latest medical research in the west showed that longevity was prolonged by avoiding red meat and eating fish – just the diet my father had followed all his life. A few months later when my father died, I recalled the conversation and realised the depths of his dejection.

Since then I have often heard such sentiments being expressed, if not in such extreme language but forcefully enough. And whenever the Indians suffer a trouncing at the hands of opposition pacemen the lament is heard that it is the lack of red meat in the diet that lets the Indians down.

Soon after the 1984 Olympics there was the all-too-familiar inquest about India's abject performance – a country of 800 million and not a medal to show for it. So great was the outcry against vegetarianism that the National Institute of Nutrition in Hyderabad issued statistics to prove that Indian vegetarian food had just as much energy – if not more – compared to meats.

Lack of a proper diet does explain the poor standard of the Indian physique. However, this is because for many Indians their diet is simply inadequate, not because they are vegetarians. Part of the Indian problem was that they ceased to believe that they could produce a fast bowler, capable of challenging the west. However Kapil Dev proved, beyond doubt, that they can. Kapil's rise has led to a new breed of opening bowlers and while none of them have achieved the status of Nissar and Omar Singh, India's hunger for fast bowlers is slowly being satisfied.

10

Gods and boys

'A boy,' said Neville Cardus, 'looks upon his heroes at cricket with emotions terribly mixed. He believes they are gods, yet at the same time he has no real confidence in them. He thinks they are going to get out nearly every ball...Strangely indeed does a boy think that his favourite cricketers are the best in the world but still the most fallible and in need of his every devoted thought.'

Cardus was recalling his agonies as a child watching Lancashire. He loved Spooner so much he never dared to watch him make a stroke, 'I probably never saw him at the moment which he actually played a ball.'

Like Cardus, I too have agonised about Indian cricket and can readily enter that special feeling, that mixture of joy and fear that is the foundation of sports enthusiasm. While age, maturity and experience do make one more cynical of joy and less frightened about fear, this feeling is part of sports watching, or at least partisan sports watching. Aside from Indian cricket my sporting loyalties are to Surrey and Tottenham Hotspur and come five o'clock on a winter Saturday evening a frisson of anticipation and fear passes through me as I await the result of Spurs. If it is right I am elated, if not depressed. As Colin Welland has said, partisan sports watching is terrible; the price of the odd moments of bliss – and no bliss could be purer, as when Tottenham beat Liverpool at Anfield after 72 years – is years of frayed nerves and black moods.

This is not a particularly Indian thing. It is a universal phenomenon, which explains the emotions that sport can generate, also the almost mystical unity between sport and superstition. Don Revie, the manager of Leeds United, always wore the same blue suit to football matches and I have sat for hours glued to one uncomfortable spot in my living room, unable to move paralysed by fear that any change would mean the fall of an Indian wicket, or a goal against Tottenham. When on that magical day at the Oval in August 1971, Chandrashekar ran through England I stood rooted at one spot, not daring to move even for a pee, till the deed was done. It made me feel I played some part in it, though no doubt millions of Indians felt the same way. It is like being part of a magic spell, recreating a mythical time that has elapsed and will never return. Human history is rooted in myth and magic and sport is the modern way of recreating something that was part of our ancestors' lives.

Myth and magic are still central to Indian life, in a way that would appear exotic in the west. Serious newspapers can review alleged books of history that seek to prove that in prehistory Indians had an Empire that included Britain. I once met the author of one of these history books and was told entertaining 'evidence' in support of such a theory. Asked why nobody else seemed to acknowledge or even mention it, he said, 'those pages of history have been forgotten'.

According to Dr Sudhir Kakar, a psychotherapist in New Delhi 'the world of magic and animistic ways of thinking lie close to the surface' in India. 'There seems,' he says, 'to be a different relationship to outside reality, compared to one met with in the West. In India it is closer to a certain stage in childhood when our outer objects did not have a separate, independent existence but were intimately related to the self and its affective states. They were not something in their own right but were good or bad, threatening or rewarding, helpful or cruel, all depending on the person's feelings of the moment.'

V. S. Naipaul has borrowed this theory to argue that Indians have a childlike perception of reality and, unlike the west, cannot describe the sex act. To them 'it happened'. Naipaul, using Kakar, makes such of the fact that in his autobiography Gandhi never refers to landscape despite his travels to England, South Africa and in India. He was too busy coping with his own turmoil produced by these travels to be able to actually describe them.

The Naipaulian point is part of a wider thesis, what may be called the Naipauls' (both V. S. and his brother Shiva) view of India. That it is a wounded civilisation whose intellectual ability is second rate, and which has nothing to offer the world except its Gandhian concepts of holy poverty and its recurring crooked comedy of holy men and, while asserting its own antiquity, needs the west for every practical assistance.

This is perhaps a more brutal, less charmingly expressed version of a theory put forward by Nirad Chaudhuri that Indians are really Europeans, in thrall to the goddess Circe. The goddess with the flowing tresses, sweetly singing before her loom has drugged Indians into forgetting their European heritage.

Chaudhuri, in the tradition of great eccentrics, suggests that if only Indians rediscovered 'our original European spirit and character' and conquered the Indian environment all would be well.

Perhaps so. I cannot accept that the Indian intellect is second rate, or that Indians need to be Europeans – in any case the type of Europeans Chaudhuri has in mind are so idealised that they are rarely found outside books. What is necessary is a greater perception of reality. But that, at least in the sporting sense, is not merely an Indian failing. In fact it is most evident in this country during the Wimbledon fortnight. Britain puts on the greatest tennis show on earth but British players fail dismally to make much of a show themselves. Yet every Wimbledon involves the same ritual anticipation and hope in the media about the British hopefuls followed by anxious, almost tearful reporting of their defeats; as one commentator said we seem to watch an endless succession of Annabels being beaten by foreigners to be succeeded by much hand-wringing and despair about Britain's failure to produce players whose tennis ability matches the organisational ability of Wimbledon.

Something similar happens in Indian sports. Like the British tennis aficionado, Indians collect the little nuggets of success, treasure them and return to them again and again puzzled and worried as to why they have not led to the sporting pot of gold that has been promised. Listen to this interview with Vijay Amritraj, published just before the 1985 Wimbledon. When Amritraj first emerged on the scene he was linked with Borg and Connors as the ABC of tennis. 'We find that B and C have done quite well,' asked the interviewer. 'What about you?' Amritraj frankly confesses that he was never in the same class and that 'it is not always that if you have three children they would perform equally well given the same opportunity'.

Yet the question betrays both the hope and despair of the Indian sports follower. A promising player emerges, the world press writes some favourable words about him, Indians immediately treasure this as an omen for the future and, when it does not materialise, bemoan their fate, the champion who has failed and the world in general. When Ramanathan Krishnan, the greatest tennis player India has produced was at his prime, pre-Wimbledon articles in the Indian press invariably asked, 'Can Krishnan win Wimbledon?' He never did, though he was in two semi-finals and Indians took what solace they could from lyrical articles, by Geoffrey Green and others, rhapsodising about the Indian's artistic touch-play. It was almost a touchstone of reassurance, something to cling to. It was much later when I read Geoffrey Green's autobiography that I realised how much of a spell India itself, had cast on certain writers.

All this has made the Indian sports enthusiast at once a hunter of nuggets about India's sporting achievements, and quite the most wide-eyed observer of the international sporting scene. Partly because of the corrosive colonial influence, partly because Indian sports journalism lacks confidence and very often substitutes coverage of home sports with reprints of articles from the English press, the Indian sports enthusiast, compared to an English one, is astonishingly well informed about the major English and international sports. He can comment intimately in a manner that would quite baffle most Englishmen.

Here is Akhilesh Krishnan, from Madras, in a letter to *Sportsweek*, about Martin Crowe playing for Somerset (15 February 1984):

> It is a real bonus for Somerset to sign the gifted New Zealand batsman Martin Crowe for this year's English County Championship matches. Crowe celebrated his selection with a timely 100 in the first Test at Basin River (*sic*), Wellington. Crowe came in place of West Indian Vivian Richards and hoped to do well as an all-rounder. During New Zealand's England tour last year Crowe registered an average of over 50 in county matches and claimed useful wickets as a medium-pace bowler. Incidentally in the first Test against England at Wellington, Crowe's elder brother and Auckland captain Jeff Crowe top scored in the first innings and his younger brother followed it up with a defiant century. Thus, the brothers played a stellar role in salvaging the reputation of the Kiwi team. Only the Chappell brothers have done better than the Crowe brothers in Test cricket. It is a real boon for New Zealand cricket and Somerset to have such a fine utility player.

All countries develop their eccentrics who know a great deal about one particular foreign country. But in India such eccentrics are the norm, and during the summer of 1984 as Gower and England lurched from defeat to defeat against Clive Lloyd's West Indians, the Indian sporting press was full of articles from sports reporters confidently opinionating about events of which they had little direct knowledge.

One can see the colonial hangover, though I have seen Indians express similar opinions about events in Russia or even America and not merely in sport. It is part of the tremendous Indian facility – something they share with Latins – of developing a quick and easy intimacy with places and people that may appear intrusive, or even rude to the Anglo-Saxon but seem most natural to the Indian. The obverse of this is that Indians themselves are tremendously susceptible to flattery, particularly if the flatterer happens to be a foreigner, and a white one, at that.

It was something well appreciated by Tony Greig during the 1976–7 England tour of India, so well indeed that he used the Indian crowds to help him inflict a crushing defeat on the Indian team, and in Robin Marler's memorable phrase became the Clive of cricket. Greig's achievements on that tour were indeed something out of fiction, transforming his team which, on paper was weaker than the Indians, into world-beaters by using what should have been the opponents' best weapon: support from the home crowd. Before the tour few could have imagined it.

A South African-born Englishman, the very epitome of the blond Anglo-Saxon, going to a coloured country and proving such a great hero that, even as he inflicted a crushing defeat on its national cricket team, he was idolised by millions of natives. Yet Tony Greig did just that in India during that winter Test series.

On the field, he inflicted one of the worst defeats ever sustained by India at home; off the field he advertised towels, creams for chapped skins, ointments for bruised ankles and even the awful Indian blades, proving that sexual appeal is not dimmed by a change of climatic zones. Calcutta's Grand Hotel where the MCC stayed, was virtually immobilised by hundreds of Bengalis screaming to get a glimpse of 'Taani', while even as India won a solitary Test at Bangalore, women of this supposedly archconservative southern city flashed their considerable bellbottomed trousered legs at Greig. As one Indian journalist put it, 'He beat our men, took our money and screwed our women', and that from a modern cricketer is something.

Much of what he did would have been banal in England, dismissed in that classic Brian Johnston phrase, 'Greig is doing his nut.' If he beat a batsman he would raise his arms and keep them raised for a minute; if he stopped a ball he would go down on his hands and knees and pause. Once, he cover-drove Bedi, going down on his left knee, and remained frozen for almost a minute, much to Bedi's annoyance. Standing at silly point, he would flex his muscles and bring a roar from the crowd, or he would turn to them and pointing at the batsman shake his knees, capturing the batsman's uncertainty.

But his gestures were discriminating, distinguishing between populist expectations and elitist tastes. In India, the cheaper stands are all to one side of the ground, generally known as the east stand. Here great masses of people are herded in like cattle – and a single movement can cause whole ranks to sway. For hours they stay rooted to one spot, ready with tiffin carriers and makeshift potties (generally empty coconuts).

When the cricket becomes boring, incidents are generated; and often during the course of a day's play there are huge roars to relieve boredom, and totally unrelated to the game. In front of the simple medieval crowd Greig performed antics which one English journalist, apologising for his fuddy-duddy image, opined no English Captain should indulge in. His favourite one was to indicate a shapely woman by rubbing the ball on his breast in a manner that was unmistakable.

For the affluent sections, which invariably included the press and players' enclosures, Greig would doff his cap or wave and smile – gentle, appropriate gestures, to a crowd aware of its own status as the leaders of modern thrusting India.

Greig's task was made easier by the fact that Bedi, the Indian Captain, was a Sikh, and subject to Irish-style comic jokes, the 'Sikh twelve o'clock'.

Once a promising Sikh cricketer dropped a sitter at precisely twelve o'clock and was so devastated by the subsequent sarcastic attacks that ultimately he retired from the Test scene.

Then in the wake of the Sanjay Gandhi-led family planning programme, a popular joke had been going the rounds. One day a very worried Sikh returns home and tells his wife, 'You know, our son is doing very badly at school. Four years ago he was in the seventh standard (roughly equivalent to the first form). Then the teacher said that he was not up to it and he was demoted to the fifth standard. Last year to the fourth standard and this year to the third standard. If this goes on it is going to become dreadful and you'd better watch out. Tie your clothes very tightly round yourself because otherwise, who knows, he may one day suddenly re-enter your womb.'

Bedi, with his idiosyncrasies, accentuated this. He always emerged ten or fifteen minutes after the lunch and tea sessions of play had commenced (the joke ran: he was still in the loo) and all this emphasised Greig's stature.

So while Bedi was often the butt of jokes, Greig was the subject of poetry, much of it terrible. In Kolkatta's popular stands he was called Greigda – a Bengali term of respect used for the older brother – which was itself some measure of the growing self-confidence of the Indian crowds. Not so long ago he would have been called Greig sahib, which is the proper term of respect for a white man, or any distinguished man in these parts.

Watching Greig on the field one began to believe in superman. From the moment he led his team on and made them bow to the crowd in the manner of a football side, you felt you were in the presence of a conjurer, his magic made possible by the receptiveness of the Indian crowds.

But though Greig's visit was deeply humiliating – and as an Indian reporting for the English media I experienced at first hand the cruel spell the white man can still cast over my fellow Indians, often at my own expense – it also marked a development in Indian crowds. *Greigda* was the cry of a Calcutta crowd that was no longer happy with the dreary draws of the 1940s and 1950s. Indian cricket, or at least its supporters, had moved into the second, more demanding phase of the game.

Dr Richard Cashman has identified four phases of Indian cricket: 1932–6 when India played 7 Tests, lost 5, used 26 players; 1946–59 when India won her first-ever Test; 1959–69, when Ramchand, Contractor and mostly Pataudi rebuilt Indian cricket and introduced a positive outlook; and 1971–9 (Cashman's book was published in 1980) when India won the Test series in England and the West Indies for the first time and the spin quartet of Bedi, Chandrashekar, Prasanna and Venkat came to the fore.

The classifications make some sense but I would personally define three phases of Indian cricket.

The first, the colonial phase lasted from 1932 to 1971 when, despite some victories and a sea-change in attitudes brought about by Pataudi, Indian crowds did not expect to win. They were happy enough with performances which stretched opponents, and brought the team good notices even if they ended in failure. But all that changed in 1971.

The transformation was all the sweeter because it was so sudden and unexpected. Before the Indians went on that West Indian tour in the winter of 1971 Pataudi was deposed as Captain – a fact that hardly encouraged the Indians to think they could take on the mighty West Indians. Certainly it was not thought so by the new captain, Ajit Wadekar who, before the crucial selection committee meeting, was not even sure he would be selected to tour. In fact, Wadekar told Pataudi that he hoped Pataudi would use his influence to see that he made the tour. Pataudi who probably sensed what was coming replied that it was more likely that he, Pataudi would require Wadekar's help to get selected when Wadekar became Captain.

So the Indians left Mumbai, in John Woodcock's memorable phrase, with a couple of useful spinners, not including Chandrashekar – he joined later for the England tour – and in six months were being talked about as world champions. This was probably not as outlandish a claim as some English critics seemed to think. India beat the West Indies in the West Indies – albeit a weak West Indian side – and then England in England, an England that under Illingworth had looked invincible and had just won back the Ashes in Australia.

Yet even at the beginning of the English tour Indians had to pinch themselves to believe that here at least was a team that could fulfil their fantasies. From the first day of the Lord's test it was clear that the Indian spinners would trouble England. When India took the first innings lead in the Test it was for the first time in forty years of Test cricket in this country and the euphoria was understandable.

It was also tinged with a feeling that it was just too good to last and I well remember the reactions of the Indian supporters on the last day of the Lord's Test. India having bowled out England were left 183 to win their first-ever Test in this country in four hours and twenty minutes. It was a chase; particularly against the weather, but it seemed attainable and after losing two quick wickets, Engineer and Gavaskar, in their very different ways, set about getting it.

I sat next to a West Indian whose drinking matched his exuberance. 'Man, you are going to win. Man, you are whipping England.' I was not so sure and the Indians around me were even more uncertain. Every time Engineer dashed down the wicket to Gifford the Indians held their breath – they knew their Faroukh, they knew how fickle their cricket gods could be. By the time rain set in at tea, India required 38 to win with 2 wickets left. My West Indian friend had long since vanished and the caution of the Indian supporters was justified. Certainly the Indians overdid the world champions hype after the Oval victory but when you have waited quite as long as that to savour success you are entitled to some overreaction.

The more significant effect was that after these victories Indians began to get a taste for them; the generation fed on draws at home and defeats abroad was a philosophical one – they didn't expect much and were thankful for what they received. But after 1971 the supporters' expectations changed; they greeted victories with theatrical euphoria and defeats with depressing fury. Thus when the Indians lost all three Tests in England in 1974, being bowled out for 42 at Lord's, there was such fury against the Captain Ajit Wadekar and the manager Hemu Adhukari that they chose to return to the country quietly – long after the team had gone. Even before they left England for home the team had discovered how fickle supporters can be. On the golden 1971 visit nearly all the Indians in England seemed to want to socialise with them. In 1974 after the 42 all out at Lord's the invitations dried up so quickly that the bereft players began courting the despised journalists – more so after they were snubbed by the High Commissioner, an action which provoked a tremendous backlash against the cricketers in India.

Indians, perhaps more than most people can veer from one extreme to another and this phase certainly saw the development of some unpleasantly ruthless behaviour, such as the sacking of Wadekar, whose record as India's Captain though brief – only three Test series – is quite the best. The Indians had discovered that their newly created gods had clay feet.

In 1983 the Indians won the World cup which marks the start of the third phase of Indian cricket. Between 1932 and 1971 Indians regarded a draw as a victory, 1971–83 introduced them to the heady delights of victory and made defeat that much more difficult to accept. The World cup triumph of 1983 delightful as it was, was also something of a trap. It made Indians think that they ought to win every match, and they began to believe their own propaganda of being world champions of one-day cricket. While there was some substance in the claim in that since the World cup India won limited-overs tournaments in Sharjah and Australia, it was significant that these triumphs had all come away from home.

At home the Indian record has been patchier and some of the blame for this must fall on the Indian crowds. As Sunil Gavaskar said after the Indians' triumph in Australia in the winter of 1984–5, at home the crowds create such pressure with their relentless expectations that they unsettle the players and force them to play in a virtual pressure cooker with inevitable loss of form and motivation. Crowds that once applauded draws, now find even the hint of defeat difficult to stomach.

This has been accentuated by the fact that the World Cup triumphs came in one-day matches where there are no draws. It has made one-day matches all the rage and depressed the worth of Test matches. In the two decades since that 1983 triumph India has became so devoted to the one-day version of the game that while stadiums are always packed for one-day internationals, Tests can see empty stands – unthinkable in my youth. So much so that in Mumbai where once they only sold a 'season ticket' for a Test, meaning you had to buy a ticket for all five days, they have long since had to start selling daily tickets.

The explanation for this is perhaps that what had been taken as genuine enthusiasm for cricket was instead *tamasha* – a wave of emotion and feeling. Indian political analysts often describe elections in terms of waves, the 'Indira wave' for the 1971 elections, the 'anti-emergency wave' for the 1977 elections, the 'sympathy wave' for the 1984 post-Indira Gandhi elections. Cricket enthusiasm too can be described in terms of waves. It developed in the mid-1960s and grew on the back of the 1971 victories and the spread of radio and television coverage. The World Cup victory shattered the Test wave and replaced it with frenzy for the new one-day stuff which seemed to better suit both pockets and social tastes.

In his autobiography, *Tiger's Tale*, Pataudi, still seeing India with the sense of wonder that Winchester and Oxford had instilled in him, wrote about Indian cricket crowds of the 1950s and 1960s thus: 'Cricket in India today is non-spectacular low-key stuff played on shirt front sun baked wickets. The crowds do not seem to mind at all. They lap it up. It may be another fifteen years before they become sophisticated and outspoken in their demands for more action and better results but it will happen.'

Tiger's prediction has come true, though perhaps not quite in the way Pataudi imagined. India has a wonderful facility for making fools of futurologists – it is a western game that sits uneasily in India. It is easy both for Indians and westerners to be swept up by Indian enthusiasms and come to extravagant conclusions. Despite the undoubted progress that the country has made, Indians show no sense of history or analysis. As technology improves, as middle India becomes stronger, even attempts at elementary analysis recede, confusing both Indians and foreigners. I can easily see why Scyld Berry should have made his confident prediction that India was destined to become the Test cricket capital in 1982 but sounded much more chastened after the somewhat different experiences of 1984–5.

I recall talking to Raj Singh, manager of the Indian team to England in 1982 and a shrewd observer of the game. The Indian tour began disastrously, India losing the one-day matches against England but Raj Singh was philosophical. The one-day game was foreign to India. Let England play this rubbish. We Indians, he said, would stick to the real thing – the Tests. Yet even as he spoke India was entering its most barren Test period – 31 Tests without a win before India beat England at Mumbai in the winter of 1984 and its greatest, most glorious moment in international cricket was just a year away in the World Cup.

Raj Singh, like Scyld Berry, was basing himself on what seemed to be unmistakable pointers. A large and growing urban population extremely fond of the game, vast facilities including stadia that dwarf most in England and the spread of radio and television, particularly ball-by-ball commentaries on radio in Indian languages that, Raj Singh felt, had made the game Indian. The commentaries were awful, the commentators very often selected by the Minister of Information on a jobs for the boys basis, but Raj Singh's point had validity. Above all there was the climate which, for most of the year, is rain free. All signs that seemed to bear out Scyld Berry's assertion in *Cricket Wallah* in 1982 that Indian batting would always remain orthodox 'because the one-day game, which grows fast in other Test countries, holds no great attraction'. The winter of 1981–2, in fact, saw India play their first one-day international at home.

The World Cup transformation came about because of the deeds of a group of highly motivated north Indians led by Kapil Dev. But it was a transformation wrought by individuals – as had always been the case in India – and it is this that makes any prediction about Indian cricket hazardous.

Cricket owes its growth in India to certain individuals – Parsees, keen to become British, the princes keen to preserve their archaic rule nourishing it as a way to curry favour with the British, and now the businessmen and industrialists of middle India who see in it vast opportunities for commercial profit. For two decades the profit potential lay in Test matches but now that the focus has shifted to one-day matches one can see that the old theory of India being the last bastion of Test cricket has little to support it.

Unlike England, Indian cricket has not developed the roots through village and club cricket that sustain the English game whatever the merits of the national team. Unlike the West Indies it is not a nationalist factor that brings together the disparate islands. Indians do not play cricket to further their national sense of identity – they suffer from a surfeit of such symbols.

Indians themselves recognise that they have failed to develop some of the attributes that form a cricketing or sporting culture. Indian defeat led to inquests about cricketers' lack of the 'killer instinct'. Almost believing their own propaganda that Indians are artistic touch-players who are a bit too gentlemanly for their opponents, Indians endlessly debate about how they might acquire the ruthlessness that marks out a Connors or a McEnroe. The foreigners' rhapsody about Indian gentleness is used as a stick to beat the failed cricketers.

Perhaps the problem is that Indians expect too much from their cricketers – expectations aroused by the generally low standards of reporting and analysis of the game in the country. Despite the growth and development of the game, India has yet to develop the sort of cricket journalism seen in, say England or Australia. It is very common for a series of Test matches in the same newspaper to be reported by different journalists reflecting the different regions of the country.

Of course, development of proper cricket journalism has hardly bothered the West Indies but India, where the game is constantly compared to England or Australia, reinforces cricket as a *tamasha fiesta*. A fiesta can take many forms, it can fluctuate from day to day, even from event to event and there are signs that this is just what Indian cricket is doing.

This would suggest that the Indian temperament is more suited to football which even as played in the west is more of a fiesta, less analytical and for-mal than cricket. Football, as we have seen, remains the most popular sport in India. England's cricketers witnessing the decline of spectator interest in recent Test series' have been surprised to find such enthusiasm for football – a game they thought was foreign in India. What it has lacked, outside pockets such as Bengal, is social acceptance and the political patronage given to cricket. But if interest in Test cricket slides, and one-day cricket does not quite fill the vacuum, then one can see football reclaiming the role that Vivekananda proclaimed for it all those years ago. Football has many hurdles to overcome, including shambolic organisation. Not least of its problems is the tremendous Indian ability to introduce politics into everything. But if it can get its act together – and it is a big if – it may be just possible to see India become the footballing capital of the twenty-first century.

It is interesting to note that as a result of the opening up of India since the economic liberation of 1991 and the arrival of satellite and cable television, Indians have been exposed to international football like never before. My brother-in-law in Kolkata watches more live matches from the English Premier league on television than I can in England. The Champion league matches are also shown live. I arrived in Mumbai not long ago and got into my hotel at two in the morning to find a live Premier league match being screened. Sometime later on a trip to Darjeeliing – a hill station in the foothills of the Himalayas – I saw a young boy wearing David Beckham's No. 7 Manchester United shirt – Beckham had not yet been sold to Real Madrid. I have found a few Indian cricket administrators who confess that their children are more attracted to football than cricket. On television quizzes for school students, questions about European football are so easy that students often yearn for something more challenging.

But this is international, European football. And the more they watch Manchester United and Real Madrid, the more they turn away from the

Indian football disillusioned by its quality. It is now so poor that far from dominating Asian soccer – as it did in my childhood – it struggles even to beat its neighbours and FIFA despairs of the way Indian football is run. The result is an Indian paradox: great enthusiasm for watching the televised European game, disenchantment with the domestic game.

Cricket in India has a vibrant international side of its own, and if Indian football could get a role model like Tendulker then it could begin to challenge cricket.

India, said R. K. Narayan, will always go on. Indian cricket too will survive but the form it will take may surprise many. Enthusiasms wax and wane in India, perhaps more so than in other countries and there are definite signs that the enthusiasm for Test cricket so strong in the 1960s and 1970s has now begun to wane. One-day cricket has replaced it but fortune is fickle and Indians could soon discover another *tamasha* to amuse and titillate them. I hope it does not happen, but I fear it might.

11

Shining India or poverty of ambition?

In the summer of 2002 I fulfilled one of my most cherished ambitions – to watch a Test match at Bridgetown, Barbados. I had seen cricket in Trinidad and Antigua but never at the headquarters of West Indian cricket. For me Barbados was the home of the cricketing greats I had long worshipped: Weeks, Worrell, Walcott, Gary Sobers and Wes Hall. The trip was made memorable by a dinner with Sobers, who for my generation of cricket lovers remains the greatest cricketer we have ever seen, or are ever likely to. Just to see him field at leg slip was worth the admission money.

The omens for the trip were also good. Just days before I arrived in Barbados India won a Test match in Trinidad, the first victory in the West Indies for 26 years, and only their third ever – all three coming at Trinidad. This gave them a 1–0 lead with three Tests to go and the victory seemed to mark a new trend in Indian cricket. After the dismal 1950s Indian cricket had always been strong at home. There had been the odd blips, like the 3–1 defeat by Tony Greig's side in 1976–7, and then the 2–1 defeat by David Gower's side in 1984–5, but for 13 years between 1987 and 2000 India did not lose a series at home. And while Cronje's South Africans dented this in 2000, the revelation of match fixing practised by Cronje put a different light on the series.

Now, under Saurav Ganguly, Indians, always such bad travellers, had begun to win abroad. At that stage Ganguly had not won a series away from home but, apart from South Africa, Ganguly had won at least a Test abroad even if he subsequently lost the series.

But the Barbados Test reawakened all the old fears. India played dreadfully on the first day and lost the match soon after lunch on the fourth. After the match I asked Harsha Bogle, the doyen of Indian cricket commentators – and one of the few television commentators who has made it without having played cricket at the highest level (the only other commentator is Tony Crozier). Bogle's reply was succinct. 'I am afraid there is a terrible poverty of ambition in Indian cricket.'

What this means is that Indian cricketers having won a Test abroad – more than previous touring Indian Test teams have managed – feel they have gone as far as they need to. The Trinidad Test was not seen as a launch paid for winning the series, as it should have been, but the peak itself. The end of that West Indies series seemed to bear out Bogle. India went on to lose the last Test and with it the series 2–1 – when with a bit more resolute batting in the final Test in Jamaica the Test and the series could have been drawn. This was all the more galling as minutes after the last Indian wicket fell tremendous rain lashed Jamaica and for days there was no cricket, washing out one-day internationals meant to be played there after the Test.

Bogle's prescient remarks also seemed to explain what for many decades was one of the oddest features of Indian batting. In a land which is often described as slow and patient, and which has produced some of the great run accumulators of the game, batsmen such as Merchant, Hazare, Gavaskar, there was no Indian score of 300 in a Test innings. For a Test batsman to score 300 is rare but hardly unusual, batsmen of all the major Test playing countries had scored 300 – I exclude countries such as Zimbabwe and Bangladesh – and many had done so not long after their teams had achieved Test status. For years I was intrigued by this Indian failure and often asked Indian cricketers for an explanation. What depressed me was that not only did none of them give me a satisfactory answer but few of them seemed to care. Some said it was the heat, but the heat is no less in domestic cricket where many Indians have scored 300. In 1948 B. B. Nimbalkar had scored 443 not out and would have passed Bradman's then record of 452 not out but for the opposing captain, a minor prince with a grand title, conceding the match after lunch. In neighbouring Pakistan Hanif Mohammed, a mere six years after his country's Test debut, scored 300 in a Test – in the West Indies. Bogle's poverty of ambition seemed the only explanation for the failure by Indian batsmen to convert their many double centuries into triples.

Eventually, in April 2004, 72 years after India's Test debut, an Indian did score 300 in a Test innings and it is in keeping with the remarkable Indian cricket story that it was the most unlikely Indian and he achieved it not at home but in the heart of India's greatest cricketing rival.

That man was Virender Sehwag. Brought up in the Najafgarh area of west Delhi, playing his cricket on the small ground there and riding into town on a scooter, Sehwag has always bucked the trend. He made his debut as a dashing middle-order batsman scoring a hundred in his first Test in South Africa. By this time a debutant Test hundred was no longer the kiss of death it had been for so long in Indian cricket although, apart from Sehwag, only three others Visvanath, Azharuddin and Ganguly have followed their debut hundreds with more Test hundreds. In England in the summer of 2002 he was suddenly converted to a Test opener and it looked like another of those short-term measures Indian cricket specialises in, which, invariably, end in tears. But it worked. However, although he hit a hundred in England and a double hundred in Australia it seemed inconceivable that his whole batting approach based on blasting the ball could allow him to go where the technically more accomplished Merchant and Gavaskar had not gone. More so as India were on their first tour of Pakistan for 15 years, a country where India had never before won a Test.

But Sehwag on opening the batting in the first Test at Multan treated the Pakistani attack as if he was back at the ground at Najafgarh, ending the first day tantalisingly close to 300. The next day, in characteristic style, he went from 296 to 300 with a 6. Sehwag's innings was the launch pad for a unique triple for Indian cricket: for the first time an Indian had scored 300 in a Test innings, India's victory in Multan was its first-ever Test victory in Pakistan and then, after another victory in Rawalpindi India won its first-ever Test series. For good measure the 2–1 victory was also India's first series win abroad for ten years.

The feat seemed to suggest Indian cricketers had at last conquered their poverty of ambition and was immediately hailed as proof a new India, both on the cricket field and off. It had come in the middle of an election campaign when the ruling party, the Bharatiya Janata Party, was seeking re-election on the slogan of India Shining The country's growth rate was over 8 per cent, higher than any other country bar China, it had $100 billion in foreign exchange reserves, its rupee was stable, its agricultural resilient and there was a vibrant Indian middle class. And in his Republic Day message of 2004 the Indian President APJ Abdul Kalam even predicted India would soon 'occupy pride of position' on the global scene. The very English phrase 'feel good' was part of the BJP's official campaign slogan with the the BJP's deputy Prime Minister L. K. Advani saying to party members, in that curious mix of Hindi-English which is now so much part of India, 'Aam aadmi ke nazariye se yahi hai pheel good'('In the opinion of everyone this is feel good'). Advani had been inspired to use the phrase having seen how effective it had proved for Margaret Thatcher in winning elections in the UK. India it seemed, had reversed the old cliché of the thin man trying to get out of a fat one, by becoming a country where a fat man of some 300 million well-off Indians was trying to shrug off the embrace of the emaciated thin men and women of more than 600 million. As it happens because of the failure to attend to the needs of these thin Indians, mostly in the rural areas, the BJP sensationally lost the election.

But despite this BJP failure, the incoming Congress government stressed that this was a new India and the mood music about India is very different to the one I heard when I was growing up. The world over, politicians, who in the past talked about the aid they needed to give to India, now warn their nations of the economic threat posed by India. As I write, this has been the theme of the remarks made by Gordon Brown, the British Chancellor, and the man in charge of the world's fourth-largest economy to the House of Commons. Western newspapers that once only spoke of hungry Indians now speak of hungry Indian businessmen seeing to take over moribund western companies with some Indian businessmen rich enough to dominate the *Sunday Times* Rich List. Eighty years after E. M. Forster's Fielding had taunted Aziz, saying India whose only peer was the Holy Roman Empire would come waddling into nationhood on a par with Belgium, India appears to be making purposeful strides to take its rightful place in the world.

It is in cricket that this power has been felt most forcefully. This was brought home four months after Sehwag's feat when a dinner was held at the home of Notts County Football ground – one of the oldest football clubs in England, and a founder of the Football League. The dinner was meant to honour the Indian team and Sehwag in particular. It was hosted by Nat Puri, an Indian born businessman from Nottingham, who is a great patron of cricket and loves the Indian game. He had promised to give £50,000 to the first Indian batsman to score 300 runs in a Test innings. Sehwag got the award from Boycott and when Boycott asked him what were his thoughts as he went to his 300 with a 6 he said, "You bat your way, I bat my." Boycott was quite stunned by the nonchalance. Sehwag then put the money in his back pocket and for days afterwards wandered about England not caring about it, before turning to a friend to ask where he could deposit the money. Sehwag, of course, declared it to the authorities.

The dinner brought together many elements that now make up Indian cricket and explain why it is such a formidable force. There were cricketers like Sehwag, a very different breed to the traditional Indian cricketers, there were the men and women of Indian origin who could consider themselves to be successful in Britain, reflecting the power of the Indian diaspora, and there was the hunger for televised cricket in India, where the sheer numbers attracted to the game – audiences of over 200 million for a game were not unknown – created an economic force world cricket had never before seen.

The very presence of the Indian team in England in the summer of 2004 testified to that. They were playing a series of one-day matches with England which were being televised live in India. The money this earned the England and Wales Cricket Board was very crucial. This was followed by the ICC. Champions Trophy where all the sponsors were either Indian companies or international companies operating in the Indian market. All these matches were also being televised and during the Champions Trophy Final, despite the fact that it was between England and the West Indies, very often names of Indian companies such as Bharat Petroleum, complete with its Sanskrit logo, would be flashed up on the Oval scoreboard To those who know how international cricket is run this was no surprise. India now provides 60 per cent of world cricket's income and it is estimated that every second person watching televised cricket is an Indian. With India's growing economic muscle, and an insatiable appetite for the one-day game, this is a market that cricket administrators round the world want to cultivate. Major cricket tournaments like the ICC Champions Trophy or the World Cup could not exist without it being sold to a television company broadcasting to India. Commercial sponsors see such events as a wonderful way to reach the growing Indian market for whom cricket, particularly one-day cricket, is now the great marketing tool.

How big this market can be was emphasised even as the Champions Trophy matches were going on in England. News began to emerge from India that a huge fight was going for the rights to televise Indian cricket over the next four years from 2004 through to 2008. Zee TV, an Indian company, had outbid Rupert Murdoch's Star by offering $308 million. Given this means a total of 108 days of international cricket, it valued each day at $2.85 million, nearly as much as Kerry Packer was prepared to pay for all five years of Australian cricket back in 1977 when the previous cricket revolution had taken place. (Packer had offered $3.25 million to televise five years of Australian cricket including the Ashes series. It was the Australian Board's refusal to even consider the offer that led to the Packer revolution.) Even allowing for inflation this shows how big the Indian cricket market. Never in its history has cricket been so lucrative.

But if Indian cricket's economic muscle is so dominant then surely Indian cricketers no longer suffer from a poverty of ambition? Sehwag clearly does not, but India's economic power is not always matched by similar dominance on the field, and what is more the Indian board continue to behave as if it was a street trader, eager for the loot but unable to either plan for it, let alone manage it. The essential contradictions of the country and its cricket have not vanished.

Change has come, enormous change, but it has come far too quickly to be assimilated. To appreciate how quickly this has happened, consider this fact. Twenty years ago India was just entering the television age, little more than ten years ago the Indian economy was closed to the world – and on the point of collapse – but now the sheer size of the market means India calls all the shots in cricket's commercial world.

India came late to television, later than most other third world countries and two decades after its neighbour Pakistan. When I left India in 1969 there was only an experimental television in New Delhi broadcasting for fewer hours than BBC television was before the Second World War. I had seen only ten minutes of television on a visit to New Delhi.

In 1977 with Kerry Packer creating mayhem in the cricket world, India had barely entered the television age. There were just 676,615 sets in a country whose population was already over 600 million. At that stage not a single ball of cricket had ever been televised in India and in any case India was dead set against Packer with no Indian cricketer recruited to play for his circus.

Today, 80 million homes have television, which means over 400 million Indians can, and do, watch televised cricket, particularly the more elaborate version of the pyjama game first devised by Packer. By the end of the decade it is estimated that a further 30 million Indian homes will have television and, given each home is meant to have five people, that will add another 150 million Indians to the numbers watching television and therefore televised cricket.

Dramatic change of this nature always catches us by surprise, but in this case the surprise is all the greater because of the way it happened. It came about quite by chance in 1991 when all the elements in Indian cricket came together matched by changes in the wider world. That year, under pressure from the World Bank, India was forced to open up its economy and allow foreign investment into what had been one of the most protected markets in the world. The year 1991 was also that of the first Gulf War, and suddenly Indians learnt it was possible to view the war on television – as opposed to newsreels, which is how they had previously followed wars and major events. They started buying television sets, and cable operators acquired dishes and simply flung cable over treetops and verandahs to provide service to the mushrooming high-rise homes in India's metropolitan cities.

Television also began to reach India's villages, and many there, who had previously never seen any television, suddenly saw in this medium a splendid new business. An article in the *Guardian Weekend*, written on 9 April 1994, captured this well. It described how a Jeet Singh in the village of Bakthawar, on the borders of Haryana and Uttar Pradesh, transformed himself from a shopkeeper into the village's cable operator:

> He used to run a general store before moving into cable in this rather more advanced village of 15,000 people. His dish cost him £750. The cabling and boosting equipment to link up another 140 houses cost him another £1,800. Total outlay around £2,400. He charges each house £2 a month, bringing him an income of £280 a month, so he has his costs covered within a year.

The year 1991 was also when cricket finally became one family, and when for the first time South Africa, having shed its sporting apartheid past, played a non-white country, launching its rebirth with a one-day series in India. That historic tour made the Indian Board realise it had television rights it could sell. Before that, Doordarshan, the state broadcaster, had televised domestic cricket and far from paying anything had often demanded fees from the board to cover the cost of production.

Now two South African television channels wanted the rights. Amrit Mathur, who worked for then Indian Board President Madhavrao Scindia has a precise recollection of what happened. Mathur recalls, 'We had to find out first who owned the rights and then how much they were worth.' Mathur discovered that the rights belonged to the Indian Board and their value was much more than what the Indians thought they were. So in one of the great ironies of cricket as South Africa at last discovered what it is to play against a non-white country, the Indians discovered that they were sitting on a gold mine they had not known existed.

But even now the Indian Board might never have begun to mine this gold but for the intervention of an Indian who had gone to live in Connecticut. Mark Mascarenhas, a Bangalore boy, who before his death in a car crash in January 2002 was to become more famous as Sachin Tendulkar's agent making him the best paid cricketer in the world, was convinced cricket rights could fetch big money

Mascarenhas's involvement illustrated the growing power of the Indian diaspora. He was very proud of his Indian roots, kept close links with his family in Bangalore, where he went back very often, he died while on a visit back home to south India, but found it easier to operate his business from Connecticut. The arrival of Mascarenhas and many other Indians in the US had been made possible by the liberalisation of American immigration laws, and in particular removal of racist laws which kept a tight lid on Asian immigration. America's celebrated call of give me your poor, huddled masses, had always been directed at the Europeans. Now in the 1960s it started welcoming educated Indians and many young middle-class Indians brought up on cricket went to live in the US. But they missed their cricket and Mascarenhas discovered they were willing to pay top dollars for sports through pay per view television. For years one of his major deals was televising Sharjah cricket. This was yet another illustration of the power of the Indian diaspora. The cricket in the desert had been created by an Arab fascinated by cricket when he went to study in Pakistan and catering for the cricket appetite of the subcontinental diaspora in the Middle East. If in the US mostly middle-class, educated Indians, had gone, the Gulf had seen more working-class Indians, but both these groups were devoted to cricket.

Mascarenhas made his mark on the world stage when he bought the rights for the 1996 World Cup held in the subcontinent. He guaranteed $10 million but delivered $30 million. At the time seasoned broadcasters thought Mascrenhas was mad but the profits he made and the huge sums the Indian board made as they ruthlessly commercialised the World Cup enabled every major cricket ground in the country to be equipped with floodlights, opening the floodgates for one-day cricket in India. Ehsan Mani, now President of the ICC, then involved in the running of the World Cup believes that the 1996 World Cup was the 'turning point' for the sale of cricket's televised rights.

By the time Mascarenhas performed his audacious coup in 1996 Indians had been fully introduced to the television age. The country had gone from two Doordarshan channels before 1991 to 50 channels – it now has over 200 channels and over 60,000 cable operators. By 1996 India had also became familiar with foreign television companies, the two most important being Rupert Murdoch's Star and Disney's ESPN. For a time in the late 1990s the two giants fought each other over cricket rights. But soon they came to a curious and interesting alliance.

They formed a joint venture company called ESPN Star Sports (ESS) and decided not to bid against each other, effectively carving up the cricket market. They continue to run their own separate sports channels but divide up Indian cricket between them. If one shows one-day internationals, then the other will show Test cricket. Both companies broadcast from Singapore and while in the early years the anchor men used to be white, now they use more Indians and an international cast of ex-cricketers led by Sunil Gavaskar and including Geoff Boycott.

Apart from sports there is little they have in common. ESPN has never ventured out of sports while Star with its global ambitions has many other channels including general entertainment and news channels. It is now the number one television company in India and its programme *Who Wants To Be a Crorepati?* modelled on *Who Wants To Be a Millionaire?* hosted by Bollywood's greatest actor Amitabh Bachchan is the most popular show in India. Star presents to a more comprehensive competition to Doordarshan than Sky presents to the terrestrial channels in the UK.

To an extent this mirrors the situation in England, with the BBC, Channel 4, and Sky all competing for cricket and at various stages being in partnership with each other, the partnership between BBC and Sky in the early 1990s having been replaced by the one between Channel 4 and Sky. However, the Indian situation has been rather more fluid. So while Doordarshan had domestic cricket for five years between 1999 and 2003, paying $55 million, ESPN and Star also had Indian cricket, but more often India's matches overseas, but with some satellite television rights for domestic cricket acquired from Doordarshan.

The whole picture changed in 2000 when suddenly another Indian television company, which had previously shown no interest, made the biggest bid cricket has ever seen.

The story of Zee TV is one of those extraordinary stories India specializes in. Its founder Subhas Chandra started an oil mill when he was 19 and then earned money exporting grain to Russia. In 1992, a year after India opened up its markets, he set up Zee TV funded by money from the Indian diaspora, having previously had funds from Sir James Goldsmith and other UK businessmen. For eight years Zee showed no interest in cricket, preferring to show movies, Indian sitcoms and other standard general entertainment programmes. Zee was very successful in this and Murdoch, himself, bought a stake in the company. At this stage and for some years afterwards Zee was convinced sports was not for it. Its forte was current affairs and films and it seemed quite happy with that mix.

But in the summer of 2000, when the ICC met in Paris to consider bids for the 2003 and 2007 World Cups and other ICC tournaments, Zee tabled the biggest bid in the history of the game: $660 million, $110 million more than World Sports, the group backed by Rupert Murdoch. With cricket rocked by the corruption tales, the ICC, unsure of the future, decided to play safe and impressed by Murdoch's backing for World Sports accepted the lower bid. Zee for most of the ICC was an unknown Indian company.

Three years later there was another surprising Indian intervention from a rival of Zee and ESPN Star. This was Sony which for some years had been running a general entertainment channel with occasional forays into cricket.

Sony bid nearly $230 million for the Indian rights for the 2003 and 2007 World Cup. The amount was all the more amazing given that GCC struggled to sell the rights in other countries. In these countries they were shown on one or the other of Murdoch's channels, for instance Sky in England. But in India Murdoch recouped nearly half of what he had paid for the entire package, testimony to the strength and power of the Indian cricket market.

Sony's chief executive, Kunal Dasgupta, makes it very clear what the logic of this huge bid was. 'Cricket is the only product in India which unites the whole country, north–south, east–west. It transcends class, religion, regional and language differences. You do not require words to explain Sachin Tendulkar or Rahul Dravid.' In a country of over 20 languages, 1,700 dialects, 5 religions and many castes and sub-castes, cricket cuts across barriers in a way that nothing else did. Indian advertisers have no doubts about cricket's drawing power and in February 2004, with an election on the horizon, the *Economic Times* reported that major companies preferred to spend more money buying advertisements spots when cricket was on rather than when election news was on. Cricket excited the viewers in the way politics did not. Just as Murdoch had used Premier League football in England to drive the sales of dishes and attract the young males advertisers find so difficult to reach, Sony was using World Cup cricket.

Sony's success seems to have rekindled Zee's interest, despite its earlier failure. In the autumn of 2004 when the Indian Board asked for bids for the rights for four years starting with the 2004 season, Zee returned to the fray determined to get cricket. After a complex series of typically Indian mauoeuvres Zee emerged on top with a bid of $308 million easily trumping Star, Doordarshan and Sony.

But if all this emphasised the selling power of Indian cricket the way the deal was done also revealed the wretched manner the Indian Board, by far the richest cricket board in the world, operates. The contract was negotiated only weeks before India was due to host Australia for what was seen as the championship of the world. Any properly run board would have had the deal signed a year, or at least a few months, before the start of India's most important season in years. But despite all the talk of planning-there is still a Soviet-style National Planning Commission – Indians have a horror of sitting down and working things out in good time. Indians are the ultimate last minute merchants, even more than the Greeks, and while very often it all comes right on the night – as the Athens Olympics did – this time things went horribly wrong with the Indian Board making a mess of its own tendering process.

The Indian Board's tender had said the rights would only go to a broadcaster which broadcasts cricket. This seemed to rule out Zee which has so far not televised cricket. So when Star lost it took the Board to court alleging it had violated its own tendering process. The Board then performed a series of somersaults ending with decision to cancel the tender process and get the rights back from Zee. Zee retaliated by taking the Board to the Supreme Court and as this is being written the matter is still unresolved. In time, no doubt, some decision will be made but whatever it is, it is doubtful if the Board can earn anything like the money Zee offered – the truly attractive element in the package the India–Australia series is history – and Board insiders freely confess that the Board started the negotiations too late and messed things up both strategically and legally.

The solution the Indians came for the Australia series illustrates the ad hoc way the Indian board can run cricket. As the Supreme Court discussed the television deal, the Australians arrived in India and Indian cricket was faced with a catastrophic television black-out. Finally a last minute compromise was worked out pending the Supreme Court judgment: Ten Sports was given the right to do the production with the matches shown on Doordarshan in India and Sony hawking the rights abroad. In the UK this meant being shown on Setanta, an Irish pay per view channel But with the main cricket commentators tied up with ESPN Star the series saw, probably, the most curious set of commentators of any recent series. Sanjay Manjrekar apart, Indians suddenly heard from cricketers who were hardly household names in India and most of them were white foreigners. There was Dean Jones, Michael Slater, and amazingly Robin Jackman. Back in the 1980s Jackman because of his links with white South Africa would not have been allowed to play cricket in India, now he was the doyen of the commentators. One ex-cricketer Michael Atherton, who had arrived in India to write about the series for the *Sunday Telegraph*, suddenly found himself being employed as a commentator. But at least Atherton had played in India. Merv Hughes had never played in India. He happened to be accompanying an Australian touring party come over to see the cricket and found himself in the commentary box. While all this was going on India's established commentators like Harsha Bogle, who has seen India play all over the world such the 1990s, was broadcasting to Australians over ABC radio. Throughout the series the Indian board gave the impression that it has just discovered the art of televising cricket. In England such a situation would have raised a tremendous outcry, in India nobody seemed bothered.

It illustrated yet another paradox of Indian cricket.

India may be the economic powerhouse of world cricket but the Indian Board remains unreformed and, as the series against Australia showed, a great liability. It continues to operate as if India was still a poor cricketing land which cannot attract regular visits from Test playing countries and has to be content with unofficial Tests against so-called Commonwealth teams organised by the old Lancashire wicketkeeper George Duckworth. The Indian Board has no proper corporate office, or even a recognisable corporate structure. It has a laughable administrative office in the north stand of the Brabourne Stadium where India has not played cricket for some thirty years. As one source said the Board continues to be run as if its entire office is located in the briefcase of Jagmohan Dalmiya until recently the Board President, now the Patron, a newly created position.

The last time we encountered Dalmiya it was the winter of 1984 and he was in charge of the Calcutta Test, talking of how he had no problems declaring 'houseful' every time a Test was played in Kolkata. Now he has no problems declaring coffers full every time India takes the field but while his money making capacity is unrivalled that can hardly be said of his organisational skills.

His money making ability first came to prominence during the 1996 World Cup. Apart from the television riches Mascarenhas brought, the tournament was marketed on a scale never before seen in cricket. There was an official sponsor for every conceivable product, including the official World Cup chewing gum. It has been estimated that India and Pakistan pocketed a profit of almost $50 million.

Dalmiya, whose official title was Convenor of the Pakistan India Sri Lanka Organising committee (PILCOM), drove this commercial juggernaut. But even as he made money on a scale never done before he revealed his inability to organise events. He was responsible for the opening ceremony in Calcutta, which was widely regarded as a disaster. The designer, an Italian who had designed the 1990 Italian World Cup opener, did not take into account that Calcutta could be windy and the compere Saeed Jaffrey got the names of some of the teams wrong.

Dalmiya's Jekyll and Hyde personality, a fantastic ability to make money but not always able to organise and manage events continued to haunt him as he rode up the cricket escalator. Dalmiya used the success of the World Cup to extend his power base by standing for the Presidency of the ICC. At that stage he was not even the Indian Board President but with the Asians angered by the ICC's impotence in the face of Australia's refusal on security grounds to go to Colombo to play their World Cup group matches urged Dalmiya to stand. The money man who had allowed others to be king now sought the throne himself.

Dalmiya ran his election as if it was an American presidential race, energetically wooing the associates, but despite twice winning the vote of the ICC members, he found the old powers reluctant to accept him. The bitter power struggle, essentially a brown versus white (and black) battle with England, Australia, New Zealand and the West Indies ranged against the subcontinent, was so vicious that it left scars which have never healed. The Asian countries resented the grudging acceptance of them by England and Australia, while the old powers felt that the new kids on the block were not following the gentlemanly ways and were also doing nothing about cricketing corruption. In the end Dalmiya was accepted but with poor grace. He never felt part of cricket's most important club and the club never felt he could ever be truly one of them.

As he had done in India Dalmiya made money for the ICC. Before Dalmiya arrived ICC's income was little more than the subscriptions the members paid. Under his leadership through initially controversial tournaments like the ICC. Knock-out tournaments – now know as the Champions Trophy – ICC began to harvest television income for the first time. But this was also the period when match fixing emerged as a great scourge and there was a lamentable failure by the cricket authorities to deal with it.

The centre of match fixing was the subcontinent and it was sustained by the Indian love for betting. Gambling comes naturally to Indians. Mahabharata, one of the two great myths of Hinduism, turns on a loaded game of dice. It was played between the Pandavas and the Kauravas, two lots of cousins who were both claiming the throne of Indraprastha, the legendary capital of ancient India. In this epic story of good and bad the Pandavas were the goodies, the Kauravas were the baddies. The leader of the Pandavas, Yuddisthara, who was the embodiment of goodness and honour – he never told a lie in his life – agreed to a game of dice with his wicked cousins to settle the fate of ancient India. The Pandavas duly lost but unknown to them a wicked Kaurava uncle had loaded the dice. When the Pandavas found out they decided the dice game could not be allowed to stand and went to war to reclaim their just rewards. It was on this historic battlefield that the Hindu god Krishna enunciated his philosophy, which is enshrined in the Bhagavat Gita, the closest the Hindus have to a bible.

In modern India, whose many laws still reflect the legacy of Britain, gambling is only legally permissible on racetracks – as it was in Britain before the betting shops were legalised in the 1960s. Outside that, all other forms of gambling are illegal. Such restrictions have not stopped gambling, merely pushed it underground. When I was growing up in Mumbai in the 1950s gambling would take place at street corners and the most popular form of gambling was betting on the closing prices of the New York Cotton Exchange. This produced a set of numbers every day and the bet involved predicting what the numbers would be. As New York is ten hours behind Mumbai, by the time the cotton exchange closed in New York it would be the next morning in Mumbai and one of my early childhood memories is the excited hubbub of conversations as the numbers came through from New York.

The closing prices of the New York cotton exchange remained the favourite bet of the Indian punter until the mid-1960s when matka, the Indian numbers game, took over. Again it was centred around Mumbai and every evening about 7 p.m. a hush would descend at street corners of the city – an unnerving sight given the constant ceaseless noise – and indeed across many street corners in urban India as the Matka numbers were eagerly awaited. Then from the secret Matka centre somewhere in central Mumbai the numbers would emerge and the hush would dissolve into a cauldron of noise – either of joy or desolation. The Matka game still goes on but in the 1980s the Indian gamblers found a new game: cricket and in particular the one-day game.

By 1996, and the heyday of the match fixer, there had been an enormous spread of such one-day matches, the greatest expansion in the history of the game, with series in places not traditionally associated with cricket such as Sharjah, Singapore and Toronto. Indians call them masala, spicy, matches and there were many reasons why such masala matches developed. Sharjah had started as benefit matches for former Indian and Pakistani cricketers who have no English-style benefit system. Toronto provided a North American haven for India versus Pakistan matches, often not possible for political reasons in the subcontinent, Singapore and other tournaments represented the commercial opportunities that one-day cricket provided to those seeking to reach the new emerging Indian middle classes.

As such matches spread, so did reports that match fixing was going on. These reports were mainly in the Indian press and it was their relentless investigation that began to provide a glimpse of what was really going on during these matches. However, even then nothing may have emerged but for the chance discovery by the Delhi police while investigating an extortion threat that some of their suspects were actually involved in fixing cricket matches. The conversations they taped revealed that the then South African captain Hansie Cronje was involved in fixing matches. Now there could no doubt that this was more than mere salacious stories in the Indian press.

This evidence emerged just as Dalmiya was coming to the end of his controversial three-year reign as ICC President. Dalmiya had long argued that he could do nothing about match fixing unless he was given proof and resented the fact that his ability to make money for cricket was overshadowed by this crisis. To be fair to Dalmiya, while he was the most prominent administrative figure in Indian and world cricket when the crisis broke, it was not all down to him. Many in Indian and world cricket – including some on his own board – refused to believe match fixing was possible. Even those who conceded it might be taking place did nothing about it. But as the man in charge of cricket Dalmiya had to take the heat and the result was that for all the money he had made for international cricket he left office with international cricket bearing the scars of match fixing. It was only after he left office that the cricket authorities began to give the impression that they were able to tackle the greatest scourge the game has known.

The match fixing saga illustrated another paradox of Indian cricket. Match fixing may have originated and been organised in the subcontinent but it was the Indian media that did much to pursue it, when the English media had ignored it as a subcontinental disease. And the corner stone of the investigations were the conversations between the fixers taped by the Delhi police followed by the comprehensive Indian CBI report. Indeed when ICC finally started to gets its act together and appointed Lord Paul Condon, former head of the Metropolitan Police, as the head of its anti-corruption unit Condon never failed to lavish praise on the Indian CBI for the sterling work it had done It is clear that without the Indian CBI, match fixing could never have been tackled. So if Indian bookies started match fixing, and the Indian Board allowed it to flourish, it was the Indian media that made the world aware and the Indian police that helped cricket tackle the issue.

The CBI was also investigating television deals Dalmiya had entered into but in this case not only did Dalmiya protest his innocence with some success but the investigations led nowhere. So for all his questionable international legacy when Dalmiya returned to India from the ICC he returned as a hero. His ability to make money for the Board now gave him unrivalled powers and he used it to make yet more money for Indian cricket and gather more power for himself. However, his failure to come to grips with the structure of the game and the need to modernise it meant that in one vital area he did not exercise complete power: this was over India's leading cricketers. The result was that India had some of the richest cricketers in the world but they were effectively outside the control of the

Indian board. This created many problems for Dalmiya, himself, but for all his money-making skills he seemed unable or unwilling to tackle it.

The basic problem stemmed from the fact that Indian cricketers had no contract with their Board. (As this book went to print they were just being agreed.) They signed up for specific tours but in between tours there was no contractual relationship. This did not matter as long as Indian cricket was poor. But when television brought its riches it also dramatically changed the life of the country's top cricketers. For the first time it brought Indian crick-eters into the homes of millions of Indians and they could see their heroes perform live in glorious colour. Before the 1991 revolution the Indian cricket follower had few opportunities to see their stars, unless they could actually go to a Test Match. And when India played overseas all they had were radio commentaries on All India Radio, which was often of dubious standard and not always available. The deeds of Gavaskar in the West Indies in 1971 could be followed at best on radio on poor quality commentaries provided by All India Radio. Indians did watch Kapil Dev's triumph in the World Cup of 1983 but the historic match against Zimbabwe when Kapil Dev took India from 17 for 5 to a match wining 266, making 175, was not broadcast by the BBC and Indians only heard dim and distant reports of it. As we have seen, even in the pre-television age Indian, cricketers were useful marketing tools but television opened up a whole new marketing world for individual cricketers and advertisers were quick to exploit it.

Tendulkar, as the outstanding cricketer of his generation, was the major beneficiary of this. Soon he could be seen on Indian television advertising almost everything and his deals were so lucrative that he became the richest cricketer in the world with an income estimated at $15 million a year. But along with Tendulkar the cricketers who made their mark in the 1990s also benefited such as Ganguly, Rahul Dravid, Anil Kumble, and then through the new century the stars that began to emerge such as V. V. S. Laxman, Sehwag, Yuvraj Singh, Mohamed Kaif and Harbhajan Singh. The Indian Test and one-day team was like a very privileged club and whenever it got a prominent member then he made it to the small screen advertising some product. Often the advertisement features the entire team.

However, with the players having no year-long central contract with their Board this meant that they earned more money from their sponsors than from their employers. And this carried the seeds of a great conflict. The players may have signed up with a company while the Board may be considering a sponsorship with a rival company. The problems this can cause first surfaced in quite dramatic fashion during India's tour of England in 2002.

The tour was to be followed by the Champions Trophy in Sri Lanka. The ICC had certain sponsors – either Indian companies or companies operating extensively in India. In modern marketing sponsors are extremely vigilant about what they call 'ambush marketing' making sure their rivals who have not sponsored an event do not use the event to advertise their product. The ICC required all the world's cricketers who were going to take part in the tournament to sign a declaration that for a period before, during and after the tournament they would not be involved in any advertising that was in competition with the ICC sponsors. But India's leading cricketers had contracts with companies that were rivals of ICC's sponsors and they refused to sign such agreements. So while India faced up to England at Headingley, seeking a win to square the series, off the field their cricketers were locked in a grim battle with Dalmiya. It was both curious and a reflection of the power of Indian cricket that when Nasser Hussain the England captain was asked about the controversy he expressed sympathy but also confessed that England's cricketers did not have such problems because they did not enjoy such sponsorships. As it happens India won a massive victory at Headingley with the cricketers saying the fight with their Board had made them more determined. The dispute lingered on as India played England at the Oval and the ICC got involved with Indian players seeking to form a trade union to press for their rights. Neither the ICC's involvement nor the demand for a trade union pleased Dalmiya. In the end a compromise solution was found but six months later the dispute flared up again during the 2003 World Cup in South Africa and this time the ICC held back money owed to India. The whole issue revealed the extraordinary management style of Dalmiya and how a man with great money-making skills can be a very poor manager of men.

But, curiously, this whole dispute revealed the managerial skills of another man from Dalmiya's part of the world Saurav Ganguly. Ganguly had emerged as the captain of India in 2000 following the match fixing allegations. With Azharuddin gone and Tendulkar after two spells, not seeking the captaincy selectors choose Ganguly. Ganguly a Brahmin, hails from a well-off Calcutta family, part of the bhadralok, gentlemanly, traditions of the upper castes of the province. His older brother had played for Bengal and like many rich Bengali kids was known as raja, king. When Saurav came along he was nicknamed Maharaja, greater king and the story was that on his first tour of Australia asked to be twelfth man he refused to carry drinks as at home that was the work of servants. Many years later Lancashire cricket was riveted by a story that when Ganguly played for Lancashire he had asked Atherton to carry his sweater back to the dressing room. Such stories may be apocryphal but they have given Ganguly a reputation in England for being snooty. I must say that when I have met him I have always found him very polite and considerate and he has always referred to me as Mihirda, da being a term of respect in

Bengal. I am not saying Ganguly cannot be arrogant but there may be a cultural factor in describing Ganguly as Lord Snooty.

I had first encountered Ganguly on India's troubled tour of England in 1996. That tour saw Navjot Singh Sidhu, the opening batsman, leave the tour in sensational circumstances not seen on an Indian tour since 1936 and the Amarnath incident.

Sidhu had been dropped for the third one-day international in Old Trafford. However, in the clumsy way the tour was managed neither Azharuddin, the captain, or Sandip Patil, the cricket manager, spoke to him. All they did was pin the team sheet up on the dressing room. The result was Sidhu, unaware he was dropped, sat in the Old Trafford pavilion expecting to play. As Azharuddin on winning the toss signalled from the middle that India would bat, Sidhu started padding up.

The rest of the team, aware he was dropped, started laughing and one or two also made jokes about Sikhs – Sidhu being a Sikh – which are common in India. Many of the remarks had come from the younger members of the side and Sidhu, a senior player, felt all the more insulted. In an Indian culture where older people expect to be treated with respect such behaviour was likely to cause grave offence and it did. Sidhu felt so insulted that despite the efforts of Board President, and fellow Sikh Inderjit Singh Bhindra, he refused to carry on with the tour.

As he left the tour he made this dramatic declaration, 'I promised my father on his deathbed that I would live my life with integrity and respect. As long as I stay on this tour I cannot do that.'

Ganguly was Sidhu's room-mate and I remember how bemused and hesitant he sounded when I tried to find out what had happened to Sidhu. At that stage he had every reason to feel diffident. Ganguly had been taken to Australia in 1991–2 then discarded. On the 1996 tour he had shown his potential in the Old Trafford one-day international – the one where Sidhu was dropped – and should have played at the Edgebaston Test, where he might have made the difference between victory and defeat. He made his debut at Lord's and was a key player, holding India together after Tendulkar fell. Batting with an elegance that comes naturally to left handers he scored a quite beautiful century on his debut. And this playing in front of a crowd that was more interested in events in a totally unrelated sport taking part at the same time in another part of north London. On that Saturday many spectators in the Warner Stand, and elsewhere at Lord's, turned their back on Ganguly and the cricket and watched soccer on television. At one stage play was stopped due to cheering as England finally beat Spain on penalties in the Euro 96 quarter final at Wembley. But Ganguly did not allow himself to be fazed by such distractions and went on to make his century. He followed this up with a century in the next Test.

By the time the Headingley Test of 2002 Ganguly was established as the captain and the Indian cricket team seemed to have developed an interesting equilibrium. Many of the players in the team, the younger players were Ganguly's men, players he had believed in and helped to mature as cricketers, both Sehwag and Harbhajan Singh were examples of such cricketers. Then there were older cricketers like Anil Kumble, widely considered the shrewd cricketer in India, who led the players' negotiations with Dalmiya. Above all, of course, was Tendulkar who was like a god king who had abdicated the throne but still exercised a tremendous influence. With Tendulkar it could be claimed the traditional pattern of Indian batsmanship had been broken. In the past, when India had produced a great batsman he always had a rival. So Merchant had Hazare, Gavaskar had Visvanath. Tendulkar is on his own. There are many Tendulkar clones, Sehwag to an extent, but no one has come close to matching his mastery of the art of batsmanship or his hold over the Indian public.

For Ganguly to hold all these elements together is quite an achievement. It is all the more an achievement because he comes from Bengal. Kolkata may have a great Test match ground but Bengal has produced few cricketers and Bengal has long been at the periphery of Indian life. Its glory days when it led British India is ancient history. Kolkata once the second city of the Empire has long been left trailing behind other Indian cities. And Bengal is on such a limb that since 1977 it has been ruled by a hard-line communist party whose name has in brackets the word Marxist – popularly know as CPI(M) – to distinguish it from the more soft-line Indian communists.

But perhaps because he is an outsider who comes from an outside province Ganguly has been able to hold the Indian team together when others who come from the centre have not. In many ways he is much more of a modern India, an Indian born long after independence, very different to an Indian like me, free not only from the shackles and taints of colonialism, but also free of the uncertainties and the enforced servility of the immediate post-independence era. But most importantly an Indian cricketer who has come to bloom after India had entered the television age.

This television age has made Indians realise that because of India's location it is India, not England, which is at the centre of the cricket world. An Indian can start the day by getting up at 6 in the morning to catch the cricket from Australia – an even earlier start is necessary if cricket is being played in New Zealand. Then at lunch-time, as the Australian day comes to a close, the action switches to South Africa. Finally, he can stay up late at night to watch cricket from the West Indies.

In addition to this, of course, there are all sorts of sports from round the world that Indians can and do watch. Apart from cricket there is live coverage of Premiership matches and matches in the Italian and Spanish leagues and sports from all over the world including American baseball, basketball and even ice hockey. This availability of international sports explains why Tendulkar's favourite sport outside cricket is Formula One and he has appeared in commercials with Michael Schumaker, something that an Indian cricketer from a pre-television age could not have contemplated.

India's rise as world cricket's greatest power does create problems for the rest of the globe but it also imposes a burden on the Indian cricket administrator. The problem for the rest of the world is that they have to come to terms with the fact that for the first time a non-white country has economic power over an international sport. This is an unprecedented situation.

Take soccer, the world's most popular sport. The economic powerhouse of soccer is Europe and other continents and countries must pay homage to it. Interestingly, cricket used to be similar to soccer. For decades the economic axis of world cricket was England v. Australia – Packer's revolution was inspired by the television rights to the Ashes series – with the West Indies providing marvellous cricketers but no money, the West Indies having no television market to exploit. In soccer it is European money allied to the flair and style of south America which, like the West Indies, has little or no money and has to sell its best players to European clubs. The rise of India means cricket is no longer like soccer. Now there is a non-European country with money which can dictate events. Given that international sports is largely run by Europe and by white men, both the IOC and FIFA are good examples of this, India's emergence as a cricket superpower is all the more difficult for the cricket world to come to terms with. To complicate the picture, the USA, the world's only superpower, remains outside international sport as the sports it plays, baseball and American football, are not international sports.

It is clear international cricket is struggling to come to terms with Indian cricket power. And this imposes an obligation on the Indian cricket administrators to make sure that Indian power is exercised with skill, style and a certain sensitivity. So far, there is little evidence to show that Indian cricket administrators appreciate the obligations India's new position in cricket demands of them.

12

My India, my England

This book began with a question: India, whose India? It is not entirely for the sake of symmetry that I seek to conclude with a personal perspective on both India and cricket. 'There was a time,' wrote V. S. Naipaul in *India: A Wounded Civilisation*, 'when Indians who had been abroad and picked up some simple degree of skill said that they had been displaced and were neither of the East nor the West. In this they were absurd and self-dramatizing: they carried India with them, Indian ways of perceiving. Now, with the great migrant rush, little is heard of that displacement. Instead Indians say that they have become too educated for India. The opposite is equally true: they are not educated enough; they only want to repeat their lessons. The imported skills are rooted in nothing; they are skills separate from principles.'

Of course it is always easy to criticise, but Naipaul has a point. Who speaks for India? Can one, who have lived much of the last 35 years in England – having left India when I was 21 – really write about India, its society or even its cricket? In India I am alternatively seen as a well-off Indian who can be sponged on during a visit to London, or a traitor who has abandoned the sweet poverty of India for the riches of the west. Like Anthony de Mello's implied criticism of Ranji some of my Indian friends think that the reason for my self-chosen exile is a romantic involvement. I am, as it happens, happily married to a wonderful English woman, but that came long after I had decided to settle in this country and after one failed marriage with an Indian.

In fact I would probably have a better lifestyle in India, I could certainly afford servants which I cannot in west London. Indians, particularly rich Indians, exalt poverty – not their own but the concept of poverty and want to believe that anyone choosing the west in preference to India must have been seduced by its material comforts. In my case the reverse is true since, as I explained, middle India, to which I belonged is about the most material place on earth.

In December 2002 with immigration once again making the headlines in the UK I wrote a piece for the *Observer* in which I said:

TWENTY-FIVE YEARS AGO, when I decided to leave India and come back to this country for good, Shiva Naipaul invited me to dinner at his flat in Maida Vale and mockingly admonished me saying, 'So you have come back for more of the old colonial lash.' Now as I try and follow the frenzied debate about immigration I have often wondered about what Naipaul said: what is it that lures so many to this country?

The way the debate about immigration is presented it would seem this is just a question of material possessions. Britain is presented as a modern El Dorado and the many hundreds of thousands attracted to it are only seduced by the prospect of making undreamt of wealth.

Such a scenario makes it easy to present scare stories of immigration but in so doing the very patriots who propagate such views are selling this country short, indeed demeaning it.

There is so much more on offer than merely the chance of making money. In fact its greatest riches are not material. In my case the colonial lash Naipaul said I hungered for was not money but success and recognition in my chosen field of writing and journalism. Had I continued to live in India I would have had a lifestyle far richer than anything I enjoy here.

Indeed, leaving India impoverished me materially but it enriched me in various other ways: culturally, intellectually and it made me realise my dream of becoming a writer, something I doubt if I could have achieved in India, or at least not without a lot more hassle.

Like many members of my family, I had originally come to this country to go to university. I had then qualified as a chartered accountant and wanted to continue living here in an effort to become a writer. But under immense emotional blackmail – the Hindu mother's capacity for such blackmail exceeds that of any other faith, even perhaps the Jewish Mamma – I was forced to return to India. My brother-in-law was then a leading chartered accountant in India and in the nepotistic way these things work there I was offered a partnership in a leading firm.

I was immediately sucked into what my brother-in-law called the good life: a very comfortable flat in the family home, servants who did my every bidding, chauffeur-driven cars and membership of clubs – indeed, there were few material wants. But when I tried to keep my dim hopes of journalism alive I found how limiting India was and how much more open and liberating England could be.

Before I had left England I had made some progress in becoming a journalist and was agreeably surprised that, despite the fact that I was an unknown, it was possible to open some very august doors.

I had become a broadcaster on the nascent London Broadcasting Corporation, persuaded the *Sunday Times* to allow me to string for them, got a publisher to commission me to write a biography of the Australian cricketer Keith Miller and even managed to interview one of my journalistic heroes: Anthony Howard, then editor of the *New Statesman*. In India, by contrast, I had, as the Indians say, no 'pull' in the media.

In business my family contacts made life easy, in the media I knew nobody and, unlike London, cold calling was not welcome. The editor of a Kolkata paper did finally see me but treated me with the sort of disdain that my grandmother inflicted on the untouchable woman who cleaned her toilets. And the head of a sports radio station made it clear to me that if I wanted to broadcast cricket commentaries I would have to keep giving him and his wife presents.

After three years of such an existence – material comfort in an intellectual desert – I decided to abandon India and take my chance at becoming a writer. When I arrived back at Heathrow I was almost the archetypal struggling writer: I had one completed book with a publisher, another incomplete manuscript in my case and pounds 400 in the bank, but no job or even offer of one.

Three months after I had given up my comfortable partnership, the *Sunday Times*, which had begun to use me, closed down for a year and I confronted the hard realities of the world of freelance journalism.

Since then much has changed for me and the partners I left behind in India. They have grown immensely rich as the Indian service sector has boomed. They earn at a conservative estimate five times what I earn, live in houses that are virtual palaces, do not have to worry about doctors' waiting lists, or traffic, as they are invariably driven everywhere. And when they travel abroad, which they do frequently, they always go first class while I rely on my wits to upgrade to premium plus.

But while I feel embarrassed that I cannot reciprocate the lavish hospitality they shower on me when I visit India, I have never had any regrets about abandoning accountancy there for journalism here.

For although I have not quite fulfilled my dreams, to be a cricket writer like Neville Cardus, a broadcaster like John Arlott, or a foreign correspondent like James Cameron – I did have the privilege of meeting all three – I like to think I have not done too badly and whatever I have done has been achieved without any nepotism or pull or toadying to unpleasant people.

I am well aware that there still remain immense barriers of colour and creed in this country and I have always felt there is a glass ceiling beyond which I cannot go, but within such boundaries it has provided me with opportunities which I would not have had in India.

It is an immensely open, intellectually alive and culturally curious country and it surprises me that in the endless debate about immigration these virtues are not talked of but the stress is only on filthy lucre.

True, the lure of money drives many immigrants to this country, but there are quite a few like us who live here not for the money but more for its values.

I was forcefully made aware of the mixture of scorn and lust that Indians have for *pardesis* – Indians living abroad – during my coverage of the Rajendra Sethia story, the Indian-born British businessman who for a time in the 1980s was the world's biggest bankrupt. At the height of the story I was visited in my London offices by an Indian doctor practising in Harley Street, who claimed to be a friend of Rajendra Sethia and who told me that as an Indian, and a fellow Bengali, I should stop writing about Sethia's business exploits. I was harming the Indian business community in London and did I really want to help the white men finish off this outstanding Indian businessman.

Some years ago a friend of mine said I was the second best known Indian professional – Salman Rushdie being the first. She was grossly exaggerating, of course, and reacting to the fact that just then, with interest in India revived and Raj nostalgia in the vogue, I found myself asked to become the expert on almost everything Indian from books, to fashion, festivals, cinema, food and, of course, cricket. Within minutes of Mrs Gandhi being shot, I was on the air explaining what it meant and how things might develop. Years later when Rajiv Gandhi was assassinated and then, later still, when his Italian wife nearly became Prime Minister I was again called on to play the pundit. The money is good, although occasionally it can be tiring. It is one thing earning money pretending to be an expert in all things Indian – it is another constantly advising friends and acquaintances which Indian take-away they should frequent but the pleasures outweigh the problems. It is certainly better than being asked by Indian newspapers to write for next to nothing – merely for the love of India.

I sometimes even become enough of a professional Indian to find myself aroused by some slight to India or Indians. When I first arrived in this country my Indian nationalism was pristine. Though born eight months before the British left India and brought up in a mixture of cultural traditions – large doses of P. G. Wodehouse and William Brown, queuing up to see the Queen, yet hailing Mahatma Gandhi as the father of the Indian nation – I, like most of my contemporaries, held the British responsible for India's problems. My contemporaries who have remained behind in India have grown ever more nationalist and bitterly anti-British, fed on a constant stream of stories of the behaviour of immigration officers. I find that apart from my loyalty to the Indian cricket team, and some personal ties, my links are less secure. Some years ago I gave up my

Indian passport – India does not allow for dual nationality – but not withstanding the ridiculous Norman Tebbitt cricket Test, which only exposes Tebitt's failure to understand sport (and which incidentally was not much talked about when Australians in England moaned about Australia's defeat by England in the Rugby World Cup) I find no disloyalty in loving India and being British. Only the petty minded or the insecure would see that as a threat to the British identity, or politicians with their own particular agenda, as Tebbitt clearly has.

When I came to England I had hoped to lose myself in the cosmopolitan world of London, but I find that I cannot. Perhaps as Naipaul says Indians do not understand the word cosmopolitan – it was a word much used in my childhood to describe Mumbai. We meant Mumbai was cosmopolitan in that it contained the different Indian communities which perhaps betrayed how we saw the Indian nation. Since 9/11 and the debate on clash of cultures and civilisations I feel Naipaul did India and Indians a disservice. I grew up with Indians but if we were all of one race what a remarkable range of religions there was: my best friends were Muslims and Catholics, and my sister's best friend a Jew. More remarkably still we never dwelt on religious differences.

London is indeed cosmopolitan, but it is also English, and I occasionally tire of those well-meaning English acquaintances who, trying to make me feel at 'home', enquire whether I 'eat everything' and solicitously ask my opinion about the latest Indian fad. That blonde who wants to see *Passage to India* with me – is she interested in me or in keeping up with Raj nostalgia; that editor who says we must talk about the Raj revival, is he offering me work or just keeping himself informed about different views?

But all exiles must feel that, except perhaps English exiles who seem to have a remarkable ability not only to carry their England intact with them, but impose it on others. My India crumbles every time I visit India, and I am very like an Israeli friend of mine who has similar feelings about his country – I look forward to going 'home', but often hate it while I am there. I resent Indians trying to label me as pro-Indian or anti-Indian – like children playing with the toy of nationalism. I hate it even more when in India – because of my name, I am not only quickly identified as a Bengali but told I must hail from Kolkata when, in fact, I consider Mumbai my home town. And I am often confused by my own reactions to the country of my birth. This was vividly brought home to me some years ago.

Some time before I left England in the mid-1970s for a brief return to India I, along with a group of theatrical friends, had put on a show called *The Black Man's Burden*, or, to give its more graphic subtitle, *It Gets Dark Earlier Since They Came*. After the first night the thing was thrown open for discussion. Somebody opined that the British reaction to India was the result of the brutalisation they had gone through as a result of climate, behaviour of natives and many other factors. I believe the man was Indian, though he had a rather English-looking wife who seemed embarrassed by his question. Nettled, I reacted angrily and played the part of the aggrieved Indian nationalist with some effect. Three months later I was in Kolkata's main street – Chowringhee.

My watch strap had broken and I had it repaired from a fairly established place. The service was courteous, I was given a bill (which has to be asked for in India) and I was reassured about the guarantee. A few days later the strap broke in very peculiar circumstances – it fell into the loo. The watch was damaged and I decided to go back to the shop. Three months had taught me a lot and I quickly worked out my strategy. The moment I entered the shop my voice was well above reasonable complaining terms and without any preliminaries I demanded to know the name of the shopkeeper's solicitor. The man, obviously puzzled and dreadfully worried, tried to mollify me: he smiled, he shook his head, he walked up and down behind his counter; with folded hands and head bowed he walked all round me; he offered me a chair. I refused to budge from the straight and narrow legal path. 'I want to know the name of your solicitor.' Even as he replaced the strap, repaired and serviced the watch and even the glass case – all at no expense – I stood fuming. As I left the shop, he smiled and bowed and I was convinced of the virtue of behaving occasionally like a colonial satrap. Later, when I wrote about it to a friend I made the point that had so nettled me in London: this is the inevitable result of living among an elite that has adopted and preserved the worst instincts of its colonial masters. The cycle was complete. Philosophically unreconciled to India, physically part of it.

Every Indian, says Naipaul, sees himself as unique, to be the only one of his sort to be recognised abroad. Nehru was often described – and liked being described – as the lonely aristocrat. Aristocracy is easy in India as the English cricketers have often discovered and Tony Lewis realises every time he visits the country, instantly surrounded by Indians who still recall his captaincy of the England tour of 1972–3. I have no illusions about my uniqueness or of being an aristocrat. English friends of mine have suggested I straddle two cultures. I doubt that – I merely exist in the slipstream of both, one ruled by caste and money and the other by class and accent.

Caste and money are the great arbiters of Indian society just as class and accent divide the English. Caste is a more invisible barrier in India than people in the west think. You cannot tell Indians' caste by their looks, and in modern, middle India, people of different castes live side by side, eat together, club together, play sport together and often do business together. Where they draw the line is marriage – then the many myriad caste and sub-caste distinctions surface to preserve the ancestral barriers. Unlike the west, integration in India stops on the threshold of the bedroom.

Outwardly, class is more manifest in England and signified, very often, by accent. I did not realise the variety and importance of accent in England until I arrived in this country. Brought up on the 'export only' version of English, I thought everybody spoke like Brian Johnston or Alvar Liddell. John Arlott didn't, but then he was the equivalent of God giving ball by ball commentary, and I can still recall the chill in my spine as that unique voice conveyed the fear of Indian batsmen facing up to the menace of Trueman. I could almost imagine them getting out before Trueman had approached the crease. To me, as to most Indians, the Scots, the Irish and the Welsh existed in the jokes told by the English, but they were not separate entities.

This idea of an English stereotype who always wore a three-piece suit whatever the weather, and read the *Times*, is even now prevalent in India and one reason why Don Mosey, the BBC's cricket commentator, found life a shade difficult in India during the 1981–2 tour of the country. The Indians were just not used to BBC correspondents who did their commentaries dressed in beach shorts and spoke in a Yorkshire accent. I can well recall the conversation of a group of Indians who encountered an Englishman visiting India during that India versus England series and could not understand why he was not interested in the score or English cricket fortunes. 'But isn't he worried about how his country is doing?' asked the puzzled Indians.

The English do have great pride in their country – as they have every reason to – despite the self-deprecatory air they normally adopt. But this pride surfaces as patriotic fervour only when England play Australia at cricket, Scotland at football or the Welsh at rugby. Then my English friends seem to discover a patriotic zeal nobody could imagine existed. The only other time I have seen it surface in this fashion was during the Falklands crisis.

The Indians happened to be touring England then and some of them were surprised by what they saw as a reassertion of the old imperial lion. I must confess I was not entirely surprised since it seemed to me very evidently a working-out of an imperial nostalgia which has lain dormant since 1947 and the withdrawal from India. For many people this is still seen as a 'loss' – an unplanned and unnecessary defeat brought about by the conspiracy of foreigners and their collaborators in this country. I do not believe the British sought the Falklands War, nor do I share the *Belgrano* conspiracy theory. The war was forced upon Mrs Thatcher, but she did understand the deep-seated British desire not to be pushed around any more. The memories of the shrinking red imperial colour on the map; India, Suez, Aden, Rhodesia, are still vivid in many minds and, as Mrs Thatcher said after the Falklands' victory 'it shows we can still do some of the things that made Britain great'. I am not saying, as Salman Rushdie said, that the British still hanker after an Empire or import immigrants into this country to indulge their empire fantasies. The British Empire was not all bad, as my father always maintained, but the point is that for many Britains the sudden change from the greatest power on earth to struggling European one is, I think, difficult to stomach. The Falklands provided an antidote and they eagerly welcomed it.

The war also brought home to me the gulf that fundamentally separates me from even my closest English friends. I was, I must confess, against the Falklands enterprise but though a good many of my English friends also felt the same way they could not but get emotionally involved with the tragedies and the successes that unfolded in the South Atlantic. I remember one night talking to a friend about this and saying, after the Argentinians had dropped a bomb which did not explode, 'You know you English are very lucky.' The friend, who I had never suspected of any patriotism, fairly flared up. 'What do you mean lucky? Luck has nothing to do with it.' What I meant is that the British are unique among nations in having avoided being conquered for nearly one thousand years – not since the Normans. Look at any other country in Europe and you will see a cycle of conquest and liberation. France was under the German jackboot some sixty years ago, Russia still mourns her war dead, and large parts of Asia, Africa and South America have been entirely remade by conquest. America has not been conquered but she is only two hundred years old.

I come from a country whose history is one of repeated conquests with supposedly superior Indian forces strangely unaccountably losing to marauding foreigners. I am no longer puzzled by it but it still pains me to read Indian history. It also gives me a certain perspective on the world, a certain way of looking at it which is different from how my English friends look at it. Some of my English friends occasionally interpret this as touchiness, a chip on the shoulder, when it really is a cry for understanding. My English friends can be sure about the world because they have made so much of it. I cannot, because I do not quite know what world, if any, my ancestors have left for me. The world I live in is the world made by others, very often by Englishmen, certainly by Europeans, and not by my ancestors. This requires certain adjustments on my part which my English friends do not have to make.

It would be nice to say this book about Indian cricket is unique. I would like to think I have said things here that have not been said before – or at least not quite in this fashion. I have avoided the grand theory because while it is tempting to do so with India, this invariably makes one look stupid. I have refrained from predictions because everyone who writes anything about India loves to predict and, in my experience, most emerge with egg on their faces. You may like the country or hate it, but it has an infinite capacity for surprise.

I wrote this book because I wanted to share some of my love for Indian cricket which has often saddened me, every now and again infuriated me, but provided rare moments of bliss surpassing almost everything. When I was young, Indian defeats would fill me with tears and in turn lead to fantasies of personal glorious deeds righting Indian cricket. Those glories never went beyond my bedroom mirror or the maidan game we played but in a way they were satisfying. Just as it was satisfying to try and imagine that I could bat like Tom Graveney and Mushtaq Ali, bowl fast like Lindwall and Miller and twirl my leg-spinners like Subhas Gupte. How I treasured Graveney's predictions in *Cricket Through the Covers* that on the 1959 Indian tour Gupte would be acclaimed as the great bowler, and how I raged when the task proved too much for him.

Even now I can barely contain myself when some ignorant English critic refuses to give Gupte his due as perhaps one of the finest post-war leg-spinners who was unfortunate enough to play in a team that could not catch – or often did not want to – and had no other bowlers. But then youthful fantasies are difficult to shake off.

Some years ago I caused a few comments in a journalists *Who's Who* by describing my fantasy of making 100 at Lord's repeatedly hooking Trueman and Statham and powering India to a great win. Every time Indians tour England and the Indians troop out to Lord's, I, for a fleeting moment, relive the fantasy – not so much scoring 100 myself but imagin-ing Indians winning the toss, batting, running up 600 for not much and then bowling out England twice by Saturday evening. It has never happened but who knows it might. Fantasies have a strange way of coming true. I doubt if any Indian could have imagined the circumstances of the Oval triumph of 1971 or the World Cup win of 1983.

Just as the West Indies started their reply to India's 183 in that World Cup final, I, tired of the rather rancid atmosphere of the Lord's press box, went for a walk. The Indians were depressed, the English and the Australians who had both been beaten by the Indians made no secret of their contempt for the pathetic Indian showing – surely their own teams would have done better. As I neared the Tavern, Greenidge got out; soon after I returned to the press box, Richards was out, the rest is history.

It is part of the magic and mystery of sport that occasionally such fantasies come true. And when that happens what matters is not the wider meaning, whether it brings nations together or even creates a nation – as C. L. R. James thought of the West Indian tour of Australia in 1960–1 – but the joy it brings to those who have loved and followed the game, a joy like no other because it is sweet, unexpected and without any obligations. It also connects you to a wider sporting family that you did not know existed and this is a family tie where the only requirement is you love and treasure your cricket team.

I don't know, of course, what fantasies, if any, the Indians will fulfil in the future. Indian cricket has always seemed to be to me a bit like Gatsby in Scott Fitzgerald's *The Great Gatsby*. Having seen the green light at the end of Daisy's dock, 'He had come a long way to this blue lawn, and his dream must have seemed so close that he could hardly fail to grasp it.' But even as Gatsby grasped his dream it was behind him and to the Indian cricket follower 'the orgiastic future' recedes year by year. But like Scott Fitzgerald's narrator, the Indian cricket follower does believe that 'tomorrow we will run faster, stretch out our arms further... And one fine morning –'.

Postscript

As this book was going to press, important changes were taking place in Indian cricket that needed to be documented. The Supreme Court after long deliberation upheld the cricket board's decision to cancel its television tender process and start again, although at the time of writing, this had yet to happen and television rights were still being sold on an *ad-hoc* basis.

Overshadowing all this was the change in the Indian Board and the end of the Ganguly reign. The battle for control had been going on for over a year. In September 2004, an election for the Board President had seen Jagmohan Dalmiya's nominee Randhir Singh Mahendra just manage to defeat Sharad Pawar, a minister in the Indian government who had once aspired to be Prime Minister. But Randhir Singh's victory was only on Dalmiya's casting vote in an election which saw Dalmiya perform the extraordinary feat of voting four times. This resulted in another court battle and, a year later in September 2005, Pawar finally gained the Presidency. Dalmiya left his position on the ICC as India's representative and also the Presidency of the Asian Cricket Conference. Yet the long shadow Dalmiya has cast on Indian cricket remains, and while the new Indian board is charting new directions, in many ways the new board is behaving like the successors of the Mughal empire, seeking to pick up the pieces and make sense of the inheritance they have been bequeathed.

As Dalmiya fell so did Ganguly, although the two events were not directly related.

One of the most interesting features about Ganguly's rise was that for almost the first time since India came into international cricket there was no jockeying for the captaincy. As we have seen, even before India made its Test debut the question of who would captain India had proved a thorny issue. There were always two contestants, each with their own camp. So if there was C. K. Nayudu, then in the opposite corner there was Wazir Ali and later Vizzy. In subsequent decades we had Merchant vs Hazare, followed by Hazare vs Amarnath, then Pataudi vs Borde, followed by Pataudi vs Wadekar, then Gavaskar vs Kapil Dev and finally Azharuddin vs Tendulkar. In the last two cases, the rivals often switched captaincy in successive seasons, so Kapil Dev took over from Gavaskar in 1983, Gavaskar returned in 1984, Kapil Dev regained the captaincy in 1985.

But Ganguly's rise had seen a new trend in Indian cricket. While Tendulkar remained in the side as the elder statesman, he clearly did not want to be captain again and nobody questioned his right to lead. So much so that Ganguly even helped his putative rival Dravid, who had made his Test debut with him at Lord's in 1996, making 95, gain a place in the one-day side.

But perhaps such an unlikely Indian scenario was too good to last. And Ganguly's fall in the winter of 2005 suggested that the old Indian ways were not dead, they were merely having a long sleep.

Although Ganguly had the best record of any Indian captain – 21 victories in 49 Tests, 10 of them coming abroad – there were murmurings even during India's tour of Australia in 2003–4, where India had come close to beating Australia. It was the return visit of Australia in 2004 that produced the first real cracks. In the crucial Nagpur Test Ganguly withdrew before the Test was due to start claiming he was unwell, although the previous day he had taken part in all the practice. His enemies have since claimed that he did not like the look of the wicket, which was far too green and suited Australia more than India. India lost the Test and with it the series, the first series defeat at home to Australia for 35 years. It is interesting to recall that the previous series defeat to Australia in 1969 had meant the death knell of Pataudi's captaincy and it is clear the seeds of Ganguly's fall were sown by this Australian victory.

It was masked for a time as Ganguly did lead India to a historic series victory over Pakistan, but this was almost a victory of an absentee landlord. He did not play in the first two Tests of the three-Test series and during the first, when Dravid's decision to declare with Tendulkar on 194 not out produced a storm with Tendulkar expressing his unhappiness, Ganguly, while not openly critical of Dravid, made comments which suggested he wanted to have it both ways. His statement, in part, read:

> We all make mistakes. I don't want to say who's made a mistake – even if Rahul's made a mistake by declaring it at 194 or if Sachin's made a mistake by making a statement... Whoever it is made a mistake it's for the team to accept it – for Rahul to accept it, for Sachin to accept it, us to accept it and go ahead.

If Dravid did make a mistake it was a mistake worth making, as India won the Test.

The dam truly broke when, in the summer of 2005, India went to Zimbabwe and Ganguly fell out quite spectacularly with the new cricket coach Greg Chappell. Ironically Ganguly had worked assiduously to get Chappell the job against the advice of Steve Waugh, who had suggested Tom Moody. Ganguly had benefited from Chappell's advice during the 2003

Australian tour and publicly thanked him. But once Chappell was coach the situation changed. Ganguly clearly found Chappell's ideas impossible to work with and Chappell had little time for Ganguly.

During the Zimbabwe tour Chappell had suggested to Ganguly he should step down as captain, a suggestion not taken up. Then, in a much publicised e-mail, Chappell set out the problem as he saw it:

> Everything he does is designed to maximise his chances of success and is usually detrimental to someone else's chances . . . This team has been made to be fearful and distrusting by the rumour-mongering and deceit that is Sourav's *modus operandi* of divide and rule.

We could be back in 1936 and this could have been Sir John Beaumont talking of Vizzy's behaviour in England during that tour. Back in India after the Zimbabwe tour, Ganguly initially did not play because he was injured, with Dravid taking the team to Sri Lanka. But then when Sri Lanka came to India for a one-day series he was dropped and Dravid given the captaincy of the one-day side. Dravid did spectacularly well, winning 6–1. Ganguly's supporters waited for the moment to pounce and when the South Africans turned up to play in Kolkata such was the anger in Ganguly's home town that the crowds treated the Indian team as if they were hated foreigners, a hatred that stunned the team. Dravid, who was booed from the ground, consoled himself by saying he and the Indian team had now attained the rank of the great Gavaskar as he had also faced such treatment from the Kolkata crowd.

The real battle came when, for the Test series against Sri Lanka, Ganguly was dropped as captain with Kiran More, the chairman of the selectors, saying it was time for a change. However Ganguly was to continue in the team. This was a messy compromise and was bound to cause problems. Ganguly played in the second Test in Delhi, helping India win, but was nevertheless dropped for the third, which India won as well. His supporters were outraged and now the nation was gripped by this soap opera. The question was would he make the team to Pakistan? In a repeat of what had happened during the Gavaskar-Kapil Dev battle in the 1984–5 season, the Board president Sharad Pawar got involved and Ganguly went to see him at his home, late one night. Pawar also spoke to Tendulkar and then said, in contradiction to what Chappell had claimed, Ganguly was not a disruptive force in the team.

The team was selected on Christmas Eve 2005 and that day I flew into Kolkata to find my fellow Bengalis talking of nothing else. At a party where I would not have expected much cricket talk, and where not many people knew much about the game, everyone had an opinion about Ganguly.

There was much talk of treating Sourav with respect – after all he was India's most successful captain. That day the selectors met and chose him for the tour. Crowds had gathered outside Ganguly's house in the Kolkata suburb of Behala and as they heard the news they converted this Christmas Eve into Holi, daubing each other with colour and dancing with joy.

The *Sunday Statesman* led with the story on its front page under the headline 'Ganguly smuggled into team for Pak sojourn'. The paper said:

> The 'five-man army' aka selectors may have been leaned on by the powers that be owing to political compulsions, even though Ganguly's inclusion was stoutly opposed by the 'team management'. A source said that certain powerful BCCI members might also have wanted to cut Greg Chappell down to size. Hence the decision to smuggle the 'Prince of Kolkata' back into the Test team. Chairman of the selectors Mr Kiran More, tried vainly to justify the inclusion of Ganguly as 'middle-order batsman' at the expense of Kaif, who became the fall guy yet again owing to his lack of both political and 'official support'.

Not surprisingly, as India began their Test campaign in Pakistan this caused more problems. Now the question was, if Ganguly played, where he would play? The middle order being settled, could he open? On the day before the Test Chappell had ruled out a place for Ganguly as opener, saying either Gautam Gambhir or the recalled Wasim Jaffer would partner Vice-captain Virender Sehwag at the top of the order. 'We have three very good openers and it's unfortunate one of them would have to be left out', he said.

On the morning of the first Test it was a very different story. Dravid, Ganguly and Chappell were caught on television having a furious argument on the field. It was explained away as one of those cricket talks players have, but it led to an extraordinary decision. Sehwag could not be dropped but Gambhir and Jaffer were dispensable. And as Ganguly could not open and had to be fitted in the middle order, on the morning of the match Dravid, probably India's best-ever No. 3, decided to open and create a middle order place for Ganguly. It revived memories of the many similar messy decisions Indian cricket has taken in the past, based more on hope than any realistic assessment of success. All of India watched this development with bated breath – Dravid opening even led the television news. There was an unspoken fear that as so often in the past when Indian cricket had much such *ad-hoc*, last-minute compromises, it would emerge looking stupid and with egg on its face. However on this occasion it worked so well that the new opening pair came within four runs of beating Pankaj Roy's and Vinoo Mankad's 413 set against New Zealand in 1955.

This does provide a warming thought that, although Ganguly's fall bears all the marks of the old India, the way the team has coped indicates that there is a new India bursting to get out. In the past India had not overcome internal dissension, indeed internal dissension was blamed for defeat. Of course it helped that the pitch for the first Test in Lahore was so batsman-friendly that only eight wickets fell in five days, but a previous Indian team faced with such a huge Pakistan score could well have crumbled. The crucial factor, arguably, was that the response was led by that very new, very shiny Indian Sehwag, batting in a style that he has made his own but which for many Indians is still wondrous to behold.

But if this is encouraging, what Indian cricket – which seeks to model itself on Australia – has to learn is the unsentimental way Australians handle change. In the last decade and half they have successfully managed the transition from Allan Border to Mark Taylor through to Steve Waugh and finally Ricky Ponting. In 2003, Ponting led the one-day side to the World Cup, winning it again. Waugh, who had won the Cup in 1999 and was still Test captain, wanted to go as a player but was not chosen. Chappell is part of that Australian school. As he said just before the first Test against Pakistan:

> There is no place for sentiment in international cricket. Whether Ganguly has been the captain before or not makes no difference. He wants to keep playing, he wants to play for India. You can't knock that. But at the end of the day, we have to pick the best team. The playing eleven will be selected purely on cricketing merit.

Indian cricket has still some way to go before it accepts such an un-Indian, unsentimental approach, an approach it would have to accept if it really wants to shed its bad old ways and see a shiny new Indian cricket emerge.

Mihir Bose
February 2006

Index